Heaven on Earth

Maharaj Sawan Singh
1858 - 1948

Heaven on Earth

Daryai Lal Kapur

RADHA SOAMI SATSANG BEAS

Published by:
S. Sewa Singh, Secretary
Radha Soami Satsang Beas
P.O. Dera Baba Jaimal Singh
Dist. Amritsar 143204
Punjab, India

First Edition   1986   15,000 copies
Second Edition (revised)   1996   10,000 copies

Printed at: Baba Barkha Nath Printers, New Delhi 110 015

To My Lord and Beloved Satguru

CONTENTS

CHAPTER ONE: BABA JAIMAL SINGH

CHAPTER TWO: MAHARAJ SAWAN SINGH

CHAPTER THREE: MAHARAJ JAGAT SINGH

CHAPTER FOUR: MAHARAJ CHARAN SINGH

PREFACE TO THE SECOND EDITION

This second English edition of *Heaven on Earth* is being released just ten years after the first edition appeared, and twenty-five years after Diwan Daryai Lal Kapur's account of the Radha Soami Satsang Beas was first published in Urdu. There have been significant changes at the Dera, namely the passing away of Hazur Maharaj Charan Singh from this earth plane, and the succession of Baba Gurinder Singh as spiritual Master. The Dera has grown and expanded, both physically in terms of its size and facilities, and in terms of the numbers of the disciples coming to attend the Master's satsangs. Following in the spirit of ultimate service and self-sacrifice exemplified by all the Masters, the present Master has established a demanding satsang and travel schedule within India and abroad, in order to attend to the spiritual needs of his disciples. The manifestation of divine love between Master and disciples is evident in all his activities as it was in the lives of the Masters who preceded him.

In preparing this edition of *Heaven on Earth*, a number of passages not included in the first English rendering have been added from the original version. Revisions made by the author to the original book before his passing in December 1978 have been incorporated also. Other minor corrections have been made, and several unnecessary footnotes have been eliminated. It has been decided to leave all references to the previous Masters at the Dera as they were given in the first edition, and no attempt has been made to bring the book up to date. These personal accounts of the Masters—the heart of any account of Radha Soami Satsang Beas—speak in the language of their time. Thus a person who has had no contact with the colony can share something of the atmosphere of that period through the particularities of Diwan Daryai Lal Kapur's style and perspective. The book should be enjoyed as a living history of the Dera and what it represents—the mastership of the Saints who lived and taught here, from the early days of Baba Ji through almost a century of his successors' living presence.

Sewa Singh
Secretary

May 1996

PREFACE TO THE FIRST EDITION

Heaven on Earth is the English rendering of Diwan Daryai Lal Kapur's popular and absorbing Urdu work, which traces the beginning and growth of Dera Baba Jaimal Singh, the centre of Radha Soami Satsang Beas.

The history of the Dera is, in fact, the life story of the great Saints whose love and grace, diligence and dedication, have developed this place—once a wilderness—into a flourishing centre of peace and beatitude. It is also the story of the expansion of Sant Mat, which, beginning from a tiny spot on the west bank of the river Beas, has spread not only to every state and town of India but also to almost every corner of the world.

Born in 1889, Diwan Sahib—as the author was popularly known—graduated in law and arts and began practice as a lawyer in Jullundur. He joined the Kapurthala State Civil Service in 1920 and soon rose to become a judge. He also served as finance minister in Kapurthala State.

Diwan Sahib retired in 1947 and began to spend more time in the Dera, adopting it as his permanent place of residence in 1957. Initiated by Maharaj Sawan Singh Ji in December 1910, Diwan Sahib was a devoted disciple and a keen satsangi all his life. During his last twenty years, he served the present Master, Maharaj Charan Singh Ji, as his personal secretary. Active even till his last, Diwan Sahib departed from this world in 1977.

Diwan Sahib's earlier book, *Call of the Great Master*, is very popular with satsangis and seekers. Several editions have been printed, and it has been translated into a number of Indian and Western languages. *Heaven on Earth* is the outcome of the author's lifelong experience on the path. Having come in close contact with the three Masters at the Dera—from the Great Master to the present Master—and having personally known many disciples of Baba Ji Maharaj, Diwan Sahib was well qualified to undertake this work.

Heaven on Earth has already been translated into several Indian languages, and we are happy to present this English translation to our Western readers. The reader should keep in mind that Diwan Sahib, in preparing the revised edition of this book, has brought the narrative up to the year 1971/72. But the Dera, under Maharaj Charan Singh Ji's kind patronage and loving guidance, has continued to develop in all directions—physical and spiritual. To narrate the story of this development and of the present Master's boundless love and grace would require another volume. In spite of all its physical growth, the Dera continues to be a centre of inner tranquillity, of love and understanding; in this world of strife and turmoil, it is truly a unique place of peace and bliss.

S. L. Sondhi
Secretary

February 1985

INTRODUCTION

The idea of writing a history of the Radha Soami Satsang Beas first came to my mind in 1912. I had accompanied the Great Master on his visit to Soami Bagh, Agra, on the occasion of a bhandara in honour of Soami Ji Maharaj. The Master's group also included devoted disciples such as Sardar Bhagat Singh, Sardar Jagat Singh (later our Satguru at Beas), Pundit Lal Chand, Lala Munshi Ram, and a few others.

We stayed in the rooms built by Baba Ji Maharaj with the Great Master's seva contribution. Although I was young (just twenty-four) and a new satsangi (initiated only two years earlier), I was thrilled to stay in those rooms and to meet the few initiates of Soami Ji Maharaj who were still living, as well as some satsangis who had personally known Baba Ji Maharaj. When Bibi Sewadasi and Seth Sudarshan Singh—both initiates of Soami Ji—would talk about Baba Ji with deep feeling and devotion, we would feel inspired and fascinated. It was during one of my sittings with them that the idea came to mind of writing a book about the Dera, Baba Ji, and the Great Master.

Although I began to note down a few incidents, no serious attempt in this direction could be made because of my worldly preoccupation. In 1964 my revered and dear friend, Rai Bahadur Shankar Dass Sondhi, wrote me that I should pay immediate attention to the proposed book on Dera and its Masters. Reminding me that during the previous seven years satsangis like Prof. Jagmohan Lal, Rai Bahadur Gulwant Rai, Lala Balak Ram, Lala Munshi Ram, and Babu Gulab Singh

—all close to the Great Master—had passed away, Rai Bahadur Shankar Dass added, "And what certainty do we have? We may be guests in this world for a few more years, months, or maybe weeks."

Within two months of my receiving this letter, Rai Bahadur Shankar Dass also left us for his final journey. Shaken out of my mood of procrastination, I took up the work in all earnestness, and the manuscript of *Firdaus-i-Barin* (Urdu) was ready in 1966.

The incidents included in this volume are based on information obtained from satsangis who have been close to the Masters at the Dera, and on my own personal experiences; for, having come to Sant Mat in 1910, I have been a witness to many things narrated herein.

The account of events before 1910 is based on information received from Rai Bahadur Seth Sudarshan Singh, Baba Garib Das, and Bibi Sewadasi—all disciples of Soami Ji Maharaj—who had close contact with Baba Ji Maharaj. Many details about the early days of the Dera and about Baba Ji and the Great Master are based on accounts gathered from Bibi Rukko, Baba Bagga Singh, "Mahant" Inder Singh, Bhai Manna Singh, Lala Parmanand Bajaj, Babu Gulab Singh, Milkhi Ram—Bibi Ralli's father—Baba Nizamuddin, Bhai Moti Ram, Munshi Chananmal, Bhai Surain Singh, and Magghar Singh, who were all initiates of Baba Ji; old satsangis from the neighbouring villages of Waraich and Balsarai, such as Sardar Lal Singh and Nambardar Jagat Singh; old attendants of the Great Master, such as Roor Singh and Banta Singh; the Great Master's family members, particularly his wife, Mata Kishan Kaur, and his son Sardar Bachint Singh; and many other prominent satsangis, such as Lala Munshi Ram, Rai Bahadur Shankar Dass, Sardar Sewa Singh, Rai Bahadur Gulwant Rai, Bakshi Chanan Shah, Bhai Shadi, and Bibi Ralli.

In his satsangs and personal talks, the Great Master would often narrate incidents of Baba Ji's life and sometimes also reminisce about his own. I have tried to make use of this precious material, which forms a part of my most cherished memory of our beloved Master.

After the second edition of *Firdaus-i-Barin,* some of my friends, old residents of the Dera, and senior satsangis pointed out certain discrepancies in the book and gave more details about Dera history and the life of Baba Ji, Great Master, and Sardar Bahadur Maharaj Ji. In view of this fresh information and suggestions from friends, I have made corrections and changes in the original text, and have also added some material.

Not much was written about Sardar Bahadur Maharaj Jagat Singh in the first two editions. Pundit Lal Chand Dharmani and the Dharmani family, Air Vice-Marshal (A.V.M.) K. L. Sondhi, and Prof. Balwant Singh—all of whom had known Sardar Bahadur Ji from his days in Lyallpur—and Bibi Ralli, Sardar Gurdial Singh, Nambardar Jagat Singh, Bakshi Maluk Chand, Ram Nath Mehta, and Dr (Miss) S. Sinha gave me some more material about him. On the basis of their information I have rewritten the chapter on Sardar Bahadur Maharaj Ji.

Similarly, I have almost rewritten the portion about our present Master, Maharaj Charan Singh Ji, and have tried to bring the narrative up to date. In this connection I gratefully acknowledge the assistance of the satsang secretaries of centres in India and abroad, and of good friends like Miss Louise Hilger, Mr H. F. Weekley, Mr Sam Busa, Mrs Bea Jauncey, Mr R. N. Mehta, Prof. Janak Puri, Mr Krishin Babani, A.V.M. K. L. Sondhi, and Mr Madan Mehta, besides many other satsangis from India and abroad.

My good friend and a very devoted satsangi, Prof. Jagmohan Lal, who was working as the present Master's personal secretary, left this world in 1958, and the Master gave me that seva. I am blessed with the rare privilege of coming in close contact with Maharaj Charan Singh Ji and have a few times heard him reminisce about the Great Master and Sardar Bahadur Ji, and also about himself. I have taken the liberty of basing some parts of my narrative on these reminiscences.

I do not claim to be an author, historian, scholar, or thinker. The urge to write this book has come from my sixty-three years of association with three great Masters at the Dera. I have no words to express my gratitude to my beloved Satguru for all his compassion and grace, which I have done little to deserve. For the many flaws in the narrative, flaws of language and style, I pray for the Master's forgiveness, as also for that of the kind readers.

In the end, I would like to submit that the history of the Dera is closely related to the life of the Masters. It may be easy to write the history of an institution, but it is not easy to depict the glory of the perfect Masters. It is beyond comprehension and beyond words. To quote Tulsi Sahib, "If anyone claims he has understood a Saint, Tulsi—dismayed—shouts in reprobation: Enough!"

It will be my great good fortune if this humble contribution to satsang literature is accepted at the feet of my beloved Satguru.

Daryai Lal Kapur

Dera Baba Jaimal Singh
October 1973

Chapter One

Baba Jaimal Singh

An Early Quest for Truth

Whenever perfect Masters come to the world, glimpses of their inner spiritual light become evident even in their childhood. The veils of mind, matter, and illusion cannot stifle the glow of their innate spiritual urge. Jaimal Singh, son of Jodh Singh and Daya Kaur, was born in 1839 in the village of Ghuman, about eighteen miles north of the present Dera. He exhibited signs of a deep spiritual thirst at a very early age, a thirst that, as we shall see, prompted him while still in his teens to undertake a long, untiring search for Truth.

When Baba Jaimal Singh was about five, his parents sent him to the Namdev shrine in the village[1] to learn to read and write from Baba Khem Das, a learned man of Ghuman. During his visits, Baba Ji (as Jaimal Singh later came to be known) would listen with rapt attention to the Saints' hymns being recited at the shrine. He would sit for hours, absorbed by the hymns and the talk of holy men who were visiting the shrine. Moved by the child's devotion, Baba Khem Das began explaining passages from the Adi Granth to him, and under his direction Baba Ji soon was able to read and recite the Adi Granth fluently.[2]

---

[1] Namdev (1270–1350) was a Saint from Maharashtra. Born two hundred years before Guru Nanak, he travelled widely in North India and spent the last eighteen years of his life at Ghuman. Some of his hymns are included in the Adi Granth.

[2] The Adi Granth, compiled c. 1604 by Guru Arjan, the fifth Guru in the line of Guru Nanak, is a collection of devotional hymns written by various Saints and devotees who lived between the twelfth and seventeenth centuries.

By the time he was nine years old, young Jaimal Singh's desire for spiritual knowledge had become so intense that he would spend almost all his time, from morning till night, at the shrine of Saint Namdev, trying to understand the meaning of the holy scriptures. The spiritual bent of Baba Ji's mind at such an early age surprised his parents, and his father, Sardar Jodh Singh, felt deeply concerned.

At Baba Ji's insistence, Baba Khem Das taught him to repeat one of the names of God, 'Sohang Satnam'. This practice enabled him to attain a certain tranquillity of mind, but what he wanted was something more.

Reading holy scriptures developed in him a vague yearning to know the Truth, to meet the Lord. Through regular study of the Adi Granth, this desire soon took shape and turned into an intense longing to realize God, to learn the true meaning of the words of the great Saints in the Adi Granth.

The more he read the Adi Granth, the stronger became his urge to know the Truth. He found frequent references to the terms *Shabd* and *Nam* in the poems of Guru Nanak and other Saints: "Through Nam everything came into being.... The one Nam emancipates all.... Nam supports all worlds and regions, Nam supports the firmament and the lower worlds."[1] He wondered what that Name was which created everything, which emancipates all, which sustains all the worlds.

Young Jaimal Singh could not accept that mere words, however holy, could have the power to create the universe and sustain it. There must be some divine power that is the essence of creation, the primordial, creative power of God, and this must be what the Adi Granth calls Nam or Shabd. Baba Khem Das, however, was unable to provide any insight into this mysterious power.

[1] Adi Granth, *Suhi*, M.3, p. 753; *Basant*, M.3, p. 1175; *Gaudi Sukhmani*, M.5, p. 284.

To find the key to the mystery of Nam became the driving passion of Baba Ji's life. He would sit for hours in the company of sadhus, faqirs, and yogis who came on pilgrimage to the shrine of Namdev, serving them and discussing spiritual matters with them. Sardar Jodh Singh became worried that his promising twelve-year-old son, influenced by the company of holy men, would renounce the world and become a recluse. To keep him away from their company, he sent Baba Ji to live with Bibi Tabo, his married sister who lived ten miles away in the village of Sathiala, not far from the present Dera.

But the changed surroundings and his sister's affection could not divert his mind from his spiritual search. The more he brooded over the nature of Nam and Shabd, the greater became his thirst to know what Nam truly was. Here also he found yogis and holy men, and started to spend most of his time in their company. He learned *pranayam* from a yogi he met in Sathiala.[1] He mastered the art so rapidly that his teacher felt he must have been a yogi in his past life. Despite the ease and success with which he performed the yogic practices, the youth gave up pranayam after a few months because the Adi Granth rejects these practices as futile, and because he soon realized that they could not reveal the mystery of Nam, the main object of his quest. Bibi Tabo soon reported to her father her concern that the boy's interest in spirituality and sadhus, instead of showing any signs of waning, had day after day increased and become an obsession. Sardar Jodh Singh, much disturbed at this, immediately came and took Jaimal Singh back to Ghuman. In spite of all his father's efforts, Baba Ji continued his spiritual quest, which now, although he was only thirteen, was the sole interest in his life—a burning flame that had completely enveloped his mind and soul.

---

[1] *Pranayam* is a yogic system for controlling and regulating the *prana*, or "vital air."

His continued study of the Adi Granth convinced him that pranayam, hatha yoga, renunciation, repetition of holy names, penances, fasting, and meritorious deeds were futile on the path of God-realization.[1] But if all these practices were useless, what was the path through which Guru Nanak, Namdev, Kabir, and other great Saints had attained spiritual perfection? What was the means that Guru Nanak had adopted to meet the Lord?

Baba Ji finally came to two important conclusions from reading the writings of the Saints: that the foremost require-ment for following the path to God-realization was a realized soul, a perfect Master; and that the key to the true path lay in the Shabd, or Nam, which was something deeper and greater than any of the names of God. His curiosity was also aroused when he found in the Adi Granth the term *panch shabd* ("the five sounds"), which was also described as *anahad*, or "unstruck," "unlimited." His quest now took definite shape—a search for the Master who could show him the path of the five shabds.

Around this time two family crises threatened to come in the way of Baba Ji's spiritual quest. He was now about four-teen and his parents tried to persuade him to marry, in the hope that he would give up his spiritual inclinations and settle down.[2] But Baba Ji, whose eyes were fixed on the high target of God-realization, firmly declined to comply with their wishes. His parents, who by now had realized the iron will and spiritual determination of their son, reconciled them-selves to his decision. Thus Baba Ji chose to live a life of celi-bacy, remaining unmarried throughout his life.

---

[1] The term "meritorious deeds" refers to feeding sadhus and brahmins, going on pilgrimages, bathing in holy waters, giving alms, reading and reciting scrip-tures, and going to temples, gurdwaras, churches, and the like.
[2] In those days child-marriages were prevalent, but the bride would continue to stay with her parents till she came of age.

After a few months Baba Ji's father died. Baba Ji was now in a dilemma. Love and duty towards his mother, Daya Kaur, were holding him back, while desire to know the Truth urged him to continue his search. He spent some time with the family, sad and restless. One day, laying his heart before his mother, he begged her to allow him to go out in search of someone who could show him the path of Shabd, or Nam. His mother, not insensitive to her young son's state of agitation, understood and gave him permission to follow his quest.

Search for a Master and the Five Shabds

One morning, young Jaimal Singh, then a boy of fourteen, set out on his long journey. The purpose of his journey was clear in his mind, but there was no fixed destination in view. He did not know where to find the object of his search. A firm determination and a strong will were his only companions.

Baba Ji went to Amritsar, where among other holy men he came across a sadhu who told him about a *shabd* (inner sound) connected with the lower *chakras*.[1] He learned how to listen to this sound, but found that it was nowhere near the path of the five shabds that he sought. Continuing his journey, he visited Nankana Sahib, Lahore, Emnabad, and many holy places in Punjab, but he failed to find any holy man who could unveil the mystery of "the five sounds." Instead of feeling discouraged, he intensified his search. At every village and town that came on his way, he would inquire if there were any holy men nearby.

Thus he scanned almost the entire Punjab, meeting yogis, ascetics, Vedantists, scholars, hermits of various schools,

---

[1] *Chakra* literally means "wheel"; the term is used to denote energy centres in the body.

and Muslim faqirs and sufis. Quite a few of them were adepts in their way of practice and had obtained miraculous powers. But nothing could impress him. Many holy men would offer to initiate him, but Baba Ji would decline, for his ideal guide was the one who could show him the true home within the home of the body and tell him of the place where the melody of the five shabds resounds:

> He who reveals the Home within the home
> (of the body)
> Is the true Master, perfect and wise;
> There reverberate the five melodies,
> There resounds the Shabd of drum.
>
> *Adi Granth, M.1, p. 1290*

As the miles of walking and futile search mounted, Jaimal Singh was guided by this single stanza from the scriptures, which became his touchstone whenever he met a possible Master.

At the age of fourteen, when most boys would be playing games and gossiping with friends, Baba Ji was wandering from place to place in search of the way to meet the Lord. Failure to achieve his objective as well as the hardships of travelling could not discourage him.

There were no trains in India at that time, and buses and cars were unknown even in the West. There were no bridges over many of the large rivers, so travellers had to cross them by ferry, and wade through streams and rivulets. Most of the time Baba Ji travelled on foot, covering hundreds of miles through wild forests, steep mountain trails, jungle wilderness, and sparsely populated areas. He walked through jungles infested with snakes and wild animals, sometimes alone, sometimes with a small group of travellers. At times he could barely cover three or four miles a day; at other times he had to walk for twelve or fourteen hours with hardly a break, in order to cover the thirty-odd miles to the next hamlet or village before nightfall.

In the face of disappointment, he would sometimes wonder if there really was a path of five shabds, but would soon remember that the words of Guru Nanak and the Saints could not be wrong. Baba Ji persisted relentlessly, the urge of his soul leading him from one place to the next. To find the adept who could tell him about the path of Shabd was the sole objective, the only aim, of his life.

At Nankana Sahib, where Guru Nanak was born, Baba Ji had learned of a sage named Baba Balak Singh of Hazro, District Attock, in the Northwest Frontier Province (now in Pakistan), who, it seemed, might be the one he was seeking. After a long and arduous journey, Baba Ji reached Hazro. Baba Balak Singh, a pious and noble soul, told him that his spiritual practice was to repeat "Wahiguru," one of the names of God. He knew nothing of the secret of the five sounds.

Continuing his search, Baba Ji visited Naushehra, Peshawar, and other towns of the Northwest Frontier Province, and one night arrived at a village in the district of Mardan. Here he met a spiritual man who was leading a householder's life, who confirmed Baba Ji's views about the path of five shabds: "Son, what you are searching for has also been my search. There is certainly a path of five shabds, and it is this very practice that Guru Nanak and his successors taught. But I have received initiation into the secret of only two shabds." A wave of happiness surged through Baba Ji. For the first time he had received confirmation of the truth of the inner sounds; now he knew he was not chasing a mirage. Desiring only the true and complete path, he was not interested in learning the secret of the two shabds and told the holy man simply, "The

Lord who has given you the secret of the two shabds will also arrange to give me the secret of the five shabds."

Leaving Mardan, Baba Ji travelled back to Punjab where he joined a group of sadhus on their way to Rishikesh, a famous place of Hindu pilgrimage. He stayed in Rishikesh for several months, meeting a number of spiritually advanced ascetics and yogis, but failed to find a Master who could satisfy his yearning. Disappointed, he was about to leave when he learned of an old sadhu who lived alone in a forest retreat about twenty-five miles from Rishikesh in a place called Tapoban. Apparently the sage never left his retreat nor did he allow anyone to approach him; he pursued his spiritual practice and lived on whatever wild fruits and herbs he could find in the forest.

Baba Ji immediately set out to find the holy man, travelling the whole day through the dense forest. By the evening he finally came to a glade where an old man was standing, partially supported by a cloth rope. The sadhu said to Baba Ji, "Why have you come? It's not safe here. Don't you know tigers and bears live in this forest?" Baba Ji replied without hesitating, "If the tigers don't harm you, why would they bother me?" Seeing Baba Ji's courage, the sadhu relented and agreed to let him spend the night there.

During the night the old man conversed with Baba Ji and was impressed by his earnestness. He listened while the youth spoke of his search for a Master with the secret of the five sounds. Moved by Baba Ji's thirst for Truth and his perseverance, the sadhu, heaving a deep sigh, said, "The thirst that has driven you from place to place also afflicts me. My long years of meditation have given me certain spiritual powers, but I have realized that without initiation into the path of the five shabds there is no salvation. Through my inner vision I have learned that a great Saint has appeared in Agra who is an adept in the practice of five shabds and initiates seekers into the same path. He has spent the last seventeen or eighteen years in deep meditation and has only just begun to give out his teachings. You must go to him, for he is the only one who can give you what you seek."

The next morning the sadhu bade a warm farewell to Baba Ji and said, "I will also come to Agra, but it will take quite some time because my feet have become heavy from years of constant standing."

Overjoyed and charged with renewed vigour and enthusiasm, Baba Ji left Rishikesh for Agra. But on reaching Agra he realized that in his great happiness he had completely forgotten to ask the name and exact location of the great Saint. For days he searched the many temples and holy places, combing the labyrinthine lanes and alleys of Agra and inquiring about the Saint, but nobody seemed to have heard of him.

Meeting With Soami Ji

One morning, after searching for several days, Baba Ji sat on the banks of the Jamuna River, deeply distressed and not knowing what to do next. He had spent almost three years in his search; he had covered thousands of miles, visited hundreds of places, and met countless sadhus, yogis, and holy men. Not deterred by hardships, not wearied by disappointments, he had continued his search with an unshaken resolve to succeed, with an inner faith that one day he would find the path that his heart and soul longed for. Now on the brink of discovery, his search seemed destined to fail. His heart was torn with desire to meet the Master he could not find. With tears rolling down his cheeks, in his helplessness he prayed to the Lord.

Suddenly Baba Ji became aware of two bathers engrossed in a discussion about a holy man and the wonderful discourses he gave. Baba Ji moved closer to them and listened for a while. Finally he asked them the name of the Saint they were speaking about and where he lived. They told him that the great Saint, Soami Shiv Dayal Singh, known as Soami Ji, lived in Panni Gali. In later years Baba Ji used to say that Soami Ji had arranged this coincidental meeting in answer to his prayer.

He quickly went to the house and found Soami Ji Maharaj sitting among his disciples, about to start the satsang. The moment Baba Ji saw him, a sense of peace filled his heart, and he approached and bowed respectfully at Soami Ji's feet. Soami Ji smiled and said, "He has arrived—my old friend!" The remark took Baba Ji by surprise as he had not seen Soami Ji before. Overwhelmed by the love and light he beheld in the great Saint, Baba Ji sat down in the group of disciples, his eyes fixed on Soami Ji's face. Soami Ji then gave a discourse on a verse from the Adi Granth, explaining the main principles of Sant Mat and the spiritual meaning and significance of the five shabds. The discourse was a revelation to Baba Ji. He had at last found what he had been looking for all these years. His doubts were resolved and his heart was filled with peace, happiness, and a sense of deep gratitude.

For several days Baba Ji attended Soami Ji's satsangs, and soon all that had been obscure and difficult to understand in the Adi Granth became clear. He knew he wanted initiation from this great Mystic but found himself hesitating because Soami Ji was not a Sikh. He could not resolve whether it was proper for him to accept a non-Sikh as his Master, despite his conviction that Soami Ji was the one who could give him the key to true spiritual knowledge.

For four days he remained in this dilemma. One day, while Baba Ji was lost in these thoughts, Soami Ji came to him and gently inquired whether he had yet decided the question of Sikh and non-Sikh. As Baba Ji had spoken to no one about his conflict, Soami Ji's loving words moved him profoundly and tears filled his eyes. Soami Ji continued, "We must look for the Truth. Seekers often involve themselves in external forms and lose sight of the true path. Just think: What difference can wearing long or short hair make on the path of God-realization?[1] Our object is to meet the Lord, not to remain tied to the formalities of long or short hair." With love and gratitude Baba Ji knelt and touched his head to Soami Ji's feet. Soami Ji lovingly placed his hands on Baba Ji's head and gently lifted him.

The next day Baba Jaimal Singh received initiation and for two days and nights remained absorbed in meditation in a small room in Soami Ji's house. He emerged transformed, his being filled with happiness and contentment. The priceless jewel he had been seeking for years was at last obtained through the grace of his Master. Bliss and rapture filled every pore of his body; he could hardly contain his joy.

Spiritual Practice

Baba Ji stayed on with Soami Ji for some time. Though still very young—he was a little over seventeen at the time of his initiation—he took up the spiritual practice in all earnestness, devoting himself almost exclusively to meditation. Except for listening to the Sound Current and seeing his Master, little else appealed to him, and his meditation rapidly bore

---

[1] It is customary for Sikhs not to cut their hair.

fruit. Soami Ji told him, "You are an old associate of mine. You have already done this practice in previous births and earned this spiritual wealth."

One day, Baba Ji was engaged in meditation when Soami Ji came by. As Baba Ji's attention was absorbed within, he failed to notice his Master standing before him. Soami Ji, through his own power, brought Baba Ji's attention down and inquired, "Are you satisfied that what I have given you is the path of Guru Nanak?" Baba Ji replied that the path was indeed the true one and that his soul went to higher regions, but there was yet some obstacle.

Soami Ji said, "The obstacle is a minor one. You have many times crossed these regions when you were with me before." Baba Ji, with some hesitation, requested proof of this. Soami Ji told him, "Well, if you want proof, again take your attention within." Baba Ji sat in meditation and Soami Ji put his hand on his head; with his own attention he removed the obstruction from Baba Ji's spiritual path.

When Baba Ji's attention came out, he said, "Maharaj Ji, my work is done. Permit me now to stay at your feet. Here I shall live, serve you, and do my meditation."

Soami Ji replied, "We must always keep a balance between our worldly and spiritual duties. If you give up everything you will have to depend on others for your living. Those who bow at your feet and bring you food will rob you of your spiritual wealth. The devotee must earn his own living. This is essential for meditation."

The Soldier-Saint

Following Soami Ji's directions, Baba Jaimal Singh in 1856 enlisted in the 24th Sikh Regiment, which was then stationed in

Agra. As long as the regiment was in Agra, Baba Ji would come daily to Panni Gali for Soami Ji's darshan and satsang.

One evening Baba Ji was so inspired by the satsang that he decided to sit in meditation for a short while before returning to his regiment. Soon it became dark and the night advanced, but he was unaware of the physical world as he was absorbed in the bliss of higher inner regions. Worried that Jaimal Singh would incur disciplinary action for his absence, some brother satsangis went to Soami Ji and expressed their concern. Soami Ji said, "Yes, you are right. Try to get him up from his meditation and send him to the barracks." But the satsangis soon returned, saying that they could not draw his attention out. At this, Soami Ji himself went, and found Baba Ji's attention so firmly riveted within that he was utterly oblivious of everything outside. Very pleased with his young disciple's deep meditation, Soami Ji said, "Leave him alone. In the morning we shall see what happens."

Baba Ji remained in meditation the entire night, and in the early morning hurried back to his regiment. Without changing into uniform, he reported directly to his sergeant, saying, "Sir, as I was absent from duty all night, I am willing to accept whatever punishment is decided for me."

The sergeant was puzzled. He looked quizzically at Baba Ji and said, "Last night you attended the rounds of the barracks with me. Then you locked the magazine and handed me the keys. You were present on parade at 5:00 A.M. and answered the roll call. Now what is this nonsense? Were any other soldier to talk like this I would be sure he had been drinking." With a quiet apology Baba Ji withdrew to his barracks, thanking Soami Ji in his heart.

In the evening Baba Ji went to Soami Ji and said, "Last night the gracious Master performed my duties for me. From now on I will serve only him and no one else." Soami Ji embraced him and said, "In the regiment, too, you are doing my work. Go, do that duty as though it were service to me."

In Soami Ji's satsang there were many great devotees, such as Rai Bahadur Saligram, Baba Gharib Das and Baba Jaimal Singh. In the circle of disciples, Rai Bahadur Saligram was known for his loving *seva,* or service to the Master, Baba Gharib Das for his learning and humility, and Baba Jaimal Singh for his meditation and high spiritual progress. Soami Ji once remarked about Baba Ji, "He is an old associate of mine. He will propagate the path of the Shabd in Punjab."

The extent of Baba Ji's spiritual wealth was related to us by Baba Hans Das, an enlightened soul, when once we accompanied the Great Master, Baba Sawan Singh Ji, on a visit to Agra. He was full of praise for Baba Ji, saying, "Soami Ji gave us the water of spirituality in measured doses in a tiny glass, but he gave to Baba Jaimal Singh in huge mugfuls— like a millionaire giving away his wealth."

In 1857, Baba Ji's regiment was ordered to move from Agra to Delhi. Baba Ji could not bear the thought of separation from his beloved Master; he begged Soami Ji to let him resign from his post and stay at his feet. Soami Ji replied, "You are not a servant of the British government. You are in my employ. I shall be with you wherever you go." Then he added, "Many souls are thirsting for emancipation and are waiting for you to arrive."

When the time came for him to leave, Baba Ji bowed his head and humbly asked for his blessings. Soami Ji told him to bring some water. Baba Ji brought water in a bowl, and Soami Ji, as a token of his grace and love, blessed it. Baba Ji raised the bowl and drank all the water thus blessed by his Master. Then, before leaving, he placed his forehead on his Satguru's feet and Soami Ji put his hands on Baba Ji's head.

After Baba Ji left, several other satsangis made a similar request for his blessings, but Soami Ji said, "The true *amrit* (nectar) has been taken away by the disciple who just left." One of the old disciples from Uttar Pradesh who happened to be a little outspoken grumbled, "I don't know, Sir, why you are so soft and gracious to Jaimal Singh. Why all this partiality towards him?"

Soami Ji replied, "There is no question of bias or favouritism on this path. It is a path of love and intense spiritual practice. He who cares nothing for public opinion, who controls his body and mind, and burns away all cravings and desires in the furnace of love, earns this spiritual wealth. Who else has done as much meditation as Jaimal Singh has? This gift of the Lord is not given away for nothing."

Whenever Baba Ji's regiment was stationed close enough, he would go to Agra for darshan and satsang. In 1857 his regiment was located in Delhi and then in Peshawar; after a brief stay at Ambala, the regiment was transferred to Jhansi in 1859 for three years. From there Baba Ji was able to spend his entire two-month furloughs in Agra, meditating day and night. Once Soami Ji saw him sitting deeply absorbed in meditation and was highly pleased with him. "He is a soldier-saint," he remarked, and recited the following verse: "The Melody of the highest region within, some soldier-saint alone will catch."[1]

In 1862 the regiment returned to Agra for a few months, and in November 1863 it was again transferred to Peshawar. The next record of the regiment shows its being stationed in Rawalpindi in 1868.

In 1869 Baba Ji met a sadhu named Sarabdayal Singh, who was an adept in the practice of pranayam and who also recited verses from the Adi Granth, giving discourses on them.

---

[1] *Sar Bachan Poetry*, p. 94:12.

He was deeply impressed with Baba Ji, and a discussion between them about the path of the five shabds came to him as a revelation. Amazed and delighted to learn the true meaning of the verses, he asked Baba Ji to initiate him. Soami Ji had already instructed Baba Ji to initiate any seekers he thought fit, but he always sent them to Soami Ji. On Baba Ji's advice, Sarabdayal Singh went to Agra and received initiation from Soami Ji Maharaj.

Baba Ji's officers always admired him for his keen sense of duty, his punctuality, and his readiness to carry out their commands. They gradually came to know that he was a highly evolved soul who had enlisted in the army just to earn his own living and avoid being a burden on others. His loving nature, noble behaviour, and saintly qualities greatly impressed them.

One of the few detailed stories of Baba Ji's army career concerns an officer who served as his superior. Once, a new major, who was harsh and irascible by nature and abused his subordinates over virtually nothing, was transferred to Baba Ji's unit. Not surprisingly, the soldiers soon tired of his abuses and went to Baba Ji, then a sergeant, whose noble manner and saintly reputation had made him revered by the men. They said, "The new major abuses us. He flares up over trifles and seems to think extra guard duty is a mild punishment, since he gives it unhesitatingly. We are miserable under this oppressive officer. Will you help us by talking to him?" Baba Ji gently explained to them that officers vary widely in their manner, but it is always best for subordinates to be patient and tolerant, for "all days are not the same."

The very next day the major happened to call Baba Ji into his office and spoke in his usual abrasive manner. "It has been brought to my notice that you don't eat meat and that the other soldiers in the regiment, following your bad example, are also giving up meat."

Baba Ji said, "Sir, vegetarianism causes no physical weakness. I am prepared to stand a trial of strength with any meat eater. Slaughtering animals and consuming their meat is a great sin."

Even though Baba Ji had spoken gently, the major reacted furiously, exclaiming, "Don't you bandy words with me! If anyone refuses to take meat this evening, he will be made an example of." Baba Ji did not reply but calmly left the office and returned to his barracks.

That evening the major went out for a drive and had not gone far when his gig overturned.[1] With great difficulty he was removed from the carriage and taken home. The military doctor examined him and found he had fractured his right leg and some ribs. His leg was splinted, and a small sack of sand was tied to his foot to hold the leg in position.[2] When the doctor left, his pain became excruciating. Groaning with pain, the major spent a miserable night, with the doctor visiting him several times but unable to give him relief.

The next day the major asked to see Baba Ji. The major felt that he was suffering because he had used abusive language towards a noble person and he wanted to apologize to him. But Baba Ji could not be found as it was Sunday, which he always spent in meditation away from the barracks. On Monday, hearing about the accident, Baba Ji went straight to the major, who was still in great pain. Baba Ji sat on the bed and comforted the officer, who said, "I have been in unbearable pain, but with your arrival it has lessened greatly. Please forgive me for the way I treated you."

---

[1] A gig is a light, horse-drawn carriage.
[2] This was a form of traction.

Baba Ji replied softly, "You did nothing to hurt me, sir. What is there to forgive?" Baba Ji's humility, generosity, and tenderness had a profound effect on the major, and he started to weep. The soldiers present could hardly believe this was the same man who threatened everyone with punishments, and cursed and abused his men at the slightest provocation.

Baba Ji said gently, "Don't give way to despair. Joy and sorrow are both states of mind. You will soon be well." After that the man's pain vanished completely. In three months, when the bone had set, the major resumed his duties, but he was not the same man. He was reasonable and even kind; a brief contact with Baba Ji had transformed him.

On 20 October 1870, Baba Ji's regiment was transferred to Mian Mir, near Lahore (now in Pakistan) and remained there for three years. In those days when his regiment was stationed far away from Agra, Baba Ji spent his furloughs meditating in a wooded wilderness between the villages of Balsarai and Waraich, on the Beas River near the present site of the Dera. In 1873 Baba Ji's regiment was transferred to Jhansi a second time, for a five-year posting. In Jhansi he was close enough again to go to Agra during his leave periods.[1] It was during one such leave period that the following incident occurred:

Once, Soami Ji had decided to sit in meditation in a small room for two or three days and had told his disciples not to disturb him until he came out. He bolted the door from the inside and sat in meditation. The very next day Baba Ji arrived in Agra on three days' leave. Whenever he came to Agra it was his practice first to meet Soami Ji, bow to him, and then to attend to other things. Upon reaching Panni Gali he

---

[1] It would be wrong to presume that Baba Ji only had two months' leave in a year; there were short leaves during the year and sometimes between postings too.

was informed of Soami Ji's orders. Baba Ji said nothing but
sat in meditation for two days without eating or drinking anything. A few satsangis urged him to have the Master's darshan
by climbing to the ventilator with the help of a ladder, as his
leave was to end that day. But Baba Ji refused, saying that one
should never disobey his Master's orders. After only a short
while Soami Ji Maharaj came out of his room, and when he
heard of Baba Ji's devotion and implicit obedience, he embraced him warmly. Then he gave him parshad and sent him
off in time to catch his train back to Jhansi.

Baba Ji used to devote all his spare time in the regiment
to meditation or spiritual discussions. Many people, greatly
impressed with him, asked for initiation, but Baba Ji always
sent them to Soami Ji. While he was still in Jhansi, Soami Ji
sent Baba Ji strict orders to initiate earnest seekers himself
and not refer them to Agra. At this time a Sikh named Inder
Singh, who came from the village of Bhandal, District Lahore, joined Baba Ji's regiment as a sepoy, or foot soldier. He
was with Baba Ji throughout his army career, from 1877 onwards. He used to narrate many incidents of Baba Ji's life during service days and would say that Baba Ji, under Soami Ji's
directions, initiated Inder Singh and one other person at
Jhansi in 1877/78, while Soami Ji was still living.[1] The name
of the first initiate cannot be ascertained, for in the list of
initiates maintained by Baba Ji, in his own handwriting, the
first few names have no dates. The first entry is of Amir Singh
of Jhelum, who presumably was in Baba Ji's regiment.

---

[1] Later many members of Inder Singh's village, Bhandal or Bhandallan (now in
Pakistan), came to Beas and received initiation from Baba Ji Maharaj. Baba Ji
would sometimes go to Bhandal to hold satsangs. His letters to the sangat of
Bhandal reveal his love for them.

Successorship of Baba Jaimal Singh

In 1875 Baba Ji was promoted to the rank of *nayak*.[1] He continued to visit Agra whenever he could get leave. At the end of one of his periods of leave in October 1877, Soami Ji said to him, "This is your last darshan. By the time you get your next furlough, I will have gone back to the true Home. There will not be another physical meeting between us." Soami Ji's words stunned Baba Ji. Only a realized soul can know the anguish of separation from his Satguru. With tears flowing from his eyes, he stood speechless. Moved by his disciple's love, Soami Ji embraced Baba Ji and said, "You are my beloved son, a *gurmukh* disciple. I have transformed you, and you are now my very own self. I am greatly pleased with you. The Almighty will always be gracious to you."

Chanda Singh, one of the disciples of Soami Ji, and a devoted soul, was present at this meeting. He said, "Maharaj Ji, you are speaking of leaving us. Who will look after us?" Soami Ji Maharaj assured him that there was no cause for worry and that all would be properly taken care of. Chanda Singh then submitted that satsang and initiation be started in Punjab also. Soami Ji replied, "This request has been accepted by the Supreme Being and this duty has already been allotted to Jaimal Singh." Soami Ji then gave his own turban to Baba Ji, along with parshad, as a token of his love and grace. Soami Ji ordered him to start satsang and give Nam in Punjab, and bade him a most affectionate farewell. Soami Ji left the mortal body and returned to his true Home on 15 June 1878.

On 1 May 1878, Baba Ji was promoted to the rank of *havaldar*.[2] The next year his regiment was stationed at Peshawar. The British government in India was at war with Afghanistan,

---

[1] *Nayak* was a rank in the British Indian Army equivalent to corporal.

[2] *Havaldar* was a rank in the British Indian Army equivalent to sergeant.

and Baba Ji's regiment at Peshawar was part of the reinforce-
ments to be sent to Kabul in case of need. Tribal Pathans used
to attack Peshawar every now and then. While stationed there,
Baba Ji would go out at night into the open and dig a small
pit in the sandy soil. With his rifle tucked under his knees, he
would sit there in meditation the whole night. Many a time
the Pathans would pass by. Nobody would disturb him, and
they would say among themselves, "He is a holy man. We
should not touch him." If there were three or four holidays,
he would devote all of them to bhajan.

In 1880 Baba Ji's regiment was transferred to Multan for
three years. After that it was successively in Mian Mir in 1883,
in Rawalpindi in July 1885, and in Sialkot in 1887. During all
these years Baba Ji spent all his time after work in meditation. As before, during his furloughs Baba Ji would stay in
Ghuman for a few days, then go to the banks of the Beas River
to meditate day and night. On 18 August 1889, Baba Ji retired
on pension after thirty-three years of army service, and went
to his village, Ghuman.

Living in Agra around this time was a Punjabi lady, Bibi
Rukko, who served Mata Radha Ji, Soami Ji's wife. She would
often ask Mata Radha Ji and Seth Pratap Singh, Soami Ji's
younger brother, to send some spiritually advanced satsangi
to her home province, Punjab, to initiate seekers: "Punjab,
once the land of great Gurus and Saints, has become a spiritual wilderness." Mata Ji would reply, "Soami Ji has already
arranged for this. Have no worry; when the time comes, your
wish will be fulfilled."

Once when Bibi Rukko made this request, Mata Ji said,
"Why don't you go yourself?" But she did not want to leave
the satsang and said, "That is a job for a perfect Saint—a Saint
with the power to soften the parched and barren soil of Punjab and move hearts of flint." Mata Ji replied, "That is exactly

the kind of great soul Soami Ji has selected. Only a few more months and you will know everything."

Some months later, when Mata Ji got up for her usual bath after midnight, she called Bibi Rukko and said, "Tomorrow the Satguru you have been praying for will arrive. He is Soami Ji's exalted son and gurmukh devotee to whom he entrusted the work in Punjab long ago. Go to the railway station tomorrow and receive him."

When Bibi Rukko went to the station she found Baba Ji Maharaj, who had come to Agra for the first time since Soami Ji's death. Baba Ji stayed with Mata Ji for a few days, spending most of his time in meditation. Mata Ji treated him with great love and respect. Then, the day before he was supposed to leave, Mata Ji sent for Seth Pratap Singh, Sudershan Singh,[1] and a few other senior satsangis. She offered Baba Ji a silken turban and said, "Shortly before his departure, Soami Ji Maharaj gave me this turban and said, 'Jaimal Singh is my beloved son and a gurmukh disciple. See that this turban is tied around his head when he comes.'" After the turban was tied on Baba Ji's head,[2] Mata Ji said, "Go to Punjab and carry out Soami Ji's orders. Spread the message of Soami Ji and initiate the thirsty souls into the path of Shabd."

Seth Pratap Singh then brought a small carpet and asked Baba Ji to sit on it. Baba Ji immediately recognized that it was Soami Ji's prayer mat, used for meditation. He folded his hands, politely refusing to sit upon it. But when Mata Ji explained that the prayer mat belonged to Soami Ji and that he

---

[1] Seth Pratap Singh's son.

[2] It is a normal practice in India that when a father dies, his turban is tied on the head of his eldest son or the person designated to be his heir. This marks the transmission of all responsibilities of the head of the family to the heir, signifying his succession to the role of the father. It is a ceremony which is conducted in the presence of his relatives and prominent members of the community.

had willed it to Baba Ji, he took the carpet in his hands, raised it to his forehead in a gesture of reverence, and gratefully accepted it. Mata Ji then instructed Bibi Rukko to go with Baba Ji, telling her to look upon service to Baba Ji as service rendered to Soami Ji himself.

While at Agra, Baba Ji Maharaj one day visited Rai Bahadur Saligram Sahib. After retirement in 1887, he had come back and started satsang in Pipal Mandi, Agra. He was called Hazur Sahib. Seth Pratap Singh Ji and Baba Garibdas Ji went along with Baba Ji. Hazur Sahib got up to embrace Baba Ji with great love and talked to him affectionately. He said, "Brother, you have truly served Soami Ji Maharaj and, by meditating, have reached the true Home." To which Baba Ji Maharaj replied "No one can serve as you have done. Soami Ji Maharaj always showered his grace on you."

The next day Rai Bahadur Saligram Sahib brought a silken gown with gold work on it for Baba Ji. But he refused to take it, saying that a poor farmer like himself had no use for it. Saligram Sahib persisted and said, "Has Soami Ji Maharaj not made you the King of kings and filled you with his spiritual wealth?" But Baba Ji did not take the gown. Thereupon Radha Ji took the gown from Hazur Saligram Sahib and gave it to Baba Ji, who then accepted it.

Soami Ji Maharaj, very pleased with Baba Ji, had earlier given him his personal shawl as a token of his love. Baba Ji would occasionally wear the shawl—a deep brown, soft wool shawl with a bold paisley design embroidered in deep green all along the border. A few months before his departure, Baba Ji gave this shawl to Maharaj Sawan Singh.

Baba Ji Settles at Beas

As long as Soami Ji was living, Baba Ji had spent his furloughs in Agra whenever possible, meditating and having Soami Ji's darshan. After Soami Ji passed away in 1878, Baba Ji adopted a different routine during his periods of leave. He would first go to his village, Ghuman, for two or three days. After that he would shift to the west bank of the Beas River, which he knew well from having spent so much time there. He would remain absorbed in meditation day and night. For food he would buy a few chapattis from Nihal Singh's stand at the Beas railway station, put them in a bundle, and hang them from the branch of a tree. After three or four days of uninterrupted meditation, when he felt hungry he would get up from bhajan, dip one or two dry chapattis in water, and eat them.

In 1889, on retirement from the army, Baba Ji went to his home village, Ghuman. Here he initiated a few seekers. Although he used to explain Sant Mat and give occasional discourses to seekers while in the army, this was now to become a regular feature of his life. But he longed to be at a quiet place suitable for meditation, where he could sit for long hours or even days, which perhaps he could not have done in his home in Ghuman.

The lonely, deserted place between the villages of Waraich and Balsarai on the west bank of the river Beas was his favourite retreat for meditation during his service days. As already mentioned, he had first adopted this spot for meditation in 1870 while his army unit was stationed in Mian Mir, near Lahore. Even much earlier than this, in the days when the bridge over the river had not yet been built, he must have passed through here on his trips to Agra in order to take the ferry from the village of Kaniewali, about two miles south of the present Dera.

For a few months, this lonely spot served as a meditation retreat for Baba Ji. He would visit nearby villages like Ghuman, Manko, Vadala, Dhaliwal, and Veela, and hold satsangs there. But as the number of satsangis increased, they started coming to Dera for his darshan, and satsangs in this deserted area became more regular.

Although Baba Ji was staying here most of the time, he had not yet decided to make it his home. Satsangis from different villages would entreat him to make their village his Dera. Quite a few satsangis used to come from the village of Dhaliwal and would always request him to settle down there. One day Baba Ji told them that their village was within the reach of the strong currents of the river and would not be a suitable place for the purpose. Baba Ji's words about Dhaliwal came true when in later years the village was considerably damaged by the currents undercutting the sandy banks.

Until the year 1891, during his visits to the site of the present Dera, Baba Ji used to stay in an improvised room dug into one of the rugged walls of the sandy ravines near the river—a room that could be described as a type of large cave. The cave served as protection against the vagaries of the weather and provided a quiet spot where he could sit in meditation as long as he pleased.

This was not an attempt to escape from worldly responsibilities and seek shelter in mountains and caves. Always averse to the parasitic life of a recluse, Baba Ji took full interest in his army service and attended to his duties faithfully. But he used to spend most of his free time in devotion to the Lord, and the holidays he got came as a God-sent opportunity to devote more time to meditation, to which he attached great importance and which he relished most in life. The lonely spot on the banks of the Beas served as an ideal place to sit undisturbed in meditation, and the improvised cave was a safe place in which to do so.

The long hours of meditation, sometimes extending to days, were not an endeavour to undertake rigorous austerities, penances, and fasting. His soul during meditation would soar to the high spiritual regions and stay there for hours or even days, enjoying inner bliss and peace. Deeply absorbed within, he would become oblivious of time and place, of the physical world and its needs.

Later, when the sangat started coming, the opportunity for such long hours of meditation became rarer. When Baba Ji accepted the request of the residents of Waraich and Balsarai to make this place his permanent residence, a small hut replaced the cave.[1]

The site where Baba Ji sat for meditation, and where the small mud hut with a thatched roof was made for him in 1891, was at that time a deserted wasteland. Snakes, scorpions, jackals, vultures, and other wild animals roamed freely, and the river was infested with crocodiles; small thorny shrubs abounded, and some of the few large trees were believed to be haunted by ghosts and evil spirits. The old men of Waraich used to tell us that skeletons of cattle and other animals, as well as of humans, had been found there, and most people avoided passing through this area even during the daytime.

---

[1] In the soft yet firmly set soil of the ravines, satsangis coming from outside the Dera used to dig out caves as living quarters. These caves were almost like well-ventilated rooms—an opening at the top or on the far side of the wall provided a constant inflow of fresh air and light, and sometimes doors were put over the main entrance, which could be locked from the outside. Such caves were still here even until 1965, but have gradually disappeared as the ravines have been filled in, with the expansion of the Dera.

When Baba Ji first came, well-wishers from the neigh-bouring villages warned him against these dangers, particu-larly against an evil spirit who killed anybody who ventured anywhere near it. Baba Ji replied, "Do not worry, the ogre will not harm me."

The old men of Waraich would also tell us about a faqir called Kahana Kamla ("Kahana, the mad one") who used to roam about in this area several years before Baba Ji came and settled here. This man, mostly engrossed in his own thoughts, would collect any brick or brick pieces, stones, and pebbles he could find in his wanderings and make piles of them at the place where Dera's first buildings were later to be con-structed. When people asked him what he was doing, he would say, "A King of kings will come and live here. I am col-lecting materials for his palace." Sometimes he would say that a large township would be built here.

Some satsangis from the cities felt unhappy at Baba Ji's decision to stay in a mud hut in such a deserted and barren land. A cloth merchant from Amritsar once said, "Maharaj Ji, what a lonely and forbidding spot you have selected. There is nothing except thorny acacias and spiny shrubs here." Baba Ji replied, "My son, this very place will one day become a centre of spiritual activity."

Early Years of the Dera

During these early days several small incidents occurred, which impressed the simple folk in this area and made them realize that Baba Ji was no ordinary person. A man from a neighbouring village once stole a new pair of shoes belong-ing to a satsangi. When Baba Ji heard about it, he told the satsangi, "It's all right. The thief will bring back the shoes himself." Early the next morning the villager came to Baba Ji with the new pair of shoes in his hand. After asking Baba Ji's forgiveness, he said, "All night long I felt the shoes on my chest. Their weight was crushing me and I could not sleep."

When a lamp is lighted, moths automatically come flying around it; wherever Saints appear, their marked souls are naturally drawn towards them. Slowly but steadily the number of Baba Ji's disciples increased, and he came to be known in the neighbouring villages and towns as a highly evolved soul. His clear exposition of spiritual truth in simple but forceful everyday language impressed all who came to his satsangs. He laid great stress on leading a pure life, earning one's own honest living, fulfilling one's family and social obligations, and attending to meditation regularly. His own life exemplified these basic principles of Sant Mat—he lived according to what he taught and he practised what he preached.

Baba Ji's personal possessions consisted of a few changes of clothes, a brass plate, a bowl, a small brass pot, a cot, some simple bedding, a pair of leather shoes, a pair of wooden sandals, and a walking stick. He ate sparingly and took little interest in food, eating whatever Bibi Rukko cooked. Sometimes Baba Ji would sit in meditation for four or five days at a time. Bibi Rukko would feel worried and express her anxiety over Baba Ji's health to the satsangis of Waraich. As with all perfect Saints, he never accepted any gifts but lived entirely on his pension, which he collected each month from Sathiala, a few miles from the Dera.[1] His personal needs were few and he would always save some amount out of his pension to give as seva for the sangat. Many close satsangis and their family

---

[1] Sathiala, about four miles north of Dera, was the nearest post office at that time for Dera, Waraich, and Balsarai.

members were treated as personal guests, and Baba Ji would rarely allow them to eat in the langar, providing meals for them from his own kitchen.

Baba Ji's disciples were simple men and women who carried out their spiritual labours with deep devotion. The Great Master often used to tell us stories about satsangis of Baba Ji's day, like the one about Machhar and Ramditta, two farmers from the village of Mandali. Both of them were steeped in love for Baba Ji, and they would never start their daily duties until they had sat in meditation for some hours and had seen the Radiant Form of their Master.

Once during the corn season when it was their turn to get irrigation water, although they had sat in meditation for a long time, they were unable to see the Master within. Ramditta said, "Brother Machhar, today Baba Ji has not given me his darshan within." Machhar said, "He hasn't appeared to me either. But if we miss our turn for water, our crop will die." At this, Ramditta said with fervour, "Everything belongs to the Satguru. Let it die if such be his will!" They both returned to their meditation, and within a few moments Baba Ji appeared to them within.

Baba Ji's Great Love and Compassion

Although Baba Ji was loved and respected by satsangis and even non-satsangis, there were many orthodox people, dominated by superstitions, who resented his teachings. In the village of Bhandal some of these people started slandering Baba Ji, which greatly upset the satsangis, who wrote to him about it. Always loving and forgiving, Baba Ji sent a reply that reveals the grace and kindness of the Saints:

*Satsangis must have love and affection for one another.
You are really all one. Have implicit faith in the Satguru;
one day he will take you with him to the true Home. Do
not be angry or perturbed if anybody speaks ill of me.
Those who have been initiated by the Saints are already
redeemed. But such is their grace that they liberate their
critics also, for there is no other way out for such people.
In this manner, even those who have not received initiation will be cleansed and liberated. Saints alone know
the working of the Saints' grace.*[1]

Many stories are told of Baba Ji's great love and compassion. Maharaj Sawan Singh once wrote that one of his colleagues was very anxious to be initiated; he looked upon Baba
Ji as a perfect Saint and longed to receive Nam in this very
birth. Baba Ji replied unequivocally, "From the day his faith
in me became firm, his destiny has been in my hands. He
will receive the benefit of initiation through the Satguru's
thoughts of mercy and grace for him, so that even if he were
to die right now, he would again receive a human birth. He
will not go into the chain of lower species."

In his compassion, Baba Ji would sometimes reveal the
working of the Saints' grace to some of his disciples. He would
tell them that there was some load of karma to undergo which
would mean a period of illness and adversity. But he would
tell the person not to worry as there would be considerable
remission, and the account of karmas would be settled
through only a few days of fever. He conveyed such hints even
in his letters.

At the same time Baba Ji was uncompromising in his
principles. Once a few satsangis brought to his notice that a

---

[1]   This letter, as well as extracts from other letters given in this chapter, are translated from Baba Ji's original letters in Punjabi.

mausoleum was being constructed in Agra in honour and memory of Soami Ji and that donations were being requested for this purpose. Baba Ji said, "The only true memorial to a Saint is his teachings. Mausoleums cannot keep his memory alive. Instead they divert the attention of the true seeker to outward rituals. Soami Ji always emphasized the need for turning the attention within and meditating inwardly." Then he said, "Do not let anyone build a memorial for me when I am gone." He always strongly forbade his disciples to indulge in outward rituals and ceremonies; likewise, meditation on photographs of Saints was forbidden. Outspoken in his condemnation of this practice, he ordered his initiates not to possess even a single copy of his photograph.

Life at the Dera, including the food and dress of the satsangis, was simple during Baba Ji's time. As there was no shop in the Dera, all groceries had to be brought from nearby villages. Except for flour, pulses, and the like, all other items of daily need had to be purchased in the towns of Amritsar or Jullundur. Even paper to write letters on had to be brought from the towns. Baba Ji used to write letters in his own hand, but when Milkhi Ram (the father of Bibi Ralli) of the village of Mithapur became a satsangi, Baba Ji would sometimes dictate replies to him.

Baba Ji used to hold satsang every day, but the number of people attending was quite small. Daily satsang was attended usually by only four or five satsangis and occasionally by as many as eight or ten. Sometimes Baba Ji would sit on the ground on a mat covered with a white cloth. Other times he would sit on a cot as he discoursed on a verse from the writings of the saints, recited by Bibi Rukko or Jwala Singh. Bibi Ralli, who has been living at Dera from the age of six and who also saw Baba Ji Maharaj, informs us that in those days the monthly satsang was attended by thirty to fifty people, and only about thirty pounds of cereal and sugar were needed to prepare the parshad. Later, as the number of initiates increased, the attendance at the monthly satsangs grew to about two hundred.[1] Today during the bhandaras, four hundred thousand people eat in the langar and almost four hundred pounds of salt alone are used for each meal.

Bibi Rukko, who served Baba Ji faithfully till the end of his life, not only had great love for Baba Ji but also was fond of the other members of his family. She wanted Swami Singh, son of Baba Ji's brother Jiwan Singh, to be his successor. But Baba Ji would explain to her that Swami Singh was not worthy of this exalted work and was not destined to live for long. Swami Singh died soon after Baba Ji.

Baba Ji had two brothers, Jiwan Singh and Dan Singh; both loved him deeply and attended his satsang regularly. He also had two sisters, Bibi Tabo and Bibi Rajo. Bibi Tabo firmly believed from the beginning that Baba Ji was no ordinary person; she used to tell the other members of the family that her brother was a great soul. Soon after Baba Ji left the world, both his brothers also passed away. Today there are no living descendants of Baba Ji's family.

Initiation of Maharaj Sawan Singh

In October 1894, Baba Ji went to the Murree Hills along with Bibi Rukko.[2] The purpose of his visit, as he told Bibi Rukko,

---

[1] Whenever Baba Ji was at the Dera on *sankrant,* the first day of the month according to the Indian calendar, he would hold satsang, which was attended by a relatively large number of satsangis. The regular "monthly satsangs" were introduced later by Maharaj Sawan Singh when he was in service. On the last weekend of every month he would get leave from his job, come to Dera, and hold satsang.

[2] Not far from Rawalpindi, the Murree Hills are now in Pakistan.

was to initiate Maharaj Sawan Singh, who was at the time stationed at Murree as a sub-divisional officer in the Military Engineering Service. Maharaj Sawan Singh, a keen seeker of spiritual truth, heard about Baba Ji and his satsangs. He came to the satsang and, after a few days of inquiries, asked for Nam. Baba Ji initiated him on 15 October 1894.[1] A devoted disciple and a highly evolved soul, Maharaj Sawan Singh was Baba Ji's chosen successor. In satsangs and informal talks with close satsangis, Maharaj Ji would sometimes narrate incidents of Baba Ji's life, some of which form the basis of this chapter.

Baba Ji once accompanied Maharaj Sawan Singh to the Murree Hills. Opposite Sawan Singh Ji's bungalow was a small hill known as Maujpuri or Mokshapuri, a place of pilgrimage for Hindus. Sawan Singh Ji, pointing to the scenery, said to Baba Ji, "Look, Maharaj Ji, what a lovely spot!" Baba Ji replied that he had seen it before. Sawan Singh Ji thought that Baba Ji might have been there when he was in the service, but when he inquired, Baba Ji said that he was referring to a time when these mountains had not yet come up and the entire place had been a flat plain. Baba Ji often declared that the Lord had sent him from Sach Khand in earlier times, too, to liberate souls from bondage.

Baba Ji and His Disciples

Though he had not undergone any formal education, Baba Ji's understanding of the various schools of Indian philosophy was profound. Through his long search and keen inquiries, he knew the intricacies and pitfalls of the many systems of yogic practice and pranayam. Once, three pundits came to

---

[1] Details of the initiation of Maharaj Sawan Singh will be given in the next chapter.

Dera to seek Baba Ji's opinion in a dispute over the interpretation of certain verses in the scriptures. One of them had suggested that since Baba Jaimal Singh was an enlightened soul, he might be able to give them the correct meaning. When they presented their problem, Baba Ji humbly said that he was ignorant of the Sanskrit language. Yet during the course of his conversation he threw such light on the disputed point that, amazed at his insight, they humbly requested initiation. Baba Ji told them that scholars are too caught up in the intellect to work hard at meditation, pure erudition being of little help on the path. At this, two of the pundits left, but the third persisted and begged for Nam. Baba Ji, acceding to his request, granted him initiation.

After six months he came again and told Baba Ji Maharaj that the path of Surat Shabd Yoga was not as high a path as that of pranayam. He came again in a few months, saying that even pranayam was useless, and begged Baba Ji to show him a glimpse of what lay inside. Baba Ji advised him to work hard at his meditation if he was keen to have inner experiences.

Several days later, while on his way to collect his pension in Sathiala, Baba Ji was accosted by the pundit. He entreated Baba Ji to give him just a fleeting glimpse of the inner regions, but Baba Ji explained that it would be harmful. The pundit insisted until finally Baba Ji made him sit in meditation and took the man's attention within. The pundit shrieked and fell to the ground, crying, "Save me, save me!" Baba Ji said, "Bring your attention out." He opened his eyes and said, "It was as if a million thunderbolts fell on me all at once." Then Baba Ji told him, "You have only three more years to live. Spend them as you wish, in meditation or worldly pursuits."

Baba Ji used to say that Sant Mat is a path of acceptance, not of obstinacy. It is wrong to press Saints to do something against their judgment; one should always try to live in their will. They will take the disciple's soul inside whenever they think it fit.

Maharaj Sawan Singh sometimes used to narrate an incident from Baba Ji's life to illustrate the great Saint's compassionate nature and how Saints often quietly undergo suffering in order to fulfil a loving devotee's earnest but obstinate demand. Once, at the request of a devoted satsangi, tailor Moti Ram, Baba Ji went to Ambala for satsang. He stayed with Moti Ram, who had a keen desire that Sant Mat should spread in Ambala. Baba Ji's discourses greatly impressed the people. A relative of the magistrate, named Hukam Singh, came to satsang every day. When he requested initiation, Baba Ji put him off tactfully. Then Hukam Singh asked Moti Ram to speak to Baba Ji on his behalf. Thinking that the initiation of such an intelligent and influential man would give a great impetus to satsang in the city, Moti Ram pleaded Hukam Singh's case to Baba Ji. He again refused. When Moti Ram repeated his request, Baba Ji said, "Ask me to initiate a thousand other souls instead, but don't ask me to give Nam to this man. His karmic load is very heavy." Moti Ram still persisted and said, "Maharaj Ji, if even you cannot lighten this man's burden, then where else can he go?"

At this, Baba Ji, who had originally intended to stay in Ambala for a whole month, said to Moti Ram, "All right, if you insist on having him initiated, I will do so. But I will leave Ambala immediately after his initiation." Moti Ram was adamant and said, "As you wish, Sir. I shall come to Beas for your darshan and shall hear your satsangs there."

The next day a tonga (horse-drawn cart) was called at Baba Ji's request, his bedding was placed in it, and the tonga stood ready to leave. Immediately after initiating Hukam Singh, Baba Ji went to the railway station and caught a train for Beas. When the train stopped at Ludhiana, Sawan Singh

Ji happened to be on the platform. He humbly asked, "Maharaj Ji, my village is only a short distance from here. Please come and give darshan." Baba Ji said, "No, not this time." And then he added, "Do not come to Dera this Sunday." Sawan Singh Ji was surprised, for he had never received such orders before; whenever he came home on leave, he always attended Sunday satsang at Beas. However, in obedience to his Master's orders, he returned to his village.

On reaching Dera, Baba Ji had a violent fever. His body burned like a furnace, giving off heat that his attendants could feel as soon as they came near. Everyone was in despair, for they had lost hope that Baba Ji would survive. When Bibi Rukko and other satsangis begged him to take medicine, Baba Ji said, "I will not take any medicine for twelve days." Bibi Rukko, distraught with grief, began to cry. Baba Ji comforted her, saying, "Don't worry. I am not leaving you."

For twelve days the fever raged and then subsided suddenly. On the thirteenth or fourteenth day Sawan Singh Ji came to Dera for the Sunday satsang and learned of Baba Ji's illness. He said, "Maharaj Ji, you forbade me to come to Dera. If I had been here, I could at least have been of some service." Baba Ji said, "The sight of my suffering would have been unbearable for you. That is why I did not let you come."

Sawan Singh Ji asked Baba Ji the cause of his undergoing such intense suffering. At first Baba Ji avoided telling him, but on seeing Maharaj Ji's anxiety, he said that the burden of Hukam Singh's karmas was so heavy that he had been destined to be roasted by Kal in the fires of hell for seven births. At Moti Ram's insistence Baba Ji took those karmas on himself.

Maharaj Sawan Singh, who never narrated this incident while Hukam Singh was living, used to say that all karmic accounts have to be cleared, for Kal demands the remittance of karmic debts to the last penny.

When Maharaj Sawan Singh was in government service, he had a watchman named Kishan Singh who served him for thirteen years. He was a pure-hearted man, very fond of reciting verses from the Adi Granth; he would get up soon after midnight to have a bath and begin his recitation. Maharaj Ji thought the man was sincere and had a devotional bent of mind, and that if he were to receive initiation his devotion would be properly channelled. During one of Baba Ji's visits to him, Maharaj Sawan Singh said, "Baba Ji Maharaj, Kishan Singh will be coming to see you." Kishan Singh went to see Baba Ji at Maharaj Sawan Singh's suggestion, sat with him for some time, but left without asking for initiation. The Saints never ask any soul to seek initiation from them, so Kishan Singh went away empty-handed.

When he returned from his office, Maharaj Sawan Singh asked Baba Ji if Kishan Singh had come to see him. Baba Ji said, "Yes, he did, but what you are thinking for him will not be possible." Maharaj Ji said, "He seems such a pure soul—he recites the scriptures very devotedly. It would greatly benefit him to receive initiation." Baba Ji replied, "Reading and reciting scriptures is one thing; Nam is something quite apart from such outward practices. He is not destined to get Nam during this birth. In fact, he will be burned alive."

Maharaj Sawan Singh used to relate that several years later he met some satsangis from Kishan Singh's village, Sayyad Kasravan, and inquired about him. They told him that one day Kishan Singh's house had caught fire. He climbed up to the roof to put out the fire but fell, and was burnt in the flames.

Hazur used to relate another such incident. In Murree, Maharaj Ji had an orderly named Hari Singh who worked with him for eleven years. Once, when Baba Ji was visiting Murree, Maharaj Ji brought Hari Singh to Baba Ji to seek his grace for the servant. After he had left, Baba Ji said, "This man

39

will not get initiation during his present birth even if he keeps listening to satsangs for a hundred years. He is destined to die by drowning." A few years later Hari Singh went to his ancestral home, where he became involved in a lawsuit. Overcome with fear and nervousness, he left a suicide note absolving others of responsibility for his death, and plunged into a pond.

Maharaj Ji used to say that the Saints do not look upon anyone as good or evil. They only look at his karmas, which they see as clearly as one sees the contents of a glass bottle.

Baba Ji's Love for Maharaj Sawan Singh

Baba Ji had great love and regard for Maharaj Sawan Singh. The letters written by him to Maharaj Ji give glimpses of the deep spiritual unity and love between a perfect Master and the disciple chosen by him to continue his divine mission:

> *Babu Sawan Singh, my beloved disciple, you are the life of my life. You are my son, the soul of obedience—a gurmukh. I am highly pleased with you. You are definitely going to reach Sach Khand and live with me for ever and ever. You are not to be given another birth.*

> *You are dearer to me than my body, dearer than the breath within it. And you will not be born again. Where I live, there you will live also. I am very, very happy with you.*

> *In every way I am very, very pleased with you. Your form is not separate from mine; the bodies appear different for the purpose of performing worldly duties.*

The letters reflect the interest Baba Ji had not only in Maharaj Sawan Singh's meditation and spiritual progress but also in his physical well-being. He instructed Maharaj Ji to write to him at least twice a month and never less than once. He was always pleased to receive letters from this beloved disciple, and would sometimes express his feelings thus: "The moment I receive a letter from you, my heart is filled with a happiness that no words can describe."

Bhai Manna Singh, who served Baba Ji for several years, once told us, "One day I saw Baba Ji reading a letter over and over again, but I did not know what it contained or who it was from. When I asked about it, Baba Ji told me it was a letter from Babu Sawan Singh, overflowing with love for the Master and longing to be at his feet. He wanted to resign his job and yearned to come to Dera to devote all his time to the Master's service. Then I said to Baba Ji, "If he is languishing there without you and yearns to spend his time at your holy feet, why not call him here?" Baba Ji replied, "He still has to fulfil his worldly obligations. But a day will come, my child, when you will see for yourself how much spiritual work Soami Ji takes from him."

Many times Baba Ji wrote to Maharaj Ji, "All the worldly work you are doing is service rendered to the Master. Meditation is also the Master's service." When Maharaj Ji asked permission to give up his job and come to Dera, Baba Ji replied: "Sach Khand is just behind the veil, not far. Why should you feel disturbed? You will definitely reach Home. You have written that you want to give up service in order to devote yourself entirely to bhajan. What is yours in the home? What is yours in the service? What is yours in the money you earn? Just think, what is there in giving them up or in keeping them? All that you see is a magician's show. The world is like a dream.... You write that you have not mentioned to anyone the money you give in seva, in case you should feel vain. Why should you feel vain? What belongs to you? All this belongs to the Master. You must look upon yourself as his agent, not the owner."

Once, when Basant Singh, Maharaj Sawan Singh's second son, failed his examinations, Maharaj Ji wrote to Baba Ji that his sons were not studying, whereas other people's children seemed to study hard. Baba Ji replied, "Do not worry about Basant Singh. Let him study and teach him draftsmanship also. What does it matter if he has failed in his examinations twice? He will get through. Who knows what is in store for him? You feel sorry that your sons are not good in their studies while those of others, much younger, study well. Just think, have those boys been blessed with the wealth of Nam? When they die they will not go Home, but your sons will go to their true Home. What comparison is there between your family and theirs?"

Baba Ji had great love and concern even for Maharaj Sawan Singh's entire family. Maharaj Ji had surrendered his heart and soul to Baba Ji and always lived in his will; and Baba Ji, as is evident from his letters, was deeply concerned about the welfare of Maharaj Ji and his family. Once Baba Ji told Bibi Rukko that the karmas of Bachint Singh, Maharaj Ji's eldest son, were very heavy and he was destined to be hanged from a tree in his own courtyard. Bibi Rukko submitted, "Baba Ji Maharaj, Babu Sawan Singh is your devoted disciple. He has surrendered his body, mind, and soul at your feet. If such a thing happens to his son, would it not cause him anguish?" At this Baba Ji became silent.

The next time Baba Ji went to Mehmansinghwala with Bibi Rukko, he sat in meditation the whole night. On getting up in the morning, he called Bibi Rukko and said, "Take the rope which my bedding has been tied up with and tie it to

42

the branch of the tree in the courtyard." When the rope had been properly tied, Baba Ji called Bachint Singh and around his neck put a noose made from the free end. Giving his knife to Bibi Rukko, Baba Ji said, "As soon as I pull the rope around the boy's throat, cut it in one stroke from the other end." Bibi Rukko did so, and Baba Ji said to Bachint Singh, "Go, my son, Soami Ji Maharaj has forgiven you."[1]

In one of his letters to Maharaj Sawan Singh, Baba Ji sent the following instructions regarding the life and conduct of an ideal disciple, a gurmukh:

> As soon as you have finished your official duties, stop your worldly routine, take your attention out of your worldly work, and begin your spiritual work. From 6:00 to 8:00 P.M. sit in bhajan. Then hold satsang from 8:00 to 10:00 P.M. After 10:00 P.M. you may go to bed or indulge in talk, but your meditation must start by 4:30 A.M. During your duties of the day, you may talk freely with others, but as soon as the day's routine is over in the office, you should observe silence and not waste your time in the company of worldly people. Eat your meals by yourself in the kitchen.
>
> You should stay aloof in this world, and yet associate with people in your work. The way you live should be an example for others. You should live in the world like the duck, which, although living in water all day, flies away with dry wings. I pray that you may receive grace and blessings.

Putting great emphasis on doing meditation while at the same time fulfilling one's worldly duties, Baba Ji would write

---

[1] As the author mentions, "Bachint Singh himself used to narrate this incident. I have heard it also from Bibi Rukko."

to Maharaj Ji to do his meditation every day punctually and regularly, and also to devote all his free time to it. However, when Maharaj Ji felt that he was not doing enough meditation due to official duties, Baba Ji wrote to him with great affection and compassion that "the responsibility for your meditation during the time you are occupied in official work is mine"—an assurance that a great soul like Maharaj Sawan Singh Ji alone was worthy of.

A Portrait of Baba Ji

Unfortunately there are no photographs of Baba Ji available, so we know of his appearance only from descriptions—and who can describe a Saint? Initiates of Baba Ji used to say that he was medium height, with a light, wheatish complexion and an attractive face highlighted by deeply impressive, sparkling eyes. His voice was deep, yet soft and caressing. His letters, mostly written to his beloved disciple Maharaj Sawan Singh, show a clear mind, facile expression, and profound understanding. They also reflect a strong sense of spiritual discipline and a deeply loving and compassionate nature.

Strict with himself but kind to others, his entire life was one of uncompromising physical and spiritual discipline. Never accepting gifts or presents from others, maintaining himself on his frugal pension, he always urged his disciples to support themselves and their families through their own honest income. "Never use anything which does not belong to you," he would remind his disciples. "Even if you happen to be the ruler of the whole world, you must earn your living through honest means. Work with integrity in your service. Use your income and also share it with others—members of your family and the sangat—as far as feasible."

Baba Ji himself followed this practice meticulously. Once a subscription for a Punjabi paper was sent, but through oversight the paper was addressed to "Sant Jwala Singh" instead of "Sant Jaimal Singh." Although several satsangis suggested that it was a slip on the part of the senders, and the paper must be meant for him since there was no Sant Jwala Singh in this small place, Baba Ji refused to accept the packet in the remote possibility that the paper was meant for someone else.

Endowed with a strong will and an immense spiritual power, Baba Ji also possessed great physical strength. His disciples used to give many accounts of his strength. Sardar Fateh Singh of the village of Dasuha was regarded as one of the strongest men of his time. He could lift with his bare hands a persian wheel with the whole round of pots full of water; he could jump over two camels standing side by side. Once, when he was riding a camel through a forest, two robbers stopped him and demanded the thick gold bangles he was wearing. He told the robbers to come on either side of him and remove the bangles. When they came close, he caught each of them by the hair and rode for quite a distance, dangling them by their hair. He let them go only after they had repeatedly begged him to forgive them.

Fateh Singh's army unit was stationed at Delhi in 1857 along with Baba Ji's. He used to narrate that once, when he was boasting about his strength to Baba Ji Maharaj—then a youth of eighteen—Baba Ji told him not to feel so much pride. "Why should I not feel proud of something that is a fact?" asked Fateh Singh. At this, Baba Ji got up and placed his foot firmly on one side of the cot he had been sitting on. He said to Fateh Singh, "Lift this end, if you can." Fateh Singh tried as hard as he could, but could not even raise the side of the cot. Then he fell at Baba Ji's feet, his pride humbled.

Baba Ji would always stress the importance of perform-ing one's worldly obligations along with meditation, and he himself followed this practice throughout his life. He would spend almost all spare time after military duty in meditation, sometimes devoting the entire night to it. Punctual and vigi-lant in performing his military duties, he was attached to no one yet was loving towards all. Maharaj Sawan Singh used to say that Baba Ji had no hostile feelings even towards the op-posing combatants; in the evenings he would sometimes go among them and they respected him as a great holy man.

Satsang Tours

There is no record available of Baba Ji's tours, nor details of his visits to various places. However, it is known that he used to go regularly on satsang tours to villages and towns in Punjab. Manko, Vadala, Dhaliwal, and Bhandallan (now in Pakistan) were some of the places he used to visit often. He would also go to Murree, Kalabagh, Khairagali, Abbotabad, Rawalpindi, and other hill areas to give darshan and hold satsangs at Maharaj Sawan Singh's request. A few colleagues and subordinates of Maharaj Ji, as well as his personal ser-vants like Roor Singh (who looked after his horse), Banta Singh, and Chanan Singh (his cook and servant), were some of Baba Ji's initiates in the hills. He would also visit Amritsar two or three times a year.

There were quite a few satsangi families in Baba Ji's home village of Ghuman, and he would often visit his village and hold satsang there. In Ghuman, Baba Ji lived in a small room, about nine feet long and three and a half feet wide. Even be-fore coming to Beas, whenever Baba Ji spent time in Ghuman, this small room was his favourite place for meditation.

Maharaj Sawan Singh had a desire that his mother be initiated by Baba Ji, but he would never ask him to do so. In April 1896, when Baba Ji first visited Mehmansinghwala, Maharaj Ji's home village, he initiated Maharaj Ji's mother, wife, and eldest daughter-in-law. After this he visited Mehmansinghwala often, and during later visits he initiated Maharaj Ji's grandfather, Sardar Sher Singh—who was then more than a hundred years old—and Maharaj Ji's sons Bachint Singh and Basant Singh.

Baba Ji's Attitude Towards Others

In Baba Ji's time the sangat was small and the relationship between the satsangis and the Master was of a close personal nature. Sometimes he would serve chapattis in the langar with his own hands. Although Baba Ji spent thirty-three years of his life in military service, on coming to Dera he had to keep the accounts, maintain a record of initiations, and plan the purchase of even the smallest items required for construction work. He used to keep a record of all money received in seva, even of a paisa or a fraction thereof, and would note the name of the person giving the seva, a record he maintained till 27 December 1903, two days before he left this world. The record of initiation comes to us from the year 1884, but old satsangis used to say that Baba Ji, on the instructions of Soami Ji Maharaj, had started initiating in 1877/78, when he was still in service.

The drawings of the various Dera buildings constructed in Baba Ji's time were supplied by Maharaj Sawan Singh. The actual supervision of work, engagement of labour, payment of wages, selection of materials—such as wooden rafters, lime, tar, iron girders, planks of wood, paint, and many small items necessary for construction of the buildings—was done by Baba Ji.

Like all Saints, Baba Ji had great personal charm. His loving nature, humility, and spirit of tolerance and understanding won the hearts of those who came in contact with him. The soldiers of his unit loved and respected him, and many continued to write to him till the end of his life. Some became satsangis, but almost the entire unit would regularly send their respects in letters written jointly. Whenever the unit passed through Beas, they would send a message to Baba Ji, requesting that he come and give darshan at the railway station, for they could not break their journey during army transfers. Baba Ji's letters to Maharaj Sawan Singh throw light on Baba Ji's affection for his co-soldiers and subordinates, and once, when the 24th Regiment was returning from China, Baba Ji cancelled all other programmes in order to meet them at the railway station.

Construction Projects at the Dera

At the time Maharaj Sawan Singh was initiated, Baba Ji Maharaj was living in a small mud hut, eight feet by eight feet and barely eight and a half feet high. There was another small hut nearby in which Bibi Rukko lived and prepared meals for Baba Ji. There were only two cots—the one used by Baba Ji, which is still preserved, and a very small one belonging to Bibi Rukko. In winter the satsangis coming from outside the Dera used to spread straw or reeds on the ground, and sheets or a thin cotton carpet to make a bed. During the cold weather they would sleep in the neighbouring villages or in small improvised caves that they hollowed out in the sandy ravines that abounded in the area.

Whenever Maharaj Sawan Singh came to Dera, Baba Ji lodged him in his own hut. Maharaj Ji would unroll his bedding under Baba Ji's cot and sleep there. Later, even when a few rooms were built, Maharaj Ji still used to sleep in Baba Ji's room under his cot. But after Baba Ji left this world, Maharaj Ji never again used the room for sleeping; instead, he would sit for meditation there.

Soon after his initiation, Maharaj Sawan Singh persuaded Baba Ji to allow the thatched hut to be turned into a permanent room. Baba Ji preferred a small room, so the length and breadth were kept practically the same, but the ceiling height was increased by a few feet. Maharaj Ji saw to it that the earth and other materials of the mud walls of the hut were not thrown away; all of it was used for the raised plinth of the new room.

One morning during his first visit to Dera, Maharaj Sawan Singh happened to see Bibi Rukko bringing a pitcher of water for Baba Ji's bath. Then after a short while she brought water for Maharaj Sawan Singh's bath. Maharaj Ji realized that such clean water could not have come from the river; Bibi Rukko must have brought it from some well. But he had not seen a well anywhere near the Dera. When asked, Bibi Rukko told him that she had brought the water from the well in Waraich. As the river water was not clean, she would daily bring water from the village for Baba Ji's bath and for cooking and drinking purposes. Maharaj Ji, distressed to learn that Bibi Rukko had to take so much trouble every day, requested her to allow him to do this seva as long as he stayed in Dera.

However, the next day when he went to Waraich to get water, the soft soil, depressions, ravines, and ridges made it difficult for him to balance the heavy, water-filled pitcher on his head. Though he was unaccustomed to that kind of work,

49

he managed to cover the mile-long distance from the well to the Dera, thinking all the while how convenient it would be for the sangat if a well were dug at Dera. After some thought, he approached Baba Ji one day and hesitantly said, "Maharaj Ji, the sangat is being put to great inconvenience because of the lack of fresh water. If you would give permission to dig a well here, the sangat would benefit greatly and Bibi Rukko would be relieved of much daily trouble."

Baba Ji said, "What is the point of sinking a well? I may not stay here long—today I am here, tomorrow somewhere else. I do not want to be tied down to a well." Maharaj Sawan Singh then said, "Maharaj Ji, I don't want to tie you down. If you even once drink the water from the well, it will be enough reward for me." Baba Ji smiled and said, "All right, get the well dug. I will not be tied down to it, but you will be."

The significance of Baba Ji's words became clear when Maharaj Sawan Singh was appointed his successor.

When the digging of the well began, a brick kiln was built to supply baked bricks for the well.[1] On 16 May 1897, Baba Ji lit the kiln with his own hands, and on 9 December 1898, he wrote to Maharaj Sawan Singh about the completion of the well:

The well is ready now. The water is seven cubits deep, sufficient for our needs. The layers of sand had ended, so the depth could not be increased. On December 8 the

---

[1] The brick kiln in those days was an open-air mound of charcoal and wood shavings, which was called *ava* in Punjabi. When the raw brick moulds were placed around it and covered with charcoal etc., it was lit. The low heat would bake the bricks in six to eight weeks. The brick kiln started by Baba Ji in Dera still continues to operate, though with an improved design and on a larger scale. The location of the kilns has been shifted from time to time according to the needs and expansion of Dera. All buildings, roads, etc., in Dera have been made with bricks from the Dera kilns.

work was completed. The first water from the well was sent to Chacha Ji[1] and will probably be distributed as parshad among the sangat. But the formal opening of the well will take place when you arrive here.

In 1898, at the request of Maharaj Sawan Singh, a small satsang hall was constructed, thirty feet by fifteen feet, to be used for satsang and accommodation. Built at the same time as the well, it served as a satsang hall for only a very short time because the sangat had increased even during its construction. Maharaj Sawan Singh, during one of his visits, mentioned the shortage of accommodation to Baba Ji and requested permission to build a few rooms for the sangat. Baba Ji replied, "But the river is too close."[2] He was quiet for a while, and then gave permission for construction of a building.

At that time the river was undercutting the Waraich land adjacent to the river. From above, the earth appeared to be solid; but at any time, houses and land would suddenly collapse into the river and be swept out of sight. Worried by this, the villagers had to keep moving their homes inland, away from the encroaching river.

The villagers came to Maharaj Sawan Singh and said, "What are you doing? You're building rooms on the very land that is being washed away by the river!" Maharaj Ji said, "If Baba Ji's sangat uses these rooms for only one day, it is enough. I want nothing more." Thus, work was begun on a building with five rooms on the ground floor and four on the first floor. It was completed in 1900.

---

[1] Seth Pratap Singh, Soami Ji's younger brother, affectionately called Chacha Ji.
[2] In those days the Beas River ran in a zigzag right through the eastern part of the present Dera, within a few yards of where these rooms were built. The river used to flow through the present langar grounds and shed area, the eye camp area, and the "thirty-six quarters."

Baba Ji always used the donations sent by the Great Master for construction at the Dera. The well, the two small satsang halls, the rooms, and other early buildings were all made with major contributions from Maharaj Sawan Singh.[1] Even in Soami Bagh, Agra, most of the money for building small rooms for the accommodation of Beas satsangis came from the Great Master's donations. While on active duty in the hill stations, Maharaj Ji would often send woollen cloth and other local products to Baba Ji as presents for Seth Pratap Singh. When Baba Ji sent these things to Agra, Chacha Ji would accept them gladly, in a spirit of love and affection.

Relationship With Soami Bagh at Agra

After the departure of Soami Ji Maharaj, Baba Ji continued to visit Agra to pay his respects to Mata Radha Ji (Soami Ji's wife), and to meet the other members of Soami Ji's family. Sometimes he would take Maharaj Sawan Singh along with him. Soami Ji's younger brother, Seth Pratap Singh, had great affection and regard for Baba Ji. Baba Ji also respected and loved him as a family member of his Master, Soami Ji Maharaj. The letters received by Baba Ji and Maharaj Sawan Singh from Agra reveal mutual feelings of deep affection and respect between Baba Ji and Soami Ji's family members.

Once, Seth Pratap Singh wrote a letter to Baba Ji asking him to be one of the ten members of a committee formed to resolve the conflicts and unite the various groups that had sprung up since Soami Ji had passed on. Baba Ji declined membership, saying he had faith only in Soami Ji Maharaj,

---

[1] The two small satsang halls are near the well, to the west of the Great Master's residence.

and in people who had received initiation as Soami Ji had instructed and who practised simran and bhajan accordingly. Since some of the proposed members of the committee did not meet these criteria, Baba Ji did not wish to associate himself with it. Baba Ji instructed Maharaj Sawan Singh to correspond with Chacha Ji and give Baba Ji's conditions for the Beas Satsang to join such a committee.[1]

Although Soami Ji's works had already been published in Hindi, Baba Ji wanted them to be available to Punjabi-speaking people also. In 1901 Baba Ji received Seth Pratap Singh's permission to publish both *Sar Bachan* prose and poetry in Punjabi script, and entrusted the task to Maharaj Sawan Singh. Baba Ji asked him not to make any changes in the manuscript, not even in a mark of punctuation. "There should, however, be one difference"—so the instructions read—"the line in the preface stating that Soami Ji had no Guru should be deleted."[2] By 1903 both works of Soami Ji had been printed and released to the sangat.

Gradually the sangat grew and Maharaj Sawan Singh asked Baba Ji's permission to build a larger satsang hall since the old one had become too small to hold the growing number of people. Baba Ji said, "Dera is at the brink of the river. Why spend so much money here?" Maharaj Ji again made the deferential response he had made before: "Maharaj Ji, if you hold satsang in the new hall even once, I will look upon my seva as fruitful. After that, if the river sweeps away the entire building, it does not matter." Baba Ji was pleased with the reply and gave his permission.

The new hall (fifty-five feet by twenty feet), built near the well, was completed in April/May 1903. As it turned out, Baba

---

[1] The gist of these letters appear in *Spiritual Letters*, numbers 97–99.
[2] Baba Ji used to say that Soami Ji was initiated by Tulsi Sahib of Hathras.

Ji did hold only one satsang in the hall. When disciples asked him to give more satsangs there, he replied, "Baba Sawan Singh will deliver discourses here now."

Last Days of Baba Ji Maharaj
Successorship of Maharaj Sawan Singh Ji

On the last Sunday in July 1903, Baba Ji ordered all his disciples to go to the satsang hall and sit in meditation. He himself did not go; nor did Bibi Rukko and one other satsangi. Baba Ji said, "You also go, Bibi, and take this satsangi with you." Bibi Rukko said, "Maharaj Ji, we will go only if you also go. Please come and give satsang." Baba Ji again told them to go, saying, "The one who is to deliver satsang is already there."

Following Baba Ji's orders, Bibi Rukko and the other satsangi went to the hall. As soon as she entered she exclaimed, "What is this change in the Master's will?" She immediately returned to Baba Ji and said, "I didn't have either your darshan or Chacha Ji's. Babu Sawan Singh is sitting on the dais."[1]

Baba Ji said, "Bibi, understand the order. Did I not tell you on the very first day when Babu Sawan Singh came to satsang in the Murree Hills that he is a highly evolved soul? Soami Ji is going to take great spiritual work from him. But keep this to yourself."

Bibi Rukko went back to the hall and asked the satsangis to sit in meditation again. When they got up from meditation she asked them whose darshan they had had within. All of them said the same thing: "We saw Babu Sawan Singh within."

---

[1]   Sawan Singh Ji was not physically present in Dera at that time.

In this way, months before he left the earth plane, Baba Ji gave the sangat knowledge of his successor's identity. On hearing about this, one satsangi said to Baba Ji, "Sir, I will recognize no authority but yours." Baba Ji told him that in that case he would never attain salvation. Dumbfounded by Baba Ji's reply, the man admitted he was confused and begged Baba Ji to explain what he meant.

Baba Ji said, "Whoever is appointed by a perfect Master in his lifetime to be his successor is in fact another form of the Master's own self. There is no difference between the two." Baba Ji went on to say, "My successor will have greater power than I. I have lived in this world keeping myself concealed; he will reveal himself in all his glory. I have mixed with all sorts of people and tried to accommodate everyone, but he will not put up with those who have no interest in spiritual matters."

Baba Ji kept silent for a few moments and then said, "Few understand what Sant Mat truly is. But what can a poor soul do? Only he understands, whom the Saints bless with the power to do so."

The satsangi then asked, "How does a Saint merge with his successor?" Baba Ji said, "Like a sugar cube dissolves in water—the colour stays the same, but the taste is different."

In August 1903, about four months before leaving this world for his true Home, Baba Ji initiated Sardar Surain Singh and Maghar Singh, who later served Maharaj Sawan Singh as his *pathis* for many years.[1]

In August, Baba Ji also went to Ghuman; this was perhaps his last visit to his home village. Before leaving for Dera, he called his youngest brother, Jiwan Singh, and told him, "Now your worldly work is almost over.[2] Tell me if you want

---

[1] *Pathis* means "readers"; it is they who recite the hymn, or shabd, at satsang.
[2] Sardar Jiwan Singh passed away soon after Baba Ji.

anything." Jiwan Singh submitted that he wanted nothing except satsang and Baba Ji's company. At this, Baba Ji said that Dan Singh (the younger brother of Baba Ji, who was a close disciple of Soami Ji Maharaj) had also made the same request.

Then Baba Ji asked his sister-in-law, Inder Kaur, Jiwan Singh's wife, to demand anything she wanted. She humbly prayed that she only wanted always to be at her beloved Satguru's feet, and nothing else. Baba Ji, much pleased with her reply, said, "Merge yourself in the Shabd Dhun. Soami Ji Maharaj is always with you." After a few moments Baba Ji said that he also had never asked for worldly things from Soami Ji, nor had he any worldly desires. He only begged for love for Soami Ji's lotus feet and implicit faith in him.

While returning from Ghuman, he said that Soami Ji Maharaj had fulfilled both the worldly and spiritual desires of all satsangis, and added, "Now I am also ready to leave."

In the last few months of 1903, Bibi Rukko and Bhai Milkhi Ram, who were worried because Baba Ji was giving hints of his impending departure and because he remained mostly withdrawn, sent Maharaj Sawan Singh letters about Baba Ji. In her letter dated 25 October 1903, Bibi Rukko wrote:

For the last three or four days, Baba Ji's surat (soul) has remained inside most of the time.[1] He says that his surat does not wish to come down. When he has to explain something, he does it thoroughly, but immediately turns his attention inwards. Baba Ji is not suffering from any disease and has no physical trouble of any kind. He takes no medicine. Once, when Bibi Devan came to have his darshan, he directed her to now take the refuge of Babu Sawan Singh.

---

[1] *Surat* means "consciousness," " attention," or "soul."

On 28 October 1903, Bhai Milkhi Ram of Mithapur came to attend satsang. Baba Ji called him and said, "I intend to reveal some inner mysteries till now kept secret by the Saints. I am doing so under the orders of Soami Ji Maharaj. Please note down what I say. Soami Ji Maharaj desires that the melodies of Shabd resounding around the Anami region be revealed.[1] As directed by him, I will now describe them."

Bibi Rukko, who happened to be present, interrupted Baba Ji, saying, "We already have the writings of Soami Ji Maharaj in poetry and prose. If Soami Ji wishes to shower his grace on us, please ask him to give us his inner blessings, not the outward grace of written words."

Baba Ji was silent for some time. Then he said, "I have conveyed your sentiments to Soami Ji Maharaj. He has accepted them."

One month before his departure, Baba Ji told the satsangis that he had completed his work in the world. His soul now had no desire to leave its Home and descend to the lower regions.

One day, when a group of satsangis were sitting around Baba Ji, a satsangi talked about a holy man, Baba Karam Singh of Hoti Mardan, who had predicted the date of his departure from the world several days in advance. Baba Ji said, "Yes, holy men do have foresight. They can, if they wish, reveal the time and date of their death several years before it is to occur." Then he said, "There are only days now, not weeks or months, before I leave for my spiritual Home."

Tears started flowing from the eyes of the satsangis. Milkhi Ram, his throat choked with emotion, asked Baba Ji, "Maharaj Ji, whose care are you entrusting us to?"

---

1   The sound and light of Anami ("nameless"), Agam ("inaccessible"), and Alakh ("imperceptible") regions have not been described by Saints, as there is hardly any way to compare them with the sounds and lights of this world.

Baba Ji said, "Have no worry. I have appointed Babu Sawan Singh as my successor. He will look after you very well. His power and spiritual splendour will be much more than mine. Through him hundreds of thousands of souls will attain salvation, and every village and city will resound with the greeting 'Radha Soami.'"

After a few moments, Baba Ji said he had only one more soul to initiate and that he would be coming soon. On 26 December 1903, Lala Mangat Rai came to Dera and was initiated by Baba Ji, three days before Baba Ji left.[1]

The Passing Away of Baba Ji Maharaj

Around the fourth or fifth of December, while a few satsangis were sitting with Baba Ji, he said, "On the night of December 28, I must leave this earth." He told them not to feel disturbed; Babu Sawan Singh would guide them and fully take care of their spiritual needs. Then he said, "The greatest *karni* for a disciple is to live within the teachings and orders of the Satguru.[2] Those who do so attain true freedom while they are in the human body."

Twelve days before Baba Ji passed away, Bibi Rukko asked, "Baba Ji Maharaj, you had said that you will appoint six successors!" Baba Ji replied that he had thought earlier that the number would be six. Now Soami Ji's wish was that only one would do, so the work of six will be done by Babu Sawan Singh alone.

---

[1]   Lala Mangat Rai from the village of Lohari (District Muzaffarnagar), on retirement from his post as inspector of police, settled at Dera and served as Maharaj Sawan Singh's first secretary until 1927.
[2]   *Karni* means practice, deed, or act.

A few days before Baba Ji left this world, his entire room seemed to be resounding with Shabd. So strong was the inner pull of Shabd and so powerful the reverberation, that with the exception of Bibi Rukko, Manna Singh, and one more sevadar, the souls of all who entered the room would be pulled within; they would fall unconscious and had to be carried out of the room by the three sevadars.

Between the night of December 28 and the morning of the twenty-ninth—the time of Baba Ji's passing away—Maharaj Sawan Singh was in Abbotabad.[1] He had once begged Baba Ji, "Maharaj Ji, please keep me at your feet during your last days." Baba Ji had replied, "No, dear child, the agony of separation would be unbearable for you. However, you will perform all my last rites yourself."

On the night of December 29, Maharaj Sawan Singh arrived at Dera. The next day it was he who placed Baba Ji's body on the funeral pyre and performed the cremation ceremony. Many times Baba Ji had instructed his disciples not to build any kind of memorial to commemorate him. Baba Ji's sacred body was cremated on the bank of the Beas River. Maharaj Sawan Singh used to say that the place where Baba Ji's body had been cremated was completely obliterated by the river, which flooded on the next day; not even his ashes could be collected.

Baba Ji's entire life was one of dedication to the cause of Sant Mat, and of love and devotion to the Lord. Thirsting for Truth at the age of nine, studying and absorbing the hymns and words of Saints at twelve, he set out to find a true guide to the Lord at the incredibly young age of thirteen or fourteen. Initiated by Soami Ji Maharaj when he was just a boy of seventeen, he soon attained high spiritual realization. He

---

[1]   Now in Pakistan.

served in the army for thirty-three years, retiring on a pension at the age of fifty. He started giving Nam in 1877/78 at the age of thirty-nine, and settled at Dera at the age of fifty-two, living here till, at sixty-four, the resplendent light of his soul merged back into its Source, the Supreme Lord. He had initiated 2,343 souls during his lifetime.

Baba Ji sometimes used to say that the results of his long hours of meditation would be revealed in their full splendour after he had left this world.

The true import of his words was to become evident in the course of time.

Chapter Two

Maharaj Sawan Singh

Early Life, Quest, and Discipleship

In Maharaj Sawan Singh, Baba Ji had chosen as successor his most beloved disciple, a highly evolved soul who bore the exacting responsibility of mastership for forty-five years with ungrudging diligence and an abundance of kindness and grace. The lamp, the oil, and the wick were ready; Baba Ji's spiritual touch kindled the flame to shine with an ever-increasing brilliance and illuminate the hearts of countless seekers and disciples.

BIRTH AND CHILDHOOD

Born on 20 July 1858 in his mother's village of Jatana,[1] Punjab, Maharaj Sawan Singh came from an illustrious Grewal family of Sikhs (from the village of Mehmansinghwala, District Ludhiana, Punjab), known for its physical beauty, moral character, and religious inclination. His grandfather, Sardar Sher Singh, lived for 115 years and passed away in 1914. His father, Sardar Kabal Singh, was an officer in the British Indian Army who rose to the post of subedar-major, the highest rank then open to an Indian serving in the army. His mother, Bibi Jiwani, was an efficient housewife; a kindhearted, affectionate person; and, as I knew her in 1910/11, a mother who respected and adored her son Maharaj Sawan Singh as the manifest form of her own Master, Baba Jaimal Singh.

---

[1] It is customary in many parts of India for the mother to return to her parents' home for the delivery of the baby and stay there for the first few weeks of the child's life.

The entire family was fond of the company of holy men and used to offer food, clothes, and other necessities to sadhus who came to their village, Mehmansinghwala. Three years before Maharaj Sawan Singh's birth, a holy man predicted that a great soul and devotee of God would be born in their family and that he would be known throughout the world.

Two days after Maharaj Ji's birth in the month of Sawan,[1] 1858, Sardar Sher Singh, his grandfather, went to the nearby village of Gujjerwal and asked the Sikh priest, as was the custom, to name the child. The priest invoked the blessing of the Lord and opened the Adi Granth; Sawan, the month when the monsoon comes, was indicated as the name for the child. Sardar Sher Singh felt very happy for he had also wanted to name his grandchild Sawan Singh, after the month of his birth.

There had been a severe drought in the previous year, and the rains were yet to come that year. Crops, plants, and trees were dying, and a famine appeared likely. On the fifth day of Sawan, the day Maharaj Ji was born, the monsoon started, and continued in abundance for the whole month. The wells and ponds overflowed and the crops prospered. The village people regarded him as a blessed child, for from the time of his birth the parched land began to blossom.

The Great Master used to say that his parents and grandparents were religious-minded and that he naturally imbibed from them a thirst for spiritual knowledge. When he was only three or four he would accompany his grandfather, holding on to his finger, to see the holy men staying in his village. Maharaj Ji's mother, Bibi Jiwani, used to tell us that even in his infancy he was unusually beautiful and captivating. Whenever he smiled or laughed, his countenance glowed. He usu-

---

[1] In Punjab, the month of *Sawan* is the equivalent of July 15 to August 15.

ally kept calm and cheerful and rarely showed signs of anger; all who saw him were eager to take him in their arms.

Bibi Jiwani was a deeply religious person—righteous, noble, and God-fearing. Like other members of the family, she also used to recite *Japji* and *Sukhmani* every morning.[1] She would rise daily much before dawn to recite the holy scriptures, and the child Sawan Singh would listen quietly whenever he was awake at that hour.

Once, when Maharaj Ji was nine, his mother became quite ill with a high fever. For two days she continued to perform her morning devotions, not allowing her sickness to interfere; but on the fourth day she was so weak she could not even get out of bed. She was much distressed at missing her recitation for the first time in years. Maharaj Ji got out of bed and came to her, as it was past her usual time for beginning her prayers. Affectionately he asked her if she were not going to recite the *Japji*. On hearing this, tears came to her eyes. Maharaj Ji then offered to do the recitation for her. She thought he might know two or three cantos from repeating them with her, but was amazed when he recited all the thirty-eight cantos with devotion and correct intonation. Moved to tears and overflowing with joy, she embraced the child and blessed him.

EDUCATION

A buoyant spirit was one of Maharaj Ji's main characteristics as a child. His sweet and happy nature drew people to him, a calm serenity imbuing his friendly cheerfulness even at that early age.

---

[1] Orthodox Sikhs start the day "in the name of the Lord" by reciting the *Japji* (by Guru Nanak) every morning before sunrise; the devout often recite the lengthy but popular composition *Sukhmani* (by Guru Arjan) in addition to the *Japji*.

He began his primary education in the school at the nearby village of Narangwal, a mile's walk from his house. After this, he joined the Middle School at Gujjerwal, a village about two and a half miles away. He would walk to school early in the morning and return in the evening.

Intelligent and industrious, Maharaj Ji was good at sports and excellent in studies. From an early age he acquired the habit of cleanliness—he kept his books, notebooks, and clothes in excellent order. He always respected his teachers as one respects parents and family elders; and his punctuality, sincerity, and attention to his studies won the hearts of his teachers. He used to reminisce about his Persian teacher, telling how he would draw water from the well for his teacher's bath and gladly do a few household chores for him.

After early schooling at Narangwal and Gujjerwal, Maharaj Ji joined the Mission High School at Ludhiana, a distance of fourteen miles from his home. The railway line joining his village with Ludhiana had not yet been laid. He would walk the fourteen miles from Mehmansinghwala to the high school early on Monday mornings, carrying flour, lentils, and other provisions for the week, and walk back on Saturday evenings. Thus, early in life, Maharaj Ji developed the stamina and liking for long walks that he continued to exhibit during the rest of his life. At an age of 80 years he would walk miles on the mountainous paths that cars or other vehicles could not reach.

Whatever Maharaj Ji did, he did in a correct and systematic manner, and wherever he went he left a deep impression. Out of the hundreds of students who must have passed through their hands, his teachers always remembered Maharaj Ji; and later on, some of them, who were still alive then, would come to Dera to meet him. Even after he had finished school, Maharaj Ji sometimes sent presents to his former teachers. Pandit Daulat Ram, one of his teachers, often came to Dera after he had retired from service. He told us that Hazur Maharaj Ji sometimes sent him bolts of woollen cloth from Abbotabad and the Murree Hills, where Hazur was stationed during his service in the army.

After finishing high school, Maharaj Ji stayed at home and looked after the family farm for a while. Then he worked for a year for the Irrigation Department in the malaria-infested district of Rohtak, but he contracted malaria and had to return home. After recuperating, he enlisted in the 14th Punjab Regiment, following his family tradition of military service. Some time later, at the suggestion of his British officers, he enrolled at Thomson Engineering College, Roorkee, to qualify as an army engineer.

At Thomson College, Hazur performed brilliantly in his studies. Pandit Bansi Lal, an engineer from Kapurthala and a classmate of Maharaj Ji at Roorkee, often came to see him later at the Dera. He said that in his college days at Roorkee, Hazur spent most of his time in studies and that his serious, serene manner impressed the other students. Bansi Lal told us how he had once asked their mathematics teacher why the teachers spent so much more time with Maharaj Ji than with the other students, when all the students paid the same fees. The teacher replied that a teacher's attention is naturally attracted by a student who has a real thirst for knowledge. Bansi Lal also said that during their college days Maharaj Ji would recite the *Japji* early every morning and repeat verses from the Adi Granth every night before retiring.

Maharaj Ji was popular with students as well as teachers. His room in the hostel was a model of cleanliness: the floor was always spotless, a clean sheet adorned the bed, and on the table his books, notes, instruments, pen, ink, etc., were kept in a systematic manner. Though restrained in speech, he was quick to share a joke. He was always cheerful, and his laughter infectious. He was generous by nature and willingly gave away anything a fellow student asked for. Bansi Lal would tell us that if any student borrowed a pencil, notebook, paper, ink, or pen from Maharaj Ji, he would never ask for it back. Once Maharaj Ji bought a beautiful new pair of English shoes —a rare thing in those days—which Bansi Lal liked immensely. Seeing this, Maharaj Ji immediately gave the shoes to him. Generous and always willing to offer things to his friends, Maharaj Ji himself never asked any favours from them.

Maharaj Ji never forgot a face, nor his childhood school friends. One day in July 1943, while in Dalhousie, he met an old schoolmate whom he had not seen in over sixty years— Sardar Bishan Singh. Maharaj Ji not only recognized him, but also greeted him with the warmth and regard due to an old friend. For the rest of his stay in Dalhousie, Maharaj Ji would meet him every day and would often invite him for lunch. And though Sardar Bishan Singh was not a satsangi, Hazur helped him during his last days, and looked after and consoled the family members when he passed away.

In 1886, Maharaj Ji received his engineering degree with high marks, returned to his regiment, and was transferred to the Military Engineering Department. He approached all his assignments with great dedication and was always keen to improve on his own performance. A few months after joining service, his superior officer was preparing to leave for a new post. Maharaj Ji went to him and said, "Sir, I want one favour from you." The officer replied that he had already handed over the charge to his successor and therefore could not do anything for Maharaj Ji now. But Hazur said, "I am fresh from college and have little experience. I would appreciate it if you would point out my defects and shortcomings to enable me to work more efficiently." The officer, who had been pleased with Maharaj Ji's work, was surprised and said,

"During all these years I have never had such a request before." He then made a few suggestions, which Maharaj Ji followed assiduously to improve his work.

Babu Gulab Singh, who served under Maharaj Ji as a clerk and storekeeper for a long time, used to describe some of Hazur's qualities as an officer. He worked with such vigour and concentration that Gulab Singh and other young colleagues would become exhausted trying to keep up with him. Whenever Maharaj Ji was given some responsible job, he became so absorbed in it that he would overlook the need for his own physical rest and nourishment. He always urged his subordinates to work seriously and devotedly as well.

Babu Gulab Singh would say that Maharaj Ji could finish in two weeks what it would take other officers a month to do, and he would often give the example of one of Maharaj Ji's early assignments, which was to supervise the construction of a cavalry remount depot at Sargodha. Three British engineers had been given this task originally but had spent seven months without accomplishing much, so the commanding officer asked Hazur to finish the job before the year ended. In the four or five months left in the year, Maharaj Ji managed to complete the construction of the entire depot.

His example inspired his officers and his subordinates to strive to be like him. Strict with himself, he was conscientious in his duties and appreciated discipline and diligence on the part of his subordinates. Yet he was not strict with them, nor did he force an unnecessarily rigorous routine on them; instead, his humility, courtesy, and sweet nature made them actually enjoy working for him. He commanded with love, and if it ever became necessary, he reprimanded with affection and understanding of his subordinates' human failings. The officers were impressed with his abilities, his sincerity in doing his duties, and above all, his personal charm; he could persuade his officers to accommodate him in whatever he wished to do.

Once, a British officer, who was notoriously unaccommodating and bad tempered, took over as their commander. Maharaj Ji's colleagues wished that he could do something to change this difficult officer. After he had worked with Maharaj Ji for only one month he began to change, and from then on would not do anything without consulting him. Hazur later always advised his disciples that success in their career would come from obeying and respecting their superiors and being sweet-tempered to their subordinates.

SPIRITUAL PURSUIT AND INITIATION

Throughout his early life and career, Maharaj Ji had been earnestly searching for spiritual truth and a way to attain it. His search included the study of spiritual books, discussions with holy men, and the study of religion and philosophy. Maharaj Ji had started reading the Adi Granth by the time he was about ten, and had read Dassam Granth, Ramayan, Mahabharat, and Bhagvat even while he was in his teens. Good books on philosophy and religion were not easily available; but Maharaj Ji, particularly during his service days, was so fond of reading books on spirituality and religion that he would obtain them directly from the various publishers and dealers in rare books, sometimes paying a very high price for a particular book.

Maharaj Ji had a good knowledge of Persian and, in the course of time, built up a small personal library.[1] This collection includes works of Shams-i-Tabriz, Maulana Rum, Khwaja Hafiz, Amir Khusro, and other Sufi Saints. Each book con-

---

[1] His personal collection is still at the Dera. It contains books in Persian, Arabic, Urdu, English, Punjabi, and Hindi. He had managed to obtain a rare edition of *Fatu-hat-al-Makki*, an Arabic treatise on religion and spirituality, and had it translated.

tains pencil markings and marginal notes in Maharaj Ji's own hand. His early copy of the Adi Granth has a blank page opposite each page of text, where in places he wrote explanations of these passages along with analytical comments and his own views. He thus acquired a profound understanding of the Adi Granth, as well as of Hindu and Muslim theology and Sufi philosophy.[1]

Before he met Baba Ji, Maharaj Ji spent much of his free time discussing spiritual matters with sadhus and holy men, serving them and offering them food and necessities for their journey. When he was transferred to the Murree Hills in 1891, he purposely rented a house near an inn where Hindu pilgrims and holy men used to stay during their pilgrimage to Amarnath. This gave him an opportunity to meet various learned men and devotees of different paths.

Although from an early age Maharaj Ji was fond of meeting holy men, he was never drawn to sham devotees or false sadhus. His innate ability to judge the qualities of a holy man is clearly indicated by a small incident which took place when he was working as the sub-divisional officer in the hills.

One day he was going on horseback in the mountains when a sudden feeling of deep happiness filled his heart. He thought to himself that this feeling could not have any physical origin; it was elevating and blissful. At the same time he experienced an exhilarating fragrance filling the atmosphere. It was the month of April and it could have been the fragrance of some flowering shrub, but Maharaj Ji had lived in the

---

[1] His first book on the Adi Granth was *Chaurasi Vishaywala Gurmat Sidhant*, published in 1920 with selections from the scripture given under eighty-four subheadings. This was later elaborated and parallel quotations from Persian Saints were added; this larger version with exhaustive notes, called *Gurmat Sidhant*, in two volumes, was published in 1943. It was this version that was translated into English and published during the 1960s in abbreviated form as *Philosophy of the Masters,* in five volumes.

mountains long enough to realize that this was not the fragrance of any known mountain flower. As he proceeded on the mountain path, the fragrance became stronger.

After a short distance, Hazur found a faqir absorbed in meditation, sitting by the wayside. The fragrance was coming from him. Out of respect for the holy man, Maharaj Ji got down from his horse and, not wishing to disturb the faqir, started to walk past quietly. The holy man opened his eyes and looked at Maharaj Ji with a smile of pure joy, saying, "It is a rare nose that can discern this fragrance."

In his pursuit of the spiritual path, Maharaj Ji associated with both Hindu and Muslim holy men with equal fervour and went wherever a mystic could be found. He was completely free of bias against any caste or religion. In his search for Truth he studied many of the major religions thoroughly. He studied Vedanta, the Upanishads, the Gita, Yog Vashist, and other Hindu sacred writings, discussing them with the most knowledgeable people he could find. According to Babu Gulab Singh, well-known mahatmas and scholars often talked with Maharaj Ji about spiritual subjects until late at night. From these studies and discussions he acquired a deep knowledge of Hindu philosophy and scriptures.

Maharaj Ji studied the Qur'an as well as the works of Maulana Rum, Shams-i-Tabriz, Mujjadid Alf Sani, and other Persian Mystics. There was a Christian clergyman with whom he discussed the Bible. He even contacted a Buddhist priest and studied Buddhism and Jainism with him. He often attended religious gatherings and occasionally worked as president or secretary of religious societies. Hazur used to say he was prepared to sit at the feet of the lowest of the low castes if only he could learn how to obtain the spiritual treasure.

During his service in Naushehra, Maharaj Ji came in contact with Baba Kahan, a highly advanced faqir who later foretold that Maharaj Ji would soon find a perfect Master. On Sundays he often went to see Baba Kahan in Peshawar, which was nearby. The Baba lived in a state of God-intoxication, oblivious to the world. He preferred solitude and would sometimes drive people away by abusing them or threatening them with a large club. But he was always very happy to receive Maharaj Ji and treated him with great love and regard.

Once, when Maharaj Ji was returning for a month's leave from an expedition to Kala Pahar (the Black Mountain) in the Northwestern Frontier Province, he had about two thousand rupees with him—his pay and allowances for the past several months. He stopped at Peshawar to see Baba Kahan and found the Baba on the railway platform. Maharaj Ji asked the Baba why he was waiting there, and he replied, "My good friend was arriving, so I wanted to come and receive him personally." With great warmth he took Maharaj Ji home with him, and they talked till late at night.

When he was about to leave, Maharaj Ji, as was his practice, offered five rupees to Baba Kahan, but the Baba said, "I will accept a full twenty—round, white, and shining." Maharaj Ji laughed and said, "Baba, you have become greedy. So far you have always taken four or five; today you want twenty!" "No, I am not greedy," he countered. "Charity must be proportionate to one's income. You have brought two thousand rupees, I have asked you for twenty."

Maharaj Ji placed twenty rupees before him. The Baba said, "If you feel unhappy, you may take them back." Maharaj Ji smiled and replied, "You know that I do not feel unhappy in giving to you. Please accept them." Baba Kahan then said, "It is not for me. I only want your income to be blessed and spent properly." As always, he did not keep the money for himself but distributed it among needy children.

One night, after Maharaj Ji had sat with Baba Kahan for a long time, the Baba asked him to go as it was past midnight. But Maharaj Ji said, "Today I will not go empty-handed. You must give me something." The Baba said, "You will obtain inexhaustible spiritual treasure, but the time has not yet come." Maharaj Ji inquired, "And when will the time come?" "Soon, very soon," was the reply.

After a few moments' silence, Maharaj Ji asked, "Will I get it from you or from someone else?" The Baba said, "Your wealth is not with me; it is with someone else."

It was the first time that the Baba seemed to be in a revealing mood. Maharaj Ji inquired, "Who is he? Where can I find him? Please give me some idea—where does he live?" But Baba Kahan would not reveal anything more. He closed the matter with the remark, "He who holds your treasure will himself come to you."

Shortly after this, Baba Kahan's prediction came true. One day in October 1894, Maharaj Ji was leaving his office in Murree and going down the hill when he passed an elderly man coming up the hill. Hazur thought that he might be some military retiree coming to collect his pension or file a court appeal with the Commissioner. The elderly gentleman was none other than Baba Jaimal Singh, who had come to Murree with Bibi Rukko.

When Maharaj Ji passed him, Baba Ji said to Bibi Rukko, "I have come here to initiate this man. He is an old associate of mine." Bibi Rukko exclaimed, "But he did not even greet you! What kind of old associate is he?" Baba Ji said, "He is as yet unaware of me—what does he know? But in four days' time he will come to me."

Hazur would relate that, three days after he had met Baba Ji on the road, he was spending the evening with a holy man, studying Vedantic scripture, his current spiritual interest.

Kahan Singh, a disciple of Baba Ji's and a friend of Hazur's, came into the room. He said, "You have been looking for a real mystic for a long time. There is a great mahatma here right now. If you want to meet him, come." At Maharaj Ji's questioning, Kahan Singh explained that this Master was of the Radha Soami path and initiated disciples into the practice of the Word—Surat Shabd Yoga.

As soon as the Vedantist holy man heard the words "Radha Soami," he began criticizing the path, saying that its followers were atheists who claimed to go around with some musical instrument inside their heads. Maharaj Ji said he had never heard of a musical instrument that could be put inside someone's head. The sadhu persisted in trying to stop him from going to see Baba Ji, but his arguments had no effect.

The next day Maharaj Ji went with Kahan Singh to Baba Ji. He listened to Baba Ji's discourses for three or four days and asked him many questions about the path. Ultimately he was convinced that it was the right path. Maharaj Ji later said that in those three or four days of association with Baba Ji, all his doubts and questions of the last twenty-five years were resolved. He humbly asked Baba Ji for initiation; one hesitation, however, remained—the name "Radha Soami" seemed strange to him. When he asked Baba Ji for initiation, he also asked not to be given the name Radha Soami. Baba Ji lovingly inquired what he had against this name, and Hazur said it seemed new and strange to him.

Baba Ji asked him if he recited any verses from the scriptures. He said he daily recited the *Japji* and the *Jaap Sahib*. Baba Ji then asked how many different names of God were used by Guru Gobind Singh in the *Jaap Sahib*. Maharaj Ji said he did not remember exactly, but there must be eleven or twelve hundred. Then Baba Ji said affectionately, "When you have nothing against using twelve hundred such names that never appeared in any scripture before the *Jaap Sahib*, what difference does it make if a Saint has given God another name out of his love for Him?" He then explained that "Radha Soami" is another name for that Lord. "Radha" denotes soul and "Soami" is the Lord. Thus "Radha Soami" means the Lord of the soul.

This conversation cleared up his doubts, and Maharaj Ji was initiated the next day, 15 October 1894. After initiating him, Baba Ji Maharaj said, "You had already earned this wealth; I have simply kept it for you. Today it is returned to you." At this, Maharaj Ji remembered Baba Kahan's words— that the one who had his wealth would himself deliver it to him.

THE DAYS OF DISCIPLESHIP
Day after day Maharaj Ji's love for his Satguru, Baba Jaimal Singh, grew deeper. Meditation became for Maharaj Ji his prime occupation in life, and Baba Ji's darshan the only desire of his heart. The letters he wrote to his beloved Master were full of love and longing:

> *The yearning for your darshan torments me day and night....*

> *Without seeing you, I am restless like a fish out of water.*

> *I do not ask even for Sach Khand. I beg only for the boon of devotion and faith, and love for your lotus feet.*

So intense became his love and longing for the Master that he would earnestly beg Baba Ji to permit him to give up his government job and come to stay with Baba Ji at the Dera, for his work did not give him enough time for meditation and kept him away from the Satguru.

But Baba Ji would reply, "Have no worry. You are always with me, not far." And he would tell Maharaj Ji to continue with his government job, looking upon himself as the Satguru's agent and keeping in mind that the job he was doing was also rendering service to the Master.

Accepting as Baba Ji's will the torment of separation from the physical form, Maharaj Ji continued with his service as an engineer but increased his time in meditation. His entire free time was devoted to spiritual pursuits. He slept very little. If sometimes sleep tried to overpower him, he would meditate while standing. He had a staff made that was five feet long, with a crosspiece for the elbows, which he would sometimes use for doing bhajan in a standing position when he felt sleepy.[1]

Banta Singh[2] used to tell us that even during the early days after initiation, Hazur's inclination was mostly towards his meditation. Though he was scrupulously regular and strict in his official duties, he had little interest in any other activity. Sometimes Maharaj Ji would tell Banta Singh to saddle his horse, as he usually enjoyed going out for a ride. While Banta Singh was out saddling the horse, Hazur would take up a book and casually read a few devotional hymns. He would be so overcome with longing that he would sit in meditation, the outing forgotten; Banta Singh would be left waiting outside with the horse.

Soon after initiation Maharaj Ji had a desire that his family members at Mehmansinghwala, and also his friends, should be blessed with the great Saint's satsangs. Once, in

---

[1] The staff is still in Great Master's room at the Dera.

[2] Banta Singh, a disciple of Baba Ji's, was a distant relation of the Great Master and was his personal attendant all through the Master's service days. When Maharaj Ji retired, Banta Singh came to the Dera, and later moved to Sikanderpur, where he stayed with Sardar Harbans Singh, the father of Maharaj Charan Singh. Baba Banta Singh as he was affectionately called by the Great Master's family members, passed away at Sikanderpur in 1951.

1896, when Maharaj Ji had come to Dera on one of his holidays, Baba Ji decided to visit Mehmansinghwala.

Because "Radha Soami" was still unfamiliar to most people as a name of God, at heart Maharaj Ji wanted Baba Ji to give his Mehmansinghwala satsang on a hymn from the Adi Granth, rather than on a verse from Soami Ji Maharaj's *Sar Bachan*.

Baba Ji knew his disciple's deepest thoughts and took a verse from the Adi Granth for his discourse. But then in the evening Bibi Rukko went up to the roof terrace of the Great Master's home and began singing hymns of praise to Radha Soami in her powerful voice, which echoed throughout the village. Whenever Maharaj Ji related this incident, he used to say that within a few minutes all concern over public opinion was removed from his mind.

Maharaj Ji had a deep desire for Baba Ji to initiate his mother, and on that first visit to Mehmansinghwala Baba Ji initiated not only Maharaj Ji's mother, Jivani Ji, but also his wife, Kishen Kaur, and daughter-in-law. Later he initiated Maharaj Ji's grandfather, Sardar Sher Singh Ji (then 109 years old), and his eldest son, Sardar Bachint Singh. During Baba Ji's subsequent visits to Mehmansinghwala, Hazur's entire family of that time was blessed with initiation by Baba Ji. Munshi Narayan Singh, one of Maharaj Ji's friends, who used to tease him about having taken up a new faith, also received initiation on one of Baba Ji's visits, and later his entire family was initiated.

The first visit of his beloved Satguru was a great occasion for Maharaj Ji. Baba Ji stayed with him, and Maharaj Ji personally took care of his entire stay, looking after all his needs. He drew water from the well for Baba Ji's bath; he ground the wheat, cooked the food, and served it to his beloved Master. Hazur's daughter-in-law, Bibi Inder Kaur, seeing him perform duties that in those days were the prerogative of the household ladies, offered to grind the wheat into flour. But Maharaj Ji said, "No, daughter, this is my service."

Even later, whenever Baba Ji visited his village, the Great Master continued to do all this seva himself.

Although devotion and meditation had become the main object of his life, Hazur was never slack in his official duties. His heart longed to be with the Satguru and his interest in meditation grew from day to day, yet he remained alert towards his other duties. He had struck an ideal balance between his first love—meditation—and his worldly obligations. His superiors, pleased with his work, would confidently give him tasks that were considered intricate and difficult to accomplish.

The water works at Murree Hills were completed under Maharaj Ji's supervision. The army engineering department was entrusted with building the water pipeline through hard rocks and uneven terrain, from a great distance, into the city. The first month's experience showed that if the work of cutting through the rock were done with chisels and other small manual cutting tools, the progress would be so slow and the cost so high that it would be impossible to finish the work within the time fixed and within the grant allowed by the government. In one month they could complete only a quarter of a mile, and one-fourth of the grant was exhausted.

In a meeting of the engineers, called to find a solution to the problem, Maharaj Ji suggested continuing the work by means of blasting, to save time and money. His proposal was accepted and he was asked to supervise the job. Under his guidance the work proceeded swiftly, until the last mile of pipeline was to be laid.

The pipeline had reached the part of that town where there were large shops, offices, and a magnificent church. Because the clergy and the British merchants had threatened to sue the government if any damage occurred, the officials ordered the blasting stopped and the hammer-and-chisel technique resumed. The stone there proved to be the hardest of all and the cost of cutting the rock was therefore much higher; within a few days it became clear that the last section of pipeline would take more than two years to complete and the cost would be exhorbitant.

Again a meeting was called, but no one seemed to have a solution to the dilemma. In the end, Maharaj Ji's chief turned to him and asked whether he could not come up with a plan to solve the difficulty. Just then an idea had occurred to Maharaj Ji and he replied that he might be able to manage the work if he were allowed to buy a few hundred wooden sleepers, to act as shock absorbers when blasting. Greatly relieved, the colonel said, "Buy any number you like. We leave this matter entirely in your hands and shall be obliged if you could help us out of this difficult situation."

Maharaj Ji resumed the blasting, putting two or three layers of heavy wooden sleepers on top of the rock to be blasted, to absorb the shock from the explosion. The trial proved successful and the work progressed well. In the beginning, Maharaj Ji supervised all the operations himself and did not leave anything in the hands of his subordinates. But by the time they reached the quarter where the big shops were situated, his subordinates and even the labourers had become efficient and expert in the technique.

One morning, when the blasting work had reached a point between the cathedral on one side and the biggest European shop on the other, it was decided to use four tiers of sleepers instead of the usual two or three. Maharaj Ji had his men place the sleepers over the first site, told them to explode the detonators that had been set, and turned aside for a few minutes to drink a glass of milk his servant had brought.

That morning he had left his house earlier than usual, before breakfast was ready, and had told his servant to bring some milk to the work site. When he turned back to the site, he found that the blasting had been a complete success.

Turning to the overseer, Maharaj Ji gave orders for sleepers to be placed in the same way on the next site, but was stunned to hear that the detonators had already been lit. There was not a second to lose. While everybody stood motionless in bewilderment, Maharaj Ji ran towards the unexploded detonators to put out the fuses if he could. On the way, one of his British subordinates caught hold of him with both hands and refused to allow him to go further, despite his struggles. Maharaj Ji once told us, "I released myself from the junior officer's grip and ran towards the spot where the detonators were. It was then that a prayer involuntarily escaped my lips. I had been recently initiated by Baba Ji Maharaj and I turned to him in all humility. 'O my Master, my honor is now in your hands. I am not afraid of being injured or even killed. What bothers me is betraying the faith my officers have put in me.'

"On getting hold of the fuses I found that they had fizzled out after burning for only a quarter of an inch. How? I do not know up to this time. There was nothing wrong with them. Afterwards those very fuses were used and they proved effective."

Maharaj Ji used to say, "The feelings of gratitude that welled up in me at that time, only my heart knew." When he told Baba Ji about the incident, Baba Ji replied that the Lord always helps his devotees in times of need and that Soami Ji Maharaj himself would successfully complete everything that Maharaj Ji undertook.

Hazur had deep love for Baba Ji, and Baba Ji cherished him as one of his finest disciples. Though we had not seen

Baba Ji, we could sometimes catch a glimpse of the bond of divine love between him and Maharaj Ji. Whenever Hazur narrated an incident connected with Baba Ji, his face would become radiant, his soft melodious voice would be charged with emotion, and his eyes would fill with tears. One such incident that he occasionally narrated in the satsang was about one of his visits to the Dera.

It was the month of June, the hottest period of summer in the Punjab when temperatures often reach 120 degrees Fahrenheit (about 50 degrees centigrade). Maharaj Ji had been stationed mostly in the high-mountain terrain of western Punjab, five thousand to eight thousand feet above sea level. He had spent all his summer months in the mountains and was not accustomed to the heat of the plains.

Maharaj Ji arrived at the Beas railway station to visit the Dera. It was noon; the sun was blazing and hot winds were blowing. He started on foot for the Dera[1]—a distance of about three miles—and had gone a short way when he thought of resting in the shade of a tree. But then he remembered the story of Sohini, who gave up her life in her love for Mahiwal.[2] To meet her lover, she tried to cross a river in spate, on an unbaked mud pitcher, knowing fully that the pitcher could dissolve. Remembering the story, Maharaj Ji continued his

---

[1] In the 1890s, the sangat would walk from the station to the Dera. There was no road; irregular footpaths, broken by fields and ravines, joined the Dera to the Beas station.

[2] Sohini and Mahiwal are characters from a popular love story of Punjab. To meet her lover, Mahiwal, every day Sohini would stealthily cross a nearby river, swimming with the aid of a large earthen pitcher. One day a relative of Sohini's, discovering her visits to Mahiwal, replaced the earthen pitcher with an unbaked mud pitcher of the same size and shape. The river was in spate, and although Sohini noticed the switch in pitchers, she preferred to risk her life than put her love to the disgrace of timidity. The pitcher dissolved midstream, but she swam on; and close to the opposite bank—within sight of her lover—she began to drown. Mahiwal, jumping into the stormy waters, reached her—but they both drowned before they could reach the banks.

journey, for he thought how unbecoming it was to seek shelter from the heat instead of going for his beloved Satguru's darshan, when worldly lovers have made greater sacrifices.

At that very moment, Bibi Rukko, as she often related, was surprised to find Baba Ji walking about in the midday sun. She requested that he come inside, away from the scorching heat of the sun. Baba Ji made no reply but continued to walk in the sun until shortly before Maharaj Sawan Singh arrived.

When the Great Master reached the Dera, Bibi Rukko said, "Brother, I knew you were on your way to the Dera." He replied with a smile, "Yes, sister, you are an advanced soul, you know the past and future easily."

"No," she replied, "It's not that. Baba Ji has been walking in the sun for almost an hour and went inside only a few minutes before you arrived. I was sure he must be protecting one of his loving devotees, taking the heat of the sun on himself."

Maharaj Ji said, "That explains why the heat suddenly lost its sting for me."

Maharaj Ji had completely surrendered himself to Baba Ji. In all matters, whether spiritual or worldly, he would act according to Baba Ji's directions. Before he was initiated, Maharaj Ji used to place his entire income before his mother, and if his wife wanted anything Maharaj Ji would tell her to go to his mother. After he was initiated, he told everybody in his family, "the Master comes first." From then on, whatever was left after deducting his basic expenses, he would place before Baba Ji. From that amount, whatever Baba Ji thought proper he would give to Maharaj Ji's family members, spending the rest in the service of the sangat. The well, the small satsang hall, the satsang hall called the Nam Ghar, the rooms east of Great Master's house, the kitchen—all were built by Baba Ji from Maharaj Sawan Singh's seva. Hazur often mentioned that as a result of this seva, Baba Ji had blessed his sons with an income of hundreds of thousands of rupees.

Maharaj Ji would not spend a penny from his salary except in accordance with Baba Ji's instructions. Sometimes Baba Ji himself would ask for details of Maharaj Ji's income for the coming year and would then tell him how to spend it. In his letter dated 25 November 1898, Baba Ji writes: "Also let me know what your salary will be this year. Is your salary separate or does it include allowances? Then I will let you know how to spend this year's income. You are my very life. You will be with me always."

At Baba Ji's instructions Maharaj Ji used to regularly send produce from his farm in Mehmansinghwala as seva to the Dera—wheat, corn, and other grains. Later, when he bought the farm in Sirsa, he continued to send provisions from there for the Dera langar. This practice is followed even now.

Whenever he could get leave, Hazur would come to Baba Ji Maharaj at Dera. Once in 1898 when Maharaj Ji was preparing to leave the Dera and return to his post, Baba Ji ordered him to go to his family home in Mehmansinghwala for a day. On his return journey when he was passing through Beas, Baba Ji met him at the railway station. Baba Ji started to say something, then stopped abruptly. When Baba Ji and Bibi Rukko were on their way back to the Dera, Baba Ji said, "Babu Sawan Singh is going to face a very hard time; but Soami Ji will take care of him."

Maharaj Ji returned to his post in Khairagali, a town eight to ten miles from Murree. The next day he was to go on an inspection tour. Since horses were the only transportation available for supervising construction projects in such a mountainous region, Maharaj Ji had become an expert rider. As his horse would run by, he would catch hold of its mane and jump into the saddle in one smooth motion. While he was at the Dera, however, the servant in charge of his horse had clipped the horse's mane and forgot to tell Maharaj Ji on his return. The next day, when Hazur tried to jump into the saddle in his usual fashion, there was no mane to hold on to and he took a bad fall. He fractured his femur and the leg was also dislocated. He was taken to the hospital, where the army surgeon set the bone and plastered the leg.

At the hospital the army doctor told Maharaj Ji to eat meat and drink wine, which Maharaj Ji firmly refused to do. The doctor warned Maharaj Ji that if he did not take the prescribed diet, he would become weak and the bone would not heal; the result would be a permanent disability. But Maharaj Ji refused to yield to the doctor's pressure.

Maharaj Ji's colleagues and subordinates felt greatly concerned. They asked him to write to Baba Ji. But Maharaj Ji, who understood the path well and knew the significance of the vows undertaken at the time of initiation, had no inclination to write to his Satguru. His colleagues kept insisting, and Maharaj Ji wrote to Baba Ji, simply informing him about the situation.

Baba Ji replied, "The Satguru's directive is only one, not many. My order is the same as it was the first day: do not touch meat and wine." Baba Ji also assured Maharaj Ji about the fracture: "Your leg will become absolutely all right. The bones will join well. No one will know that it was ever broken." When the plaster was removed after three months, the leg had healed completely, as Baba Ji had said it would.

But the fracture in the leg and the tedium of lying in a cast for three months was not as painful as his inability to visit Dera and meet the beloved Satguru. Baba Ji himself, greatly concerned about his beloved disciple's well-being, kept writing to him regularly and told him to take milk and ghee in enough quantity to maintain strength during convalescence.

When Maharaj Ji was discharged from the hospital, Baba Ji came to Khairagali and spent a few days with his dearest disciple.

Maharaj Ji's service career was a balance between the performance of worldly and spiritual duties. Baba Ji had instructed him that after his official duties were over, he should not waste his time in social visits and idle talk. Keeping this in mind, Hazur always arranged to live in an isolated area, usually away from the city.[1] Once when he was posted in Khairagali, he found a vacant house outside the town, which was said to be haunted by a ghost who drove people away by throwing stones at them. Maharaj Ji rented the house, saying he could live with the ghost.

One night he heard what sounded like a shower of stones hitting the corrugated iron roof. Banta Singh became quite nervous and hurried outside. Hearing the noise, Hazur went out to see who was there. He found that the "ghost" was a wild tree with hard, walnut-like fruit; some of its fruit-laden branches hit the roof whenever the wind blew. The next morning the overhanging branches were cut and there was no more trouble from the "ghost."

Maharaj Ji had neither time nor inclination for idle conversation but would spend hours talking about the Master and the teachings. He respected all religions and often discussed spiritual matters with Hindus, Muslims, and Christians. He would never criticize any religion. There was a Christian clergyman who enjoyed initiating discussions with Maharaj Ji and often asked awkward questions. Once when Hazur ran into the clergyman at the Beas railway station, the man asked him who was the greatest—Guru Nanak, Kabir,

---

[1] Satsangis who accompanied Hazur on his tours to Kalabagh remember that his bungalow was the only house on a completely isolated part of a hill, away from all habitation.

or Baba Ji. Maharaj Ji replied, "Bring all three before me and I will answer you." Puzzled, the minister asked, "How can this be done?" Maharaj Ji said, "I have only seen Baba Ji. To me he is the greatest Saint. What I have obtained spiritually is from him; to me, he has no equal."

Maharaj Ji was adept in conveying his message in a few words. During his posting in Murree, a Muslim colleague and close friend informed him that he was going on a pilgrimage to Mecca and asked Hazur if he wanted anything from there. Maharaj Ji said, "Please give my regards to the God of Mecca." The man was puzzled: "Is there a different God in Mecca?" Maharaj Ji smiled and said, "Then why go there?"

Hazur's approach towards the orthodox was one of tolerance and understanding. He was both convincing and kind in his dealings with people. Once Maharaj Ji was on leave because of ill health. His substitute at work stayed at Maharaj Ji's house with him until he was well. His name was Kaithal Ram and he belonged to a village near Khanna in Punjab. The man worshipped a stone idol that he carried with him in a box, and Maharaj Ji gave him a small room near his own for his lengthy morning and evening worship of the idol. One night the man asked the servant to bring him his night cap, but the servant by mistake brought him the cap used for covering the idol. Cursing the servant, the man ran to the box and apologized profusely to his god for having awakened him.

Mohan Singh, a clerk with a wry sense of humour, who was working under Maharaj Ji, happened to be there at the time and overheard the man. He remarked, "You needn't worry. Your god will never wake up—he sleeps all the time." The man was deeply offended and complained to Hazur about the clerk. Maharaj Ji gently explained to him what constitutes true devotion and what the true temple of God is. The man was convinced and decided to give up idol worship.

Later, Maharaj Ji spoke to Mohan Singh and told him it was not proper to hurt anyone's feelings.

Installation as the Master

At the time Baba Ji Maharaj passed away, Hazur was stationed at Abbotabad. From the letters of Bibi Rukko and Milkhi Ram, Maharaj Ji had understood that Baba Ji had decided to leave the world, and though there was no illness, his decision appeared to be final. Hazur was restless, his heart longed to be near his beloved Satguru, but, as narrated earlier,[1] Baba Ji had clearly told him that he did not want Hazur to be present at the Dera during his last days.

Hazur, therefore, silently bore the agony of impending separation from Baba Ji, spending all his free time in solitude and meditation. On receiving the telegram of Baba Ji's departure, he went immediately to Dera, and all the last rites of Baba Ji were performed by him.

The formal ceremony of installing Maharaj Ji as the Satguru was performed with quiet dignity. He was offered Soami Ji's turban and shawl as a token of the responsibility of the mastership—a responsibility that Hazur was to fulfil for forty-five years with great devotion and diligence, humility and compassion. The lamp of spirituality lit by Baba Ji shone with great brightness in Hazur, combining the brilliance of Baba Ji's meditation and spiritual power with that of his own.

Whenever Maharaj Ji came to the Dera during Baba Ji's lifetime, he did all possible seva with other satsangis. He would draw water from the well of the neighbouring village and himself carry it for Baba Ji's bath. And after the first Dera

---

[1] See Chapter One, p. 59

well was completed, he would draw water from the well for his Satguru's bath and then join the sangat in drawing water for the langar. On becoming the Master, he continued for nearly a decade the practice of drawing a few buckets of water for the langar.

Whenever Maharaj Ji came to Dera after Baba Ji passed away, he spent almost all his time in meditation. Bibi Rukko would sometimes feel concerned about his health and write to Seth Pratap Singh at Agra. In reply to one of her letters, Seth Pratap Singh wrote, "It gave me great pleasure and my heart blossomed with joy to learn about Babu Sawan Singh's great interest in meditation and of such absorption within that he at times does not come out of the room for four days at a stretch."

Maharaj Ji did not initiate anyone for some time after he became the Master. Seth Pratap Singh asked him to start initiations, saying, "You have the blessings and all the spiritual power of Soami Ji and Baba Ji with you, besides your own."

Hazur had to continue with his army service for at least another eight years to qualify for a pension. While he was stationed at Kalabagh, Maharaj Ji sometimes used to hold satsangs at his bungalow, but he did not reveal that he was the Sant Satguru, for Saints do not go out to declare that they are Masters. He was now devoting more time to meditation and had further reduced his association with people.

In those days Babu Gajja Singh was also in Kalabagh.[1] Once in a while he used to hold satsangs in his own house. The people were fond of Gurbani (the Adi Granth) but had little idea about a living Master. One day, in 1904, Babu Gajja Singh dwelt at length on the need for a living Master and his qualities. After satsang, two or three people stayed on and said

---

[1] Babu Gajja Singh was an initiate of Baba Ji's. He lived for a long time with Maharaj Sawan Singh.

to Babu Gajja Singh that he had talked so much in praise of a living Satguru—but did such a person really exist? "Yes, he does exist," replied Gajja Singh.

They were anxious to know who he was and where he could be found. Two of the inquirers were working in minor jobs in Hazur's office. Gajja Singh asked them to go to their boss, for he held the treasure of true Nam with him.

They met Maharaj Ji and begged for initiation, and after a few days they were initiated. Thus the Great Master granted initiation for the first time in 1904.

On becoming the Satguru, Maharaj Ji began to spend all his holidays at the Dera. Satsangis and seekers gradually began to flock around him. Maharaj Ji also tried to visit Agra occasionally, as had been Baba Ji's practice, where Seth Pratap Singh Ji received him with great affection and respect. During one of Hazur's visits, Chacha Ji, deeply impressed with Maharaj Ji and overcome with emotion, offered to give anything Hazur wanted. Maharaj Ji said that he desired nothing except his blessings and grace. When Chacha Ji pressed him again to ask for something, Maharaj Ji said the only thing he could think of to request was Soami Ji's copy of the Adi Granth, from which he used to deliver satsangs. Chacha Ji gave it to Hazur and, with tears in his eyes, said, "You have already taken Soami Ji away. Now you are also taking this precious memento from us."[1] He then embraced Maharaj Ji and said, "The grace and blessings of Soami Ji will always be with you."

Gradually the work at the Dera began to increase, and the disciples grew restless during Maharaj Ji's absences, for he could only spend his holidays at Dera. Maharaj Ji was only fifty-three then and had two more years before his retirement. Even though his fellow officers begged him to stay on, Hazur

---

[1] This copy of the Adi Granth is preserved in the Dera archives.

retired in April 1911 in order to devote himself entirely to the
great spiritual duty entrusted to him by his Satguru.

Now Maharaj Ji's entire time was dedicated to satsang,
initiation, guiding the sangat, organizing seva, and to his own
meditation. He slept very little, at times attending to the queries of seekers until late in the night and then getting up at
3:00 A.M. His diet, already sparse, was now even further reduced. Satsangis close to Maharaj Ji would feel worried, but
he would assure them, "Do not worry. The nectar of Nam
will not let the body become weak. Nam sustains the entire
creation; it is not difficult for Nam to sustain the human body,
provided one is fully attuned to it."

But Banta Singh, who in the early days was also Hazur's
cook, would remonstrate: "Maharaj Ji, you eat and sleep very
little. Do you not feel hungry or sleepy?" Hazur would reply,
"Food and sleep are things that a person can increase and
decrease as he wishes. The body does not need much food
and sleep to keep healthy. Bhajan automatically reduces the
need for food and sleep."

Maharaj Ji ate very little food, and also paid little attention to its taste. Banta Singh sometimes used to narrate small
incidents to illustrate this. Once he prepared *kheer* (rice pud-
ding) for Hazur and took it along with the rest of the food.
Maharaj Ji ate the sweet dish after his meal. But later, when
Banta Singh was eating, he was crestfallen to discover that he
had put salt into the sweet dish instead of sugar. He could
not eat even a spoonful of the kheer, while Maharaj Ji had
eaten it without complaining or exhibiting the slightest sign
of discomfort.

Banta Singh ran to the Master and apologized profusely
for his lapse. Maharaj Ji consoled him with the words, "Do
not be upset, Banta Singh, I found the kheer all right." Banta
Singh used to tell us of other similar lapses on his part—like

the time he mistakenly put cream of wheat (*suji*) instead of sugar into Hazur's milk—but again, Maharaj Ji did not appear to notice and never complained.

Once, in some other context, Hazur told us that Saints live in the world but their attention is always absorbed inwards. They eat, but are not concerned with taste. They mostly stay at a higher plane and act from there.

Now that Maharaj Ji had retired from service, new seekers started coming to the Dera in large numbers. They absorbed his satsangs and sought the blessing of initiation. Old satsangis—the disciples of Baba Ji—generally looked upon Hazur as the same power as their own Satguru, for, in the words of Baba Ji, on the high spiritual plane Great Master had become one with Baba Ji. Like sugar in water, the colour of the water stays the same, but the taste changes.

In those days the incident of Hukam Singh confirmed that the Master and his successor are spiritually the same. Hukam Singh was a disciple of Baba Ji. He was a keen satsangi who never remained idle. He would spend the entire day in seva of the sangat, and almost the entire night in meditation. His efforts were rewarded, the inner door opened, his soul soared into the spiritual regions of sound and light. But he could not digest it; overcome with excitement, he started narrating his experiences to others. Baba Ji said to him, "Hukam Singh, digest what you have been given." Beside himself with joy, Hukam Singh declared, "Sir, even if a scholar of all the Vedas were to come before me, he would not be able to speak." He then loudly started narrating his experiences before others.

Baba Ji Maharaj stopped his inner progress. Hukam Singh tried his best, but could not go within. He approached Baba Ji, but the Satguru knew that it was not in the disciple's interest to reopen the inner door. The precious wealth was not meant to be squandered. However, Hukam Singh could not understand; upset and annoyed, he left the Dera and went back to his village.

After Baba Ji Maharaj left the world, Hukam Singh again came to the Dera and resumed seva here. Although the door to the inner path was closed, he persevered with his long hours of meditation and ceaseless seva. During his last days he became ill, and Maharaj Ji used to go and see him daily.

One day as Hazur was about to go to see him, Hukam Singh himself came. Maharaj Ji said, "Hukam Singh, I was just coming to see you ..." Hukam Singh said, "Hazur, I have come to beg for one thing from you." When Maharaj Ji inquired what it was that he wanted, Hukam Singh submitted, "My Master, my lord, please allow me once to bow my head at your feet." Maharaj Ji tried to explain that he never liked satsangis to touch his feet, much less the initiates of Baba Ji Maharaj.

At this Hukam Singh said, "If your form is the same as that of Baba Ji and if your body belongs to Baba Ji and not to you, then allow me to touch your feet; if it is not so, I do not insist."

Maharaj Ji, who had surrendered his entire being to his Satguru, could not say that his body did not belong to Baba Ji. He closed his eyes, remembered his Master, and said, "All right, you may." Hukam Singh bowed and knelt down, putting his head on Maharaj Ji's feet. The next moment when he got up, his face was radiant with joy. He said, "The inner path, which has remained closed for sixteen years, has now opened! My time has come and my beloved Satguru has promised to take care of me."

As scheduled earlier, the Great Master left for Agra that day. Hukam Singh passed away a few days later. Before death he was in ecstasy. Full of praise for Maharaj Ji, he had a radiant smile on his face.

Hazur's Family and Marriage

Hazur's father, Sardar Kabal Singh, came from a respected family of Jat Sikhs from the village of Mehmansinghwala (District Ludhiana, Punjab). He served in the British Indian Army and, as already mentioned, rose to the highest post open to an Indian officer in those days. Known for his intelligence, courage, and integrity, he was an extremely religious-minded person, giving respect to his own religion as well as to the leaders and sages of other religions. During his childhood, the Great Master used to accompany his father on visits to holy men who espoused various paths. Unfortunately, Sardar Kabal Singh passed away at a young age, when he was in his forties.

Maharaj Ji's mother, Jiwani Ji, an initiate of Baba Ji Maharaj, was a kind-hearted, dignified, and devoted disciple. From the time Baba Ji appointed Maharaj Sawan Singh as his successor, Hazur's mother no longer regarded him as a son but treated him with the reverence due a Master. I can still vividly recall an episode when Maharaj Ji, dressed all in white, came out into the courtyard and stood with his hands folded respectfully in front of his mother. Although Hazur was mature and stately, he stood before his mother like a loving child. His mother, also dressed in white, folded her hands in reverence to Maharaj Ji. Maharaj Ji said, "Mother, please don't fold your hands like this." In a tone of affection and respect, his mother said, "Please permit me—you are more than a son to me."

Maharaj Ji's grandfather, Sardar Sher Singh, who lived to the ripe old age of 115 and maintained reasonably good health till the last, looked after the family farm at Mehmansinghwala and also brought up Maharaj Ji, because Sardar Kabal Singh used to be away from the village on army duty for long periods. He was initiated by Baba Ji in 1900, when he was well over a hundred years old.

When Maharaj Ji was about twenty-five, his parents arranged his marriage with Bibi Kishan Kaur, whom the satsangis later called Amma Ji, or "mother," out of respect and affection. She was a kindhearted, soft-spoken, affectionate lady—an ideal wife—devoted, obedient, and understanding.

The Great Master had three sons. The eldest, Sardar Bachint Singh, an initiate of Baba Ji Maharaj, earned great social respect in Sirsa, where he settled in 1915 and rose to become an honorary magistrate under the British rule. He was bold, outspoken, and courageous. He had great respect for Maharaj Sawan Singh Ji and Sardar Bahadur Jagat Singh; and later, when Sardar Charan Singh was appointed Satguru at Beas, Sardar Bachint Singh was one of the first to pay homage to him. Sardar Bachint Singh's only son, Sardar Nagendra Singh, now a venerable elderly gentleman, is looking after the farms near Sirsa.[1] Sardar Bachint Singh passed away in 1952.

Sardar Basant Singh, Hazur's second son, was initiated by Baba Ji at a young age. He was an engineer, well settled in government service, when he passed away at the age of thirty-two. His son, Sardar Satnam Singh, is looking after his father's large farm in Sirsa district.

Maharaj Ji's youngest son, Sardar Harbans Singh, was quite young when Baba Ji passed away, and though he came in close contact with Baba Ji along with the other family members, he was later initiated by Hazur Maharaj Ji. Intelligent, sober, and hard-working, humble and straightforward, he was an example of devotion to the Master. He always looked upon the Great Master as his Satguru, and gave the same love and respect to Sardar Bahadur Maharaj Ji and to his own eldest

---

[1] Sardar Nagendra Singh passed away in 1986.

son, Maharaj Charan Singh, when he succeeded Sardar Bahadur Ji in 1951. When the Great Master purchased the farmland in Sirsa district, Sardar Harbans Singh looked after it
and was the one mainly responsible for turning the barren
wasteland into large agricultural farms, which today yield excellent crops. Sardar Harbans Singh had three sons—the eldest one, Sardar Charan Singh, became the spiritual head of
the Radha Soami Satsang and our beloved Sant Satguru. The
second son, Sardar Purshottam Singh, now a retired army
officer, is known for his bravery, efficiency, and hospitality.[1] The
youngest son, Sardar Jagat Singh, passed away at the young
age of seventeen, when he was still completing his education.

The Passing Away of Hazur's Mother

Shortly after his retirement, Maharaj Ji had to visit Kalabagh
for a few days. Here he received a telegram that his mother
was seriously ill. He immediately went to see her in Mehmansinghwala. She told Hazur that her time to depart had come,
but did not say when it would be. Maharaj Ji asked if she was
in pain. She said, "No, except that for the last three months I
have not had Baba Ji's darshan within. This was a great torment for me. But today he gave me darshan, so now that pain
has also gone."

Maharaj Ji told his mother to ask Baba Ji why she had
been deprived of darshan for so long. She closed her eyes for
a few minutes, then conveyed Baba Ji's reply, that during sickness the Satguru sometimes withdraws his darshan even from
a satsangi who daily sees him inside, so that the disciple, overcome by pain, does not ask that the pain be taken away.

---

[1]   Sardar Purshottam Singh passed away in October 1990.

Then Hazur said to his mother, "Ask Baba Ji Maharaj when he will be taking you." The reply was, "The day after tomorrow, at night." Seeing that Maharaj Ji was silent, his mother asked him if anything was wrong. He said, "If such is Baba Ji's will and he is with you, I feel no regret at your going. The only worry is that the day after tomorrow is the monthly satsang at the Dera, and the sangat will go away disappointed if I am not there. Yet I feel I cannot leave you now."

At this Mata Ji again turned her attention within and after a while said, "Go without any hesitation. Baba Ji says that he will take me only on your return after the satsang." Hazur said that he would return after the satsang, reaching Mehmansinghwala by the evening.

Maharaj Ji came to the Dera and gave satsang the next two days, but he was detained afterwards because of some important administrative matters of the Dera. He decided to finish the Dera work since Baba Ji had said that he would take Mata Ji only after Hazur's return. However, after he had finished the work it was too dark to travel to Mehmansinghwala.

The next day he went back to Mehmansinghwala and asked Mata Ji how she was. She said Baba Ji had come the day before and had asked if Babu Ji had returned. When she said he had not, Baba Ji said, "It does not matter. Tomorrow when he comes I'll take you."

In her last moments Maharaj Ji's mother was very happy. She asked everyone in the room to sit in meditation. When they came out of meditation, she had gone.

Purchase of Land in Sirsa

It was a year or so later that Maharaj Ji purchased the land at Sirsa. Even while he was in service, Maharaj Ji had wanted to buy some land for his family's financial security. He had thought of buying land in Montgomery or Sargodha, but when he sought Baba Ji's permission, Baba Ji said, "That land has many times flourished and has many times been laid waste. I will get you land at a place you will not be required to leave."

Finally in 1912/13, shortly after retiring to the Dera, Maharaj Ji bought some land near Sirsa, five or six miles from the town. It was very cheap as it was covered with sand dunes and prickly shrubs and had no water supply. To cultivate the land was hard, and to go and live in the inhospitable, wilderness-like surroundings, which were infested with scorpions and highly poisonous snakes, was a discouraging and almost frightening prospect. Even the inhabitants of the neighbouring villages seemed unfriendly.

When Hazur returned to see the land again with Sardar Bhagat Singh and Rai Sahib Munshi Ram, Sardar Bhagat Singh said, "Maharaj Ji, even if someone gave me this land free, I would not take it." Hazur laughed and said, "Only a farmer knows the value of farmland. With a little hard work it will become highly productive land."

The reaction of Sardar Bachint Singh, Maharaj Ji's eldest son, was, "What sort of place is this? It is surrounded on all sides by non-satsangis. Mehmansinghwala was better than this." Maharaj Ji said, "Don't worry, son. Every thorny shrub here will one day resound with the greeting, 'Radha Soami.'"

The other members of the Master's family said, "Maharaj Ji, Sikanderpur is a village owned by Muslim farmers and criminal tribes. How will we get along with them?" "With love," Hazur replied. "We will share their joys and sorrows. If they have troubles, we will try to help them."

And with love the Great Master won them. They were overwhelmed by Maharaj Ji's kindness and concern for them. Whenever he went there, they would all flock around to see him. They would often sit with him until eleven at night or even later, telling him their problems and discussing spiritual matters. Soon they began to treat Hazur's family also with great respect and affection.

Boons From Baba Ji

Once Maharaj Ji revealed that he had asked four boons from Baba Ji. First he had asked about the langar. Hazur submitted to his beloved Satguru, "I have never begged for anything from anyone. Pray grant your blessings that your langar continues regularly and I may never be required to tell the sangat that such-and-such article is needed for the langar." To this Baba Ji replied, "My son, there will never be any shortage in your langar. It will run regularly." And exactly as Baba Ji said, there has never been any shortage of anything in the langar. Hazur used to tell the sevadars to serve food to the sangat "with affection and large-heartedness, because Baba Ji's treasure is inexhaustible."

Second, Maharaj Ji had asked that if any injurious remark should inadvertently escape his lips, the words should not cause any harm to anyone.

Third, he had asked that his children should never be required to spread their hands before others for material needs. Maharaj Ji, on another occasion, remarked that he was grateful to the Lord, for his children were able to support themselves and freely offer money and provisions in seva without any desire for reward.

Fourth, he had requested that the souls he initiated be protected and taken care of at the time of their departure from the world.

During the same conversation, Baba Ji told Hazur, "My child, the construction work you have started here will continue without a break."[1] From the time Baba Ji allowed the Great Master to build the well and the first buildings, the growth of the Dera has been continuous, and, as revealed by Baba Ji, the work of development and construction has continued without a break.

Maharaj Ji's Love and Dedication

In the early days the only buildings at Dera were the ones Hazur had built during Baba Ji's time: the small satsang hall, a larger hall, the well, and a two-storey building to the east of the small satsang hall. The satsangis who came for a few days of satsang stayed wherever they could find space—in the satsang hall, the initiation hall, doorways, and verandas. There were few satsangis then—Baba Ji had initiated two thousand three hundred and forty three—so about two hundred people attended the Sunday satsangs and could thus fit into the small satsang hall.

Government officials and educated gentry stayed in the rooms to the east of Baba Ji's room, all sleeping on the floor. There were no bathrooms; the sangat bathed in the river, and

---

[1] The exact words used by Baba Ji were, "My child, trowel and hammer will constantly be in operation here."

Hazur at the well. There was no electricity; lanterns, small oil lamps, and candles were used to dispel the darkness. The river was so close that the sound of the flowing waters could be heard in almost every part of the Dera. The Dera lands were very small; the river was close by on one side and the well was the boundary on the other. The rest of the present Dera site was all fields, barren land, and ravines. A narrow bridle path, skirting the river and passing through the fields, was the only "road" connecting the Dera and the Beas railway station.

When Hazur came to stay at the Dera, he devoted his attention to two major areas of activity. The first included conveying the message of the Saints to the people, helping seekers, giving discourses on Sant Mat, guiding initiates, solving their inner problems, and generating in their hearts love and devotion for the Lord. The second included providing shelter, accommodation, and amenities to the ever-increasing number of seekers and satsangis who were coming to the Dera.[1]

Maharaj Ji's entire life was now dedicated to spirituality, and seva of the sangat. His own comfort, well-being, convenience, and even health became secondary for him. Endowed with an extraordinary willpower, Hazur had a great capacity for hard work. He would endure any amount of physical discomfort and hardship while carrying out his duties. He would completely disregard extremes of weather—heat, cold, heavy rains; nothing could deter him from his mission of satsang, initiation, and seva. He would stand in the summer sun— sometimes it is 120 degrees Fahrenheit in June—without an

---

[1] When Baba Ji settled down at Dera, it was on a very small piece of land between the villages of Waraich and Balsarai. Hazur Maharaj Ji gradually bought land from the farmers with Dera's funds. In 1952/53 Dera's land holding was consolidated. Today the land measures several hundred acres and is bounded on all sides by a wall. Besides this there is more land belonging to Dera outside the Dera boundary wall. Barring a small portion near the Beas River, a ring road runs around Dera.

umbrella, for hours at a time, supervising the harvesting. Once when I put an umbrella over his head, he said, "No, son, I do not need it. Don't you see the sangat is doing seva in the sun?" With Hazur looking on, seva that would normally take two days to finish was done in half a day.

Another time, after blessing the langar food, Maharaj Ji went to give darshan to the women baking chapattis over the pits of burning wood. In order to be visible to the ladies, he had to stand in the thick smoke coming from the damp fuel in the ovens. I myself was hardly able to breathe or see because of the smoke, and I requested that Hazur move to one side, away from it. He refused, saying, "The smoke doesn't bother me."

Nothing seemed to disturb Maharaj Ji's equanimity—hunger, thirst, illness, loss of wealth, even the death of a son.

Maharaj Ji's second son, Basant Singh, was very ill, and Hazur was bringing him to the Dera. When the Dera was still two miles away, Basant Singh's condition started deteriorating. Maharaj Ji realized that the end was approaching. He thought that if he reached the Dera with Basant Singh in this condition, Bibi Rukko would start crying and could insist that he be given a new lease on life. The Master, always resigned to his Satguru's will, stopped under the shade of a tree. After a short time, Basant Singh informed him that Baba Ji Maharaj in his Radiant Form had arrived to take him. Maharaj Ji said, "Son, if Baba Ji Maharaj has come, then with pleasure go with him."

The death of a young son of thirty-two, educated and well-placed in government service, leaving behind a young wife and small child![1] Who would not have been shaken? But

---

[1]   Sardar Basant Singh's wife died soon after him; his son, Sardar Satnam Singh, was a big landholder in Sirsa.

Maharaj Ji was absolutely unperturbed and calm. He would sometimes reminisce about that moment, saying, "I examined myself carefully and found my heart free from either joy or sorrow. My mind was like a clean slate with not a mark on it."

The Masters are always more concerned about the needs of their disciples than their own. I remember once Maharaj Ji had a cold and high fever; some of us begged him to rest and not to go to satsang that afternoon. He said he was all right and must go to satsang. Bibi Ralli and a few close satsangis knew that he was far from well and was in great discomfort. They almost insisted that Maharaj Ji stay in his room and rest. But he replied, "The more this body is utilized in seva the better. After all, it will be consigned to flames one day. I should never neglect the duty entrusted to me by Baba Ji." At satsang his face was radiant and his voice so powerful that the sangat did not suspect that he was ill.

Later in the evening as I was coming out of the Master's residence, a man approached, running, and said that he had just arrived and must see the Master. I told him that Hazur was ill, had just given a two-and-a-half-hour satsang, and it was not proper to trouble him now. But he would not listen. He said he had to report on duty at Meerut Cantonment the next morning. He became very insistent in his demands, so I bolted the door on him.

When I returned to Maharaj Ji, he said, "There is a man outside who has come from a long distance. Please bring him to me." I replied that I had already sent him away, but Maharaj Ji told me to find him and bring him back. I looked everywhere, and only after giving up the search did I see him on Hazur's veranda, the very picture of misery. I apologized to him and told him that Maharaj Ji wished to see him. He was overjoyed. With tears of gratitude in his eyes, he went upstairs with me to Maharaj Ji's room.

The man requested initiation. Hazur agreed and asked him to sit down. Anxious for Maharaj Ji's health, I begged that the man be initiated the following morning. Though unwell and looking tired, Maharaj Ji overruled my suggestion and initiated him.

A few weeks later the Master gave me a letter to read. The man had died just ten days after initiation. He had had a fever for only two days when he announced to his wife and brother that his inner eye had opened and Hazur was with him. He told them that his end had come, and asked them not to grieve over his death. His wife asked what she would do without him. He said, "Go to the Satguru at Beas and take his refuge." To his brother he said, "If you want liberation, you should also go to Beas and get initiation."

A lump rose in my throat as I read the letter. Now I realized why the Master, in spite of his own ill health, had initiated the man so late in the night.

Maharaj Ji was extremely compassionate and loving. When people came to him and confessed their failings, he would graciously forgive them. At the same time he would remind them that the mind is a powerful enemy and a disciple should always be alert to its deceptive stratagems. He would tell them not to repeat their transgressions, but to do bhajan and simran with love and devotion, and the Lord would forgive them. Although our karmas were as clear to him as the contents of a glass jar, he would never speak of our shortcomings, even indirectly. He took care not to hurt anyone's feelings. I never heard him speak ironically or cynically, nor say anything critical of others. He used to say, "Saints never look at our failings. If they did, who would come to them?" Like all great Saints, he would see only our virtues. He would say, "Every soul is virtuous. Our eyes and heart are at fault if we fail to see a person's worth, for God himself sits in every human heart."

Maharaj Ji's love and compassion flowed to everyone. He could not tolerate others' suffering and, moved to mercy, often took heavy karmas on himself. However, he would not permit these things to be discussed.

I remember a small episode in my own life that illustrates Maharaj Ji's compassion and his concern for his disciples even in minor, unimportant matters. I was on summer holiday at the Dera in June 1911 or 1912. I arrived after lunch; it was noon, the sun was at its zenith, the temperature must have been over 115 degrees Fahrenheit, and hot winds were blowing. Everyone was resting, so I found a mat and lay down on the veranda of Hazur's house. Maharaj Ji was resting in a room upstairs in his house. For the first time in eighteen years he was spending the entire summer in the hot plains rather than in the hills where he had been stationed during his service days.

The heat was too intense for me to rest, let alone to sleep. The floor was burning and hot winds were blowing; it was a real furnace. My eyes burnt and my throat was parched with thirst. In my misery I shut my eyes, and then suddenly opened them to find Maharaj Ji standing beside me.

I stood up hurriedly. Hazur asked, "Why are you lying here in this terrible heat? Come with me." Maharaj Ji had Banta Singh put a cot for me in a hut behind the house, sprinkle the room with water, make the bed, and bring a jug of cold water. With relief from the heat, a deep peace and coolness filled me as I absorbed Hazur's sweet and loving concern. Like a mother rushing to a crying child, he had come to allay my physical agony and to fulfil the desire of my heart for his darshan.

It is difficult to describe Maharaj Ji's physical charm and personality; the magnetism and radiance of his face cannot be captured in words. He was tall and slim, with a well-proportioned body. His broad forehead, fair complexion, flowing white beard, and a certain spiritual glow were captivating. His eyes radiated a purity that, as any disciple knows, is indescribable. He dressed in white *kurta* and white *salwar* which, with his white turban and beard, seemed to us all the more radiant.[1] When he laughed, which was often, his face sparkled with an infectious, childlike joy. His long, sharp nose and his white moustache and his flowing white beard enhanced the beauty and awe of his face. Even kings bowed in reverence on beholding his countenance.

Maharaj Ji's spiritual beauty and magnetism would draw the attention of people who casually looked at him, and would at times hold them spellbound. Once, Sardar Bhagat Singh and I were at the Jullundur railway station to see Maharaj Ji off. It was 1914/15, when I was practising as an advocate in Jullundur. A fellow lawyer from the city, Chaudhari Rahim Baksh, was also on the platform with his spiritual mentor, a Muslim faqir of considerable spiritual attainment. When the faqir saw Maharaj Ji, he began gazing at him. Wherever Maharaj Ji turned, the man moved so that he could still see Hazur's face. Finally he approached us and said to Maharaj Ji, "Sir, your face is shining with a divine light; I cannot stop looking at you." Hazur replied, "This only reflects your generous nature and purity of heart; there is nothing special about me." The faqir said, "Only saintly persons speak with such humility." The next day, Chaudhari Rahim Baksh told me that his Murshid had said that Maharaj Ji was a king among saints.

---

[1] *Kurta* and *salwar* are the traditional shirt and pants worn by men in northern India.

Dr Johnson, the well-known American satsangi who came to the Dera in June 1932, attempted to describe Maharaj Ji for the satsangis in America, who had never seen Hazur:

And how I wish I could really describe him to you or tell you of my impressions. But did you ever try to describe a beautiful sunset?.... No king could be more graceful and dignified, and yet that dignity is so tempered with sweet humility that one is drawn to him. His voice is low and clear as silver bells. His smile is extremely gracious and one can see that his heart holds only lovingkindness for all.... He is to be seen and not described. Since seeing him I can think of nothing else. His image lingers before me all the while. I have never seen such a face before, nor imagined there was one like it among the sons of men. If ever there was a face combining old age (he is now seventy-four years of age) with beauty, majesty and calm power, it is his. But beyond all of that there is a sort of spiritual radiance which no words can describe, but which gives one a feeling of deep peace, as if the discords of earth were no longer possible in his presence. As you look into his face you lose all desire to talk, even ask questions. You simply absorb the light. His voice is vibrant with love and his smile seems as if it lights up the room.[1]

Maharaj Ji's discourses were logical, interesting, and persuasive. In a sweet, melodious voice, he would speak for two to three hours without tiring. One had such a sense of lightness during his discourses, as if many burdens had been lifted. The following are some of the observations of

---

[1]   Julian P. Johnson, *With a Great Master in India*, Letter One.

Maharaj Charan Singh about the impact of the Great Master's satsangs:

I vividly recall Hazur Maharaj Ji's satsangs. For four decades they were looked up to as nothing else had been by tens of thousands of people. Every word and every syllable that he uttered became the very life of his disciples. The satsangs thrilled. They inspired. They enthralled the minds and hearts of all. They answered all their questions. They resolved all their pressing problems. They met all their needs. Every word was a healing balm that soothed their anguished hearts. Every word was an ambrosial drop that quenched their thirsty souls. It was a memorable sight to watch the vast multitude listening with rapt attention—men, women, and children sitting in pindrop silence, their faces lit with light, love, and peace. The deep and melodious voice of the Master created a musical effect that completely magnetized the audience.[1]

His keen sense of humour delighted the sangat, and when he laughed, his eyes, lips, his whole body, radiated joy. Who could resist laughing with him? Once an old lady, a simple uneducated villager, stood up during satsang and said, "My Emperor, you used to give me darshan inside every day, but you have not appeared for the last few days." Maharaj Ji said, "Daughter, you must have done something wrong."

She replied, "A few days ago my young son died. I took it as the will of the Master and refused to weep and wail. My neighbours said I was hardhearted and rebuked me, but I didn't let that disturb me. Then I accompanied my family

---

[1] Maharaj Charan Singh, *Discourses on Sant Mat*, Foreword.

members to Hardwar to immerse his ashes in the sacred Ganges, and there, out of fear of public opinion, I performed ritual worship and offered some money. From that day you have stopped coming inside."

Hazur said, "All right, touch your ears and promise you will not do it again." The old lady put her hands to her ears, a gesture of remorse in India, and said, "I am sorry for what I did. But you also put your hands to your ears and promise that you will not go away from inside again." Amused at the woman's innocent words, Maharaj Ji burst out laughing, and so did the sangat.

Like his own Master, Maharaj Ji continually stressed the importance of earning one's own living. He lived within his own income, not accepting even small presents from others. He never accepted offerings from disciples, nor ate at any-one's house. Whenever he left the Dera for a short time to give satsangs, he took his food along with him. For longer tours, he took his cook, along with necessary provisions.

If in a special circumstance Maharaj Ji had to accept a present, he took it only after paying for it in full. Satsangis coming from mountainous regions would sometimes bring him honey, almonds, grapes, and other things. Maharaj Ji would pay them much more than their value if he accepted the articles. He would say, "What I treasure most is your love, not these gifts." Bibi Ralli often reproved them, saying, "Maharaj Ji never eats anything you bring; he feels he must pay you twice as much money if he takes them. Don't bring them in the future unless you are asked to." Maharaj Ji always enjoined on the disciples to live on their own honest and rightful earnings. Sant Mat does not teach us to become para-sites. We must earn our own living, support ourselves and our family. Strict adherence to clean, pure food and honest earning is a must for spiritual progress.

Maharaj Ji would never initiate men who begged and lived on the offerings of others. Thus priests, sadhus, and other so-called holy men who lived on gifts and charity from others would not be accepted for *Namdan*.[1] He used to say that if a sadhu eats even a grain of food belonging to someone else, he will have to account for it before he can go back to the Father.

Once such a faqir, Sain Sharafuddin, asked Hazur for initiation. He was a Muslim holy man, who wore a long gown of rough cloth and carried a begging bowl in his hands. In spite of his repeated requests, Hazur refused to initiate him, and finally told him: "Living on one's own income is necessary for the practice of Nam. What good is it to give Nam to one who lives on others' charity?" The next day the man discarded his holy gown for ordinary dress and started working as a woodcutter. After a few days Hazur initiated him. He worked persistently at the path, spending part of the day cutting wood to sell and the rest of the day in meditation. He used to tell other faqirs that his Master had given him in forty days what books could not give in forty years.

Maharaj Ji would often say in satsang that the Satguru never accepts a single penny from his disciples; he supports his family from what he earns and gives away the rest in charity. A man who lives on the offerings of his disciples is not a Guru but a beggar; the Guru is always the giver. Saints have always supported themselves and their families through their own honest earnings. Saint Namdev used to print cloth, Kabir supported himself through weaving, Saint Ravidas by making shoes; Guru Nanak and his successors worked for their own living. Baba Jaimal Singh served in the army and lived

---

[1] *Namdan:* Literally, "the gift of the Name"; initiation into the practice of Surat Shabd Yoga.

on his meagre pension. And in the tradition of past Saints, Hazur through his own example showed us how to live on one's own earnings.

This high ideal and great tradition is being firmly adhered to even today by the Satgurus at Dera. Maharaj Ji often quoted Maulana Rum in this context, who has said, "In order to be able to truly pray to God, it is imperative to earn an honest living. Honest earnings give rise to knowledge, love and devotion, as well as a longing to serve the Master and merge with the Lord. It cleanses and purifies the mind, fills it with love for the Lord, and the eyes sparkle with spiritual bliss. My friend, if your living gives rise to jealousy, laziness, and ignorance, consider it to be improper."

Maharaj Ji also laid great stress on giving regular time to meditation. While speaking about meditation, he once remarked, "I have hardly done any meditation; I have received from Baba Ji his own hard-earned treasure." Banta Singh objected, saying he had seen Hazur doing six to nine hours of meditation for days at a time, with little interest in food and sleep. "And Hazur calls it nothing!" Maharaj Ji replied, "Little do you know how precious Nam is. If one can get it by offering one's head on a platter, it will be a bargain."

When Banta Singh told us tales of Maharaj Ji's meditation, his zeal and discipline, a thrill of joy would pass through us. Hazur used to say, "Meditation means dying a living death in the prime of life. It means staying awake, eating sparingly— in short, restraining the mind's cravings and bringing it under control. All this is no child's play. It is only possible when love for the Satguru takes possession of your heart, driving out all other attachments. To attain this state you must watch every thought and account for every breath. Be alert and do not let the mind think of anything except the Master; contemplate only on his form. Become attached to the Master and turn your mind away from the world. Only in such soil can the seed of Nam sprout."

We often wanted to ask Maharaj Ji why he spent so much time in meditation even after he became the Master. Saints are Saints from birth, yet Hazur spent much time in meditation each morning. Once when five or six of us were waiting for Maharaj Ji in his room, we asked Mr Mayyadas of Rawalpindi, who had served under Hazur for many years, to ask him this question. At first Maharaj Ji said, "Meditation must be done by everyone. What better way is there to spend one's time?"

But Mr Mayyadas was not so easily satisfied; he pointed out that Baba Ji had told Hazur when he initiated him that he was returning Maharaj Ji's wealth to him, that it was already earned and had been given to Baba Ji to keep for him. During his last days Baba Ji had even told the sangat that his successor would have great spiritual power and grace. Where was the need, then, for Hazur to do meditation?

Baba Nizamuddin of Multan, an initiate of Baba Ji and an evolved soul who was present there, said, "All this meditation is done for you and me because we are weak. By their own example Saints teach us how to meditate and develop love for God. If they were not to inspire us through their own example, how could we learn?"

Maharaj Ji laughed and said, "It is a rare one who learns even through example." Baba Nizamuddin replied, "That is another reason why you meditate."

Maharaj Ji always laid great stress upon bhajan and simran. In 1920, when I rose to a good position in Kapurthala State, I wrote to Hazur, thanking him for his grace in giving me the job, and he replied:

My dear Babu Daryai Lal,

Radha Soami. *May grace from the Satguru be showered on you. I received your affectionate letter and I am
glad to learn that you have a good and comfortable job.
Now that the Lord has given you material ease and comfort, it is incumbent on you to do your meditation; for
without meditation the soul will find neither peace nor
a resting place. In worldly matters a satsangi tries to be
punctual, industrious, and attentive. But when it comes
to meditation, I get letters asking me to take care of bhajan for them. No, this is not the right attitude. This is
not true discipleship. Just as a satsangi is not slack in his
worldly pursuits, he should not be slack in meditation.*

*What a pity that meditation, which is a satsangi's
prime duty, is neglected. Deeply concerned with succeeding in worldly jobs, earnest prayers are addressed to
God; but concern for meditation is missing. It is because
the worldly jobs are taken as important and the real
duty—meditation—is taken casually. Just as you attend
to worldly matters with zeal and determination, so too
pursue meditation with love and regularity.*

*Start today. Fix a time for your daily meditation and
hold to it. Meditation can only be done if you are punctual. If you miss meditation, consider your food unearned
for that day. This is the way to control the mind; this is
the prescription to tame its waywardness. Put this into
practice, dear son. Keep your mind in meditation throughout the day, even while walking about and working.*

Radha Soami from the sangat,
Sawan Singh
3.11.1920

Satsang Tours

In 1910, at the time Maharaj Sawan Singh started satsang and initiation, the people of Punjab—once the land of great Mystics and Gurus—had forgotten the real teachings of the Saints. Superstitions had made them oblivious to the importance of actual experience. The inner path shown by the Saints had been veiled by the heavy mist of orthodox beliefs and external observances. The true meaning of Nam and Shabd was lost to them, and the concept of the living Master—a prime necessity on the spiritual path—was relegated to a position of no importance.

The land where once the Gurus and adepts had sown the seed of Nam had been made barren by prejudices and outward formalism. With great perseverance and dedication, Maharaj Ji applied himself to the task of making this land fruitful through the ambrosial showers of his satsangs. For over forty years he went from town to town, from village to village, and even from house to house, carrying the message of the Saints. It is because of his simple yet inspiring discourses, his bold and dynamic yet kind and loving personality, and his untiring efforts that Sant Mat began to spread in India and take root abroad.

In 1910 Maharaj Ji began going on satsang tours, which at first were mostly of the cities, towns, and hill regions of what is now Pakistan, and a few cities and villages of East Punjab. Although the development of the Dera demanded most of his attention, he tried to go on tours whenever he could find time.

When Maharaj Ji visited Amritsar, Jullundur, Ludhiana, Ambala, Lahore, Lyallpur, Abbotabad, and Rawalpindi, the satsang was held in some satsangi's house. There were only four to five satsangis in Amritsar, five or six in Jullundur, and three in Kapurthala.

Hymns of the Gurus and Saints were read in practically every house in Punjab, but people had little idea of the message they conveyed. When Maharaj Ji, analysing these very hymns, began to explain Nam and Shabd and the significance of a living perfect Master, people were struck by the real meaning of the compositions they had sung and recited for so long.

Sometimes learned men would come and argue with Maharaj Ji; they would even allege that the hymn Hazur took for satsang was not in the Adi Granth. Hazur would listen with great patience, explain with affection, and show them the hymn in the Adi Granth. Persons who had read the Adi Granth more than two hundred times would argue that the term *Shabd* ("Sound" or "Word") implied only the words uttered by the holy Gurus or the hymns recited by them. Maharaj Ji, with his deep study of Gurbani, would quote extensively from the Adi Granth and explain that the Shabd that "creates and dissolves the world" and the Nam that is "supporting all physical and spiritual planes"[1] cannot be a written or spoken word. Hazur would express his point of view in a friendly, conversational way, never creating rancour or ill will, rather leaving an impression of his love and humility.

Once, an aged Sikh met Maharaj Ji and said that he had read the Adi Granth from the beginning to the last page, eight hundred times. Hazur said, "Brother, I respect you for your achievement. But please tell me, has your soul ever gone within? Have you ever been able to see the inner light?" The old man looked puzzled and replied, "No."

When Maharaj Ji went on satsang tours of Abbotabad, Peshawar, Rawalpindi, and other cities now in Pakistan, devout Hindus, Arya Samajis, Vedantic scholars, and Muslim

---

[1] Adi Granth, *Majh*, M.3, p. 117; *Gaudi Sukhmani*, M.5, p.284.

theologians would come to listen to his discourses and discuss spiritual matters with him. He had a good knowledge of all these paths and religions and would always give a patient hearing to their views, explaining the Sant Mat teachings with reference to their own respective faiths. He would never try to force his views on others nor enter into heated arguments.

One evening in Wazirabad, a Muslim holy man came to meet Hazur. Maharaj Ji answered his questions, giving extensive quotations from Persian Mystics like Rumi, Shams-i-Tabriz, and Hafiz. After two hours of conversation, the holy man thanked Hazur, bowed to him, and while leaving walked backwards up to the door as a mark of respect for the Master.

A group of orthodox Sikhs once came to satsang during Maharaj Ji's discourse. Maharaj Ji offered to stop his discourse so that they could ask questions, but they requested that he continue. After satsang they questioned Maharaj Ji about his interpretations of the scriptures. Finally one of the group said, "Where is the proof that Shabd refers to something within us?"

The Master asked, "Do you have faith in the Adi Granth?" The man replied that he did, so Maharaj Ji read him the following verses from the Adi Granth:

> He who reveals the Home within the home
>   (body)
> Is the enlightened and true Master;
> There, within, ring the five melodies ever
>   resounding,
> Marking the source of the Shabd.
>
> *Adi Granth, Malar, M.1, p. 1290*

The man then agreed that Hazur had spoken the truth.

Whenever a satsangi complained to Maharaj Ji about un-friendly or rough behaviour from non-satsangi relatives, Hazur would reply, "Attend regularly to your bhajan and simran with love and devotion. Be humble and loving with everyone and do not enter into arguments about Sant Mat. Leave everything to the Lord."

Maharaj Ji never stopped any disciple from going to temples, gurdwaras, or mosques. When Hazur himself had to visit a temple or gurdwara to attend a marriage or other social ceremony, he would offer obeisance and sit on the floor with the other guests. Once, questioned by a satsangi, he replied, "We should never be disrespectful towards any religion nor criticize it. We should think of our Master and bow our head, so that we do not hurt anyone's feelings."

Gradually, educated young people were also attracted to Maharaj Ji's discourses. A journalist who had read the Vedas and other holy books got into a discussion of the Sant Mat teachings with a satsangi friend of his in Amritsar. Impressed by the teachings, the journalist decided to visit Beas to see Maharaj Ji. He wrote down fifty or sixty questions he planned to ask Hazur, for questioning and arguing were central to his work as a newspaperman.

The first satsang answered most of his questions; never-theless, he wrote down a few more. The second satsang an-swered all the rest. Not ready to give up, the journalist wrote a few more and asked for an interview with the Master. After putting him at ease with some personal queries, Hazur said, "Is there anything you would like to ask?" The journalist re-plied, "Well, I did have a few questions ... " Maharaj Ji told him that he was welcome to ask any questions he wanted to. But the satsangs had satisfied his queries; he had forgotten the new questions and was in no mood to ask anything. Ob-serving his silence, Hazur said, "Son, do not hesitate, take the piece of paper out of your pocket and ask whatever questions you have." Overwhelmed, he tearfully requested initiation.

Often people who received initiation in those early days were criticized, even treated harshly, by their family and friends, because the path was so little known. Sometimes the very people who criticized would come to the Dera to scrutinize this unusual and unorthodox path, and would be so impressed by Hazur's personality and discourses that they would seek initiation.

Once, the wife of a business executive from Central India received initiation from Maharaj Ji. When her husband, who had practiced idol worship and recited scriptures for years, learned of her initiation, he was furious and threatened to turn her out of his house. She said to him, "Please do one thing first. Go to Beas, see my Satguru, and listen to his discourses. After that I will gladly submit to whatever punishment you may choose to give me." He would not agree to her proposal until the other family members persuaded him that her suggestion was reasonable. After hearing just one of Maharaj Ji's satsangs, the executive asked Hazur's forgiveness for his behaviour and begged for initiation. In such cases, Maharaj Ji's mercy and grace helped the initiates to overcome opposition from their family.

The opposition to the Sant Mat teachings was particularly great in the isolated mountainous areas, citadels of orthodoxy and superstition. Idol worship, animal sacrifice, and various forms of external rituals were commonly practised in the mountains of Himachal Pradesh. Maharaj Ji used to undertake satsang tours of these hills very regularly, and today the entire mountain region has a large number of satsangis.

One such place is Chalate, in the mountains of Himachal Pradesh, inhabited by Rajputs who were devoted to hunting and to external religious rituals. A distinguished resident of Chalate, Mian Amar Singh, became the first satsangi in the area after he found out about Sant Mat from a satsangi in his army regiment. A few days after Amar Singh's initiation, his parents were also initiated. Amar Singh's elder brother, however, was upset at their initiation. He denounced the teachings but soon visited the Dera to see things for himself. After hearing satsang for a few days, he submitted to Maharaj Ji, "I too want to be initiated, but on two conditions. First, I will not give up hunting, for King Ramchandra, the incarnation of Lord Vishnu, used to hunt. Second, I have been repeating a mantra for the last many years, which I will not give up."

Maharaj Ji explained to him the relentless law of karma: how mighty kings, learned men, rishis, and even incarnations had to account for their actions, and how one has to pay the price of killing animals and eating meat. Maharaj Ji added, "As for your repetition, I will teach you the method of a much more effective and fruitful repetition."

Mian Amar Singh's brother still had some hesitation. After a few more days of satsang, however, he came to Maharaj Ji and said, "O King of kings, I give up meat and wine—I have no conditions. Please initiate me." And he received initiation.

In 1926, at the request of Amar Singh and his family, Maharaj Ji visited their village, Chalate, for the first time. Travelling partly on horseback and partly on foot, he gave darshan and satsang in villages on the way. When he reached Chalate the people welcomed him with a band. They danced and sang with joy at his arrival. The priests of Chalate, however, tried to keep the people away from Hazur by announcing that whoever attended satsang would be fined fifty rupees—a very large sum in those days. The next day only one lady, though not a satsangi then, dared come to the satsang.[1] Inspired by her example, others began to come on succeeding days to hear Maharaj Ji's discourses. The number grew, the fine became ineffective, and many men and women received initiation.

Bhota was another village where antagonism to the teachings dissolved because of Maharaj Ji's humility, love, and tolerance. In 1917/18, three or four villagers from Bhota came to the Dera and were initiated. On their return they met with resentment from their friends and relatives, who were deeply attached to orthodox forms of worship and a non-vegetarian diet. Gradually a few more villagers came to Maharaj Ji and received initiation. Because of opposition, they were afraid of being known as satsangis; but their new way of life, abstaining from meat and wine, gave away their secret, and they faced harassment and even social ostracism.

Much upset and concerned, they came to Dera and narrated the tale of their suffering and humiliation at the hands of the orthodox and the priestly class at Bhota. Hazur reassured them and decided to visit the village.

On the way to Bhota, the Master stopped at a number of large and small villages. Sometimes riding on horseback the whole day, sometimes walking eight to ten miles at a stretch, Hazur would stay for one, two, and sometimes three nights in a village. Many village people walked with Maharaj Ji and his party, and when Hazur initiated at Singian and Santokhgarh—two of the villages—the number of initiates was as much as a thousand.[2]

---

[1] Bibi Dharam Devi, the widow of Sepoy Ram Singh. A keen and devoted satsangi, she did a lot of seva in the hills and many came to Sant Mat through her. Later, Hazur asked her to look after the satsang hall at Kalu-ki-Bar, where she lived till her death in 1956.
[2] Seven hundred at Singian and three hundred at Santokhgarh.

Maharaj Ji stayed at Bhota for a little less than a week, and people from nearby villages, hearing about the visit of a great Saint, came to satsang in large numbers, many receiving initiation. Today there are over twenty thousand satsangis in that area. The satsang hall, built through voluntary seva by the sangat in Bhota, is one of the most beautiful buildings in the region.

Hazur thereafter visited Bhota and other mountain villages in Himachal Pradesh regularly. During one of his visits to Bhota, Maharaj Ji met a sadhu who wished to discuss spirituality with him. When the sadhu, expounding from the Vedas and other Hindu scriptures, finally exhausted his learned arguments, Maharaj Ji asked, "Sir, how far does your spirit rise inside? Have you ever gone inside?" "Inside what?" the sadhu asked in a puzzled tone.

Maharaj Ji used to say that scholars and learned men often engage in intricate philosophical discussions with no personal experience of the path within. They are being robbed every moment of their own inner wealth, while trying to guard the houses of others. Once, in the course of conversation, he said, "Scholars are the watchmen of the gates of the Lord. Themselves powerless to go within, they refuse to believe that others can."

In Sujanpur Tehra, a hill village, a large section of orthodox persons were harassing the satsangis so much that they had to hide that they were followers of Sant Mat. Maharaj Ji visited this village in 1939. Driving to the riverbank opposite the village, Maharaj Ji crossed the river by boat and found about a thousand men, women, and children waiting on the other side. Tulsi Ram, a holy man well known in the area, was among them, waiting for Hazur with a bouquet of flowers in his hands. When Maharaj Ji landed, Tulsi Ram bowed at his feet, offered the flowers, and tried to say something, but his voice was choked with tears. Hazur stepped back and greeted him with "Radha Soami." After satsang, Tulsi Ram went to Maharaj Ji for darshan, and the Great Master affectionately talked further to him about the Sant Mat teachings.

The local priests, much perturbed at the impact of Maharaj Ji's discourses on the villagers, got together during the night and decided to interrupt Hazur's satsang the next day, argue with him, and prove to the local people the value of idol worship. The next day Maharaj Ji gave a discourse on Kabir, taking a hymn that explains the futility of mechanical repetition and describes the location of the various Hindu gods and goddesses within the body. As planned, a priest stood up and gave a short talk on the benefits of idol worship. Maharaj Ji replied very sweetly that the real temple of God is the human body. The outer forms and temples remind us that the real deity is within. These idols and temples are man-made; they are artificial, not real. The real abode of God is the human body—it is the temple designed and made by the Lord, and it is in this temple that He presides. We must search for Him in the place where He actually dwells, not in things created out of dead matter with our own hands.

Speaking about the importance of a living Master, Maharaj Ji said: How is it possible for a student of today to learn from a teacher who passed away a thousand years back, or for someone to have his complaint decided by the ancient king, Vikramaditya, or for a sick man to be treated by the mythical physician, Dhanvantari?

Most of the priests were greatly impressed by the Master's talk and a few of them asked for initiation. Two or three of them, however, went to Mahatma Tulsi Ram and said, "You should be ashamed. You, a Brahmin, bowing at the feet of a Sikh!" Tulsi Ram replied, "Just look at him with my eyes— what do you know of his greatness?"

Today there are many satsangis in the villages of this area. In every bhandara satsang at the Dera, thousands come from the hill towns and villages of Bhota, Sujanpur, Bilaspur, Hamirpur, Parore, Mandi, Nurpur, and numerous other small villages of Himachal Pradesh.

The people of Ghuman, the village of Baba Ji's birth, always had a special place in Maharaj Ji's heart. And the villagers, whether they were satsangis or not, respected and adored him. Hazur often used to visit Ghuman and give satsangs there. Such visits were always an experience for us. The entire village would come to the satsang and the atmosphere would be surcharged with love and devotion.

On one of Hazur's visits to Ghuman, the villagers had spread silken fabric, embroidered sheets, and colourfully printed cloth in the satsang. Their faces were glowing with happiness, and such an atmosphere of love and devotion prevailed that Maharaj Ji said, "I am deeply moved by your love and devotion. I am very happy with the devotion of the people of Baba Ji's village. You are all members of Baba Ji's large family ..." As he said this, tears trickled down his cheeks.

After the satsang a satsangi submitted on behalf of the sangat, "Maharaj Ji, Baba Ji's house in Ghuman is old. Pray, have it rebuilt into a strong brick-and-mortar structure." Maharaj Ji replied, "I would gladly do that to keep Baba Ji's memory fresh. I would cover the entire house with gold leaf if he permitted. But it is not his will."[2]

Another time one satsangi voiced the feelings of the sangat in Ghuman to Maharaj Ji: "We are weak-willed peasants; we can hardly live up to the high teachings of satsang, let alone do our meditation. You are all-forgiving. Please

---

[2] Although Dera has built a beautiful modern satsang hall at Ghuman, the old house of Baba Ji is carefully preserved in its original condition.

forgive and save us." Maharaj Ji replied with great affection, "You are Baba Ji's own family. Don't worry, I will take care of you. Even the dogs of Ghuman will some day be saved."

The entire population of Ghuman—satsangis and non-satsangis—had deep love for Maharaj Ji and great affection and regard for the Dera. The villagers of Ghuman have been rendering service to the Dera from its very inception and continue to do so even today. The present villagers are the third generation of Baba Ji's disciples, but their devotion to the Dera and its Masters is the same as before. Whenever any important job arises, requiring dedication and hard labour, the villagers come to the Dera and stay here till the work is accomplished.

The impact of Maharaj Ji's satsangs and personality was always profound. He was kind and compassionate towards everyone, his love touching all levels of society—high and low, rich and poor. His affection and understanding transformed a number of thieves, criminals, and even dacoits into devoted satsangis. Maharaj Ji himself once said, "Soami Ji has entrusted to me some souls with most unbecoming karma."

A robber named Labh Singh, after hearing Maharaj Ji's satsang, sold his land and all other possessions in order to pay back what he had stolen. Then he asked for initiation and was blessed with Nam by Maharaj Ji. Balwant Singh of Ghuman was a notorious thief and bully. He once came to Hazur's satsang, and his eyes opened to the truth; repenting for his deeds, he begged for initiation and became a devoted satsangi. Though he was an uneducated rustic, through his meditation and through Hazur's grace he acquired a good understanding of Sant Mat and was asked by Hazur to give satsangs in his village. People who had feared and disliked the man developed respect and affection for him.

The episode of Gangu the notorious robber was well known to the sangat. Gangu happened to have a glimpse of

Maharaj Ji on a road in Amritsar, came to him, and was initiated. Earlier he had committed many robberies and had more than once escaped from jail. A few years after the Great Master's passing away, he was arrested, tried, and sentenced to death. He had a mind to break out of the jail and escape, as he had done previously; but Hazur appeared to him and asked him to accept the punishment of his karmas gracefully, which Gangu did, serene in his Master's will.[2]

Spirituality is not the prerogative of the high caste, of the rich, or even of the learned. Maharaj Ji's grace and blessings were not constrained by any social or economic factors, or by any external considerations of caste, creed, or colour. Lehna Singh of Ghuman, a sweeper belonging to the caste of untouchables, was a devoted satsangi who often came to the Dera for satsang and darshan. Poor, simple, and uneducated, but keen and regular in his meditation, Lehna would come and sit quietly in the back row. Even there people avoided sitting near him because he looked ragged and unclean. Seeing this, Maharaj Ji once told him to come and sit in the front. Lehna Singh hesitated at first, but when asked again by Hazur he came and sat in the front. A few educated, well-placed gentlemen drew away from him. At this Lehna smiled but said nothing. Seeing him smile, Maharaj Ji asked him to reveal his thoughts, saying, "Lehna, come out with whatever is on your mind." Lehna folded his hands and submitted, "Hazur, my hut of hay and reeds is rickety, my cot is broken, and my quilt is tattered." Pointing to the gentlemen, he added, "Pray, tell them that the one whom they seek is always in my lap."

Once, a police inspector was driving through Beas with a dangerous thief whom he had just captured. The robber said

---

[2] A detailed account of Gangu the robber appears in the author's book *Call of the Great Master*.

he had heard that a great Saint lived in Beas and asked the inspector to let him have Hazur's darshan. The inspector saw no harm in it and turned the vehicle towards the Dera. When they arrived, they went to the Master and the inspector said to Hazur, "This depraved robber has committed many crimes. Please bless me, Sir, so that our case is successful and he is convicted and hanged for his crimes." Maharaj Ji smiled and said, "Brother, in the court where I serve, there is nothing but forgiveness." A case was filed against the man, but he was acquitted by the judge. He came straight to Dera. After a few satsangs, he was a changed person and asked for initiation. The Master blessed him with Nam and he became a devoted disciple.

From 1911 to 1932, Maharaj Ji's attention was directed primarily to the development of the Dera, where new buildings and individual houses for satsangis were coming up regularly. His tours during this period, though many, were of shorter duration than the tours he would undertake later, between 1932 and 1946. Most of Maharaj Ji's satsang tours were in areas that are now in Pakistan. Rawalpindi, Lahore, and other cities and large towns of West Punjab had excellent satsang buildings and property, even before the foundations of satsang halls were laid in important cities of East Punjab, like Jullundur and Ludhiana. Also, there were many small towns and even villages in West Punjab where there were satsang properties. Hazur used to visit Lahore at least three or four times a year for satsang, in the course of his satsang tours.

Maharaj Ji's tours in far-flung villages were rigorous, involving transportation by bus, train, horseback, and on foot, and accommodation was often uncomfortable and inconvenient. In many villages Maharaj Ji slept in huts hardly large enough for his cot. Improvised bathrooms were made by leaning two cots against each other and covering them on the open sides with a white sheet. Once, on a cold winter morning in the mountains, I remember going into one of these bathrooms to wash; I was shivering—and with the icy cold water, the most I could manage was a hasty washing of my face and hands. But Maharaj Ji, without any complaints about the inadequate and cold "bathrooms" and the ice-cold water, would take a bath at five in the morning and be ready to meet the sangat at about six.

These tours required incredible endurance by Hazur. When he was on long tours he frequently arrived around the time for satsang, had a brief rest, and went straight to satsang, leaving orders that his travelling companions should have dinner immediately. He would not eat, as he always left a space of two hours between a meal and satsang. By the time satsang ended, it would be 4:00 P.M. Then he would go to the langar to bless the food. There were usually interviews and visits to satsangis' homes after that, so he often did not eat until 6:00 or 7:00 P.M., with only a glass of milk taken in the morning to sustain him. Through all of this he was smiling and cheerful, and satsang organizers never knew that he had not eaten or rested.

Walking with Hazur on the hilly tracks of Simla and Dalhousie was a challenging experience. He would climb so fast and with such agility that even young soldiers were reminded of their rigorous army routines. A short account of one of Maharaj Ji's tours will give an idea of his great capacity for endurance. He was just finishing a tour in Abbotabad and planned to return to Beas after delivering the morning satsang. His day began, of course, with meditation early in the morning. After giving satsang in Abbotabad, Hazur went by car to Rawalpindi, where he gave an unplanned two-hour satsang, and drove to Lyallpur, three hundred miles from Abbotabad. At Lyallpur he gave his third satsang of the day and left immediately afterwards for Beas, driving through the night and arriving at 4:30 A.M. At 6:00 A.M., he was ready to proceed to Kapurthala to attend a marriage ceremony. From Kapurthala he went on to Jullundur, arriving there at about 11:00 A.M. Dismissing the driver he had been given at Rawalpindi, the Master gave him a turban and some money as a gift. The driver, a hardy Pathan from Jalalabad (Afghanistan), said to Hazur, "Sir, remember me again. Though I am only thirty years old, I am utterly exhausted from trying to keep up with you. You did not eat or sleep, yet you do not seem tired. You are not a human being. To look at you is to look at God himself." At that time Hazur was over eighty years old.

Hazur used to go on extensive tours of the areas which are now in Pakistan. He visited Lahore, Rawalpindi, Lyallpur, Sialkot, Peshawar, Naushehra, Quetta, Multan, Karachi, Abbotabad, Kalabagh, and many small towns of this area. He would often break journey to visit small towns and sometimes even villages that happened to be on his way.

One of Hazur's tours is recounted by Dr Johnson in his book *With a Great Master in India*. It was October 1932 and Maharaj Ji was going to Kalabagh, a hill station where he had been posted for a long time during his service days. On the way to Kalabagh, Hazur gave satsang in Rawalpindi for five days, attracting people from all religious backgrounds.

The trip to Kalabagh was particularly interesting to us because we saw a number of construction projects that Maharaj Ji had supervised during his service days: the road we travelled on had literally been cut out of the mountains, since Kalabagh is at eight or nine thousand feet above sea level; and a large resting place for travellers, located next to a spring, had also been cut out of rocks. All along the road Hazur had planted trees, now fully grown and beautiful. At Kalabagh we stayed in a stone house which was Hazur's personal property, acquired by him while he lived there during his service days. This house was built on an isolated hill away from the town with deep valleys on three sides.

People came from near and distant villages surrounding Kalabagh to hear Maharaj Ji's satsang, their faces bright with love. There was even time for the Master to take Dr Johnson to the place where Baba Ji used to give satsangs whenever he came to Kalabagh. On 14th October 1932, Dr Johnson witnessed an unusual event. At eight in the morning, Maharaj Ji gathered the children of the satsangis and, teaching them the way to listen to the Shabd, he connected their souls to the Sound Current.

From Kalabagh, Maharaj Ji went to Abbotabad and gave satsang. Here several old gentlemen came to meet Hazur; they had worked under him during the period of his service. It was a sight to see, how after so many years Hazur recognized each one of them, greeted them with love, and inquired about their welfare; and also to see the affection and respect with which they met Maharaj Ji. Here during satsang a few people tried to interrupt and engage in arguments, but when Hazur lovingly answered their queries, they were satisfied.

Before Kalabagh, as already mentioned, Maharaj Ji had visited Rawalpindi, where he stayed in the satsang hall—at that time one of the most beautiful buildings in Rawalpindi. Hazur gave satsangs from October 6 to 11. The satsangs were mostly attended by Hindus and Muslims, but soon Sikhs also started coming in large numbers. The lucid exposition of Guru Nanak's teachings and Maharaj Ji's magnetic personality drew them to the satsangs.

On the early morning of the twelfth, Maharaj Ji left for Kalabagh, but before leaving he informed the sangat that he would return to Rawalpindi on October 24, give satsang in the evening, and leave the next day at 6:00 A.M.

A group of Sikhs felt worried at the impact of the Master's satsang and, fearing that many Sikhs would become satsangis, called meetings of the local Sikh leaders. It was decided by them that they would try to disturb and disrupt Hazur's proposed satsang on the twenty-fourth.

As scheduled, Maharaj Ji returned to Rawalpindi on the afternoon of October 24. At the evening satsang a number of armed Sikhs spread themselves among the sangat, a few making disturbances during Hazur's discourse. The satsangis tried unsuccessfully to quiet them. Soon a few other Sikhs joined in, shouting and waving their swords. Just as it looked as if violence might break out, the police arrived and the disturbing group slipped away. During the entire disturbance Hazur sat on the dais, unperturbed and calm, his face glowing with spiritual radiance. Several Sikhs, only a few feet from Hazur, had been shouting with their swords drawn, but nothing could disturb Maharaj Ji's serenity and composure.

Those who saw the Master then said they would never forget the beauty and radiance of his face at that time. When some satsangis said that they had seen a venerable elderly gentleman standing behind Hazur, Maharaj Ji revealed that it was Baba Ji himself, protecting them. With the agitators gone, Hazur began satsang again in his calm, sweet voice. It seemed as if nothing had happened; and though he had not previously planned for one, Hazur announced another satsang for the following morning. Satsang the next morning passed peacefully and, if anything, the number of Sikhs interested in the teachings had increased.

After the incident, the sangat in Rawalpindi flourished, with many prestigious members of the Sikh community becoming satsangis. When Hazur returned to Rawalpindi several years later, some satsangis described how everything had become peaceful after the initial opposition, and how satsang in Rawalpindi had developed. They said that it was all the result of Hazur's personal magnetism, blessings, and grace. Maharaj Ji replied with his customary humility, "Brother, the credit goes not to me but to the beauty and depth of Guru Nanak's Bani, which is full of profound spiritual meaning."[1]

Hazur had undertaken intensive tours of West Punjab and Northwest Frontier Province (now in Pakistan), and of East Punjab and Himachal Pradesh (in India). Beginning from 1905/06, such tours increased as the sangat grew. He would often visit very small villages in the hills, sometimes spending the night in a small hamlet of only a few huts, situated in isolated hills or valleys.

On one such tour of the hills in April 1933, Maharaj Ji visited about twenty towns and big villages, and over fifty hamlets. During this tour of twenty-nine days, he usually delivered two satsangs every day, and at times even three—all in different places—giving initiations in the larger villages in open places under trees—places away from settlements. In all, Hazur initiated four thousand seekers on this tour, one of the many tours of the hills that he undertook.

Always close and dear to his sangat, Maharaj Ji not only inspired love in the disciples but also gave them his love and grace in return. Every disciple felt a closeness with the Master, and as the sangat was small, the disciples had the benefit of personal contact with him. A langar was organized in almost all the places Maharaj Ji visited, and sometimes Hazur used to distribute chapattis with his own hands.

It was the beginning of Sant Mat in the hills. The simple village people had been deeply involved in external observances, idol worship, and rituals. Hazur had to do the spadework,

---

[1] Guru Nanak's Bani are the writings of Guru Nanak as contained in the Adi Granth.

and it was hard work, too. The seed was sown by him, and today there is hardly a village in Himachal Pradesh that does not have scores of satsangis.

Deeply concerned with his sangat's welfare, Maharaj Ji never forgot a face. In the winter of 1933, Hazur was on his way to seva when, just beside the Dera library, an old woman came and bowed at his feet. Maharaj Ji said, "Sister, why have you been so long in coming? When I initiated you in the village Ghoda Dhaka near Khanspur fourteen years ago, you asked permission to come to Dera. Where have you been all these fourteen years?... I am glad you have come and hope you are well." At Hazur's recognition after so long a time, the lady was in tears and almost speechless. Finally she told him how domestic and economic obstacles had kept her away. We had never even heard the name of her village.

Rao Bahadur Shivdhyan Singh, a prominent landlord of Pisawah (Dist. Aligarh, Uttar Pradesh) and a devoted disciple of Hazur, once requested Hazur to visit Pisawah also. Maharaj Ji replied, "Yes, Rao Sahib, I will also visit your home town some time." After this Rao Sahib repeated the request two or three times and was given the same assurance, but no confirmed dates.

When Rao Sahib accompanied Maharaj Ji on one of his tours in the hills, he saw the poor quality of accommodation provided for the Master—sometimes in small congested rooms, sometimes under a thatched roof. Seeing this, Rao Sahib, already feeling that the Master was being evasive about a visit to Pisawah, was unable to understand what possible objection Hazur could have to staying in his palatial house if he did not mind these dingy rooms and thatched huts.

When they returned to the Dera, he again asked the Master to visit Pisawah, but again Hazur put him off. Rao Sahib felt deeply hurt at what he took to be a rejection. He used to tell us that when he went to bed that night he was feeling dejected and depressed. Had he done something to annoy the beloved Satguru? If Hazur could visit tiny villages in the remote hills, why could he not come to Pisawah? Sad, almost in tears, he kept brooding over these things until he fell asleep. That night Maharaj Ji appeared to him in a dream and said, "Rao Sahib, you are proud of your mansion and large rooms. But what interest do I have in them?"

The next morning Rao Sahib went for Hazur's darshan and, his eyes filled with tears, submitted, "Beloved Satguru, please forgive me. I was proud of ..." But Maharaj Ji did not allow him to complete his sentence. He affectionately seated Rao Sahib beside him and, turning to his secretary, Rai Sahib Munshi Ram, asked him to note down the dates for the Pisawah satsang and make the necessary arrangements. This Pisawah tour was Maharaj Ji's first visit to the state of Uttar Pradesh.

At the request of Diwan Tejumal Bhawnani, Hazur visited Karachi, a city on the Arabian Sea in what is now Pakistan. So few satsangis were there in those days that the attendance at the first satsang was very small. Diwan Bhawnani, who had tried to inform all his friends and acquaintances, felt perturbed at the small turnout and asked Maharaj Ji, "Hazur, perhaps I should print leaflets to announce the remaining satsangs so that people will know you are here." Hazur smiled and said, "Be a little patient. Our publicity agents are already working."

The next day handbills were distributed by some orthodox religious groups in Karachi, saying that a Radha Soami Guru had arrived who was misinterpreting the scriptures and misleading the people. These circulars advised everybody to avoid his satsang. As a result, people came to Maharaj Ji's satsang out of curiosity, so much so that the satsang was overcrowded and had to be held outside. The sangat began to grow after that, and today there are a large number of satsangis from this area.

Maharaj Ji, until 1943, would spend a short while each summer in Dalhousie. Even during that brief "vacation" from his duties, satsangis would go to Dalhousie, and the Master would give satsangs and interviews and explain Sant Mat to seekers, attending with patience to their numerous questions. In 1943 Maharaj Ji became very ill and his doctors advised him to find a hill station at a lower altitude for the summers, rather than Dalhousie.

A large uninhabited tableland, surrounded on all sides by valleys, was selected and purchased; Hazur began to give satsangs there two or three times a year. Known as Kalu-ki-Bar, the land was cleared and levelled and soon a satsang hall was built there. There is no habitation around Kalu-ki-Bar, but a large number of satsangis and seekers came from nearby villages and towns.

Not only Kalu-ki-Bar but also the entire Kangra hills were areas where ritualism, worship of deities, and animal sacrifices were prevalent. Drinking and meat eating were common, and superstitions and caste differences prevailed. But Hazur's satsangs changed the people, and today there are over twenty thousand satsangis in these hillside villages.

The simple, clean-minded hill people absorbed the Master's teachings and changed their way of life. Maharaj Ji's satsang at Kalu-ki-Bar was always a memorable spectacle. Once, while Hazur was in Kalu-ki-Bar, Master Tara Singh and a few other eminent Sikh leaders came to meet him. They attended the satsang, in which Hazur gave a discourse on a shabd from the Adi Granth. For two hours the sangat sat in pindrop silence, with their gaze fixed on Maharaj Ji's face, oblivious of all else. After the satsang, the Akali leaders said to Hazur, "We are surprised to see that these illiterate and simple hill folk understand the Bani of Shri Guru Sahib and listen to the discourse with such rapt attention. Tears were flowing down the cheeks of many of them and they appeared to be unaware of their surroundings."

Maharaj Ji replied, "Yes, love for Guru Nanak's Bani has been generated in their hearts by the satsang." And Hazur added with a laugh, "Now if you feel the necessity, you may teach them the traditional form of living." Then Hazur explained that one becomes a true Sikh by understanding Guru Nanak's Bani and putting it into practice, not by adopting mere external forms.

Whenever Sardar Amar Singh Grewal, a relation of the Master, came to the Dera, he reported to him about Mehmansinghwala, Hazur's native village. He once told Maharaj Ji that a few people from the village asked Mahant Mitt Singh why such a large number of people flocked around Babu Sawan Singh. Mitt Singh replied, "I have also been to the Dera twice, and on making inquiries learned that Babu Sawan Singh has a magic book with him. When he reads it and looks at a person, that person comes under his spell." When Maharaj Ji heard this, he laughed and said, "True, Amar Singh, perfectly true. What magic could be greater than the Bani of Guru Nanak?"

In November 1945, Maharaj Ji undertook a tour of Peshawar, the areas of the Northwest Frontier, and upper Punjab. It was his last visit to the Frontier Province.

In this long tour, Hazur visited Lahore, Muridki, Kamoki, Gujranwala, Wazirabad, Gujrat, Jhelum, Rawalpindi, Haripur, Kalabagh, Nathiagali, Abbotabad, Peshawar, Shaido, Jahangean, Hazro, Gujjarkhan, Sialkot, and a number of towns and villages on the way.[1] Giving satsangs in all these places and

---

[1] All these places are now in Pakistan.

initiation at most of them, and also meeting satsangis and seekers, Hazur, who was now eighty-seven, undertook what appeared to some of his close disciples to be one of his most strenuous satsang tours.

As always, his satsangs were attended by large crowds, not only Hindus and Sikhs, but also Muslims and Pathans. Hazur had respect for men of all faiths. At Peshawar, a holy man, Baba Jagir Singh, attended the satsangs and requested that Maharaj Ji visit his village, Shaido. But Hazur had no time, as the next two days were fixed for initiations. Baba Jagir Singh was very keen that Hazur come to his village and give darshan and satsang there; with folded hands he prayed again, and Maharaj Ji had to give his consent.

The Master completed two days' programme in one day by giving Nam to seekers in three sittings, and then accompanied Baba Jagir Singh to his village. Here the satsang was attended mostly by Muslims and Pathans, some of whom sought personal interviews with the Master. In spite of the heavy schedule and physical strain, Maharaj Ji looked cheerful and radiant in satsang, his face shining with love and kindness.

From Shaido, Maharaj Ji went to Hazro, one of the many places visited by Baba Ji Maharaj during the period of his long search for a perfect Master. Here Hazur was received with great love and respect by Baba Wazir Singh (the successor of Baba Balak Singh), who attended satsang and recited a poem in Hazur's praise. In Hazro, Maharaj Ji initiated fifty seekers.

Ram Nath Mehta, who was with Maharaj Ji on this tour, relates an anecdote of the trip. One night Maharaj Ji stayed in a very small village near Peshawar. Some Pathans came to meet Hazur, and one of them stayed on till almost midnight, asking numerous questions about the path. Maharaj Ji answered patiently, giving examples from Persian Saints to show that the teachings of all Saints are the same. Maharaj Ji also told him the Persian names for the inner regions. The conversation continued till midnight. At last the Pathan gentleman said that what Hazur was saying appeared correct, but he asked, "What is the proof that the path you speak of is the correct path to meet the Lord?"

At this, Maharaj Ji told him about the method of simran, asking him to repeat every day for two hours any name of God that he liked. Hazur also told him to completely abstain from meat, eggs, and alcohol. The Master then said, "Do this repetition for forty days, and if at the end of this period you do not obtain proof of the correctness of the path, then you may come to Beas and openly accuse me of falsehood."

The man was an earnest seeker and started the practice with enthusiasm. Hardly a month had gone by before he appeared at the Dera. He told Maharaj Ji that during the prescribed practice he had now started seeing Hazur inside. His face glowing with love, and with tears in his eyes, he asked for initiation and was blessed by Hazur with Nam.

In 1947, during the great upheaval caused by the partition of India, this Muslim satsangi saved the lives of many Hindu satsangis in Shaido, Hazro, and other villages in the area, helping them escape to India. Hazur continued to visit Pakistan up to October 1946. In November 1946 he fell ill, and after 27 November he stopped going on satsang tours.

Besides visiting West and East Punjab, the Kangra Hills, and cities and towns of the present Haryana, Maharaj Ji used to visit Delhi regularly. He also undertook satsang tours to Jammu and Srinagar; Pisawah, Bulandshahar, Khurja, Meerut, and other places in Uttar Pradesh; Gwalior, Ujjain, Dewas, Indore, and villages like Deoli, Kanasia, Chidawat, and Bilawali in Madhya Pradesh; and Bombay, Pune, Sangli, and Amravati in Maharashtra. In almost all these places Maharaj Ji gave initiations and daily met many seekers.

When Maharaj Ji took up the mantle of mastership there were about twenty-four hundred satsangis and the attendance at bhandara satsangs used to be about two hundred. But soon the number of disciples and seekers began to increase and the satsang hall near the well became too small even for the weekly satsangs.

In 1933/34 the big satsang hall—Baba Jaimal Singh Hall—was built to accommodate ten thousand people. But even before the hall was ready in 1934, the attendance at bhandara and monthly satsangs had increased to over twenty thousand. Hazur said that no matter what the size of halls one makes, satsangs will now have to be held in open fields.

Alarmed at the increasing size of the sangat, an orthodox group of people started to criticize and preach against Sant Mat. This, however, had little effect on seekers, who continued to come in large numbers. Ultimately, some over-enthusiastic young men formed a committee in order to dissuade seekers from going to the Dera. Putting up posters, shouting slogans, and indulging in malicious propaganda through fiery speeches, they tried to disturb the satsangs. Finding these methods ineffective, they organized games and wrestling matches just outside the Dera during the satsang hours.

The sangat became agitated. Maharaj Ji told the satsangis not to interfere in these activities, but to maintain peace and act with love and tolerance, keeping in mind the high principles of Sant Mat. He also directed the sevadars to serve these young men food in the langar, and if they came to satsang, to receive them with affection.

As there was no arrangement for food nearby, the young men would come to eat in the langar. Impressed by the devotion of the satsangis and their loving behaviour, some of them began to attend the satsang and soon asked for initiation. People who came to witness the wrestling bouts also started coming to satsang out of curiosity, and the attendance at satsangs began to increase. Seeing this, the opposition was withdrawn. Some time later a few of the organizers, greatly moved by the Master's lovingkindness and magnetic personality, came and sought his forgiveness for their behaviour.

Hazur's satsangs—his simple and lucid exposition of the teachings—drew seekers from all walks of life: the educated and the learned as well as the simple and devout. Lawyers, professors, government officers, businessmen, judges, scientists, intellectuals, and persons from the ruling class, all came and listened to his discourses with great devotion. Hazur's very presence filled his surroundings with a wave of spirituality.

There are no words to convey the inner blessing and grace that satsangis received from him—the help and guidance, the protection in times of danger, and the unique grace at the time of the disciple's departure from the world. All of these remain an untold story, too personal to be shared with others.

Sant Mat in the West

The year 1911 has special significance in the history of Sant Mat, for it marks the beginning of Sant Mat in America and other countries in the West.

Sardar Kehar Singh Sasmus, a devoted disciple of Maharaj Sawan Singh, was serving in the Canadian Steamship Lines. In 1911 he was given a job in the Canadian Pacific Railroad which required him to visit the state of Washington in the northwestern United States.

One evening, while he was walking on a street in Port Angeles in Washington State, an American couple, Dr and Mrs Brock, happened to see him. What drew their attention to

him was no ordinary sight. Over his head they saw a beautiful radiant face with a white beard and a white turban. Unable to restrain themselves, they stopped him and asked,
"Who is the beautiful figure we see over your head?" Kehar
Singh was puzzled at first, but thinking that it must have
been the will of the Master to reveal himself to this American
couple, he said, "It is my Master, Maharaj Sawan Singh Ji."

Sardar Kehar Singh's reply did not satisfy the Brocks; its
brevity only whetted their curiosity and they wanted to know
more about this Indian gentleman's Master. Kehar Singh began to tell them about the teachings and the Master, and they
met him as frequently as possible to learn more about the
path. Gradually they realized the significance of a perfect
Master and the meaning of the terms *Nam* and *Word*. Soon
they became restless and began longing for initiation.

Seeing their impatience for Nam, Kehar Singh wrote to
Hazur about them. In reply, the Master directed Kehar Singh
to initiate Dr and Mrs Brock on his behalf, and he did so in
1911, acting as the Great Master's representative. When seekers gradually started coming to the Brocks, the Master appointed the Brocks as his representatives in America.

For about twenty years the Brocks carried out this seva in
America. They would send Maharaj Ji a full description of
initiation applicants and, after receiving the Master's permission, would give the instructions. Sometimes when the seeker
could not come to them, they would travel as much as two
thousand miles to give initiation.

Perhaps the best-known seeker of the Brocks' time was
Dr Julian Johnson, who had once served as a Christian mis-
sionary in India. It was after years of seeking a true spiritual
guide that, in 1929, Dr Johnson visited Mrs Julia McQuilkin,
an eighty-year-old satsangi in Ashland, Oregon, who had
been initiated in the early 1920s. He was deeply interested in

her explanations of the Sant Mat teachings and expressed a great desire for initiation. Mrs McQuilkin told him to contact Dr Brock, who later initiated Dr Johnson on Maharaj Ji's behalf on 21 March 1931. The same year, Mr Harvey Myers of southern California was also initiated. He was later appointed the Master's representative in southern California, and many seekers came to Sant Mat through him.

In 1932, Dr Johnson wrote to Maharaj Ji for permission to visit the Dera, as he strongly felt the necessity of meeting his Master in person. When permission was given, he sold his lucrative medical practice, his private hospital, and his house, and left for India. His friends thought him mad to give up all that for a Master he had never even seen, and they tried their best to change his mind. Dr Johnson, however, was determined to meet his Master and spend the rest of his life with him if possible. And once in India, he never thought of returning to America, as he wished to give his life to the study and practice of Sant Mat.

On coming to the Dera, Dr Johnson devoted his entire time to satsang, meditation, and seva. He used his medical knowledge and experience to serve the sick, free of cost. Though the amenities then available were limited, he stayed here till the end of his life in 1939. He was a devoted disciple and, under Maharaj Ji's guidance, made good progress on the spiritual path.

Until the arrival of Dr Johnson at the Dera, there were no books in English explaining the path. The letters written by the Great Master to the Brocks and other satsangis and seekers were the only literature available to them. Copies of relevant portions of these letters were often circulated among the American satsangis, who avidly read them over and again. Dr Johnson was asked by Dr Brock and Mr Myers to send detailed information about his experiences with the Master and about life in the Dera. These letters were later published in book form as *With a Great Master in India.*

During his years at the Dera, Dr Johnson also wrote his well-known treatise on Sant Mat, *The Path of the Masters,* which was the result of his deep study of Eastern and Western religions, his association with the Master, and the Master's satsangs. At that time Sardar Seva Singh, a judge in the Sessions Court, translated Soami Ji's *Sar Bachan Prose* into English; Dr Johnson assisted him in this project.

The Sant Mat teachings continued to grow, abroad as well as in India, during the 1930s and 40s—through the foreigners who had discovered Maharaj Ji and the teachings while they were stationed in India. These initiates then returned to their own countries, taking the teachings with them.

Colonel Sanders, who introduced Sant Mat to Great Britain, was serving as an officer in the British Army in India from 1937 to 1943. He met Maharaj Ji and received initiation in 1938, later introducing various people, including Miss Flora Ruegg, to the teachings. When he retired to England in 1943, the Great Master made him his representative there. Only a few days after returning to England, Colonel Sanders initiated Colonel Martin and Miss Ruegg on behalf of Maharaj Ji. Colonel Sanders later added to the literature on Sant Mat in English by writing a booklet for seekers, called *The Inner Voice.*

Between 1935 and 1940, Sant Mat was introduced to South Africa as well, through Sir Colin Garbett,[1] who was deeply interested in the Bible and spirituality. In 1935 he was serving the British Government in India and was appointed Financial Commissioner in the Punjab. During this time he came in contact with Maharaj Ji and the Dera, and learned about

---

[1]   Sir Colin Garbett passed away in August 1972 at the age of 91.

the teachings. He became convinced that the esoteric path hinted at in the Bible is identical with Sant Mat, and requested initiation. About the same time, two other Englishmen were initiated—Maj. E. P. Little and Dr Lander (principal of the Agricultural College in Lyallpur, where Sardar Bahadur Maharaj Jagat Singh was serving as professor). Sardar Bahadur's character and purity were instrumental in leading Dr Lander to seek initiation from Maharaj Sawan Singh. After their retirement, all three of these satsangis settled in South Africa and played an important role in spreading Sant Mat there.

Satsangis in India would often request Maharaj Ji that he allow himself to be photographed, but he would dismiss their entreaties, saying that people would start turning their attention outside and even begin contemplating on the photographs. Satsangis from abroad also longed to see their Master, and many who could not undertake the long voyage to India because of ill health, age, finances, or other problems, kept on requesting a photograph. But Hazur's reply was always in the negative.

Once, a satsangi from abroad sent a description of Maharaj Ji, saying that this was the form that had appeared to the writer inside, and inquired if it was the form of Maharaj Ji. At this, some satsangis close to Hazur begged that a photograph be sent to the Western satsangis so that they would at least know what their Master looked like. Maharaj Ji, moved to mercy, permitted a photograph to be taken. This photograph, meant for foreign satsangis, also began circulating among satsangis in India.

When the Mehta brothers—Ram Chand Mehta and Ram Nath Mehta, both eminent photographers—were initiated, Maharaj Ji gave permission for his photographs to be taken, and these photographs became available to everyone. But

Hazur always cautioned satsangis that they should never contemplate on the Master's photograph; they should keep it as one keeps the photograph of a friend or member of the family. The Mehta brothers also took great pains to make movie films of Maharaj Ji, and his disciples see these films today and refresh their memory of their beloved Satguru.

The Passing Away of Mata Kishan Kaur

Mata Kishan Kaur, the Great Master's wife, was an extraordinarily pure soul and truly a mother to all of us. With sweetness and affection she would always ask us about our families, visibly pleased to hear of their well-being. She spoke with equal affection to all of us, regardless of our position. Like Maharaj Ji, she could not bear to see anyone in distress. Whenever one of us expressed his pain to her, she affectionately called him *bachu* ("my child"), and then suggested ways to relieve the problem. Her cheerfulness, serenity, and great love inspired us all. During the twenty-five or thirty years that I knew her, I never saw a sign of anger or frustration in her face. She embodied all the qualities one might expect in the wife of a great Saint.

During the last two or three years of his sojourn in this material world, Baba Ji had started giving hints about the identity of his successor—Maharaj Sawan Singh. But the first disciple to whom this was clearly revealed was Mata Kishan Kaur, the Great Master's wife.

Sometime during the year 1898, Baba Ji called Bibi Kishan Kaur to him and most affectionately told her that he had chosen her husband, Babu Sawan Singh, to continue the divine mission of initiation and guidance of the sangat. He further added, "From now onwards, I want him to adopt a life of celibacy. Tell me if you have any desires to the contrary."

Though still young—only thirty-five—Mata Ji was a keen devotee and an ideal satsangi. During all these years of her married life she had occasion to stay only three or four times with Hazur, and that too for periods of two to four months each time. Like her husband, she was fully devoted to the Sant Mat way of life and had great love for Baba Ji.

In reply to Baba Ji, Mata Ji folded her hands and humbly said, "My Satguru, I have no desire. My only desire is to obey your orders and to live in your will." Her answer pleased Baba Ji, who, expressing his happiness, offered to give her any boon she wanted. Mata Ji had no desire for worldly things; she only wanted undying love and faith in the Satguru.

One thought, however, was troubling her: When Hazur took up the duties of mastership at the Dera, who would look after her three young sons? The youngest, Sardar Harbans Singh, was only four or five years old. Baba Ji placed his hand on her head and said, "My dear child, have no worry. I will be responsible for the upbringing of your children."

From that day onwards, Mata Kishan Kaur never looked upon Maharaj Ji as her husband, and when five years later the responsibility of mastership descended on his shoulders, Mata Ji accepted him as the personification of her Satguru, Baba Jaimal Singh. If Hazur ever introduced her to a newcomer as his wife, her simple mind would object and she would protest to Hazur for calling her his wife, for she saw herself as only one of his many disciples.

Mata Kishan Kaur was especially fond of her grandson, Maharaj Charan Singh, and had a keen desire to see his marriage before her death. She was overjoyed when he was engaged to Bibi Harjeet Kaur in June 1943. When Bibi Harjeet first came to Dera with her father, Mata Ji embraced her as lovingly as she would her own daughter. After this Mata Ji used to ask the Master, "When are you going to fix the date of Charan's marriage?" Hazur would reply, "Withdraw your thoughts from these things. He will be married in due course of time."

Every year Mata Ji used to come to Dera from Sikander-pur and spend six months here—from March to September. She used to stay with Bibi Ralli. When she came to Dera in 1944, she fell ill during the third week of August. A few days before her sickness, she said to Sardar Charan Singh, "I had wanted to leave only after witnessing your marriage, but such is not the will of Baba Ji." She then gave him four hundred rupees, saying, "Buy a gift of your choice with this money and give it to your bride on my behalf."

During Mata Kishan Kaur's illness, Maharaj Ji came to see her every morning and evening. Because of weakness, she could not get down from the bed and bow to Hazur, so she would implore him to raise his feet and let her put her forehead on them. Yielding to her entreaty, Hazur would raise his feet one at a time, and Mata Ji, taking his foot in her hands, would lower her head and place it upon Hazur's foot with great devotion.

For several months she wanted to leave this world. During the period of her illness, she would request Maharaj Ji to take her away, but Hazur knew that she had a keen desire to see the marriage ceremony of her grandson; he would just say, "Ask Baba Ji Maharaj." When she would ask Baba Ji within, he would reply, "I have no objection, but you must obtain Babu Sawan Singh's permission." And when she would again ask Hazur, the reply would be, "Not yet."

Three or four days before her death she became impatient and asked Hazur, "Why are you stopping me from going?"

The Master replied, "Very well, now keep your attention within." Her attention turned inwards, she became absorbed within—oblivious of the external world—and stayed in this state till the last.

On 7 September 1944, when Mr Ram Nath Mehta of Delhi went to Maharaj Ji for darshan, Maharaj Ji took him aside and said, "Today your Mata Ji will leave this mortal world. Go to Lahore and bring motia flowers[1] and other fragrant white flowers available there." Hazur also gave him a list of a few other items and told him to return to Beas by the 5:00 P.M. train, and that a tonga would be waiting at the station to bring him back to the Dera.

Just then Mr Mehta saw the doctor coming with a box of medicine for injections. The doctor assured Maharaj Ji that Mata Ji would surely improve with these injections. When the doctor left, Mr Mehta said, "Maharaj Ji, you say that Mata Ji is to go today. Then why let the doctor disturb her with these painful injections?"

Hazur replied, "If I don't allow the injections, the doctors will say that she could have been saved. Let them do their job. Do not worry, her attention is firmly fixed within. They may give her any number of injections, she will not feel them." Mr Mehta then left immediately for Lahore.

Around 4:00 P.M. Mata Ji's breathing became slow and subdued. Bibi Ralli went upstairs and told Hazur that Mata Ji, it seemed, was gradually sinking. In the summer Maharaj Ji sometimes took a bath in the afternoon before going to satsang. He said, "I will come downstairs after my bath."

Saints do not want the satsangi's attention to turn outside at the time of death, not even towards the physical form of the Master; that is why Hazur did not come down immediately.

---

[1] Motia flowers are a variety of small, white, very fragrant flowers.

When he came down after his bath, Mata Ji had passed away. A few minutes later the bell for satsang sounded. The Master did not want the sangat to be disturbed before satsang and therefore asked Bibi Ralli not to tell anyone of Mata Ji's death; he would himself give the news after the satsang. The Master then went to satsang and gave his discourse as though nothing had happened.

When Mr Mehta returned in the evening from Lahore, he found the tonga waiting as promised. He asked the driver if there was any news from the Dera, as he wondered if Mata Ji had indeed passed away. After hearing that the driver had no news, Mr Mehta began to worry about what the sangat would think when he arrived with all the funeral materials. When he reached the Dera and found that Hazur was already giving satsang, he really began to wonder whether Mata Ji had departed as Hazur had said, she would. When the satsang ended, Maharaj Ji announced that Mata Ji had died and that the cremation would take place immediately.

Mata Ji's body was covered with Maharaj Ji's white cotton shawl and her bier was heaped with white jasmine and motia flowers—symbols of her pure spirit.

Growth of the Dera

When Hazur Maharaj Ji came to the Dera for the first time, the colony consisted only of a mud hut and a small shack, both with thatched roofs. The hut was for Baba Ji, and the shack for Bibi Rukko, where she also cooked food for Baba Ji and herself.

The hut in which Baba Ji used to stay when he first came to the Dera in 1891 was originally built by Baba Ji himself as a temporary structure with thatched roof and walls. Maharaj

Sawan Singh Ji, during Baba Ji's lifetime, had the thatched walls replaced by bricks laid in yellow earth and plastered with mud. Later, he persuaded Baba Ji to make it a more lasting structure with brick and mortar.

When permission was granted by Baba Ji to rebuild the hut into a small room, the Great Master took care that none of the bricks, stones, or earth from the hut were thrown away. All of it was used in the foundation and the plinth of the new room. After Baba Ji's departure, Maharaj Ji never slept in this room; whenever he went to give initiation or travelled away from Dera, he always went into Baba Ji's room and sat in meditation for a while.

Both huts were rebuilt in brick by Maharaj Ji during Baba Ji's lifetime, and another room was built by the side of Bibi Rukko's hut. When Hazur took up the responsibility of mastership in 1903, the Dera had grown to include the well, the two satsang halls, a two-storey building with nine rooms, as well as Baba Ji's room. In 1911, when Maharaj Ji retired and came to live in the Dera, the building activity received a new impetus, fulfilling Baba Ji's prediction that the mason would always be at work in the Dera. With Hazur's blessings, there has been no let-up in the construction work, which is continuing even to this day at an ever-increasing tempo.

After 1911, the first building that was erected was the present library building. In those days there were fields, wasteland, deep pits, and ravines on the present site of the Dera; and the boundary of the colony on the southwest was marked by the well, known as Soami Sagar, and the two small satsang halls. Towards the west, the Dera land ended with a small ridge of ground about two and a half feet high, crowned with *phulahi*, a species of acacia tree, which formed a hedge. The ridge ran in front of the houses of Rai Bahadur Gulwant Rai and Rai Bahadur Shankar Dass. From here a narrow bridle path led to the village of Waraich, and from Waraich onwards the path went through fields and skirted the river, taking the traveller towards the village of Buddhatheh, near the Beas station.

Gradually the Dera began to grow, and new houses were built. The Dera was still surrounded by wilderness on three sides—north, west, and south—and on the east the river ran dangerously close. The Great Master purchased wastelands and fields from the villagers, and under his inspiring guidance and with the sangat's loving seva, the area was gradually developed into fertile farmland.

The Beas River was causing damage to the neighbouring villages. The Dera is at a much higher level than the river, yet flood waters would sometimes make inroads into the land on the east side of the Dera, sweeping away some portion of the earth. Although Dera did not suffer any damage from the river waters, its closeness to the river was a subject of talk among some of the non-satsangi villagers.

Sardar Amar Singh Grewal, a distant relation of Maharaj Ji, once told the Master that a so-called holy man in Mehmansinghwala was saying, "These people have built their Dera on the bank of the river Beas. I would like to see their faces when the river floods and washes their colony away." Hazur said in a firm tone, "Is the force of the river greater than the power of Baba Ji Maharaj?"

In the early years, the sangat had to cross the river in boats to collect grass and reeds—which were used as fuel in the langar—as they grew only on the opposite bank. Crossing the river was frequently difficult because of the swift current and stormy weather, and often the sevadars who went to collect the reeds would return late in the evening, sometimes as late as 11:00 at night. Maharaj Ji would always wait for the safe return of the sevadars, not retiring even if it was midnight.

Once, when they got back very late, one of the sevadars said, "Hazur, the current was very strong; it took us a long time to get across. The river creates so many problems for us." Maharaj Ji said, "Do not worry. If it is Baba Ji's will, the river will recede, and the grass and reeds will begin to grow on the Dera banks in the future."

Indeed, gradually the river began shifting, and now it is about two miles away from the Dera. The reeds and other thick grasses used for fuel grow on the Dera side of the river, and crossing the river is no longer necessary.

Maharaj Ji was himself an efficient and experienced engineer. The layout and the master plan of all the new buildings were drawn by Hazur himself. All buildings erected in the Dera during his time were personally supervised by him. He would stand for hours, giving detailed directions to masons and engineers on the most minute points. The big satsang hall, called Baba Jaimal Singh Hall, is the most remarkable of the Master's creations and is regarded as one of the most beautiful and majestic buildings in Punjab. The entire design and plan for this was made by the Master himself. Adorned with well-proportioned minarets and crowned with golden spires, the building combines both medieval and classical styles. Its flawless finish and the chaste design compel one's wonder and admiration.

Hazur laid the foundation of this hall. It was an inspiring sight and the sangat's hearts were charged with love and joy. Maharaj Ji himself laid the foundation stone and bricks around it, and he himself carried the first five baskets of earth to fill the foundation. A marble box was placed in the foundation trench, containing the book *Sar Bachan Poetry* by Soami Ji Maharaj and a note giving a brief history of the Dera. At the end of the note, the Master put his signature after writing the word "approved." He then laid the bricks around the marble box.

Maharaj Ji was reluctant to follow any formal procedure of laying the foundation, but prominent satsangis, the secretary, Dera officials, and the sangat were keen that Hazur lay the foundation stone. Yielding to their entreaties, Hazur agreed to do so. But on 30 September 1934 at 1:30 A.M., Maharaj Ji visited the spot in the company of a few satsangis, stood with closed eyes for some minutes, and invoked the grace and blessings of the Lord. This was the real foundation ceremony—if one can use the word "ceremony"—for what better start to the new project could there be than remembering the Almighty and praying for His mercy and grace?

The next day, at the time of the formal function, Rai Sahib Harnarayan informed the sangat in a short speech that Hazur had very kindly acceded to the organizers' request to lay the foundation stone. Giving a brief account of the development of the Dera, Hazur's secretary informed us how the sangat had grown: About sixty thousand people had come into the fold of Hazur's disciples, and attendance during bhandaras and monthly satsangs had risen from a few hundred to about ten thousand; from a few mud huts in the 1890s, the Dera had sprung up into a well–laid-out colony with over a hundred houses; and the message of the Saints had spread to every corner of Punjab as well as to many other parts of India and the world.

Continuing, Rai Harnarayan spoke about Hazur Maharaj Sawan Singh who had adopted the human form to emancipate souls pining to meet the Lord. Hazur's ceaseless efforts had brought a new wave of spirituality, and his mercy and grace had enabled thousands to come to the path. "All those who have had the darshan of Hazur are fortunate; they are truly blessed who have gained faith in him and follow his teachings with love and devotion; and blessed is the present time when the Lord has come in human form to guide his children. Who can enumerate the qualities of Hazur or gauge his boundless spiritual power and grace? Can one illustrate the brilliance of the sun by lighting a lamp?"

In the end he requested the Master to lay the foundation of the new satsang hall. Before laying the foundation, Maharaj Ji gave a short reply to the secretary's speech:

I have no words to express my gratitude and happiness at performing this function. I am full of many failings and shortcomings. The growth of satsang and the sangat is not because of any ability or power in me; it is the achievement of that great Saint, Baba Ji Maharaj, who spent all his life in meditation.

My father was fond of the company of sadhus and sages. He longed to meet some perfect holy man. Being a member of a Sikh family, I started reading the Adi Granth at the age of seven. I was also interested in Vedant, and I had a chance to keep the company of holy men of many religions and paths. I had no prejudice against any faith or community and held wise and noble men of all religions in reverence. I was anxious to meet a perfect Mahatma—I was not concerned or bothered whether he was an Arya Samajist, Sanatanist,[1] Sikh, Muslim, or whether he belonged even to the lowest caste of the untouchables. Twenty-two years passed in this search; I could not find the holy man I sought, the perfect guide who could give satisfactory answers to my questions. I met many high souls, but not the perfect one I wanted.

---

1. A Sanatanist is someone who follows the orthodox Hindu religion, involving acceptance of the ancient Hindu Scriptures.

Then Hazur briefly related how Baba Ji had met him in the Murree Hills and blessed him with initiation. Speaking about Baba Ji Maharaj, Hazur's face radiated love and his sweet voice was full of emotion.

Baba Ji Maharaj went to Agra and received initiation. To support himself he served in the army for thirty-three years. At the same time he devoted these thirty-three years to regular meditation. His eleven years here in the Dera were devoted to meditation.... I mean to say that it is not my power; all this development is the grace of that great Saint, it is the fruit of his meditation, the manifestation of his divine power. The farmer puts up a scarecrow to protect his field; I am a scarecrow put up by Baba Ji in his field of spiritual activity. Baba Ji is doing everything; I am only his slave and am grateful to him for appointing me as a humble servant of the sangat.

Our great Satguru's words, full of humility and overflowing with love and devotion for his own Master, deeply moved the sangat; our throats were choked and tears flowed from our eyes.

After this brief but touching address, our beloved Master —an ocean of compassion—in deference to our keen desire, laid the foundation of the satsang hall.

The imposing building was built under the personal supervision of Maharaj Ji. Every morning Hazur would be at the site from about seven till midday, and again in the afternoon from three till six or seven in the evening, except for an hour and a half of satsang. He would explain the various aspects and technical details of the construction to the engineers and masons. The sangat did seva with great enthusiasm and love, and the major part of the work was done by voluntary service from the sangat. Maharaj Ji was much pleased with the sangat's seva. In fact, Hazur always laid stress on seva and used to say that seva is a cash transaction; he who does seva is never a loser.

Dera Management and the Great Master's Wills

The Dera made such incredible growth under Hazur's mastership that considerable property was acquired. Although Maharaj Ji, as the Master, was the legal owner of all these resources, he strictly avoided using any of this property or other material given in seva for himself or any member of his family. Looking upon himself as the guardian of these resources, he worked hard to develop and increase them. At the same time he regularly gave part of his pension, as well as provisions from his farm, to the Dera in seva.

By the year 1937, besides the Dera itself, the satsang had properties at various places in the then-undivided India. The Great Master also had his personal property at Sirsa, acquired through his army income and benefits received at the time of retirement. From time immemorial, all gifts given in seva by devotees to their Satguru were regarded as the property of the Sant Satguru, who had all rights to their use, development, and disposal. Like his predecessors and all great Saints of the past, Hazur Maharaj Ji never touched a penny of the gifts received; he held them as a sacred trust of the sangat and used them judiciously for the sangat's benefit.

In 1937, Maharaj Ji felt that in order to avoid any future confusion, the properties held by him as the Sant Satguru and those held as personal properties should be properly defined. Accordingly, at the age of seventy-nine, Maharaj Ji executed his first will, defining the two kinds of property and clearly stating that his personal property at Sirsa and Mehman-singhwala would be inherited by his sons and grandsons. Giving a detailed list of satsang properties, the Master declared that, after him, this property would be "inherited and owned by that person whom I shall nominate and appoint as my successor by a separate will to be the spiritual head of Dera Baba Jaimal Singh."

By 1942, more properties had been acquired by the satsang through the grace of Maharaj Ji, and the Master decided to add them to his will of 1937. He executed a codicil, duly registered in 1942, giving the details of the additional properties that had been acquired. And again he reiterated that "After me the ownership of these properties will vest in my successor, nominated by me." Maharaj Ji further stated that the Saints, though the owners of the entire property, have never used it for personal purposes, and no perfect Saint would ever do so:

This is an ancient tradition handed down by the Shabd Margi Saints whose real home is Sach Khand and Anami, that they are regarded by their followers and disciples as the very manifestation of God. Accordingly all religious property standing in their name is considered their personal property in respect of which they have full right of transfer and disposal, and no one has any right whatsoever to interfere in the exercise of those absolute powers of theirs. However, such Saints, in spite of being absolute owners, seldom use these properties or their income for their personal benefit, but utilise all such properties and the income thereof for the uplift, welfare, and well-being of their satsangis and for religious purposes. My Guru, Baba Jaimal Singh Ji Maharaj, the founder of Dera Baba Jaimal Singh Beas, has been one *of such perfect Masters, whose line is being perpetuated till today, and will continue to be perpetuated in future. I too have been following the same principle and have been meeting my expenses and those of my dependents from my personal income and the income from my own agricultural lands and other personal properties, details of which have already been given in my previous will. Religious properties owned by me and the income therefrom have never been used for my personal purposes or those of my children.*

Before leaving for Amritsar for medical treatment in September 1947, Maharaj Ji drew up a well-considered and comprehensive scheme for the administration and management of the Dera and its satsang centres. Under this scheme Maharaj Ji appointed three committees: A General Committee, consisting of prominent satsangis from all over India; it was to act as a general advisory body and meet at least once a year. Second, an Administrative Committee, consisting of prominent satsangis who had been associated with the Dera and seva in the Dera for a long period; each committee member was the head of a department in the Dera administration, with clearly defined duties. Third, a Managing Committee, the executive body to control and direct all Dera administration work. Hazur Maharaj Ji was the President of all three of the committees, and Sardar Bahadur Jagat Singh Ji the Vice-President; Rai Sahib Munshi Ram was appointed the Secretary and Treasurer.

This document was written out by Malik Radha Kishan Khanna, Advocate, High Court. Besides being signed by the Great Master at the end, it bears his signature on every page. It was witnessed by Rai Sahib Munshi Ram, P.C.S. (Retd) and by Malik Radha Kishan Khanna.

This administrative scheme was prepared by Hazur about six months before his departure from the world, and the document clearly indicates Hazur's decision to appoint Sardar Bahadur Jagat Singh as his successor when it states that "after me Sardar Bahadur Jagat Singh shall be the President of all these three committees, and all the above-mentioned religious properties shall be transferred to him and mutated in his name in Government records."

Hazur Maharaj Ji confirmed this scheme by a will executed on 24 September 1947, reiterating that Sardar Bahadur Jagat Singh would be the President of all the three committees after Hazur's departure, and all religious properties would be transferred to him.

The natural corollary to these wills was the Great Master's final will of 20 March 1948, appointing Sardar Bahadur Jagat Singh as his successor, to continue satsang, initiation, and guidance of the sangat.[1]

Some Dera Sevadars

BIBI RUKKO

From an early age Bibi Rukko had turned away from worldly pursuits and absorbed herself in devotion to God. She spent many years in the service of Mata Radha Ji, the wife of Soami Ji Maharaj. When Baba Ji retired from military service, Mata Radha Ji sent Bibi Rukko with him to Punjab, telling her to look upon service rendered to Baba Ji as service to Soami Ji.

A keen devotee, Bibi Rukko had acquired an indomitable courage and fearlessness through her love for the Satguru and

---

[1] All these documents have been reproduced by Radha Soami Satsang Beas in the book *Origin and Growth*.

her long hours of meditation. In the early days, when Baba Ji used to go on tours, she would live all alone in the deserted wasteland which the Dera was at that time.

She served Baba Ji and the sangat with great devotion and dedication. She used to fetch water and cook food for Baba Ji and the sangat, clean utensils, and look after the Satguru and the visiting satsangis. At times she used to act as *pathi* in the satsang, reciting the hymns from which Baba Ji would give his discourse. Her voice was loud and powerful, yet sweet, and her rendering of the hymns often brought tears to the eyes of the sangat. Always alert and willing to work, even at the age of seventy and seventy-five she had the stamina and energy of a woman of forty. Probably due to her long years of meditation, she displayed, even in her seventies, the same fearlessness and dynamism that characterized her youth.

Bibi Rukko lived a simple life and was not in the least impressed by social status; she treated everyone the same, no matter what his position. I remember once I had come with my wife to attend satsang at the Dera. I had just been initiated, and both my wife and I were very particular about our dress in those days; I was wearing a suit made out of imported cloth, and my wife was in a silk sari and adorned with quite a bit of jewellery. Bibi Rukko welcomed her by saying, "Dress simply when you come to the Dera. You can dress like a queen when you are at home."

Because of her failing eyesight, during the last six months of her life (in 1933/34) Bibi Rukko stayed with Sardar Ganda Singh, a satsangi in Amritsar whose wife looked after her. Sardar Ganda Singh's wife, who was with Bibi Rukko in her last moments, used to tell us that on the morning of the day of her death Bibi Rukko looked very happy and said, "Today I am going to depart from here." During her last moments her face was radiant with joy. She told Ganda Singh's wife that she was having the darshan of both Baba Ji Maharaj and Maharaj Sawan Singh Ji. On learning of her death, Hazur sent a car to bring her body to the Dera and she was cremated here.

BIBI RAKKHI

Another highly advanced soul at the Dera in those days was Bibi Rakkhi, the daughter of Sardar Mangal Singh, a tailor in the village of Barapind, District Jullundur. Widowed at an early age, she moved to the Dera shortly afterwards. She used to spend all her time in meditation, satsang, and seva. By the Master's grace, she put her whole heart into meditation and was blessed with good progress within. Such was her absorption in meditation that in the beginning her attention would stay inside for several days at a time and she would be oblivious of her surroundings. Later, when she made more progress within, she gained greater control and began to take part in seva at the Dera. Though she was retiring and withdrawn, she took part in seva in the langar.

A kindhearted, affectionate satsangi, Bibi Rakkhi used to assist the ladies during initiations. She was one of the most devoted disciples of the Great Master and was loved and held in esteem by the sangat. She passed away in 1956.

BHAI SHADI

An account of the Great Master's life would not be complete without mentioning Bhai Shadi, a great devotee who spent most of his life in the Great Master's company and service. Bhai Shadi was born in a poor Muslim family of the village of Dhaliwal, about five miles from the Dera. From the days of his childhood he liked wrestling, which he learned from his uncle, whose conditions for taking Shadi as a pupil were that he remain celibate and always sleep outside the village in the fields. For his trade, Shadi became an expert mechanic by apprenticing himself first to a British engineer and later to a mechanic in Amritsar. On weekends he spent most of his time getting into mischief in his village. When he was twenty-one, Shadi moved back to his village, where he became a local tough, bullying, fighting, and even occasionally robbing people.

It was through this behaviour that Shadi came to the Great Master, for he began to harass satsangis on their way to the Dera. One day, when a satsangi named Bhai Mela Ram complained to the Master about Shadi's bullying, Hazur replied, "If he stops you again, ask him to come to the Dera."

A few days later, Mela Ram was on his way to the Dera when Shadi blocked his path and threatened to beat him if he did not give him some money. Mela Ram said, "Brother, I am no match for you. If you want someone to test your strength against, come and see my Master at the Dera. You will find him a much stronger opponent than I." Shadi at once accepted the challenge and said that he would go to the Dera soon.

Shortly after this, Shadi went to Sathiala to watch a wrestling match. Being so close to the Dera, he remembered his promise and decided to go on to the Dera with his uncle and a few others. When they arrived, satsang was in progress in the open area east of the library and Hazur was giving the discourse. Shadi sat down with his companions. Hardly attentive to what was being said, Shadi's eyes were fixed on Maharaj Ji's face. After the satsang, Shadi's friends were ready to leave, but Shadi very much wanted to meet Hazur. He said, "When you come to a man of God, it is not good to leave without paying your respects to him." Since his friends insisted on leaving, Shadi was reluctantly going with them when Maharaj Ji happened to pass by, and after some formal inquiries he suggested to Shadi's uncle that they stay at Dera for the night, as it was late. Shadi's uncle, however, declined and they all went back to the village.

Although Shadi had not spoken a word to Maharaj Ji, the Master's magnetic form kept hovering before his mind's eye. He became restless and after three days he quietly left his village for the Dera, never to return. At that time he was only twenty-three. At satsang that day he heard Maharaj Ji say, "Those who rob others receive punishments and have to atone for every penny they have taken." Shadi wept throughout the satsang. The next day he asked for initiation. It was a great event in Shadi's life, changing him completely. He became sweet-natured and humble; abandoning his aggressive behaviour, he devoted himself seriously to his meditation.

Maharaj Ji took special care of Shadi, making him his personal attendant. For the rest of his life Shadi was inseparable from the Master. When Maharaj Ji travelled by car, Shadi always sat next to the driver. If Maharaj Ji was in his room, Shadi could always be found sitting outside the door.

A single day's separation from Maharaj Ji was unbearable for Shadi. Whenever he had to leave the Dera during the day, he returned before evening. Once he received news from his village that his mother was very ill and on her deathbed. He left the Dera for his village to see his mother, but returned after going part of the way. The day he had come to the Master's shelter he had left everything—home, relations, and possessions. No attachments, no thoughts of the world, could take the place of the Master. He was everything to Shadi— father, mother, brother, friend.

Shadi quietly came back to the Dera and resumed his duty of attending on the Master. That night Hazur called Shadi, who used to sleep outside Hazur's room, and said, "Shadi, your mother has just died. The Master has taken charge of her soul."

At the same time that he lived at the Dera, he was also able to earn quite a comfortable living as a mechanic. He was adept at running and repairing lathes, tractors, and diesel engines. He would buy broken-down lathes and engines and repair and sell them, thus supporting himself on his own income. He also used his skills in seva for the Dera. He bought a tractor, repaired it, and presented it to the satsang. It was used in the cultivation of Dera fields for many years. Once while in Lahore with Maharaj Ji, Shadi found an old generator which he repaired and used for supplying power to the Master's residence and a part of the Dera. He also installed a motor for grinding wheat into flour.

Following Hazur's example in every possible way, Shadi was very careful never to accept gifts from anyone, not even food or drink. When outside the Dera with the Master, he would buy his food at the market; during tours he ate from the Master's own kitchen.

Because of Shadi's skill as a mechanic he often received offers from the Muslim blacksmiths of Batala to come and work with them and earn thousands of rupees; factory owners would also offer him a handsome salary if he would come and join them. But Shadi would reply, "I do not feel like leaving the service of this King of kings and going elsewhere. The salary he gives me is not available with anyone else in the world."

Bhai Shadi dedicated his life to satsang, seva, and meditation. Rai Sahib Munshi Ram wrote in *With the Three Masters*: "When we travelled with Maharaj Ji, Shadi and I would stay in the same room. If I looked at him at night, I always found him sitting in meditation; hardly ever did I see him sleep."

Shadi had no formal education; he was almost illiterate, but he had great inner perception. He could talk at length on any aspect of Sant Mat and his talks revealed his intelligence and insight. He would talk about Muslim Saints, quote from their compositions, and narrate anecdotes from their lives.

163

He had a good knowledge of the hymns of Indian Saints and could recite by heart the compositions of Guru Nanak and his successors.

Many times Shadi had marriage proposals from prosperous Muslim families, but he was not interested. When I told him he should get married, his reply was, "I am myself *Shadi*"—a word meaning marriage—"Why do I need another *shadi*?" He actually had a great aversion to women, which acted as a shield for him. His life was one of purity and simplicity, entirely dedicated to the service of the Satguru and meditation.

Maharaj Ji had great affection for Shadi, and Shadi had a great devotion for his Master. Once, when we were walking from Sikanderpur to Sirsa, Shadi was bitten by a poisonous snake. He fell immediately and changed colour. Maharaj Ji was on horseback ahead of us, but Shadi would not let us tell him what had happened. He said, "I don't want him to take this poison on himself. Don't tell him!" and became unconscious. Just at that moment Maharaj Ji turned and saw us. When he came back and found out what had happened, he told us that a branch from a neem tree was supposed to be an antidote for snake poison. Since there were no neem trees, we could only fetch a twig from a bush. Hazur passed it over Shadi's body, saying that he had heard that by doing so the effect of poison was negated. After a while Shadi regained consciousness. Greatly displeased with us for telling Hazur what had happened, he said to Maharaj Ji, "O my King, why did you take this on yourself?"

When Maharaj Ji purchased land in Sirsa, Bhai Shadi used to accompany him and work in the fields. He would run the tractor and, whenever necessary, repair it. When the sugar factory was installed at Sikanderpur, Shadi helped in the maintenance of the machinery. He had great affection for

Hazur's family members. In the words of Rai Sahib Munshi Ram, "He would do anything for the family. It made him very happy to eat or share a cup of tea with the Master's sons and grandsons, and he was always concerned about their welfare. Seeing them prosper, Shadi would rejoice as if he himself had obtained great wealth. He used to say, 'Hazur will take great seva from Sardar Charan Singh.'"

After Hazur's passing away, Shadi served both Sardar Bahadur Maharaj Jagat Singh and then Maharaj Charan Singh, but he was deeply unhappy on being separated from his Master. In 1952, when Maharaj Charan Singh was preparing to go to Sirsa, Shadi came to him and said, "Maharaj Ji, here is my savings of four thousand rupees; please accept it as seva. I have a flour mill in the Dera also, which I would like Bibi Ralli to have."

Maharaj Ji asked, "Why are you in such a hurry to go? Why not stay a little longer?" Shadi replied that without his Master, he had no desire to stay in this world. Then he laughed and said, "All my life I have hated women, but the Dera people will cremate me at the women's *ghat!*"[1] In those days all cremations were done by the riverside, near the ladies' bathing place.

Maharaj Ji replied, "Do not worry. I will come and arrange your cremation at some other place." Bhai Shadi paused and after a few moments said, "Hazur, they will not wait for you; they will do the cremation before you come."

After a few days' illness, around midnight on 25 November 1952, Bhai Shadi left this world—the devotee returning to the Beloved. During his illness his attention was mostly turned inwards. When anyone asked how he was, Shadi would reply, "I do not wish to come out from within."

---

[1] A *ghat* is a bathing place on the banks of a river.

As soon as the Master received the telegram telling of Shadi's death, he left Sirsa for the Dera. But the Dera staff, not being aware of Shadi's wishes, had already cremated the body at the women's ghat before Maharaj Ji's arrival.

BIBI RALLI

One of the most remarkable sevadars is Bibi Ralli. During Baba Ji's time she used to come to the Dera with her father, Bhai Milkhi Ram, when she was an infant of about two years. When she was five years old, she would sometimes join the ladies in rolling chapattis for the langar in the company of her older relatives, whenever she was brought to the Dera. Once, while she was trying to make chapattis, Baba Ji Maharaj happened to look at her and inquired, "Who is this child?" When he was told she was the daughter of Bhai Milkhi Ram, who was working as the scribe of Baba Ji and also doing various tasks connected with the Dera, Baba Ji Maharaj looked at her for a moment, smiled, and said, "This girl is meant for the Dera."

After a year or two, when she was about to be engaged to be married by her parents, Bhai Milkhi Ram came to Baba Ji Maharaj for his blessings and permission for the engagement. Baba Ji said, "This child is not meant for worldly pursuits."

Yielding to social convention, however, her father married her off when she was about eight or nine, as was the prevalent custom. But before she could attain maturity and go to her in-laws' house, her husband died, perhaps only a few months after the marriage. Widow remarriage was practically unknown then; and so her father, seeing the child's deep spiritual bent, brought her to the Dera at the age of nine, when the Great Master had assumed the responsibility of mastership. She served the Great Master from that age, and as she grew she took on more responsibilities, such as cooking the food in the Great Master's kitchen for Hazur and for his guests, who at times numbered as many as one hundred; looking after the lady sevadars who had retired and were living in the Dera; and keeping the keys of the Great Master's cupboard, which contained the belongings of Baba Ji—his shawl, shoes, clothes, and utensils.

From that early age, Bua Ji[1]—as the sangat affectionately calls her—has been rendering service to the Masters at the Dera. She used to run the Great Master's entire household at the Dera, serve all his guests and family members, and take care of all the Great Master's personal things; she also brought up all the family children—Maharaj Charan Singh Ji, his brother, and cousins. She is a dearly loved foster mother to the children, and all family members of the Master treat her with great love and respect.

She combines great affection and a sense of humour with a very strong sense of discipline and propriety. The sangat has always loved and also feared her, for fear is an essential part of all selfless love. Many times in the early days of the Great Master, Bua Ji would read shabds in the satsang. Her melodious voice was bold and loud and she seldom needed a loudspeaker in those days.

Sardar Bahadur Maharaj Ji also greatly respected Bibi Ralli. He would rarely go out of the Dera on a tour without first meeting her and asking her formal permission, and would make it a point to meet her immediately on his return. Bua Ji on her part looked on Sardar Bahadur Maharaj Ji as the form of her Master, and for all of us she was an example of love and devotion for him.

When Maharaj Charan Singh became the Master, Bua Ji also accepted him as her beloved Satguru, in spite of the fact

---

[1]   *Bua Ji* means "auntie," or "father's sister."

that she had brought him up from early childhood. Maharaj Ji also had great affection and regard for her and treated her as one would one's own mother.

Bua Ji has looked after all the precious belongings of Baba Ji Maharaj, the Great Master, and Sardar Bahadur Maharaj Ji; and the keys of the Great Master's house are always kept in her possession.

Always busy in some work or the other or in meditation, Bua Ji cannot be mistaken for a Dera sevadar as such. Her service has always been rendered personally to the three Masters, in the household, and she is essentially a sevadar of the Satguru, treated by all the Masters as a very close and respected family member.[1]

Accounts of the Master's Grace

The accounts of the Great Master's grace and concern for his disciples are numerous and could fill volumes. Here I am including the accounts of two satsangis whom I know personally. Their devotion for the Master and the Master's grace on them have always been a thrilling recollection for me.

Babu Bua Das, a new stationmaster at the Beas railway station, believed in following the regulations very strictly. He often refused to sell tickets to the satsangis when they came from satsang at the last minute to catch a train. He would be rude to them, and if they ran across the railway line in their hurry to catch the train, he would threaten to arrest them and at times even carried out his threat. Once when some satsangis complained about him to Hazur, Hazur said, "Do not worry, I will ask him to be a little more courteous."

---

[1] Bibi Ralli passed away in September 1983.

168

Shortly after this, one Sunday afternoon Bua Das appeared at the Dera. He came with a railway officer to see what he called "the fair" at Dera. I was sitting on the veranda next to the Master's house. He introduced himself and his companion to me and started making general inquiries about the path. In my explanation of Sant Mat, when I came to the need for a living Master, he summarily closed the talk by saying, "I am a Brahmin. Brahmins are themselves born gurus. I don't need a guru."

Just then Hazur came out of his house and looked penetratingly at Bua Das. When I said that he was the new stationmaster, Hazur replied, "Yes, I know. Have you offered them tea?" Hazur asked me to give them tea and bring them to satsang.

That day Maharaj Ji discoursed on two hymns, one about the importance of Shabd and the other about devotion to the Guru. After the satsang, Bua Das, who had listened with rapt attention, asked me, "How did he know of our conversation? His discourse referred directly to what we had been talking about. And he answered some of my questions as soon as they came to my mind." I told him to ask Maharaj Ji, for he knows all our questions, and answers them for us. While leaving for the station he said that as his officer was staying at the Beas station for two more days and wanted to attend satsang, he too would come with him for the next two days.

The next day Hazur spoke even more specifically in the satsang about resistance to accepting a Guru. "Consider the ignorance of the world. Some orthodox people say that a woman's guru and spiritual guide is her husband, and she needs no other guru. But if the husband is a slave of the senses or a drunkard, how will he guide his wife on the spiritual path? Similarly, some intelligent men, because they are Brahmins by caste, claim they do not need a guru since they are born to be the guru and guide of others. But how can a man who has never learned to steer a boat, ferry others through the stormy ocean? How can a Brahmin who has passed a few examinations and taken a job, and who works for his living almost day and night, guide others on the intricate path of spiritual practice only by virtue of his birth? He has no time to educate his own children, how can he enlighten others? How can a man who has himself lost the way lead others to the destination?"

This satsang changed Bua Das completely. He begged for initiation and was blessed with Nam by Maharaj Ji. Now it became his practice to ride his bicycle and come to the Dera every evening for satsang and then rush back to the station immediately after satsang to attend to his duties.

After initiation Bua Das was completely transformed, spending all his spare time in meditation. His mind was engrossed in simran to such an extent that while sitting in his office, he would sometimes be absorbed within for hours. His manner became gentle and affectionate, and his subordinates began to like him.

One evening a young, educated satsangi from Ambala arrived to find no coolies or tongas at the station. As he stood looking about helplessly for a way to the Dera, Bua Das, who was off duty and was therefore wearing ordinary clothes and not his uniform, happened to walk by. He asked the young man where he wanted to go and, when he learned the youth was going to the Dera, offered to carry his baggage for him. The young man asked what he would charge, thinking he was a coolie. Bua Das said he would take whatever was offered. Unaccustomed to such work, Bua Das, walking slowly and taking frequent rests, carried the man's trunk and bedroll halfway to the Dera. The young man became frustrated with his slow pace, thinking he would be late for the satsang, and berated him. At this point they met Sohan Singh, Maharaj Ji's special sevadar, whom Hazur had just sent to the railway station for no apparent reason.

He immediately recognized Bua Das and took the luggage from him. Greatly embarrassed to find out that his coolie was actually the stationmaster, the young man apologized profusely. Bua Das said, "Don't feel sorry. It is a privilege to serve one of my Master's devotees." When Hazur came to know about the incident, he was highly pleased with Bua Das for his humility and spirit of seva.

Once, after the 5:00 P.M. satsang, Bua Das felt such love for the Master that he sat in meditation with his attention completely absorbed within and failed to report to the station for his night duty. The assistant stationmaster came to Dera to find Bua Das but could not rouse him from his meditation. He went to Maharaj Ji and said, "Bua Das has night duty today, and the traffic inspector, who is a strict British disciplinarian, has come to inspect the station. What shall I do?"

Maharaj Ji said, "Draw his attention out and send him to the station in the Dera transport." The assistant stationmaster said he had tried everything to awaken him, even shouting in his ear, without any success. At this Maharaj Ji replied, "All right, let him be. We will see in the morning."

The assistant stationmaster knew the inspector was to go through the station records during the night. He would have taken over the duty for Bua Das, but the inspector knew he was on leave. That night the assistant stationmaster was miserable, thinking that Bua Das would surely be dismissed. The next morning he was finally able to rouse Bua Das, who refused to go to the station without having Maharaj Ji's darshan first. Hazur came out after 8:00 that morning. When he saw Bua Das, he told him to report to work immediately and never miss his duty again.

The stationmaster arrived around 10:00 A.M. to find the inspector resting in the waiting room. After putting on his uniform, he took out his records and asked the inspector to check them. The inspector roared, "What are you talking about, man! You know very well I went over these books with you last night." Unable to withhold his tears of gratitude to the Satguru, Bua Das excused himself and left.

The inspector reported that Bua Das was the most efficient stationmaster he had found in this division and recommended him for promotion. The next month Bua Das was made a senior grade stationmaster and was asked to choose a bigger station. When he said he did not want to leave Beas, he was confirmed in his Beas posting and still given the senior grade.

Now for Bua Das his first duty was to look after the needs of satsangis coming to the Beas station, even putting them up in his home when they arrived at night, and taking care of their children. He spent most of his money in seva to the sangat.

Another incident connected with Bua Das illustrates how the Master takes care of us when we have full faith in him. One winter during the World War days, there was an acute shortage of kerosene. Without the deputy commissioner's permit, no one could purchase kerosene, and even then, a family could buy only a few bottles of kerosene each month. At Dera the December bhandara was approaching and there was no kerosene in stock. The district commissioner had given a permit for only one tin of kerosene, that is, about sixteen litres. There was no electricity in the Dera in those days. The satsang organizers were worried: How would they provide light in the langar, in the streets and courtyards, and in the rooms and sheds where the sangat was to stay? How could one tin of kerosene serve the purpose when the sangat would be about fifteen to twenty thousand?

Bua Das heard of the shortage at the Dera and, on inquiry from the organizers, was told that at least twelve cans of kerosene would be needed to meet the bhandara needs. He had six cans in his stock at the station, for lanterns, signals, etc. He pleaded with the stationmasters of neighbouring stations—Dhilwan, Hamira, Kartarpur, and Butari—and borrowed eight cans from them for a few days, sending the fourteen cans of kerosene to the Dera.

However, a clerk at one of the stations reported Bua Das's action through an anonymous letter to the railway inspector's office. It was decided to send an officer to check the store at all these stations. All the stationmasters who had loaned kerosene began to demand it back because it was now impossible to obtain kerosene. They sent frantic messages that if the kerosene was not replaced immediately, they would be dismissed and also prosecuted. The only thing Bua Das could do was to go to the Master and confess what he had done. Maharaj Ji said, "Why did you steal from the government and give the plunder as seva? Now you have landed yourself in trouble and will bring a bad name to the Dera as well. What can we do now? You had best face the consequences of what you have done."

When Bua Das went to work that day, an inspector had already arrived. He said, "I have been forced to inspect all the stations in this area because of some rumour that you have been stealing kerosene. I have inspected the stores of all the other stations and have found their store of kerosene intact. I suppose I must check yours as well." Bua Das thought the other stationmasters must have somehow borrowed kerosene and completed their stock, so he boldly confessed that his stock was short by six cans. However, when he looked at the stock, the inspector found it complete. Bua Das thought he must have counted the empty cans by mistake, so he said,

"Sir, it seems you have counted the empty cans also. I do not want to deceive the authorities." The inspector examined the cans again and said, "They are full, Bua Das. We know you are an honest and efficient officer. If we ever find the culprit who gave the false report, we will take strong action against him."

Bua Das then ran to Maharaj Ji and told him what had happened. He kept repeating, "Glory be to my Satguru!" Hazur said, "I don't know anything about this. It must have been some other power that showered his grace on you." Then he said quietly, "Such things must be kept to yourself. Don't tell anyone about this."

The other account of the Master's grace was given to me in writing by Sardar Gurdayal Singh, Deputy Superintendent of Police, who was stationed in Jhang near Lyallpur. I reproduce it in his own words:

I was initiated by Hazur Maharaj Sawan Singh Ji in 1936. At the time of Partition I was posted at Jhang as the District Inspector of Police. In July 1947 I had come to Dera for Hazur's darshan and to ask him if, in view of the riots and violence in the country, it was wise for me to continue with my job in Pakistan. Hazur closed his eyes for a few moments, then replied, "Very well, go back, but do not take your family. Always keep the Satguru in mind."

This was the last time I saw Hazur in the physical body. Had I known that he was soon going to leave us, I would never have returned to Jhang. On my return, I found the conditions of violence and lawlessness appalling. On 15 August 1947, the country was partitioned. Earlier I had opted for service in India, but there was no response to my application from the higher authorities.

The situation became so dangerous in Jhang that one day I had to arm and barricade myself in my house. On August 25, a Hindu policeman knocked at my door begging me to allow him, his wife, and children into the house to save them from rioters. As I opened the door, instead of the policeman, I found a crowd armed with swords and batons who forced their way in and began looting the house.

Two constables who were my subordinates in the police department pointed at me and shouted, "Let us first dispatch this Sikh." I was terrified; I did not know how to save myself. Just then Maharaj Ji appeared before me and said, "You have the service revolver with you. Take it out and scare them. Don't worry, you will not be harmed."

I jumped on a table and fired a few shots in the air. The rioters immediately ran away and I again bolted the door of my house. Two hours later a Pakistani military patrol surrounded my house. I was disarmed and arrested on a false charge of murder. I was sent to the jail and incarcerated in a cell.

I wrote a full report of the incident to my boss, who was a just and noble Englishman, one Mr Rhine. But my report was not forwarded to him. I was denied basic amenities. I requested the authorities for my salary of the month so that I could pay for some of the things I needed. But in those days of communal hatred, Hindus and Muslims had both lost all human feelings of kindness and sympathy.

I thought that my influential and well-placed friends would soon try to help me out of the situation, but no one came to my aid. Riots had spread throughout the Punjab. Hindus from Pakistan and Muslims from India were leaving their homes and running away to save themselves. Gradually I lost all hope of release from the jail. I felt desolate and forlorn. Lonely, desperate, and friendless, I requested the jail authorities to present me to the court of law. They told me that I would not be able to reach the court; the mob would kill me on the way.

Although I was initiated in 1936, I had had no inner spiritual experience nor did I expect any, for I had neglected my meditation. Now, when I felt the dark shadow of impending doom gathering to engulf me, I felt repentant; I had whiled away my time in extraneous pursuits.

One night, in the last week of September 1947, I was lying on the earthen platform in my cell, brooding over my state. My heart was crying. There was no one to whom I could look for help, even consolation. Suddenly I saw Maharaj Ji standing before me; his face was shining in its own light, from his eyes were coming radiant rays of love and kindness, and I clearly heard his sweet, melodious voice, "Do not lose heart. Everything will be all right."

With these words, the brief vision faded away. I was thrilled and also perplexed. It was not a dream, for I was wide awake; nor was I engaged in meditation.

This incident gave me consolation and courage. Despondency gave way to new hope, and the agony of prison life was a bit alleviated. I was told that negotiations between the governments of India and Pakistan regarding exchange of prisoners were afoot, and I would soon be released in exchange for a Muslim doctor of Delhi who was also accused of murder. My joy knew no bounds; soon I would be free, back in India with my family and friends.

I had started to sit in meditation from the day Hazur appeared to me in September. It was the second or perhaps third day of November, a little after sunset; I was sitting in bhajan when suddenly the cell was filled with light. I saw my beloved Satguru standing before me. But this time he said, "Have patience. You will have to stay in jail for one more year."

Although the happiness at the thought of early release vanished, the ineffable joy of Maharaj Ji's darshan filled my heart. I resigned myself to the Satguru's will. Meanwhile the details of the exchange of prisoners between the two countries had been worked out and I was told that I would be released on April 4, 1948.

I had written many letters to Maharaj Ji, but had not received any reply. In early March I received his letter. Hazur wrote, "I have replied to all your letters. Do not worry if you have not received them. Have faith in the Lord and continue your meditation."

After a few days my younger brother, Major Sardara Singh, came to meet me. He informed me that Hazur was seriously ill. And soon after, on April 3, 1948, I got the heart-rending news that my beloved Satguru had left us.

My anguish at Hazur's departure was further intensified because I now lost all hope of getting out of the prison. I felt I was completely ruined and now I had no friend or sympathizer in my misery. My condition was like that of a young widow—forlorn and despondent.

On April 4, early in the morning, a number of prisoners were released and sent to India, but my turn did not come. At about 10:00 A.M. the prison officer came and told me and a few other prisoners to get ready immediately to be sent to India. Our lunch was being prepared and was soon ready, but in our enthusiasm we decided to forego it, for we would be in India within two hours and could eat in our own country. I recollected that Maharaj Ji had appeared to me in November 1947 and told me that I would be in jail for one year more, but my mind dismissed the thought, for here we were, ready to board the bus and proceed to India.

We were put in the police lorry and told that we would be taken directly to India. But after a short distance the lorry turned onto a road going in the opposite direction from India. We all became nervous. Some prisoners were in tears for they concluded that we were being driven to a secluded spot and would be done away with. I was relaxed and happy, however, for I remembered that Maharaj Ji had told me that no harm would come to me.

By midnight we reached Rawalpindi, hungry, thirsty, tired, and above all greatly disappointed. We were put in the Rawalpindi jail and confined to dark, narrow cells. I was exhausted and sleepless, and in spite of all efforts to console myself, felt like a bird in a cage. Suddenly in the dark and quiet of the night, I heard the clear sound of the gong resounding in my forehead. I had no idea what the melody of Shabd was, and remained absorbed listening to it.

In the morning I felt fresh, all physical discomfort had vanished, and all worries had disappeared. I was relaxed both physically and mentally. From then on I was not troubled with any anxiety about my release from the prison.

Now the only pain I felt was the pain of separation, for my Master was no longer on earth. I had also learned that Sardar Bahadur Jagat Singh Ji was Hazur's successor.

But I felt that my Master has gone, why need I go to Beas now, who is there for me now? If my Master were living, I would have gone and bowed at his feet, but now I would not bow this head to anyone else. What if Hazur had appointed someone as his successor—for me Maharaj Sawan Singh Ji was my Master; I would not accept anybody else in his place.

These thoughts continued to hover in my mind and I became more and more disinclined to accept Hazur's successor as my Master. One day as I was sitting in meditation at 3:00 A.M., I had an unprecedented experience. Hazur suddenly appeared to me in his Radiant Form. His face was shining in extraordinary brilliance; there was a halo of dazzling light around him. He was dressed in luminous clothes of amazing beauty. Every pore of his body appeared to be throwing out numerous rays of light. The Radiant Form of my Satguru stood before me for quite some time. But then the Form slowly began to change and soon took the form of Sardar Bahadur Maharaj Ji. He had the same radiance and brilliance. Then I heard Hazur's voice, "This body also is mine. Don't be deceived."

I was thrilled at this experience. At the same time there was a feeling of remorse at not accepting Hazur's successor. In the morning I wrote a letter of apology to Sardar Bahadur Maharaj Ji. I also wrote a letter to Sardar Bachint Singh giving full details of my experience.

I was now a changed person. Courage and renewed faith in the Master made my remaining six months in jail comparatively easy. All I longed for was to go to Beas and bow at Sardar Bahadur Ji's feet.

On 3 November 1948 I was taken to Ferozepur, a border town in India, and set free. I went straight to

Dera and paid my respects to Sardar Bahadur Ji. He received me with great love and kindness. In the evening I attended the satsang. Sardar Bahadur Ji began the discourse, and within a few minutes I saw that Maharaj Sawan Singh Ji was sitting on the dais instead of Sardar Bahadur Maharaj Ji. I was amazed. Tears flooded my eyes—tears of love and joy.

Later when I met Sardar Bachint Singh, he told me that he had wanted to read out my letter in the satsang, but Sardar Bahadur Maharaj Ji had not permitted him to do so. He took my letter from Sardar Bachint Singh and kept it with himself.

(Sd) Gurdayal Singh
Deputy Superintendent Police, Hissar

Last Days and Passing of the Great Master

Much before leaving this world, Hazur Maharaj Ji had begun to give hints about his decision to give up the mortal body. Whenever a close sevadar would look at his health and the strain of work and implore him to take some rest, he would reply, "This body has become too old. Now I will manifest myself in a young body."

On 28 November 1946, when Hazur reached Sikanderpur after a trip to Lahore, he became unwell. The doctors felt that he must have been ill for quite some time. During October, Maharaj Ji had undertaken a tour of Gujranwala, Wazirabad, Lyallpur, and Lahore, followed by another tour of Parore and Kangra. After the busy programme of the monthly satsang in October, Hazur again undertook a satsang tour, visiting Kot

Hakam Rai, Anandpur, Ropar, and Amritsar. Maharaj Ji visited Lahore on November 26 and 27, his last visit to the area that is now Pakistan.

After this tour, Maharaj Ji drove directly to Sirsa to attend the marriage of Sardar Bachint Singh's granddaughter. Shortly after arriving in Sikanderpur, Maharaj Ji became unwell. From early December 1946 until the time of his departure in April 1948, he remained ill. The doctors persevered with their medicines, but there was no lasting effect.

Despite sickness, pain, and weakness, Maharaj Ji continued with his satsang routine as much as possible. On December 12, 1946, Maharaj Ji left Sikanderpur for Dera very early in the morning. Although he was not at all well, he stopped at Sirsa, Malot, Muktsar, Kotkapura, Panjgrain, Bodian, Moga, Ludhiana, Phillaur, Phagwara, Jullundur, and Kapurthala to meet the sangat that had gathered. At Dera, Maharaj Ji became busy with the December bhandara and, unmindful of his own health, he fulfilled the duties of satsang, seva, interviews, and initiation with his usual vigour.

In the months preceding and following the partition of India in August 1947, there was tremendous violence and bloodshed. During this time an incredibly large number of Muslims of India and Hindus of Pakistan were forced to leave their homes and go to their new country. Most satsangis then lived in the part of India that was to become Pakistan. There was hardly a big city in Pakistan that did not have satsangis, and in small hill areas there were thousands of satsangis. Lahore, Rawalpindi, Lyallpur, Abbotabad, Sialkot, and a few other large cities had beautiful satsang halls; and even in smaller places like Jhelum, Hazro, Wazirabad, Kalabagh, Naushehra, Montgomery, and Gujranwala, the satsang had land and satsang halls.

A year and a half before Partition, Hazur had been giving hints of the approaching turmoil. He used to say, "A terrible hurricane is coming, but Baba Ji will protect the satsangis."

By the December 1946 bhandara, the sangat had come to know that Maharaj Ji was not well and that the doctors were worried, but no one suspected that his condition was as serious as it was. When Hazur was giving parshad to the sevadars after the bhandara, one of the older satsangis said, "Hazur, please so will it that no disease should attack your body." Maharaj Ji replied, "Tell me, when someone relates to you the account of his sickness, poverty, or misery, would you not feel pity for him? Would you not wish that his miseries be removed?"

In January 1947, when pre-Partition riots broke out all over India, news came to us of the terrible conditions during the forced migrations. Maharaj Ji gave the sangat instructions about living through these times: "Do not look upon anyone as your enemy. Do not let any feelings of ill will enter your heart. Love everyone and do not injure or harass anyone. Even to hurt someone's feelings is considered a great sin in the court of the Lord."

In January 1947, Maharaj Ji went to Sikanderpur. There were no signs of improvement in his health. News of riots and bloodshed were coming from all sides; they were grim and distressing. Yet satsangis were being saved by the Master. Along with these accounts, letters giving details of how Hazur had appeared to them at times of calamity and saved them were also being received.

On February 16, Maharaj Ji went on a trip to Oto at the request of some Namdhari Sikhs there. Because of the strain of the journey, Hazur's condition worsened. Still he followed his daily routine and stopped at stations on the way to give darshan, arriving back at the Dera on February 27. He went out again on March 6 to give satsang in the morning at the village of Vila Vajoo and at Ghuman in the evening. The doctors were giving him injections and medicines regularly, and Hazur was continuing his programme of satsang and interviews. At times he would feel very weak and take a little rest, only to resume his work with his usual dedication.

Maharaj Ji again visited Sirsa on 19 April 1947, returning on the twenty-fourth to Dera. This was his last visit to Sirsa. During this visit, as well as during the last few visits, Hazur supervised construction and expansion work on the bungalow, Grewal House. On these visits he would urge his family to finish the house as soon as possible, "for," he would add, "I do not have much time."

Maharaj Ji had planned the expansion of his house at Sikanderpur much earlier than 1947. In 1945, during his last long tour of the northeast areas of the present Pakistan— Abbotabad, Kalabagh, Peshawar, Wazirabad, and other towns —he had called Sardar Harbans Singh (his youngest son) and Milkhi Ram (a contractor) to Jhelum in order to purchase wood for the construction work at Sikanderpur. While Hazur was calculating with Milkhi Ram the quantity of wood required, Sardar Harbans Singh submitted, "Maharaj Ji, Charan Singh stays away from Sikanderpur because of his law practice, and Purshottam Singh because of his army duties. What will be the use of such a large building for me alone?" Maharaj Ji replied, "Where will my sangat stay?"

The satsangs in April, May, and June 1947 were held as usual. Maharaj Ji carried on with his Dera routine as well as he could, but there was no improvement in his health.

One day in June 1947, we were sitting in the office with Maharaj Ji. Hazur had not given Nam during the last two monthly satsangs. While we were talking about this, Gyani Karam Singh remarked that Hazur had initiated 125,375 souls.

Hearing this, Hazur said, "That is nothing: not even a few inches of sliver out of the lot has been spun."[1]

A little later one of us said that the burden and strain of satsang activities had been progressively increasing, and Maharaj Ji all these years had worked very hard to meet the ever-increasing responsibilities; but now, in view of his age and health, he should subject himself to less strain. Great Master kept quiet for a few moments and then said: "I have carried on somehow. What will the one who comes after me do?"

These words of Hazur alarmed us. A few years earlier, also, we had heard similar words from him, but this time there was a poignancy and finality in the words that chilled our hearts.

One day, Hazur gave forty rupees to a sevadar named Gopal Singh Latha and said, "When I was in service an orderly in my office gave me this money to keep for him. Then he went on leave and never again reported for duty. I looked for his relations to give them the money but could find no trace of them. Now take this money to Rai Sahib and ask him to deposit it in seva."[2]

September 17, 1947 was the satsang of the first day of the Indian month of Asoj. Maharaj Ji was feeling very weak. He did not give the discourse, but after satsang said to the sangat, "As directed by Baba Ji Maharaj, all my life I have lived strictly on my own income. I have never taken even a single paisa of the sangat for my personal use, nor have I ever borrowed money from the satsang funds. For going out on satsang tours I have no doubt used the Dera car, and it is likely that sometimes Bibi Ralli may have taken and cooked vegetables from

---

[1] Slivers are rolls of cotton, about one inch by ten inches, from which thread is spun by hand.
[2] Rai Sahib Munshi Ram, the Dera secretary.

the garden. For these two lapses I ask the sangat's forgiveness. If anyone owes me money, I absolve him of the loan. If I owe anything to anybody, I request him to let me know and take payment from me." After a pause Maharaj Ji added, "If I have spoken harsh words to anyone, I request him to please forgive me."

Hearing these words the sangat was struck dumb. Throats were choked and eyes were filled with tears. Next day, hearing about the Master's announcement in satsang, a large number of satsangis rushed to the Dera. Their faces reflected their sadness and anxiety.

In those days Maharaj Ji used to give darshan every morning from the balcony of his house. At the time of darshan, Nambardar Jagat Singh, a sevadar in charge of agriculture in the Dera, went up to the balcony, and in the presence of the sangat, prayed, "Beloved Lord, hearing your words the sangat is greatly upset. Please annul your words and tell the sangat that all is well."

Maharaj Ji said to the sangat, "Whatever I had to say, I have said. Nambardar, here, wants me to tell a lie, which I cannot. I am resigned to Baba Ji's will."

In the afternoon Maharaj Ji sorted through his books, keeping those he had bought with his own money, sending the rest to the Dera library.

A month earlier, on August 15, 1947, when India proclaimed her independence from Britain, Pakistan officially came into being. Communal clashes between Muslims on the one hand and Hindus and Sikhs on the other accelerated to such a degree that Hindus and Sikhs had to flee from their erstwhile homes in West Punjab and Muslims from theirs in India. Many Muslims left their homes in nearby villages and cities and sought refuge in the Dera. Maharaj Ji took care of them with great love and sympathy, listening to them and consoling them. In the langar he gave them clothes and money as well as food. Many Hindus and Sikhs, forced to leave Pakistan for India because of communal atrocities, also received asylum in the Dera. Here, Hindus and Muslims forgot their differences and lived in peace together. On Maharaj Ji's orders the sevadars looked after the needs of both communities affectionately. Food was served in the langar throughout the night, and ladies made chapattis night and day, almost without a stop.

When the Muslim refugees wanted to leave the Dera for Pakistan, Maharaj Ji advised them not to go until they had a military escort to accompany them. He told them, "Please stay here without hesitation till proper arrangements for your journey are made. Have no worry, you are safe here."

Near the Beas railway station a camp for Muslim refugees had been set up by the government. It was being guarded by armed soldiers and officers of the Baluchi Regiment, a military unit from the state of Baluchistan in western Pakistan. Vigilant throughout the day and night, they would shoot at any intruder. One day Maharaj Ji drove straight into the camp and met the commander of the regiment. Hazur said to him, "Please do not despair; have courage. We have all suffered greatly, but such was the Lord's will. Take full care of the poor, forlorn Muslim refugees at your camp. Console them and be kind to them. Many Muslims have also come and taken refuge with us at the Dera. Please take them with you when you leave for Pakistan. Take proper care of them and treat them with love and affection."

The young commander was moved by Hazur's loving advice. He respectfully bowed his head to Maharaj Ji and, his eyes filled with tears, expressed his gratitude.

When the Baluchi army men came to Dera to take the Muslim refugees, the sangat bade farewell to them with great affection. Later many letters were received from them, giving information about their safe arrival in Pakistan and expressing gratitude for Hazur's kind help and the sangat's loving hospitality. Some Muslims were not prepared to leave Dera; they settled here and they and their family members are still living here.

In Sikanderpur and other neighbouring villages, there was a large population of Muslims. As the riots started they left their homes and came to Sikanderpur to take refuge in Maharaj Ji's house. Hazur's youngest son, Sardar Harbans Singh, gave them shelter and provided them with food, clothing, and other necessities.

When Maharaj Ji came to know about this, he was very pleased. He sent a message to his son and also to his grandson, Sardar Charan Singh, asking them to look after the refugees with great care and affection, to protect them and to keep them in the house till arrangements for their safe journey to Pakistan were made.

Sardar Harbans Singh kept them with him for over three months and provided them with milk, tea, food, medicines, and clothes, free of cost. When the situation improved a little, he sent them to Pakistan via Rajasthan. He gave them flour, lentils, and other provisions for the way, and sent an escort of his trusted men to conduct them safely for many miles through some of the troubled areas. They reached Pakistan safely and wrote letters of praise and gratitude for the loving kindness and generosity of Hazur's family.

For over forty years the Great Master had toured the areas of the present Pakistan and had sown the seed of satsang and Nam. As a result of his untiring efforts and his unlimited grace, the seed had sprouted and grown into a vast tree bearing flowers and fruit. The ruthless storm of Partition suddenly uprooted the mighty tree, and it appeared that years of labour had been lost. But the strong winds that uprooted the tree also spread its seeds far and wide. Driven away from their homes, the satsangis spread throughout India. Their migration to various parts of India brought thousands of people into contact with the teachings of Sant Mat. A few satsangis even emigrated to Indonesia, Singapore, Thailand, Hong Kong, and Japan in the East, and to countries like the United Kingdom, Canada, the United States, and the West Indies in the West. In all these places Sant Mat began to spread, and today there are satsangis in most countries of the world.

As Pakistan came into being, the homes of satsangis were destroyed and their properties ransacked, yet the satsangis were saved from physical harm. Through the grace of Hazur, they came to Dera from distant places in Pakistan, experiencing the protecting hand of Maharaj Ji all through their perilous journey. Almost all of them gave accounts of their personal experiences of Hazur's help and protection. The sangat was saved; yet the debt of karmas had to be paid. Our merciful Master shielded his disciples and their near and dear ones, but in doing so, perhaps, took upon himself the blows of karmas destined for them.

On September 20, 1947, Maharaj Ji summoned Malik Radha Kishan Khanna, Rai Sahib Munshi Ram, and a few other prominent satsangis to draw up a well-considered and comprehensive plan for efficiently managing the Dera and its allied institutions. He set up three committees to carry out this administration: the Managing Committee as the main body for managing the Dera and its sister institutions in India and abroad; the Administrative Committee with twenty-five members, all heads of major departments within Dera; and a General Advisory Committee with members from all over India. For all three committees Hazur was designated as President and Sardar Bahadur Jagat Singh as Vice-President.

The Great Master confirmed this plan through a will executed on September 24, 1947, about six months before he left the world. Reading this will and the plan of administration in the context of Maharaj Ji's earlier wills, it became evident to many of us that Maharaj Ji had decided to appoint Sardar Bahadur Jagat Singh as his successor.

In his will dated 30 November 1937, the Great Master had clearly stated that the religious property belonging to him as the Sant Satguru "shall be inherited and owned by that person whom I shall nominate and appoint as my successor by a separate will to be the Spiritual Head of Dera Baba Jaimal Singh." Maharaj Ji reiterated this in his codicil of 7 July 1942 by declaring, "After me the ownership of these properties will vest in my successor, nominated by me. He will have the same right over these properties as has been exercised by me during my lifetime."

Thus, as early as the year 1937 Maharaj Ji had made it clear that he would appoint his successor through a will and that all satsang properties would be transferred to him. Hazur's will of 24 September 1947 clearly indicated the name of his successor when he declared, "After me Sardar Bahadur Jagat Singh shall be the President of all these three committees, and all the above-mentioned religious properties shall be transferred to him."

Since Hazur's condition was continually growing more serious and painful, on the morning of 29 September 1947, a month and a half after the partition of India, he went to Amritsar for medical tests and treatment. He stayed in the satsang hall there. The hall, small rooms, verandas, and even the open areas in front and around the Amritsar satsang hall were packed with satsangi refugees from Pakistan, as Amritsar is close to the Pakistan border. The accounts of their hardships were appalling and painful. Most of them had arrived without any money or belongings. When the riots broke out they ran away through the back door of their homes, in whatever condition they were. Each person had his own story of Hazur's protection and guidance through the chaos and bloodshed of the riots.

Under Hazur's directions the langar was run in the satsang hall at Amritsar and free food was offered to the sangat. In spite of his own illness and extreme weakness, Maharaj Ji gave darshan to the refugees two or three times a day, and often met the new arrivals, giving them words of encouragement and comfort.

While in Amritsar, the Master called his grandson, Sardar Charan Singh, from his law practice in Sirsa. He remained with the Great Master constantly during his last six months, serving him day and night. Because of the apparent helplessness of the doctors in treating Hazur, Sardar Charan Singh suggested sending for Dr Pierre Schmidt, a satsangi living in Geneva, Switzerland, who was a famous homeopath. After consulting with other family members and receiving Hazur's permission, he sent a cable to Dr Schmidt asking him to come.

By the third week of December it was felt that the Master's health was a shade better. He was still very weak, but Baba Ji's bhandara was on December 29 and Hazur was anxious to be at the Dera, for he did not want to disappoint the sangat coming from outside by staying on in Amritsar. He therefore returned to the Dera on December 24. In spite of his weakness from the journey, he gave darshan to the sangat immediately on his arrival.

On December 29, the day of the bhandara, Hazur came to the satsang but did not give the discourse himself. After the satsang, which was given by Babu Gulab Singh, a detailed note from Hazur was read out to the sangat. It was in the form of a letter in which the Master gave details of his fourteen months' illness and treatment. A few excerpts from Hazur's letter are given below:

Dear brothers and sisters and beloved sangat of my Satguru: Today is the bhandara day, which we observe every year with great enthusiasm. But alas, this year the sangat has undergone great misery; such has been the Lord's will. People have been forced to flee from their homes; a few could bring their belongings, many could not. I feel distressed and sad, but we are helpless before God's will. We have to bear the suffering.

If the people have suffered a lot, seeing the terrible misery of the sangat during the last fourteen months, I too have suffered.... My beloved Satguru must have seen some ultimate good in my illness and through it must have removed some burden or the other.

In the note, Maharaj Ji explained that he became unwell when he went to Sirsa in November 1946. Giving details of the illness and the various treatments given by the doctors, Hazur added that when no treatment was of any help, "I accepted it as the Lord's will and carried on with the satsang duties as best I could." Further, the Master informed the sangat about his trouble, which increased in Amritsar, and the treatment given during his two-and-a-half-month stay there. He also thanked the doctors who treated him and the satsangi brothers and sisters who looked after him during his illness. Hazur concluded the note with the words, "As I am unable to meet satsangis individually, I request the sangat to forgive me."

Dr Pierre Schmidt arrived at Dera from Geneva on December 29. He examined Hazur for two days, diagnosed the disease, and began the treatment. From then until the end,

Dr Schmidt attended on Maharaj Ji with a spirit of devotion and service. Hazur was greatly pleased with him and asked his grandson, Sardar Charan Singh, to look after the doctor and make him as comfortable as possible. One day Hazur said to him, "I also want you to look after Dr Schmidt after I am gone. Please take good care of him and show him whatever places in India he wants to visit; and when he desires to go, send him off with love and respect." Sardar Charan Singh followed Hazur's instructions faithfully and lovingly. He took Dr Schmidt to Simla, Delhi, Agra, and various other places, and at the time of the doctor's departure from India, personally saw him off.

From December 1947 till the end, Hazur stayed in the Dera. During these last few months he often attended satsang though he did not give discourses. He attended to his correspondence regularly and would sometimes explain certain aspects of Sant Mat to Dr Schmidt and answer his questions. Even when he was too ill to move about, he gave darshan twice a day, sometimes from his balcony and sometimes from the window of his bedroom; he also gave interviews to those with pressing problems and discussed Dera matters with the secretary. Just before retiring in the evening, he would meet members of his family and satsangis close to him.

Although Hazur had decided to leave the world, he submitted to the doctors' treatment so that the sangat would not feel distressed. One day Bibi Ralli requested, "Maharaj Ji, you have become very weak; please try to take more nourishment at shorter intervals." Maharaj Ji replied, "No, my child, this garment of the body has become too old; now I will appear in a new garment."

During the period of Hazur's illness, Sardar Charan Singh stayed with him from October 1947 to 2 April 1948. He was constantly with Maharaj Ji, and served and looked after him with great love and devotion. He was the only member of Hazur's family who was with him continuously during this period. Sohan Singh Bhandari and Dr Hazara Singh were also with Hazur and served him with great dedication till the last.

Maharaj Ji's family looked upon him as the Lord in human form and regarded it as their duty to obey and please him. Only a few days before his death, when Hazur said he would announce his successor, someone suggested he keep the succession within his own family. The members of his family who were present responded, "Maharaj Ji, spirituality cannot be inherited like worldly goods. We pray you will appoint someone spiritually capable." Hazur was pleased with these words.

On 20 March 1948, Hazur Maharaj Ji appointed Sardar Bahadur Jagat Singh Ji as his successor and executed a will to this effect. Maharaj Jagat Singh had been living at the Dera since his retirement, spending all available time in meditation. He was known for his love for the Master and for his humility, devotion, pure living, and meditation. This decision of the Great Master was welcomed by all Dera officers and satsangis staying here. Many advanced satsangis had known much earlier that Sardar Bahadur Jagat Singh Ji would be entrusted with the duty of satsang and initiation. The will was prepared by Rai Sahib Munshi Ram, who had been Maharaj Ji's secretary for several years. Here is Rai Sahib's account from his book, *Ruhani Diary*, translated from the original Urdu:

Yesterday, Saturday, 20 March 1948, Maharaj Ji sent for me for the purpose of writing his will. I hurried to his house and found Sardar Bahadur Jagat Singh sitting in the outer room, covered from head to foot as though absorbed in bhajan. Sardar Bachint Singh and Charan

Singh were also in the room. I went into the next room where Hazur's bed was placed. Dr Schmidt was also present. Hazur asked me to prepare his will. When I inquired, "In whose favour?" Hazur said, "In favour of Jagat Singh." I returned to the office, took out of the safe the two wills Hazur had already made, and studied them. It was clear that a detailed will was not needed, as Hazur had given precise instructions about the disposal of his two types of property—spiritual and worldly—in the wills he had made out several years before. All that was needed was to announce the name of his successor. I therefore prepared a brief will and took it to Hazur.

Dr Schmidt, Hazur's son Sardar Bachint Singh, and grandson Sardar Charan Singh were also present there. Hazur was lying in bed and had to be supported to sit up. Hazur picked up his reading glasses and read the will twice and then directed me to read it aloud to those present. I read it out and again gave the document to Hazur. Sardar Charan Singh had Hazur's fountain pen and he gave it to him to sign the will. But Dr Schmidt presented his own pen to Hazur saying, "Let me have this privilege." At this, Maharaj Ji took his pen and signed the will. We asked Dr Schmidt to certify that Hazur was writing the will in full possession of his senses. He gave the required certificate on the will, which was then signed by Sardar Bachint Singh and Sardar Charan Singh, as witnesses.

After checking it, Hazur gave it to me to keep safely.

March 28 was the last Sunday of the month and the day of the monthly satsang. Rai Sahib Munshi Ram's entry in his diary about this day reads:

March 29. Yesterday was the last Sunday of this month. Hearing the news of Hazur's illness, a large number of satsangis had come to the Dera. On Saturday night Bibi Ralli, Sardar Bachint Singh, and I felt that since Hazur had appointed Sardar Bahadur Jagat Singh as his successor and made a will to that effect, and as this news had reached all the prominent satsangis, it would therefore be better to inform the sangat about this on the next day—Sunday—at the monthly satsang. We called Malik Radha Kishan, Advocate of Multan, and Sardar Kirpal Singh into the office room so that we could confer with them too. We had also asked Sardar Bahadur, but he did not come. We suggested that the next day at the end of the discourse, Sardar Kirpal Singh should announce to the sangat that Hazur had appointed Sardar Bahadur Jagat Singh as his successor by a will. But Malik Radha Kishan and Sardar Kirpal Singh objected to this, saying that on hearing this announcement the sangat would be in tears; only this much should be declared—that Hazur has appointed his successor. So the next day, Sardar Kirpal Singh made that announcement at the end of the satsang.[1]

Although Sardar Bahadur Jagat Singh's name was withheld in the announcement, the sangat came to know the name of the successor chosen by Hazur, and within a few hours his name was on every satsangi's lips.

Hazur's last will is as follows:

---

[1] Translated from the original Urdu version of *With the Three Masters; Ruhani Diary,* II:309 (1976).

I, Sawan Singh, son of Sardar Kabal Singh, caste Grewal Jat, Gaddi Nasheen (Present Master at the Spiritual Centre) of Dera Baba Jaimal Singh, in the Tehsil and District of Amritsar, do hereby make the following will:

Before this, wills concerning my private properties and that of satsang properties, have been made by me, but up to this time I have not nominated any person to succeed me as the Gaddi Nasheen [Spiritual Head] of the Dera. So, now, in my full senses and with my free will, I do hereby appoint Sardar Bahadur Jagat Singh, M.A., Retired Professor, Agricultural College, Lyallpur, as my successor at Dera Baba Jaimal Singh and all the satsangs connected with it. After me he will perform all the acts and duties that I have been performing so far.

In witness thereof, I made this will to be of use when needed.

Dera Baba Jaimal Singh	**Scribe**
Dated 20th March, 1948	Munshi Ram
	Secretary

Signature of the Testator
Sawan Singh

Witness	**Witness**
Bachint Singh	Charan Singh
(Eldest son of the Great Master)	(Advocate)

Note on the will by Dr Schmidt:
The testator, who is under my treatment, read this document twice himself in my presence, and it was read over to him by his Secretary, Lala Munshi Ram. The Testator, Sardar Sawan Singh, put his signature on it in my presence.

I certify that he is at the time in full possession of his senses and signed it on his own free will.

(Sd) Dr Pierre Schmidt
(of Geneva, Switzerland)
1:30 P.M. 20th March, 1948

Seal of the Registrar,   *(Sd) Gurbachan Singh*
Jullundur   *Sub-Registrar*

On the night of March 31, Bhai Bhan Singh, Hazur's *pathi*, was asked to recite Soami Ji Maharaj's shabd, *"Dham apne chalo bhai"* ("Brother, turn thou homewards now"). During this time, satsangis had been sitting in the open space outside Hazur's house. When they heard the words of this hymn coming from one of the upper rooms, their hearts sank; they realized that Hazur had finally decided to leave them and journey back to his eternal Home. Although the doctors had given up hope much earlier, we still prayed and hoped that Hazur would change his mind and stay with us. The long months of sickness had made Hazur physically weak, yet when he gave darshan from his bedroom window, many loving disciples would see the same beauty and radiance on his face that had always been the characteristic of his magnetic personality. How could they believe that their beloved Satguru would be with them physically for only a few more days?[1]

On the morning of 2 April 1948, we congregated outside Hazur's house. When Hazur's grandson Sardar Charan Singh Ji came down the stairs, a look at his face told us that Hazur was no more. The entire atmosphere was filled with sobbing and tears.

---

[1] Dr Pierre Schmidt's detailed account of Hazur's departure from the world appears at the end of this chapter.

Some satsangis suggested that the cremation be delayed by a day to allow the sangat coming from distant places to have Hazur's last darshan. But soon we received news that two or three satsangis who were on their way to Dera had heard the news of Hazur's departure and jumped into the Beas River and died. A few more had taken poison and killed themselves. Upstairs in Hazur's residence, Sardar Bahadur Maharaj Ji was sitting with other family members near Hazur's body. When he heard of these incidents, he got up, bowed at Hazur's feet, and directed that the cremation be done that same day.[1]

When the cherished body of our beloved Satguru was placed on the bier, the entire Dera echoed with the heart-rending cries of the sangat. Men, women, young and old, all were in tears. Even the children, who had learned to love Hazur through the love of their parents, were sad and speechless. Receiving the news by telephone and telegram, satsangis rushed to Dera by car, bus, train, and plane from various cities and towns all over India, filling the Dera till it seemed Dera could hold no more. It appeared that nature also shared our grief; strong stormy winds began to blow, thick clouds of dust arose, and the sky became overcast.

The cremation took place on the riverbank about two miles from the Dera. When the pyre was ready, Sardar Bachint Singh, Hazur's eldest son, asked Sardar Bahadur Ji to light it. Sardar Bahadur Ji declined, because according to Indian custom it is the right and duty of the eldest son or of a close relative only. Sardar Bachint Singh asked him again, saying, "You are Maharaj Ji's true spiritual son. Our relationship is

---

[1] Much later, with reference to these incidents of suicide, Sardar Bahadur Maharaj Ji commented that however noble and loving their instinct may have been in killing themselves, they would have to come back to the world again to atone for this karma.

of the world, but your relationship with Hazur is true and sublime." At this, Sardar Bahadur Maharaj Ji lit the pyre.

When we returned after the cremation, Dera appeared barren and desolate. The soft breeze of spring had ceased and the fragrance that had filled our life was no more. We longed to see our beloved Satguru's radiance, to hear his melodious voice, to feel the warmth of his affectionate look, which for years had been a sustaining force in this world of misery and turmoil.

For forty-five years, Hazur Maharaj Sawan Singh graced the Dera with his sublime presence. He had dedicated his entire life to the great mission allotted him by his Satguru. Unmindful of his own health, accepting the ceaseless strain of satsang and initiation, Maharaj Ji till the very last served the sangat with love and humility.

He gave himself to the disciples but never accepted anything from them. All his life he supported himself, joining the service as a military engineer at the age of twenty-eight and retiring at fifty-three after twenty-five years of service. He was initiated by Baba Jaimal Singh Ji when he was thirty-six and was given the responsibility of mastership when he was forty-five. Hazur came to Dera permanently in 1911 and lived here for thirty-seven years. After guiding disciples and giving spiritual light to seekers for forty-five years, at the age of ninety the radiant light of our beloved Satguru merged in the Supreme Light.

The Great Master initiated over one hundred and twenty-five thousand souls and shattered the chains binding them to the domains of the negative power. There are many more, hundreds of thousands, who had the benefit of his satsang and darshan. The passing away of the Master was a great shock for the satsangis, but many others who had seen him or heard his discourses were equally sad. When the news was conveyed to a journalist for announcement in the newspaper, he broke down, unable to hold back his tears. He was not a disciple; he had met Hazur only twice.

The ashes were collected on 4 April and consigned to the Beas River. The ground where the cremation had taken place was scraped, about two feet of earth was dug up, and after dispersing it in the river water, the pit was filled with fresh earth and the ground was made level. Some sevadars, however, marked the spot with flags on bamboo poles so that it could be found again. Satsangis began to visit the spot to bow down or to sit in meditation there; some even suggested that a mausoleum in memory of Hazur be built at the spot. But Hazur Maharaj Ji often used to tell us that after him, no *samadhi*, or mausoleum, should be raised.

After two days a sudden storm and rains came, the bamboos and poles were uprooted and swept into the river, and it became impossible to identify the place.

The remarkable efforts of Maharaj Ji to accomplish his great mission; his pure and sublime life dedicated to the high ideals of Sant Mat and moulded according to the high principles he taught; his clean and honest living; his simple yet inspiring words; his boundless love and mercy towards one and all—these provided for us a living example of the ideals of Sant Mat and form the most precious memorial of our beloved Hazur Maharaj Sawan Singh.

The Passing Away of the Great Master
(From the Recollections of Dr Pierre Schmidt)

Dr Pierre Schmidt, who came from Switzerland to attend to Maharaj Ji in the last four months of his illness, wrote an account of the last days with the Master, which is reproduced below:

The Great Master died peacefully despite the serious condition of his illness. He went to his rest quietly, without pain or anguish, the pulse and respiration gradually subsiding like a lamp which burns itself out.

Two weeks before his death, on the afternoon of the twentieth of March, as he was more himself and at ease mentally and physically, he was able to sit up in bed and gave his darshan to a large number of satsangis from his window. Then at 1:30 P.M., in the presence of his eldest son (an elderly white-bearded man of sixty-eight), his grandson, his private secretary, his devoted sevadar Bibi Ralli, and myself, the secretary handed him the paper on which he had written the last wishes of the Master, which he had issued the previous evening.

The Master asked for his spectacles; then, having quietly and carefully adjusted them, he took the paper with a slightly trembling hand. He read slowly and with the greatest care each line from beginning to end; then, looking at the secretary, he handed him back the paper without speaking. He rested then for a good five minutes, blinking and looking before him as though he seemed to be reflecting, while everywhere there was an intense and unusual silence. Then he asked for the document again, read it with the same care and handed it back to the secretary, asking him to read it aloud, which he did. When he had read out the document, the secretary asked the Master, "Is it all right?" and the Master replied, "Yes," making at the same time the sign of acquiescence with his head. Then he asked for his pen. I handed him mine. Pen in hand, he looked interrogatively at his grandson, in whom he had always had the greatest confidence, and signed the precious document signifying the choice of his successor and his last wishes.

*I endorsed this signature with an important decla-
ration that the Master was in full possession of his faculties and had signed of his own free will and under no
constraint or pressure.*

*What dignity in a serene and transcendent atmos-
phere; what a noble expression in his look, in his ges-
tures, although tremulous, and in his whole attitude. It
filled us to overflowing and brought us to his holy feet
with hands joined and hearts full of emotion at the act
which he had just completed. To think that he was there
alive and that what he had just done announced that
soon he would no longer be with us in the flesh!*

*I will never forget this silence and, even more so, the
complete peace which seemed to permeate us with an
infinite blessing.*

*Seated across his bed, supported on a big cushion of
blue velvet, wrapped in a shawl of white angora wool,
bareheaded without a turban, and with an ineffable
look in his eyes—from which radiated his supreme authority and his spiritual power—from him emanated
something I cannot describe, it was so profound and
supernatural. We felt very small and very negligible before one who knew all. Then we became, as it were, permeated by a serenity, an inner peace, which made us
forget the world wherein we live; we ceased to be conscious even of ourselves; our eyes filled with tears of joy,
bathed as we were in the beatific atmosphere of this
Great Master.*

*When the Master drew his last breath, I was sitting
cross-legged on a little stool holding his holy hand
and looking deeply into his eyes, the pupils of which
contracted and then opened widely. I saw the last inspiration and felt the last beat of his heart. I stood up and,*

in profound silence, conscious of my incredible privilege, looked around at all the disciples who filled the room as well as the adjacent ones, which too were full of kneeling satsangis with moist eyes. I bowed sadly with a broken heart in reverence to the Master, meaning "all is accomplished".

It was 8:30 A.M., the second of April 1948 at Dera Baba Jaimal Singh.

What a pathetic moment! What a terrible blow to every satsangi's heart! Was it really true? For a few seconds we all felt dumbstruck, every moment expecting a miracle. And suddenly, signs of desolation, loud cries, all expressing the terrible grief felt at the loss of the beloved Master, announced from the upper rooms the fatal news to the crowd outside in the courtyard.

For the last two days the Master's room and apartment were full of satsangis watching him day and night, taking no food, for the Master had expressed the wish sometime previously that he should be surrounded only by people doing simran in silence.

The three bibis (ladies) who had been the devoted sevadars of the Master since he came to Beas, and his sons and grandsons hastened round him to lay out his holy body. Bringing water and soap, they began to wash him completely and then to dress him in white shirt and his dark clothes. While everybody was thus feverishly occupied (each one wishing to do his best in the absence of any special arrangements, one washing the Master's head, another his beard, here the arms, there the chest), his faithful male nurse and compounder, Hazara Singh, had retired to a corner of the room completely prostrated with grief, unable to utter a word or even to move. In another corner I was kneeling, meditating beside Sardar

Bahadur Jagat Singh Ji. Suddenly the new Master rose, calmly removed his shawl, took a small brass vessel (called a lota*), filled it with water, and went quietly through the crowd to the feet of the Master (where there was no one), uncovered them and piously washed, for the very last time, his holy feet, collecting carefully this precious water. What dignity in the way he performed this act! What a contrast to the feverish activity of all the others! And this devoted and significant duty was done so humbly and so unostentatiously that, I am sure, nobody marked it. His sacred function fulfilled, like a shadow he slid back, wrapped his shawl around himself, and came and sat by my side again, leaving everybody to their busy tasks.*

It was due to foresight that great strapping men were placed at the doors of the Master's apartments on the first floor, keeping them from being smashed in as the huge crowd, almost wild, rushed around, trying to enter and see for themselves their beloved Master. We could hear shrieks, vociferation, a big roar, and loud clamour with extreme excitement around the rooms and in the courtyard. I remained wisely quiet inside.

One of the grandsons of the Master went immediately to Beas railway station and thence to Amritsar, twenty-seven miles distant, to send telegrams to the main satsang centres announcing the event, and to bring sandalwood as well as the paraphernalia necessary for the funeral.

Meanwhile an incredible crowd gathered in the village. I was the spectator of the most heart-rending manifestations that any man could witness in this life. The news spread at once to the small colony and it was most painful to listen to the cries and lamentations of all the people of the village, shrieking their desolation. Within one hour, more than three thousand people came in, and by ten o'clock ten thousand had arrived from all the towns and villages nearby. The clamour of this big crowd, all in tears and manifesting the deepest grief and chagrin due to their high devotion to him, was appalling. Many swooned; a young satsangi in the village took some drug and died, not being able to live without his Master. The scenes of desolation were indescribable.

After the laying out of the Master's body was completed, it was brought down to the court of his residence for us all to behold and see. A large and beautiful hanging tapestry surrounded the bed on which his body lay in state; it was placed on a huge oriental carpet on the porch of the entrance and the crowd was allowed to pass by. One by one they filed past for more than five hours, an uninterrupted concourse of satsangis who had come to pay their last homage at his holy feet and contemplate his visage, which, though like marble, still expressed a deep serenity.

The scenes of lamentations, the cries and the desolation of his disciples, were beyond description, and there I realized what the words devotion *and* love *really mean. From the lowest class to the very highest, from the untouchables and the sweepers to the Brahmins and the Pundits, Muslim as well as Hindu and all religions, everyone came and bowed humbly before his holy body. It was a real prostration. Everyone was wishing to see and even to touch him. To preserve order, a special organization was established to shepherd the throng of people, as everybody wanted to assure himself with his own eyes that he really was dead, not being able to believe the implacable reality. Everyone laid flowers and* perfumes near him, while aromatics were prepared to put around his body for the cremation.

Then he was placed in a beautiful and imposing catafalque surrounded by red drapery adorned with silver and gold decorations.

Now a decision was required as to whether the cremation ceremony should be carried out the same day or later, because numerous satsangis begged and insisted on its postponement for some days in order that their friends and families, who had not yet been notified of the death, could arrive and see the Master for the last time. But custom in India requires that the cremation be effected on the same day—in fact, with the heat and climate prevailing in the country, it would be difficult to postpone; consequently it was decided to cremate the body at sunset that very evening.

At 5:00 P.M., in very windy, grey, and stormy weather—all Nature being upset and in movement—the precious body was coffined, and the catafalque, marvellously decorated, was carried by twelve of Master's most intimate satsangis—the new Master included—to be transported from the village to the edge of the Beas River, down to the sandy cliffed shore—four miles from the Dera—in the old bed of the river. The coffinbearers had to cross sand hills and water up to their knees, and the journey took them one and a half hours, hemmed in by twenty thousand people, throwing flowers, vociferating, jostling and hustling, raising clouds of dust around and hiding almost completely the catafalque and its porters, who had to be replaced during the crossing.

A barrier of ropes had been put around the funeral pyre, but the crowd was so great that in a moment the ropes had been surmounted, as everyone wished to be nearest to the pyre, which was being erected with precious woods, especially sandal—the wood which perfumes the very axe that cuts it. When the pyre was completed, the body of the Master was placed upon it and covered with other pieces of wood. All interstices were stuffed with twigs of sugar cane mixed with clarified butter to which were added aromatics and precious oriental perfumes. And then the fire was lighted.

I, along with my faithful assistant, Dr Puri, had retired to the back of this noisy multitude. We were as though isolated, praying silently in our hearts to our Master, seemingly out of this world. I felt like a poor foreigner, wondering if I were still living. I was saying to myself, "I am now orphan-like, having lost everything, abandoned, with nobody from whom to seek advice and help, a poor soul lost in the desert." ... And at this very moment the crowd opened up, making way for a white-clothed personage followed by quite a lot of people, and with an expression of divine goodness and love. It was the new Master coming with outstretched hands and asking me—can you believe it?—if he could sit beside me! What a response to my broken heart and my despair! What a touching and moving symbol of the Master's blessing! We remained silently seated, attending piously the ceremony, hearing the crackling of the flames mixed with the singing of the people. It was windy and raining slightly; all nature was sad and dark.

After a little while, the Master rose and asked me to follow him. I walked near him holding my umbrella against wind and rain, lifting, like everyone else, my trousers with one hand to prevent them from getting too dirty, when suddenly, as we stopped and looked backward at the glow of the fire, the storm—the rain and the wind—ceased, and behind the Dera a most extraordinary sunset allowed us to see the satsang hall, built by our Master, profiled in black over a blood-red sky, making an awe-inspiring and grandiose scene. On one side was the multitude, surrounding the mortal remains of their venerated Master, still being consumed by the flames, and on the other, the fiery sky as an echo to this unforgettable ceremony.

A guard of four men had been placed over the pyre, which burned for a day and a half. The night of the second of April was appalling, with terrible sandstorms, rolling claps of thunder and flashes of lightning, and then water-spouts of rain. In spite of all this, the four satsangis squatting down remained throughout the night around the pyre, watching the sacred mortal remains of the Master still burning, completely unconcerned with those bursting and breaking elements of Nature.

On the afternoon of the fourth of April, the ceremony of collecting the ashes was performed. Milk was thrown over the sacred bones to cool them. Then the intimate disciples and members of his family, one after another, after filling many buckets, passed them over to a long row of satsangis, who numbered three hundred, strung across the river, and the ashes with the sand were immersed into the river. This ceremony lasted the whole afternoon.

They very kindly gave me a horse to ride back to the village, and I felt deeply touched by the many delegations of people who came to thank me for attending to the Master during those three months. The new Master came personally to my bungalow and, taking me in his *arms, thanked me in the most touching way. This very moment, this—as I might say—"transformation" from one Master to another, impressed the very depth of my heart and I shall never forget this instant, which I felt was sacred and like an infinite blessing.*

Hazur Maharaj Sawan Singh Sahib was a real and great Master. He is still in the hearts of all his initiated disciples till they shall meet him in his Radiant Form.

Chapter Three

Maharaj Jagat Singh

Early Years and Education

By their example, Saints show us how to follow the path of God-realization. Sardar Bahadur Jagat Singh, our Satguru at the Dera from 1948 to 1951, inspired everyone whose life he touched, with his wonderful example of purity, detachment, and one-pointed devotion. He was born on 27 July 1884 in Nussi, a village in the Jullundur district of Punjab. His father, Sardar Bhola Singh, was a prosperous landowner from one of the most respected families in the area. From early childhood Sardar Bahadur was cheerful, composed, and soft-spoken. His mother died when he was five and his father's aunt brought him up with great care and affection.

As with the Great Master, from early childhood Sardar Bahadur came in contact with mahatmas and holy men, for his family liked serving them, often providing them with food and other necessities. Young Jagat Singh frequently went with his father to have the darshan of holy men visiting their village.

Sardar Bahadur's education began with his study of the Punjabi language with a priest of the local *gurdwara*.[1] Later he joined the Mission School in Jullundur, where he excelled in academics, always making the highest grades; he also excelled in sports, playing field hockey, soccer, and tennis. After leaving the Mission School in 1909, Sardar Bahadur went on to earn an M.Sc. degree in chemistry from Government College, Lahore. His former classmates used to say that his

---

[1] A *gurdwara* is a Sikh temple.

distinctive qualities as a student were discipline, simplicity, humility, and a subtle but winning sense of humour. With these qualities he combined a life based on the lofty principles of honesty, truthfulness, and purity, and because of these qualities even in college his friends addressed him as "Guru Ji."

After receiving his master's degree, Sardar Bahadur stayed on at the college in Lahore as a research scholar. However, when Dr Barnes, the principal of Government Agricultural College, Lyallpur, visited Lahore as an examiner for practicals, he was so impressed with Sardar Bahadur that he insisted on his joining the college in Lyallpur as assistant professor of chemistry.

Sardar Bahadur took to his work with great enthusiasm and thoroughness. His ability to make his subject both interesting and simple made him popular with his students. Even the principal, Dr Barnes, would sometimes quietly come into his class to listen to him. The students not only respected Sardar Bahadur but also had much affection for him and were always prepared to do whatever he asked of them. Strict with himself, he inspired discipline in his students. He treated them with great affection and was always concerned with their well-being. After class time he willingly taught, without any charge, students who needed extra help.

Sardar Bahadur was an example even in sports. He was an excellent field hockey and tennis player while a student in college at Lahore and was also a leading player on the Lyallpur hockey team when he was professor there. He was known for his fairness and treated his teammates as equals. The students would feel that they were playing with a fellow student, not one of their professors.

Initiation by the Great Master

The year 1910 was an extremely significant one for Sardar Bahadur: in addition to completing his education, he came in contact with Maharaj Sawan Singh and the spiritual path he had been seeking all his life. This first meeting with his Master occurred in Abbotabad where the Great Master was stationed, not yet having retired from military service. Sardar Bahadur went there to attend Maharaj Ji's satsang with his brother, Sardar Bhagat Singh,[1] and Rai Sahib Munshi Ram. Greatly impressed by Hazur and his satsang, he asked for initiation and received the gift of Nam in Abbotabad.

Initiation completely changed the direction of his life. He began to work at meditation with the same sincerity, zeal, and thoroughness he had shown as a student and teacher. From his childhood, Sardar Bahadur had been drawn towards spirituality, and although he took a keen interest in his studies, sports, and friends, he always had an inner sense of detachment and was almost indifferent to worldly objects. A few days after initiation, Sardar Bahadur attended a recitation from the Adi Granth and heard the following passage, which made a deep impression on him:

> No practice has any worth
> Save the practice of Nam
> In the company of Saints;
> So take refuge in the Master
> And cross the ocean of life,
> Lest you waste this human birth
> Drowned in illusion.
>
> *Adi Granth, Asa, M.5, p. 12*

---

[1] Always known as brothers, Sardar Bahadur and Sardar Bhagat Singh were actually first cousins.

Contemplative by nature, he always tried to mould his life according to his ideals. He realized that no task but meditation is of any value and began to shape his life according to the high principles of the path. He entrusted the management of his household affairs to Pundit Lal Chand,[1] a friend and associate, and devoted all his free time to meditation.

Marriage

While Sardar Bahadur was still in his early teens, his father had engaged him to be married. Now that he had completed his education and begun his career, the elders of his family wanted him to marry. Sardar Bahadur, completely absorbed in his duties in the college, and in meditation during his free time, had no interest in marriage. They nevertheless tried to persuade him, but he firmly declined.

Sardar Bhagat Singh, his elder brother, was an intelligent and practical person. One day, in the presence of Sardar Bahadur, he submitted to the Great Master, "Hazur, many years ago my father and uncle engaged Jagat Singh to a girl from a very respectable family. Now if the wedding does not take place, the girl will not find another suitable husband, and by breaking the engagement our family will lose their good name." Hazur turned to Sardar Bahadur and said, "Even the Gurus and most of the Saints were married. A householder's life is better for meditation. It is good for a disciple to marry."

---

[1] Pundit Lal Chand Dharmani was a student of Sardar Bahadur Jagat Singh at Agricultural College, Lyallpur, and later became a teacher at the same college. He was close to Sardar Bahadur and would always be found with him. He used to come to Dera with Sardar Bahadur; deeply inspired by the high ideals and way of living of his friend and mentor, not only Pundit Lal Chand but also his parents and other members of the family became disciples of the Great Master.

Hearing these words, Sardar Bahadur bowed his head in sub-mission to the Master's advice and gave his consent to the marriage.

His marriage to Sada Kaur, a noble-hearted, gentle lady, occurred soon after that. She also received initiation from the Great Master and spent almost all of her time in meditation. She would never sit idle: whenever her household duties were over, she devoted herself either to meditation or spinning. She did not want to hinder her husband in his pursuit of Truth, so she lived with Sardar Bahadur for only a few months; and after their son, Sardar Jaswant Singh,[1] was born, she stayed either with her parents or with Sardar Bahadur's family members at Nussi. She never went to Lyallpur again.[2]

The Perfect Disciple

Sardar Bahadur Jagat Singh's entire life was dedicated to med-itation. He had no interest in the pleasures and attractions of the world. Neither fond of expensive clothing nor of rich food, he spent most of his income on others. Conscientious about his college duties and meditation, he was unaware of other things around him. If he was ready to go to the college ten minutes early, he would utilize the time in meditation; while his servant would heat his food, Sardar Bahadur would sit in meditation. If someone happened to accompany him on his evening walk, Sardar Bahadur rarely said anything, for

---

[1] An exceptionally capable and intelligent man, Sardar Bahadur's son later held one of the highest engineering posts in the Punjab State Government and played an important part in the construction of the Bhakra Dam. He was a man of character and a devoted satsangi.

[2] Mata Sada Kaur spent the last years of her life at the Dera. She had deep affec-tion and respect for Maharaj Charan Singh. In March 1964, at the age of eighty, she passed away in a state of great inner joy.

he was busy in simran. As soon as he returned, he would go to his room and sit in bhajan.

Whatever happened in his life, Sardar Bahadur accepted as his Satguru's will. Happiness or pain, prosperity or sickness—he would accept everything with an unshaken composure. He never complained about anything; he never appeared to be discontented or disappointed with anything. In 1920, fairly early in his teaching career, Sardar Bahadur was selected by the Imperial Agricultural Service Commission for the Indian Agriculture Service. It was a prestigious post, but even as the letter of appointment was being written to Sardar Bahadur, the post was given to another person because of his political influence. Sardar Bahadur's friends and colleagues were much upset and urged him to protest against the injustice and apply to the higher authorities for a revision of the decision, but he refused.

The following Saturday, while on their way to Beas, Pundit Lal Chand several times urged him to stand up for his rights. Sardar Bahadur's only reply was, "My officer is Hazur Maharaj Ji. What has happened has happened at his command." In Beas, when his brother, Sardar Bhagat Singh, told Maharaj Ji the whole story of Sardar Bahadur's being unjustly superseded, the Great Master turned to him and said, "What about it, Jagat Singh?" Sardar Bahadur replied, "What Hazur has done, has been well done." Greatly pleased, Maharaj Ji said, "Good, Jagat Singh! This is how a satsangi should be."

For the thirty-two years he was at Lyallpur, Sardar Bahadur would leave for Beas on Saturday afternoons after college hours, arriving around 10:00 P.M., and would return on Sunday night to Lyallpur. He always went upstairs for Hazur's darshan before having his dinner, and Maharaj Ji always waited for his arrival before retiring.

Once, Maharaj Ji directed him that before coming to the Dera, he should ask the college principal's permission to be out of town on Sundays.[1] Following the Master's instructions, Sardar Bahadur went to Dr Lander, the principal, every weekend for permission to visit the Dera. This became such a regular practice that after a while, whenever Sardar Bahadur would enter the principal's office on Saturday afternoon, Dr Lander would say, "Yes, you may go to Beas," before Sardar Bahadur had uttered a word. On one occasion, as Sardar Bahadur left the principal's office, he remembered that Monday was a holiday, so he went back to ask for leave for Monday as well. When Dr Lander saw him again, he stared at Sardar Bahadur's forehead for several moments. Then he said, "Yes, you may have leave for Monday also. In the future, don't come to me for leave on holidays. You have my permission to spend all your holidays in Beas." Later Dr Lander revealed that when Sardar Bahadur had come back to his office, he had seen Hazur Maharaj Sawan Singh on Sardar Bahadur's forehead, surrounded by an aura of light.

Sardar Bahadur regarded his Satguru as the Lord himself and followed his orders implicitly. He was an example of the perfect disciple. When he went to the Great Master's room for darshan, he would sit quietly in a corner and keep looking with unblinking eyes at Maharaj Ji's face. He never requested a private interview with the Master, never asked him a question, and never initiated a conversation with him.

---

[1] In the days of British rule, it was a convention—almost a rule—for government officers to leave their station of duty only after taking permission from their superior officers. Sardar Bahadur, though appointed as the professor in charge of the chemistry department, was also unofficially entrusted by Dr Lander with the post of vice-principal, and thus shared the responsibility for the entire college administration with him. It was in view of this that the Great Master must have thought it proper for Sardar Bahadur to request formal permission from the principal before leaving Lyallpur.

Before Sardar Bahadur did anything, even rising from his seat to leave a room, he would momentarily close his eyes, first contemplating on his Master's form within.

On Maharaj Ji's order, Sardar Bahadur gave satsang in Lyallpur, always sitting in meditation for at least an hour beforehand. His simple and inspiring discourses attracted many people to Sant Mat. Most of the people from the Lyallpur area who came to Beas for initiation were drawn by Sardar Bahadur's satsangs, and even more so by his exemplary and pure life. Sometimes seekers would call on him to learn more about the teachings. Listening to him talk about the path and the Master, and asking him questions, they would sometimes sit much beyond midnight; but promptly at 2:00 A.M. Sardar Bahadur would excuse himself so that he could sit in meditation.

Once a satsangi who was worried about his son's education and career plans went to Sardar Bahadur to seek his advice. Sardar Bahadur patiently listened to him till the satsangi, in the course of his conversation, remarked, "I also sought the advice of Hazur Maharaj Ji about this." On hearing this, Sardar Bahadur stood up and said, "What! Do you imagine I could give better advice than my Master? Why have you come to me after knowing his opinion?"

Sardar Bahadur was a living example of perfect faith in the Master. An incident narrated by Pundit Lal Chand and other satsangis from Lyallpur illustrates his unshakable faith.

A Muslim faqir of high spiritual attainments, Sain Lasoori Shah, lived in Lyallpur. He had great respect for Maharaj Sawan Singh Ji and used to say that Hazur was an emperor among holy men and that all other mystics were subordinate to him. Sardar Bahadur Ji would sometimes call upon the Sain, who had great regard and affection for him. Sain Sahib used to say, "Generally people do not know how to even sit in the presence of holy men. They should learn from Sardar Jagat Singh. He is an example." Sain Lasoori Shah would often tell Sardar Bahadur Ji, "Convey my salaam to the Emperor when you go to his radiant court at Beas." And the Great Master, during his visits to Lyallpur, sometimes used to meet the Sain. Much before Maharaj Ji's arrival, the Sain would come out and stand at the door to receive him, and on Hazur's arrival he would bow his head at Hazur's feet with great devotion.

Sain Lasoori Shah would send a message now and then concerning spiritual matters to the Great Master through Sardar Bahadur, who would convey the message to Maharaj Ji on his trip to Beas and bring back his reply for the Sain. Once Maharaj Ji's reply pleased the Sain immensely; embracing Sardar Bahadur with rapture, he offered to saturate Sardar Bahadur with the hue of spiritual radiance. Sardar Bahadur politely declined to accept the faqir's offer. The Sain, however, repeated his offer a second time. In a calm but firm voice, Sardar Bahadur again said no to him.

The Sain, in the same state of ecstasy, again said, "A third time I ask you. Just say yes and I will dye you in spiritual radiance instantly." Sardar Bahadur stepped back and said, "No, don't dye me; even if you want to, do not dye me." Then he added in clear terms, "My Satguru, the great dyer, will himself imbue me with his radiance when he thinks best."

At these words Sain Lasoori Shah was both moved and pleased. He exclaimed, "Well done! A perfect disciple of a perfect Master. I was testing your faith."

Sardar Bahadur often said that Sant Mat needs no publicity, for a satsangi's character should reflect the lofty principles of Sant Mat; people will naturally be attracted to him because of his lofty moral purpose. Sardar Bahadur's life was a silent but dynamic illustration of this principle, for quite a few of his students and colleagues received initiation because of the influence of his clean way of living. Dr Lander, for example, never discussed the teachings with Sardar Bahadur but was so deeply impressed by his chaste life and personality that he made inquiries and came to the Dera with Pundit Lal Chand to study the teachings for himself. He later received initiation.

In all its aspects Sardar Bahadur's life reflected the Sant Mat teachings, offering us a real example of how a satsangi should live in the world. Although he was thorough in carrying out his teaching duties, he did not involve himself unnecessarily in the world. He never carried a penny with him and used to give his entire salary to Pundit Lal Chand, who had instructions to spend a part of it on Sardar Bahadur's household expenses and the greater part on aid to needy students. Pundit Lal Chand would purchase all articles needed in Sardar Bahadur's kitchen, pay the bills, and even buy clothes for Sardar Bahadur Ji. Whenever Sardar Bahadur learned about the financial difficulty of a student, he would help him and send money through Pundit Ji. He would also try to help his students in any of their problems in the college. After these expenses, the balance was sent every six months to his brother, Sardar Bhagat Singh.

As Professor at Lyallpur Agricultural College

On one occasion, a student from Baluchistan did not pay his college admission fee, his monthly tuition, and his hostel fee for many months, in spite of repeated reminders. The amount due swelled to two hundred rupees,[1] and the college

---

[1] Two hundred rupees was a fairly large sum of money in those days.

authorities decided to debar him from appearing for his examinations. When Sardar Bahadur happened to learn about it, he asked the student why he was not paying the college fees. The boy said that he had not received a cheque from his father so far.

When Sardar Bahadur Ji told the boy to send a telegram to his father for the money, the young man, who was himself much worried, replied, "Sir, you too are my father." Hearing this, Sardar Bahadur immediately deposited the money in the student's account.

After a few days the boy received the money from his parents. He went to Sardar Bahadur and quietly placed the amount on his desk. Sardar Bahadur gave it back to the boy, saying, "If I was your father then, am I not your father now?"

At another time, a student who is today a senior officer in the Government ran short of money when his father passed away—so much so that he had problems continuing his education. When Sardar Bahadur Ji came to know about this, he paid the boy's college and hostel fee for three years and never mentioned it to anybody.

While serving in the college at Lyallpur, Sardar Bahadur Ji paid the expenses of about 25 to 30 students for their entire studies. He would help to pay the students' expenses through Pundit Lal Chand, and they never knew who was helping them. He sent two students abroad at his expense for higher studies. He sent his Lecture Table Assistant, M.S. Nasir, to study in England. Even Pundit Lal Chand was not aware of this. On his return, Nasir told him about Sardar Bahadur Ji's graciousness.

Sardar Bahadur Ji was always concerned with the welfare of his students. Once he noticed that one of the students in his tutorial group was looking very sad and dejected. After the class Sardar Bahadur came up to the student and inquired in his usual kind tone, "You look sad; something is bothering you. What is it, son?" Sardar Bahadur's affectionate words moved the boy to tears and he could not reply. Sardar Bahadur did not ask him anything more but quietly made inquiries from the boy's friends and learned that his family was poor and he did not have money to continue his education. Sardar Bahadur paid the boy's fees and kept on paying them for the next two years until he was able to graduate. As soon as he got a good job, the young man took his first salary cheque to Sardar Bahadur. "What is this?" he asked. The boy replied, "It's my salary cheque. I owe you a large amount of money." Sardar Bahadur laughed and said, "I am not a professional money lender. Please forget it. Send the money to your father; he needs it."

Sardar Bahadur, by nature compassionate and forgiving, had faith in the innate goodness of human beings. Once a student from an affluent Bengali family had a very expensive camera, which was stolen by another student. The principal sent for Sardar Bahadur and told him the theft would give the college a bad name. He felt that somehow the thief must be caught and the camera recovered. Sardar Bahadur replied, "Sir, the camera will be recovered, but on the assurance that you will neither punish the thief nor ask for his name." He then announced to the students, "This theft will ruin the reputation of the college. I appeal to the student who took the camera to put it in my laboratory. There will be no punishment." The next day the camera was returned, but several faculty members insisted the student be punished.

The principal asked Sardar Bahadur to reveal the name of the boy who had stolen the camera, but Sardar Bahadur Ji reminded him that the condition was that he would not be required to reveal the thief's name. The principal accused Sardar Bahadur of protecting and encouraging a thief who must be punished for his deed. At this Sardar Bahadur said, "I am not protecting a thief; I am trying to save the boy from becoming a confirmed criminal. Punishment will ruin his life, and instead of reforming him it will have the opposite effect."

The next day the student who had taken the camera confessed to Sardar Bahadur and asked forgiveness. Sardar Bahadur told him to forget what had happened and to put himself firmly on the path of honest living. Today the student has risen to a very high post in the Indian government.

Sardar Bahadur was strict but at the same time loving in dealing with his students, and they adored him. His superiors, colleagues, and subordinates held him in great esteem for his sincerity, large-heartedness, and consideration. His punctuality, attention to duty, efficiency, and spirit of dedication to the job of imparting knowledge to students inspired all other members of the staff. These qualities, along with his personal charm, had created an atmosphere of purity and serenity in the educational circles of Lyallpur. Although he never called on high government officers and had no contacts in the official circles, his contribution to the field of education could not go unnoticed, and the British government conferred on him the title "Sardar Bahadur."

Pundit Lal Chand often recalls the advice Sardar Bahadur Ji gave him when he joined the staff of the college in Lyallpur: "Always be truthful. If you are at fault, admit your mistake at once. Look upon your job as a service to the Satguru. Be punctual and never be slack in the fulfilment of your duties. Avoid negligence and shun dishonesty. Always respect your superiors."

Sardar Bahadur never spoke ill of others, nor even criticized anybody. Always tolerant and amiable, he looked upon slander as a sin and rancour as a sentiment unbecoming to a human being. Pundit Lal Chand recounts his own experience:

In 1921 he had reasons to be unhappy with one of his laboratory superiors. One day, he complained bitterly to Sardar
Bahadur Ji about the behaviour of his senior colleague. Sardar
Bahadur listened quietly to him and then said, "Every man's
mind and understanding are conditioned by his own previous karmas, and though he tries to project himself in his best
light before others, he thinks and acts according to his karmas. If you do not approve of a person's thoughts and actions, it does not mean that you should hate him, nor does it
entitle you to speak ill of him. Never hate anyone; any caste,
creed, race, or nation. Slander and hatred are unpardonable
sins." Then Sardar Bahadur urged Pundit Ji to go to his colleague and seek his forgiveness for speaking ill of him.

When Pundit Ji went to his senior colleague and apologized, the man was deeply moved, and from then onwards he
always treated Pundit Ji with affection and respect.

Sardar Bahadur Ji was always a loyal and affectionate
friend. If he formed a friendship, he maintained it all his life.
Once, a friend of his, a fellow lecturer, went to England for
further training in sericulture. Before leaving, he borrowed
large amounts of money from Sardar Bahadur and a few
other people, as well as taking a loan from a bank. Once he
reached England he took a job, never returned to India, and
never repaid any of the loans. The subject came up at a gathering of friends that Sardar Bahadur was attending at Rai
Bahadur Shankar Dass Sondhi's house. Rai Bahadur said,
"Professor —— turned out to be a great cheat. He not only
embezzled money from the bank, but also took money from
Jagat Singh and never bothered to return it." At this, Sardar
Sant Singh,[1] who was also present, asked Sardar Bahadur Ji,

---

[1] Sardar Sant Singh was a prominent person of Lyallpur. He was a friend of
     Sardar Bahadur and Rai Bahadur Shankar Dass Sondhi.

MAHARAJ SARDAR BAHADUR JAGAT SINGH

"Well, Guru Ji, how much money did he take from you?" Sardar Bahadur replied, "He did not take anything from me."

When everyone else had left, Rai Bahadur Shankar Dass said, "Jagat Singh, why did you say that? You know you gave him money, and now you deny it." Sardar Bahadur quietly answered, "How could I tell a friend's secret in public?" Rai Bahadur was silent for a moment and then said with great respect, "Guru Ji, only you are capable of such consideration and tolerance."

Although mostly withdrawn and reserved, Sardar Bahadur was at the same time sociable and would mix freely with colleagues and friends. He had quite a few friends and was a regular visitor at the house of Rai Bahadur Shankar Dass Sondhi even when Rai Bahadur was not a satsangi. With his keen sense of humour, he would enjoy a joke and share humorous anecdotes with friends. Yet, a man of few words, he was essentially a person given to the duties he regarded as the service of his Satguru—his job as professor, and meditation at all available times.

Well known for his hospitality, Sardar Bahadur accommodated his friends and acquaintances in a separate guest room in his own house during their stay in Lyallpur. His servant had standing instructions to look after all their needs, serving breakfast, tea, and other meals at their convenience. But Sardar Bahadur never let his hospitality interfere with his meditation and college responsibilities.

Sometimes his guests would stay at his house for days without being able to meet their host. Once Dr Jagannath Chawla, now a high-ranking government officer, stayed at his house for ten days without seeing him. When he was leaving Lyallpur, he met Sardar Bahadur, who greeted him and asked, "When did you arrive?" When Dr Chawla replied that he had been in Lyallpur ten days, Sardar Bahadur said, "Where have you been staying? You should have stayed with me."

His daily routine automatically shut out contact with the world. Once Sardar Sewa Singh, a friend of Sardar Bhagat Singh, went to stay with Sardar Bahadur during his month-long training in Lyallpur. On hearing that he was sent by Sardar Bahadur's brother, the servant opened the guest room for him. He stayed there a month without meeting his host even once, as Sardar Bahadur would go to his room and sit in meditation as soon as he came home from the college, and the servant would put food in his room for him to eat when he had finished meditating. In the morning, after his meditation, Sardar Bahadur would drink a glass of milk and go immediately to the college.

Finally, on the day Sardar Sewa Singh finished his training, he met Sardar Bahadur and said, "Sir, I am going back today." Sardar Bahadur asked, "What brought you to Lyallpur?" He replied, "I have been here for a month's training. Sardar Bhagat Singh sent me to you and ..." Hearing the name of his brother, Sardar Bahadur interrupted, "If you were sent by my brother, you should have stayed with me." Sardar Sewa Singh replied, "But, sir, I have been staying with you for the whole month!"

Sardar Sewa Singh was surprised, for he had presumed that Sardar Bahadur's servant must have informed him about his staying in the house. The servant, however, knew that his duty was to look after the guests well and not to disturb Sardar Bahadur. Such incidents occurred frequently with Sardar Bahadur.

On the subject of carrying out our worldly duties, Air Vice-Marshal (A.V.M.) K. L. Sondhi, the son of Sardar Bahadur's friend Rai Bahadur Shankar Dass Sondhi, recalls that when he was a student at Lyallpur, Sardar Bahadur would advise the students after they were initiated that "whatever you do, whether it is your bhajan and simran or whether you are studying for an examination or doing any kind of official work, it must be done in the name of the Master or for the Master. It must be regarded as the Master's work and not your own. If you regard any duty as the Master's work, you cannot but do it with the fullest love and devotion, and therefore to the utmost capability that you have."

Sardar Bahadur lived according to this advice. Nothing, not even illness, could keep him from performing his duties. He was a prominent member of the University Military Training Corps and every year accompanied the trainees for their fifteen-day training camp. In 1941 he was very unwell and in pain. In view of his ill health, the hardships of camp life, and the rigorous work involved, the principal suggested that he need not go. Sardar Bahadur did not reply to the suggestion, but when the students left for the camp, he was with them and performed all his duties as usual.

After thirty-two years of service at the college, Sardar Bahadur retired in July 1943 on pension. A passport-size photograph was needed for his pension papers; accompanied by Pundit Lal Chand, Sardar Bahadur went to the city to have one made. In their conversation, he mentioned to Pundit Ji that he was entering the city for the first time after seventeen years! The college campus with its agricultural fields was situated outside the city of Lyallpur, and even for getting his clothes made Sardar Bahadur would not go to the city; whenever his wardrobe required a change, Pundit Lal Chand would buy the cloth for Sardar Bahadur and have the new suit made. Though simple in habits, Sardar Bahadur always dressed well and gracefully, as befitted his status as a professor in those days.

Sardar Bahadur's colleagues and friends were keen to arrange an elaborate farewell party for him, and the principal wanted to put a large colour portrait of Sardar Bahadur in the main hall of the college. But Sardar Bahadur, always humble and unassuming, quietly slipped away to Dera in order to avoid the praise and adulation attendant on such functions, and also the sadness that his friends and students would have felt.

Before leaving Lyallpur, he put his entire house, his furniture, and the things he would not need at Dera in the hands of Pundit Lal Chand, telling him to keep any belongings he wanted for himself and then send everything else to his brother, Sardar Bhagat Singh, in Jullundur. He never inquired from Pundit Ji what was done with the furniture and other items, and never looked at the articles sent to Jullundur.

From the very beginning Sardar Bahadur had little interest in money and wealth and was completely indifferent to worldly objects. His share of the income from the family farm and other properties—a substantial income of thousands of rupees—went directly to his brother, Sardar Bhagat Singh, who spent it as he thought fit. Sardar Bahadur never asked how much the income was and how it was used. As already mentioned, Sardar Bahadur used to hand over his salary to Pundit Lal Chand for household expenses and to help needy students. Every six months Sardar Bahadur would put the balance in an envelope and send it to his brother, and would never ask for an accounting. On retirement, Sardar Bahadur received thousands of rupees from his provident fund deposits. He deposited this amount in his brother's bank account through his clerk without even telling him. Later, when the clerk told Sardar Bhagat Singh about it, he was deeply moved.

At the Dera

Sardar Bahadur had centred his life so firmly around meditation, satsang, and seva that his move to the Dera required no change in his routine. He simply continued his life of devotion, with the added benefits of daily darshan and more time for meditation. He continued to handle the foreign correspondence with Professor Jagmohan Lal, a seva he had been doing for many years. In addition, Maharaj Ji put him in charge of running the langar, which he did with great love and devotion. At Hazur's bidding, Sardar Bahadur had been giving satsang for many years in Lyallpur, but at Dera he never gave a discourse, because he could not bear to sit on the dais at the same level as his Master.

The day he arrived at the Dera, Maharaj Ji said to him, "Jagat Singh, you should grow a beard now." Although he had been clean-shaven since his youth, he immediately began to grow a beard.

On 20 September 1947, only a few days before going to Amritsar for treatment of his illness, Maharaj Ji set up a plan for the Dera's administration under three committees, with Hazur as the President and Sardar Bahadur as Vice-President of each committee. When he left for Amritsar he asked all the Dera's administrators and main sevadars to continue their seva under Sardar Bahadur's supervision and gave directions that none of them should come to Amritsar.

In the first week of October, Sardar Charan Singh arrived at Dera on his way to Amritsar from Sikanderpur. He found that except for Sardar Bahadur, there was no other administrator or responsible sevadar present in the Dera. Not knowing that Hazur had directed all sevadars and officials to remain at the Dera, he asked Sardar Bahadur Ji, "Why don't you come to Amritsar with me in my car? I'll drive you back here this evening." Sardar Bahadur replied, "Maharaj Ji's orders are to stay in the Dera. I cannot come with you."

Sardar Charan Singh drove on to Amritsar. He narrated his conversation with Sardar Bahadur Ji to the Great Master and informed him that Sardar Bahadur was the only sevadar present in the Dera. Tears came to Hazur's eyes; he said, "Of all the people in the Dera, only Jagat Singh has obeyed me." All the other Dera administrators were in Amritsar on one excuse or another.

The next day the Great Master told Sardar Charan Singh to drive back to Beas and bring Sardar Bahadur to him, but Sardar Charan Singh said that without clear, unambiguous orders from Maharaj Ji, Sardar Bahadur would not leave the Dera. Hazur then had Rai Sahib Munshi Ram note down a letter for Sardar Bahadur, asking him to come to Amritsar. On reading the letter, Sardar Bahadur accompanied Sardar Charan Singh to Amritsar. During this short visit, Hazur arranged for all Dera bank accounts to be operated by either himself or Sardar Bahadur, or the survivor of the two.

At the Dera on 20 March 1948, about two weeks before he was to leave us physically, Hazur Maharaj Ji summoned Sardar Bahadur Ji and asked him to assume the burden of mastership. Sardar Bahadur replied with folded hands, "Hazur, this Emperor's throne befits only an Emperor. May you live with us forever. I am only a slave." Choked with emotion, he left the room. Maharaj Ji sent for him again, repeated what he had said before, adding, "These are my orders." Sardar Bahadur bowed his head in submission at Hazur's feet and left, tears streaming from his eyes.

Succession

Hazur Maharaj Sawan Singh left us for his true Home on 2 April 1948, assigning the duties of satsang and initiation and other responsibilities to Sardar Bahadur's care.

In a simple ceremony on 13 April 1948, Sardar Bahadur Ji was formally installed as the Master. All the members of the Great Master's family were present; representatives from other spiritual groups also came—Baba Deva Singh, Guru of Taran-Taran; Maharaj Pratap Singh of the Namdharis; the secretary of the Dayal Bagh (Agra) Guru—and numerous people from various parts of the country. Sardar Bachint Singh, Hazur's eldest son, gave a short speech. He said, "Beloved sangat of Hazur Maharaj Ji, on March 19 Hazur Maharaj Ji sent for me and said, 'I am happy that my sons are obedient and devoted. Just as you and Harbans Singh are my sons, so also is Sardar Bahadur Jagat Singh. Always obey him in all matters. Increase your love and devotion for him and look upon him as my own form.'" After conveying the Great Master's words to the sangat, Sardar Bachint Singh said, "As directed by Hazur Maharaj Ji, I offer this holy turban to Sardar Bahadur Sahib on Hazur's behalf."

Sardar Bahadur Ji accepted the turban, humbly touching it to his forehead, closed his eyes for a few minutes and then tied it on his head. Sardar Bachint Singh bowed to Maharaj Jagat Singh, and the sangat also bowed before him.

Rai Sahib Munshi Ram then read out the Great Master's will dated 20 March 1948, and explained that Hazur had ordered Sardar Bahadur to take up the responsibility of satsang and initiation and to fulfil the obligations of Satguru that Hazur had been carrying out all these years.

Sardar Bahadur Ji briefly addressed the sangat, describing how he had refused the mastership but had to submit when

Maharaj Ji firmly said, "Jagat Singh, these are my orders." Sardar Bahadur Ji added, "I am chronically ill and incapable of doing much, but it is my duty to obey Hazur's orders. The sublime dignity and glory of this turban can only be maintained through your affection and cooperation. I request you to continue with your meditation and seva as before."

Sardar Bahadur Maharaj Ji devoted himself to the duties of mastership with the dedication, self-discipline, and earnestness he had displayed in carrying out his college duties. The only difference was that in his college days he was younger and his health was much better. But neither age nor ill health could prevent him from hard work and service of the Satguru's sangat. All his life Sardar Bahadur Ji had looked upon himself as a slave of the Master and a sevadar of the sangat. The first letter he wrote to some American satsangis reflects his humility and love for Hazur Maharaj Ji:

My beloved brothers and sisters of America,
    You must all have been deeply grieved at the departure on April second of our late beloved Master from this physical plane. The satsang suffers an irreparable loss. The enchanting figure is no longer before our eyes. But the Master never dies. His radiant Shabd Form is within every one of us. He is functioning from the higher planes and is helping his disciples. They should diligently work upon his instructions and they will find him within themselves. He has commanded me to be at your service and I will do my best to carry out his command.

We all deeply felt the loss of the Great Master. Once, when Rai Bahadur Shankar Dass Sondhi's wife visited the Dera a short while after the Great Master's death, she went to call on Sardar Bahadur Maharaj Ji. On seeing him, she was so strongly reminded of the Great Master that she burst into tears. Sardar Bahadur said quietly, "Bibi Ji, you are fortunate, for you can lighten your heart by weeping. I am not permitted to do even that."

Sardar Bahadur Kartar Singh, director of the Department of Agriculture in Punjab, was a friend of Sardar Bahadur Maharaj Ji's. Although Sardar Bahadur Ji never spoke to Sardar Kartar Singh about Sant Mat, he, like many others, was greatly influenced by Sardar Bahadur Ji's noble qualities and pure life. He came to Dera to meet his friend's Satguru and was initiated by the Great Master. Sardar Kartar Singh had great regard for Sardar Bahadur Ji and used to say that there were only two persons in the world he loved deeply, and they were the only ones he feared—his mother and his friend Sardar Bahadur Jagat Singh. When Sardar Bahadur Ji became the Master, Sardar Kartar Singh wrote to Pundit Lal Chand, "I cannot put into words the profundity of my shock at Hazur Maharaj Ji's leaving us, and now with Sardar Bahadur's succeeding Hazur, I have lost my dear friend also, for he is now my Master."

Many old satsangis who were close to the Great Master no longer felt any enthusiasm for coming to Dera. When, however, they did come to the Dera, they saw the Great Master sitting in the place of Sardar Bahadur Ji. Sardar Bahadur Maharaj Ji gave the same love and affection that they used to receive from the Great Master. Soon the sangat began to come to Dera with their old joy and happiness, and began to look upon Sardar Bahadur Maharaj Ji as the manifest form of their own Master, Maharaj Sawan Singh.

Sardar Bahadur gave initiation for the first time on 30 December 1948, to six people. Dr (Miss) Sinha, who was among them, gives an interesting account of her initiation. She had come to Beas in 1947 and sought initiation from the Great

Master. Hazur, who was not well and had stopped giving Nam, promised to initiate her, saying, "For the present I have stopped giving Nam. When I become well and begin to initiate again, you will be the first to receive it." On three occasions after that she came to Dera seeking initiation, but Maharaj Ji's health did not improve and he left us all in April 1948. Miss Sinha was disappointed and much distressed. She kept asking herself how it was that the Master had not initiated her as he had said he would. She told no one, however, about his promise and decided to attend the 29 December 1948 bhandara with her cousin and some friends. The next evening Sardar Bahadur Maharaj Ji summoned her and her cousin and initiated them along with three others, thus fulfilling the Great Master's promise. Those initiated with Miss Sinha were Mr Kumud Kumar Ghosh, her cousin; Miss Vidyavati of Muzaffarpur; and Captain Raghunath Singh and his wife Premlata. The next day, Sardar Bahadur Maharaj Ji began to initiate on a larger scale.

The following letter from Sardar Bahadur Maharaj Ji to the sangat at Panipat reflects his love, kindness, and humility, and also refers to the beginning of his granting of initiation:

My dear and revered satsangis, nurtured and blessed by our beloved Satguru,
During the illuminating discourses of Hazur Maharaj Ji, you must have heard a number of times:

I am the lowliest of all;
Except for me, all are good.
O Kabir, he is a friend of mine
Who in this realization liveth.

Adi Granth, Slok, Kabir, p. 1364

Therefore, my brothers, if there is any sinner, worthless and guilty, it is I. Why? Because according to the Bani,

One should die before one's beloved.
Despicable is life and all the world
If one lives thereafter.

Adi Granth, Siri Rag, M.2, p. 83

Hazur, however, teaches us that, in Sant Mat, greatness lies in surrender to the will of the Master. I am powerless by myself to carry out his commands, and it is his benign grace alone that enables me to do his bidding.

Further, as to your inquiries about Nam, what shall I say, save repeat to you the words of Hazur Maharaj Ji. On reference being made to him that until one had attained Par Brahm one should not grant initiation, he replied, "The real Nam should be dispensed only by one who has reached Sach Khand and that, too, with the Master's explicit permission. Without this, bearing the karmic burden of the initiate is no easy task. I also entrust to the care of Maharaj Ji (Baba Jaimal Singh) whomsoever I initiate." Now, when this Param Sant has thus enjoined, the disciples and devotees can draw their own inferences. I did not grant initiation for nine months, though Hazur Maharaj Ji himself, while in his mortal frame, bade me do so, and even left the command in writing. The reason for this had better be left unexplained.

This Dera belongs to our gracious Satguru and is our holiest shrine. Hazur Baba Ji Maharaj and Hazur Maharaj Ji have sanctified this place with sixty to sixty-five years of meditation and bestowal of the gift of Nam to seekers. Whatever service of the sangat Hazur

Maharaj Ji has entrusted to me, I shall carry out with his grace and sustenance as long as he wills; and when he calls me, I shall depart.

At His behest I came;
When He beckons I shall leave.
Adi Granth, Sarang, M.2, p. 1239

There is nothing to be perturbed about. The Satguru, who rescued us from the raging fire of Pakistan and sacrificed his own life to atone for our sins, is every moment watching over and protecting us.

Transcending the cycle of births and deaths,
Came our Redeemer.
He gave us the gift of Nam and devotion,
And merged us with the Lord.
Adi Granth, Suhi, M.5, p. 749

Do not miss bhajan and simran. You have already witnessed the catastrophic happenings in the world around; and as for the future, who knows? The only wealth that can accompany us is our bhajan and simran. Even the body that we nurture night and day will have to be left behind. Nothing here is ours. Only two things belong to us—Satguru and Nam; but for these two things, we have little love. Whether the mind likes it or not, you must give full time to spiritual practice regularly and without fail. At the time of meditation, try and make your mind motionless, and hold the form of the Master in your eye centre. Gradually, the mind will give way and become still. This is not a day's job— it calls for the labour of years.

Satsang and Daily Routine

On becoming the Master at Dera, Sardar Bahadur Ji's daily routine was completely changed. Dera work, correspondence, interviews with satsangis and seekers, seva, satsang, and initiation kept him engaged from morning till night. In spite of poor health, he continued to attend to his responsibilities regularly. While selecting candidates for initiation, he would try to talk to each candidate, and during initiation would explain the path and method of meditation in great detail, giving long hours to this important function of the Satguru. The initiations would sometimes continue till past midnight; he would miss his meals, and on returning to his room he would sit in meditation. And the same routine would begin again the next morning.

Even after becoming the Master, Sardar Bahadur Maharaj Ji continued to live in the rooms of his own house for many months. The sangat and some older satsangis kept asking him to move to the Great Master's house, but he would not agree. Sardar Bachint Singh, the Great Master's eldest son, also requested of Sardar Bahadur Ji to shift to the Great Master's house. Sardar Bahadur Maharaj Ji had great regard for Sardar Bachint Singh, and when he insisted, Sardar Bahadur Ji could not ignore his requests; finally, after six or seven months, he moved into the house in which the Great Master had lived.

His life in that house showed clearly Sardar Bahadur Ji's love and respect for his Master and his great humility. He never used those rooms of the house in which the Great Master had lived, but stayed in a small room in the back. He never used the Great Master's bed, cushions, or sofa. He never sat in his chair; when he gave interviews, he sat on the floor by that chair. He even avoided stepping on Hazur's doormat. When he travelled in the Dera car, he was careful not to sit on the side where Hazur used to sit. Sardar Bahadur Ji would not even refer to Maharaj Ji by name.[1] When Hazur's name appeared in a letter or article he was reading aloud, he would pause and say, "Next, we have the name of my Lord and Master." Then he would continue reading.

Sardar Bahadur Maharaj Ji's satsangs were simple, straightforward, and logical. He was a person of few words and his satsangs were short and to the point. They usually lasted for no more than forty-five minutes. He used to say that since most people can listen attentively for only that length of time, why force them to sit longer? His voice was sweet and melodious, and though never unduly critical of any formal religion, he would convey his thoughts with an un-hesitating directness.

In spite of indifferent health, Sardar Bahadur Maharaj Ji undertook tours outside the Dera, visiting Delhi, Amritsar, Jullundur, Phagwara, Hoshiarpur, and other cities of East Punjab, and the hills of Kangra in Himachal Pradesh. The satsangi refugees from Pakistan had come and settled in the cities and towns of Punjab, and Sardar Bahadur Maharaj Ji would often meet them on his tours and try to console them.

Simplicity, Compassion, and Humour

Just as Sardar Bahadur Ji's satsangs reflected great simplicity, so did his dress. He kept very few clothes—only two or three sets of kurtas and pyjamas. Once when Bibi Ralli wanted to get four more pairs made for him, he said, "Bibi, what do I need so many clothes for?" Another time, Sardar Charan

---

[1] In India it is traditionally a sign of respect not to use the name of an elder person; particularly, a woman will avoid using her husband's name.

Singh brought six handkerchiefs for him. Bibi Ralli said to Sardar Bahadur Ji, "Hazur, Charan Singh has brought a few handkerchiefs for you." Sardar Bahadur Ji replied, "I have two handkerchiefs—one is in my pocket and one has been washed and is drying on the peg. When this one is on the peg, the other one will be in my pocket. What would I do with more?"

He was very fond of Sardar Charan Singh. According to Pundit Lal Chand, Sardar Bahadur Maharaj Ji would some-times say, "What to say about Charan—he is an Emperor."

Once Sardar Charan Singh bought a pashmina shawl from Kashmir for Sardar Bahadur Maharaj Ji. While he was asking Bibi Ralli to convey to the Satguru his desire to present it to him, Sardar Bahadur Ji himself came down to go to the satsang. Bibi Ralli said to him, "Hazur, Sardar Charan Singh has brought you a shawl." He replied, "I already have one— what will I do with another?" Then he saw Sardar Charan Singh standing there with the shawl in his hands. Sardar Bahadur Ji paused for a moment, smiled, took off his own shawl, put it on Sardar Charan Singh's shoulders, and took the new shawl from his hands. Wrapping it around his shoul-ders, he left for satsang.

Always stressing a disciplined life, hard work, and medi-tation, Sardar Bahadur Maharaj Ji, like all Saints, was loving and compassionate. Once a sevadar who had had a dispute with another sevadar came to him and said, "Maharaj Ji, I want justice." Sardar Bahadur Maharaj Ji smiled and said, "That commodity is not available here." The sevadar insisted, "Hazur, I have already told you what happened and what is needed to set things right. Now I beg you to give me justice." Sardar Bahadur Maharaj Ji repeated, "Brother, I have already told you, justice is not available here." The man exclaimed, "Hazur, if justice is not to be found at your door, where else will I find it?" Sardar Bahadur Ji replied gently, "My good friend, in Hazur Maharaj Ji's court nothing is available except mercy and grace. Justice is available in Kal's court."

In these few words, Sardar Bahadur Maharaj Ji revealed a profound truth. And indeed, during the Great Master's forty-five years' tenure of mastership, Hazur had never adopted the role of a judge or sat in judgment on anyone. He had used gentle persuasion to end disputes, had offered suggestions and understanding and love, and had given help with his grace and compassion. The same tradition of grace and compassion was continued by Sardar Bahadur Maharaj Ji and is continuing even today.

Sardar Bahadur Maharaj Ji's sense of humour was keen but gentle, free from ill will or contempt. His disciples narrate many instances of his sense of humour. Once a satsangi said to him, "Maharaj Ji, when I sit for meditation, my soul withdraws to my knees, yet I do not see anything inside." Sardar Bahadur Ji replied, "Brother, the Lord, it seems, has erred a little. He put the eyes too far away, high up in the face. If he had put them in the knees, you would surely have seen something." Then he affectionately told the man to try to attain more concentration in meditation and come up to the eye centre. He further added, "When you come to this point you will hear the Sound and also see the Light."

On another occasion Sardar Bahadur Maharaj Ji was sitting on the veranda in front of his office with the Dera secretary, Rai Sahib Munshi Ram, and a few other satsangis. A couple was approaching from a short distance away, laughing and talking as they came. Seeing them, Sardar Bahadur Ji said to Munshi Ram, "Look, Rai Sahib, how happily they are both coming here. But as soon as they come to me, they will begin to cry." This is exactly what happened. They bowed to Maharaj Ji and started weeping. Sardar Bahadur Ji said, "There must be something wrong with me that the moment you saw me you started crying. A few yards away you were laughing." They felt ashamed and stopped crying. Sardar Bahadur Ji then listened attentively to what they had to say and consoled them lovingly.

Another time a lady from a well-to-do family brought an expensive silk quilt and a velvet mattress as a present for Sardar Bahadur Maharaj Ji. She submitted, "Sir, during bhajan the Great Master ordered me to bring a quilt and mattress to you." Sardar Bahadur Ji laughed and said, "Sister, Maharaj Ji also told me you would bring the quilt and mattress, but he said I must not accept them." Then he told her very sweetly, "I only use quilts and mattresses made of cotton. What will I do with all this silk?"

With his sense of humour Sardar Bahadur Maharaj Ji combined a direct, forthright manner of expression. He would clearly convey his thoughts in a few precise words. Once the *pathi* was reciting a hymn which has the refrain, "Even if there is gale or storm, hail or rain, I will go for my Satguru's darshan." The sangat was repeating the refrain with great fervour. It was the rainy season and suddenly it started to drizzle. Everyone got up and scurried to the verandas for shelter.[1] Sardar Bahadur Ji, who had already arrived at satsang, continued sitting on the dais; he smiled and said, "A moment ago there was such brave talk of love for the Guru. Now that love is drowned by a few drops of rain!"

Once Sardar Bahadur Maharaj Ji was giving satsang a few days before the July bhandara. The weather was very hot and the monsoons were eagerly awaited. It started to rain during the satsang; many unfolded their umbrellas while others began to run for shelter. Sardar Bahadur Maharaj Ji said, "For days you have been complaining, 'It's too hot, it's too hot,'

---

[1]   In those days, daily satsang was held in the open yard, east of the library.

and you have been wishing for rain. Now that the Lord has sent cooling rain, you are running for shelter." He continued the satsang, sitting calmly on the dais. The satsangis who had fled to the verandas returned, and the others folded their umbrellas. It continued to rain throughout the satsang; and though drenched, the Master continued the discourse, and the sangat sat and listened attentively. At the end of the satsang Sardar Bahadur Maharaj Ji smiled and said, "Only this much tenacity is needed for going within."

Once a satsangi came to Sardar Bahadur Maharaj Ji and said, "I am a sinner. I am a wretched fool ..." The man continued in this vein, using disparaging terms about himself to describe his faults. Sardar Bahadur Ji smiled and said, "My friend, you have criticized yourself and used strong words to vilify yourself. But the real indication of your humility would be when someone else says the same things to you and you do not feel annoyed."

By nature fond of discipline, Sardar Bahadur Maharaj Ji always felt very happy to meet satsangis serving in the military. After the partition of India, Beas became a centre for army regiments moving from one part of the country to another. Often even non-satsangi soldiers and officers came for his darshan, and the Master always treated them with great affection. Once when a satsangi asked him why he respected the army satsangis and gave them so much attention, Sardar Bahadur Ji replied, "Baba Ji Maharaj and the Great Master served for many years in the army and supported themselves through a hard-earned, honest income. Why should one not have regard and consideration for the sangat also serving in the same line?" He added that men serving in the army have a real sense of duty and discipline.

Once, a few years after Partition, great tension developed between India and Pakistan, and the armies of the two countries were moved to the border. People of the border towns and cities panicked and left for safer places in the interior. Some satsangis thought they should leave the Dera for a safer place because the Dera is so close to the Pakistan border. They went to Sardar Bahadur Maharaj Ji and asked if war was coming. He smiled and said, "Brothers, for predictions you should consult an astrologer. I only know this: even if the Dera and all adjoining villages are abandoned, I will stay here because that is my Master's order."

Last Days

From July 1951, Sardar Bahadur Maharaj Ji's health began to deteriorate, but he continued to carry on with his duties of satsang, initiation, interviews, correspondence, and Dera administration. In spite of the excessive heat of July, he undertook a tour of Kalu-ki-Bar. Because of his weakness, he had to lie down in the Dera van during the journey. He reached Hoshiarpur at noon and found that the sangat had made arrangements for an unscheduled satsang and that satsangis were waiting for him. Sardar Bahadur Maharaj Ji could not disappoint the sangat, and in that midday heat gave a satsang. In a similar manner, he had to give another satsang at Gagret, a few miles further on. He then gave discourses at Kalu-ki-Bar every morning and evening for ten days and initiated seekers. The Master returned to Dera on July 23.

There was no improvement in Sardar Bahadur Maharaj Ji's health all through the months of July and August. Not sparing himself—as he looked upon satsang and service of the sangat as supreme—he continued his busy daily schedule. Besides the regular workload of the Dera, the Master was obliged to hold lengthy discussions with the revenue officers and villagers, as the process of land consolidation had been initiated by the government. Often the officers and non-satsangi villagers would inquire about the teachings, and Sardar Bahadur Ji would patiently hear their queries and talk to them at length about Sant Mat, till they were satisfied.

There were a few military camps in and near the Beas railway station. Sometimes army men would come to Dera for Sardar Bahadur Ji's darshan, seek an interview, and express a desire to know about the path. Sardar Bahadur Ji would talk to them, at times for two to three hours. If some of them asked for initiation, he would overlook his own state of health and initiate them right then, for he knew that they were in transit and might not have an opportunity to come to Beas again.

In view of the declining health of the Master, some senior satsangis requested of him to reduce his satsang activities, such as seva, interviews, and work related to the Dera administration. But Sardar Bahadur Maharaj Ji continued with his daily routine as before. An older satsangi, one day, tried to persuade him to work less and take more rest, saying that he should at least avoid meeting the army satsangis and refugees who came at odd hours and took much of his time, disturbing him even during the few moments of his free time. Sardar Bahadur Ji replied with emotion, "I feel ashamed that I have not been able to serve my Satguru's beloved sangat well and could not give them as much love and affection as Maharaj Ji used to."

In September 1951, Sardar Charan Singh was asked by a leading political party and by prominent citizens of Sirsa to run for a seat in the State Assembly. Accompanied by his father, Sardar Harbans Singh, and uncle, Sardar Bachint Singh, he came to Dera to seek Sardar Bahadur Maharaj Ji's permission and blessings. Sardar Harbans Singh said, "Hazur,

Charan Singh has been asked to run for the State Assembly. If you give your permission, he would like to enter the election."

Sardar Bahadur Maharaj Ji, not pleased at the suggestion, sat up and said very firmly, "No, certainly not! This work is not for you. Give up the idea. Wait and see what Hazur Maharaj Ji's *mauj* is."[1]

Sardar Charan Singh bowed to the Master in obedience and left. When everyone else had gone, Bhai Shadi said to Sardar Bahadur Ji, "Hazur, what is the harm in Sardar Charan Singh's running for that office? He seems to be interested and he is sure to win. You refused him permission with very harsh words."

Sardar Bahadur Ji replied, "Who will stop him if I don't?" He paused and then said gently, "Bhai Shadi, Hazur Maharaj Ji has to take a lot of work from him. Just watch and you will see."

About six months before Sardar Bahadur Maharaj Ji left this world, he sent blank signature forms to Sardar Charan Singh Ji through Rai Sahib Munshi Ram. The accompanying two-line note said that Sardar Bahadur Maharaj Ji desired Sardar Charan Singh to sign the blank forms and return them. Nothing was said about the purpose for which the signatures were required. Sardar Charan Singh Ji, in obedience to the Master's directions, signed and returned the forms. As soon as they were received, Sardar Bahadur Ji changed the Dera bank accounts into joint accounts to be operated either by Sardar Bahadur Ji or Sardar Charan Singh Ji, or the survivor.

By the middle of September 1951, Sardar Bahadur Maharaj Ji had become very weak and everyone felt anxious about his health. After September 20, his health further deteriorated. He could not give satsang, nor did the doctors allow him to. His son, Sardar Jaswant Singh, called in a doctor from

---

[1] *Mauj* means "will," "desire."

Kashmir, Dr Balwant Singh, who had treated Sardar Bahadur Ji before.

On 30 September 1951, Sardar Bahadur Maharaj Ji decided not only to go to satsang that day, but also to give the discourse. The doctors advised against his even going down the stairs, but Sardar Bahadur Ji said he must attend the satsang. Refusing to be carried on a chair, he descended the stairs with the assistance of Pundit Lal Chand and went in a car to satsang where he talked in a clear, strong voice for about half an hour on a hymn of Soami Ji—"Take the refuge of the Satguru, dear friend, that the debt of karmas be cleared."[1]

After the discourse, Sardar Bahadur Maharaj Ji returned to his house and climbed the stairs unassisted. The doctors, quite anxious, examined Maharaj Ji but found that there were no ill effects from his exertion. This was Hazur Maharaj Jagat Singh's last satsang.

Since Sardar Bahadur Maharaj Ji could not attend satsang, one day in early October 1951 Bhai Shadi requested that Sardar Bahadur Ji give darshan to the sangat from the window of his house, as the Great Master had done during his illness. Sardar Bahadur Maharaj Ji's reply was, "Shadi, I cannot do that. Hazur Maharaj Ji was an emperor. How can I be his equal?"

Sardar Bahadur Maharaj Ji still attended to his mail, opening it with his own hands, but sometimes with great difficulty, for the incoming letters were numerous. Seeing how weak he was, Bhai Shadi once brought a letter opener from the Great Master's desk. Sardar Bahadur Ji held it in his hands, adjusted his reading glasses, and looked at it for several minutes. Then with deep reverence, he touched it to his forehead and gave it back to Bhai Shadi, saying, "Brother, please put it back on Maharaj Ji's table."

---

[1] *Sar Bachan*, Hindi edition, Shabd 13, Page 82.

By the end of July 1951, some old satsangis at Dera had begun to feel that Sardar Bahadur Maharaj Ji's health was far from satisfactory. They approached him and suggested that in view of his health, he should reveal the name of his successor and execute a will to that effect. The Master replied, "Do not worry. Everything will be revealed at the proper time." When Sardar Bahadur Ji's health showed no signs of improvement, the anxiety of these satsangis increased. In September, an old sevadar was sent to him with the same request. Sardar Bahadur Ji smiled and said, "I will make a perfect arrangement before going. I will not go unawares."

By the beginning of October, everyone was worried about Sardar Bahadur Maharaj Ji's health. The doctors attending him felt doubtful about his recovery. The same satsangis sent for Bhai Surain Singh, a much-respected satsangi of Baba Ji Maharaj, and asked him to persuade Sardar Bahadur Ji to name his successor. He met the Master and said, "Sir, your health is causing anxiety; I request you to please make some arrangement for the future." Sardar Bahadur Maharaj Ji replied, "My respected brother, these people have put you to unnecessary trouble. I have already told them that I will make an excellent arrangement before I go."

Maharaj Jagat Singh gave his last initiation in mid-October. On October 14, Mr Jerry Seffens, a keen seeker and senior officer of the American consulate in Bombay, came to Dera to meet the Master and discuss the teachings with him, but Sardar Bahadur Ji's lungs and throat were so congested that he could not talk with Mr Seffens. Later in the afternoon Mr Seffens told Prof. Jagmohan Lal that he wanted initiation very much, but had to leave for America in a few days. The professor did not encourage him because of Sardar Bahadur Maharaj Ji's condition and did not mention anything to Sardar Bahadur Ji about the request for initiation. The next evening,

15 October 1951, Maharaj Ji himself called for Mr Seffens and, in a clear, firm voice, initiated him. Mr Seffens left on 16 October 1951.

Mr R. N. Mehta of Delhi, who had come to Dera around the middle of October, narrated an inspiring conversation he had with Sardar Bahadur Maharaj Ji. Under the influence of some interested person, an old and senior satsangi of Delhi had started speaking ill of Sardar Bahadur Ji. When the satsangi told similar things to Mr Mehta, trying to raise doubts about Sardar Bahadur Ji's honesty and integrity, Mr Mehta felt much annoyed with the satsangi. Greatly distressed at these attempts to malign the Satguru, he decided to inform Sardar Bahadur Ji about the slanderous talk initiated against him. When Mr Mehta told Sardar Bahadur Ji about these remarks, the Master made him sit down beside his bed and said sweetly to him, "Please tell this man that he will gain nothing by saying such things." Then he paused before continuing, "Perhaps I should not say this, but since I will be leaving this world soon, there seems little harm. This white, spotless beard my Master has given me, I will soon submit at his feet—pure and without a stain." This was about ten days before he passed away.

After the doctors had examined Sardar Bahadur Ji on the morning of October 21, Dr Balwant Singh said, "Maharaj Ji, your condition is critical. We cannot say what might happen within the next few hours. You should name your successor now." Maharaj Ji smiled and said, "Doctor, you believe I will go in a few hours. Have faith. I shall be a guest in this world for another day."

In the evening Maharaj Ji drew his attention inside. When two satsangis from Waraich, Fauja Singh and Chanan Singh, came for darshan, they were so upset at his feeble condition that they started weeping. Sardar Bahadur Ji opened his eyes and said affectionately in a clear voice, "Brothers, go and sleep peacefully. I'm not leaving tonight."

Sardar Bahadur Maharaj Ji's Will

Early in the morning of October 22, the doctors examined Sardar Bahadur Maharaj Ji and left after a short while. At 8:00 A.M. he again called them and said, "Doctor, today you can ask me what you wanted to know yesterday." He then called Rai Sahib Munshi Ram and told him to prepare a will in favour of Sardar Charan Singh, son of Sardar Harbans Singh Grewal of Sikanderpur, and to send him a telegram summoning him to the Dera. Hearing these words, there was a stunned silence in the room; it became clear that Maharaj Jagat Singh Ji had decided to leave us that very day.

Sardar Bachint Singh, the Great Master's eldest son, who was now settled at the Dera, had come earlier for darshan and returned to his house. The news of Sardar Bahadur Ji's will spread in the Dera within a few moments. On hearing of it, Sardar Bachint Singh hurried back to Sardar Bahadur Ji. Eyes filled with tears, he submitted, "Hazur, Maharaj Ji entrusted us to your care. Please do not go so soon. Become healthy and continue to protect us and shower your grace on us." Then after a pause he added, "Sir, Charan Singh is still quite young. Please appoint some elderly satsangi as your successor." Sardar Bahadur Ji raised his hand and said firmly, "Bhai Sahib, what I am doing is not according to my own will; I am following the orders of Hazur Maharaj Ji and Baba Ji Maharaj."

The following extract from Rai Sahib Munshi Ram's diary, under the date 22 October 1951, gives an account of the preparation of the will:

When I was removing my clothes this morning to take a bath, Gandhi and Manohar, personal attendants of Sardar Bahadur Ji, came to me and said that Sardar Bahadur Ji had called me. I put on my clothes and hurried to where he was lying on his bed. He asked me to prepare a will and bring it to him. "In whose favour?" I inquired. He replied, "In favour of Sardar Charan Singh." I did not ask any more questions because I knew that he had already transferred through me all Dera accounts in favour of Sardar Charan Singh Grewal, the son of Sardar Harbans Singh.

I went to my room to prepare the will, when a messenger arrived asking me to hurry up. Then a second messenger came, and I wrote the will in a hurry and took it to him. I did not notice anything that indicated he was about to leave this world. Shri Daryai Lal, Sardar Gurdial Singh (Sardar Bahadur Ji's nephew), Dr Balwant Singh, Pundit Lal Chand, and others were present. I first got the will witnessed by the doctor, and then read it word by word to Sardar Bahadur Ji in the presence of all. Sardar Bahadur Ji then asked for his glasses, put them on, and himself read the entire will very carefully, from beginning to end. He then signed the will in the presence of everyone who was there, after which all those present also affixed their signatures.[1]

Sardar Bahadur Ji's will reads as follows:

I, Sardar Bahadur Jagat Singh, s/o Sardar Bhola Singh, caste Jat Sikh, Spiritual Head of Dera Baba Jaimal Singh, Tehsil and District Amritsar, do hereby declare:

---

[1] Rai Sahib Munshi Ram, *With the Three Masters*, III: 182–183.

That I am seriously ill these days and there is no knowing how long I shall live, wherefore, being in full possession of my senses and of my own free will and consent, I make this will.

That so long as I am alive, I shall be the absolute owner of Dera Baba Jaimal Singh and all the properties appertaining thereto. After me, Sardar Charan Singh Grewal, s/o Sardar Harbans Singh Grewal, caste Jat Sikh, resident of Sikanderpur, Tehsil Sirsa, District Hissar, will be the Spiritual Head of Dera Baba Jaimal Singh, and will be the sole and absolute owner of all properties, movable and immovable, cash, deposits in the banks, and all the satsang ghars attached to Dera Baba Jaimal Singh in the same manner in which the late Baba Sawan Singh Ji and myself have been their owners. However, this will not affect in any way my personal and ancestral properties. Hence I have executed this will to serve as a record of my intentions.

I also declare that Sardar Charan Singh will also hold satsangs and bestow initiation as I have been doing.

Scribe	*(Sd.) Jagat Singh*
(Sd.) Munshi Ram	*22–10–1951*
Secretary, Dera	
22–10–1951	

I certify that testator S.B. Jagat Singh has been for the last month and still is under my treatment and that he is in full possession of his senses at this time.

Dt. 22nd October 1951
Balwant Singh, F.R.C.S.
Retired Chief Medical Officer, Kashmir

Witnesses

Daryailal Kapur
Ex-Finance Secretary
Kapurthala Government
at present at Dera
22–10–1951

Gurdial Singh
Notary Public
Jullundur, 22–10–51

Lalchand Dharmani, P.A.S.
Agricultural Chemist II, Punjab
on leave at Dera

Bachint Singh Grewal
22–10–51

According to Pundit Lal Chand, after the will was completed Sardar Bahadur's face was radiant with joy. When all the other satsangis had left, he folded his hands and said, "I am happy and grateful today. The wealth that belonged to Hazur Maharaj Ji has again reached him."

It seems clear that Sardar Bahadur Maharaj Ji postponed making the will and announcing his successor so that Sardar Charan Singh would not be present in the Dera to refuse the mastership, for Sardar Bahadur Ji knew that Sardar Charan Singh would not accept it and would press him to change his decision. Sardar Bahadur Ji also realized that Sardar Charan Singh's parents would have been shaken at the thought of their son's being burdened with the heavy responsibility of the mastership at the early age of thirty-five. On October 21, therefore, Sardar Bahadur Ji had told Sardar Harbans Singh, "I am feeling much better now. You had better leave for Sikanderpur today because they need you there." Obedient to the Master's orders, Sardar Harbans Singh went to pack and then returned to see Sardar Bahadur Maharaj Ji before leaving. Maharaj Ji asked him to give a message to Sardar Charan Singh: "Please tell him not to feel disturbed or upset.

What I said about the election was for his own good and on the orders of Hazur Maharaj Ji. Wait and see what Hazur's will for him is. I am very pleased with him."

Later that day Sardar Bahadur Maharaj Ji also told Sardar Charan Singh's mother, "I am much better now. You had best leave for your parents' home in Moga tomorrow morning." In obedience to the Master's directions, she left for Moga very early on the morning of October 22.

It was also the Master's divine working that Sardar Charan Singh did not reach the Dera until after the cremation, because of mechanical trouble with his car. About Sardar Charan Singh's late arrival, Rai Sahib Munshi Ram wrote in his diary:

> *This had no doubt been arranged by the Satguru with a special purpose. If Sardar Charan Singh Ji had come before Sardar Bahadur Ji Maharaj died and he had asked him to assume the successorship, then it was just possible that Sardar Charan Singh Ji might have flatly refused, just as Sardar Bahadur Ji himself had done earlier to Hazur Maharaj Sawan Singh. Bibi Rukko once told me that in 1903, even as Hazur Baba Sawan Singh Ji was being installed as the Master, tears were flowing from his eyes.[1]*

The Passing Away of Sardar Bahadur Maharaj Ji

Sardar Bahadur Maharaj Ji, late in the morning of October 22, gave the following instructions to Bibi Ralli and Pundit Lal Chand: "After I go, the cremation is to take place as soon

---

[1] Translated from the original Urdu version of *With the Three Masters; Ruhani Diary*, III:207–08 (1977).

as possible. Don't wait for the arrival of any relatives or satsangis. Do not bathe the body; do not cover it with silk, woollen, or any costly material. Do the cremation on the riverbank.
The ashes must be immersed in the river immediately, leaving no trace of the cremation site."[1]

Bibi Ralli said, "Hazur, it would help if you also told the
Dera administrators your wishes." So Sardar Bahadur Ji sent
for Sardar Bachint Singh, Babu Gulab Singh, and a few others, and asked Nambardar Jagat Singh, a sevadar, to repeat
the instructions about the last rites that Sardar Bahadur Ji
had given to the Nambardar many days before. All assured the
Master that his instructions would be carried out faithfully.

After everyone else had left, Maharaj Ji said to Pundit Lal
Chand, "Pundit Ji, this diseased body has become useless. Of
what use is it now? Should I not leave it?" Pundit Ji replied,
"It is as you will, Hazur. If you wish it, you can be well again."
At this Sardar Bahadur Ji said, "No. Do not think on those
lines."

In the afternoon Miss Hilger and the Raja and Rani of
Sangli came to have Maharaj Ji's darshan. He talked with them
until around three o'clock. After they left, Rai Sahib Munshi
Ram and a few other satsangis arrived. Though Hazur's
breathing was now laboured, he still spoke with his visitors.
Bibi Ralli asked, "What are your orders for me? Where shall I
live now?" Sardar Bahadur Maharaj Ji replied, "Stay in the
Dera in this house as before." Rai Sahib asked about Maharaj
Ji's personal sevadars, Gandhi and Manohar, and he replied
that they should stay in the Dera also.

That evening around eight o'clock, Rai Sahib Munshi
Ram came again to discuss Dera affairs with Sardar Bahadur

---

[1] Traditionally, the body of the deceased is bathed, dressed in new clothes, and
then covered with a costly piece of material. Two days after the cremation, the
ashes are collected from the cremation site and immersed in a river.

Maharaj Ji, who was resting under the covered veranda because it was hot inside the rooms. Just before leaving, Rai Sahib said, "Hazur, for three years I have laboured so much to get the Dera's property ownership changed to your name and now you are going, leaving us with such a young successor." Maharaj Ji told Rai Sahib affectionately, "Do not worry, have faith in the new Satguru, and you will see what the Lord is going to do."

Rai Sahib had scarcely left when Nambardar Jagat Singh arrived, and after bowing to the Master, quietly sat down. After a while, Sardar Bahadur Ji said, "Nambardar, it's time for you to go and sleep." He replied, "My true Emperor and Lord, the first wound of losing the Great Master has not yet healed and you are planning to give us another blow. Have mercy on us and recover your health." Sardar Bahadur Ji said lovingly, "Maharaj Ji's will, that is what is important. It is for the good of all ..."

A little before 9:00 P.M., Sardar Jaswant Singh (Sardar Bahadur Maharaj Ji's son) and Prof. Jagmohan Lal arrived for darshan, leaving after some time at Sardar Bahadur Ji's order. Then Maharaj Ji drank a small amount of milk, rinsed his mouth, and again reclined on his bed. Turning to the doctor in attendance, Dr Hazara Singh, Maharaj Ji smiled and said, "This is the night I will go." Dr Hazara Singh later told Pundit Lal Chand that Sardar Bahadur Maharaj Ji had told him several days earlier that he would leave this world that morning, between 2:30 and 3:00 A.M. He had also revealed the name of his successor to the doctor, telling him not to say anything about these things.

That evening Maharaj Ji's face reflected the profound tranquillity of the soul within. He was smiling and happy, and one felt serene in his presence.

At 9:15 P.M. Sardar Bahadur Maharaj Ji said to Pundit Lal Chand, "I am sleeping for a short while; do not disturb me." He closed his eyes and turned his attention within. At 11:00 P.M. he called Pundit Lal Chand and asked him to see whether the house had cooled off inside. Pundit Ji reported that it was still somewhat hot there, but the Master said, "It doesn't matter. Let us shift inside." He then directed that his bed be placed in the room, close to the window.

Sardar Bahadur Maharaj Ji asked Dr Hazara Singh to give him an enema, after which he had Pundit Lal Chand sponge his body and dry it thoroughly. He used a new towel to wipe Maharaj Ji's mouth, beard, and head, after which the Master put on a new shirt and pyjama. At that moment, the Master's face was radiant. He smiled at Pundit Ji affectionately and said to him and the doctor, "Look, now I am clean and have changed into new clothes. Do not wash the body or change the clothes after I go."

Sardar Bahadur Maharaj Ji told Gandhi Ram, his personal attendant, "I shall give you a sign when I leave my body." Then he said to Gandhi affectionately, "Santo,[1] I am going to sleep. Don't wake me now." Turning on his right side and covering himself up to the shoulders with his shawl, he told Pundit Ji and Gandhi to sleep also. Then he took his attention inside. Obeying the orders of the Master, they both lay down by Sardar Bahadur Ji's bed.

At exactly 2:38 A.M., Sardar Bahadur Ji knocked once on the window by his bed. Both Pundit Ji and Gandhi got up. Pundit Ji took his pulse. After a beat or two, his pulse stopped. The Master's face reflected spiritual beauty and profound peace. He had discarded the physical body to merge back into

---

[1] *Santo* literally means, "O saint"; Sardar Bahadur Ji used to call Gandhi by this affectionate term.

the Source—the Lord. It was forty minutes past two in the morning.

Hearing the knock, Bibi Ralli came upstairs. As the news spread, the stream of visitors to the room gradually increased. Sardar Bahadur Maharaj Ji's body was therefore moved to the veranda of the Nam Ghar to accommodate the sangat coming for darshan.

In accordance with the Master's orders, the bier was kept plain, and a white sheet was spread over the body. A little before noon the body was taken to the bank of the Beas River, about two miles away from the Dera. Sardar Jaswant Singh, Sardar Bahadur Ji's son, lit the pyre. Right after the cremation, the pyre was cooled with milk and water, and the ashes and remains were consigned to the river.[1] And, again in pursuance of the Satguru's desire, a channel was dug to flood the area with water, leaving no trace of the spot where the cremation had taken place.

Sardar Bahadur Maharaj Jagat Singh Ji was initiated by the Great Master at the age of twenty-five, and from that time onwards he devoted all his free time to meditation. After serving at Agricultural College, Lyallpur, for thirty-three years, he retired when he was fifty-nine, came and settled at the Dera, and lived here till the end of his life. Appointed as the Master in April 1948 at the age of sixty-four, he initiated 18,111 seekers during his short tenure of three and a half years. He left us for his eternal Home in the early hours of 23 October 1951 at the age of sixty-seven.

Sardar Bahadur Ji's life was that of one-pointed devotion. As a disciple he was quiet and withdrawn; he would seldom talk about Sant Mat to others unless someone was genuinely

---

[1] The ashes are usually collected two days after the cremation; but this was done straightaway, in compliance with Sardar Bahadur Ji's wishes.

interested. He devoted long hours to meditation, but very few of his friends knew that he would at times spend his entire night in bhajan. For him, the Master came first, the Master was everything, and his one-pointed love for the Master was inspiring for those few who knew him closely. He would often tell satsangis coming to him, "When you come to Dera, wear blinders on your eyes, so that your eyes, your thoughts, stay fixed only on the Satguru, and your mind looks and longs only for him."

As a Master, endowed with immense spiritual power, he was always humble, attributing all that he did to the grace and blessing of the Great Master. He taught the high principles of Sant Mat in a precise yet simple manner, and lived his life according to what he taught.

Chapter Four

Maharaj Charan Singh

Childhood and Education

The life of the present Master, Maharaj Charan Singh, differs from that of his predecessors in that, from its very beginning, it is closely interwoven with the life of his Master and the story of the Dera. At an early age he was brought to the Dera to be raised in intimate contact with the Great Master, his grandfather. The eldest son of Sardar Harbans Singh and the grandson of Maharaj Sawan Singh, he was born in his mother's home at Moga in the Ferozepur district of Punjab on 12 December 1916. Dr Tirath Ram told us many times that when the infant was only two months old, he was taken to the Great Master. Greatly pleased to see the baby, Hazur picked him up and said, "This child is blessed, for he will amass much spiritual wealth and enrich others from his treasure house."

For the first few years of his life, this child-saint stayed with his parents in Sikanderpur, where his father ran the family farm. In 1920/21, when he was about four or five years old, the Great Master suggested to his parents that they bring him to the Dera and leave him in his care so that his schooling and upbringing might be done here. Sikanderpur, about eight miles away from the nearest town, Sirsa, was at that time a tiny habitation with a population of less than two hundred, with no educational facilities available. His parents, always obedient to their Satguru's will, gladly accepted the suggestion, and Maharaj Charan Singh was brought to the Dera to be raised under the supervision and patronage of the Great Master, in the spiritually surcharged atmosphere of his physical presence. Thus the period of his childhood until the years of his early youth was spent at the Dera under the Great Master's loving guardianship, and in his close contact and inspiring company.

Maharaj Ji, though so young, settled into his new home and, showered with the love of the Satguru, did not miss his mother or father. The Great Master did not send him alone to visit Sikanderpur, but always took the child with him whenever he went there and then brought him back with him. Bibi Ralli tells us that for years Maharaj Ji thought the Great Master was his father.

Even when Maharaj Ji finished his secondary education at the school in Baba Bakala and joined the college in Kapurthala, later doing his B.A. in Rawalpindi, he spent all his vacations at the Dera in the Great Master's company. So deep was his love for the Great Master that for him the Great Master was both father and mother, and the Dera his home.

Shortly after Sardar Charan Singh's arrival at the Dera, the Great Master taught him the method of meditation, telling him to keep his attention at the eye centre and adding, "If you see any light or hear any sound, give your attention to it."

Bibi Ralli looked after Maharaj Ji during his childhood days, and since then he has always had great affection for her, calling her Bua Ji out of love and respect. Bibi Ralli was extremely loving but at the same time very strict. Although he was given all freedom to move about in the Dera and play with the other boys, the Great Master had instructed Bibi Ralli that the child should attend satsang regularly and should sit in meditation for fifteen minutes every day. Bibi Ralli saw to it that this routine was regularly followed by Maharaj Ji.

The Saints have their own ways to groom their successors, and if Baba Ji with his loving but strong letters to Maharaj Sawan Singh Ji gave him strength and inner force to look upon meditation and satsang as the prime duty in life, it appears that the Great Master chose to groom the future Satguru of the Dera from the impressionable age of five. Sant Mat became a part of his education, spirituality his upbringing, and love for the Master the way of his life.

When he was a little less than six, he joined the primary school at Balsarai, a village about a mile's walk from the Dera. His out-of-school time was spent with the Great Master. From childhood Maharaj Charan Singh was calm, affectionate, and cheerful.

Many satsangis in the Dera had foreknowledge that he would some day be the Master. Once, in Dalhousie, at the insistence of Prof. Jagmohan Lal and myself, the Great Master revealed that Sardar Charan Singh would one day be the Master.[1] Malik Radha Kishan told me, after Sardar Bahadur Maharaj Ji's appointment of Maharaj Charan Singh, that the Great Master had also revealed to him several years earlier that Sardar Charan Singh would one day be our Satguru.

Baburam,[2] an advanced initiate of Baba Ji Maharaj, used to relate a personal experience which reveals that even as a child, Sardar Charan Singh was chosen by the Great Master to be the guide of our spiritual destiny. Once, Baburam had come to the Dera for satsang and darshan. As the Great Master was sitting on his second-storey terrace, Baburam went upstairs, bowed at the Master's feet, and sat on the floor. At that moment young Charan, then only five or six years old, passed by, absorbed in play. Baburam looked at the child, stood up, and bowed at his feet. Seeing this, the Great Master said, "Baburam, why did you do that?" Baburam replied,

---

[1] For details, see Daryai Lal Kapur, *Call of the Great Master.*
[2] A tailor by profession, Baburam was initiated by Baba Ji at the age of about seventeen; he lived in Lucknow and used to recite shabds for the local satsang. He was over ninety years old when he passed away in the late 1960s.

"Hazur, it appears to me that he is the one." The Great Master smiled and said, "Baburam, what you saw is correct and what you did is right."

Bibi Ralli used to recall that young Charan Singh was calm and detached at an early age. If a playmate took one of his toys, he would not even mention it nor would he ask for it back. And though the other children of the family often took his clothes or school pens, he never complained.

When he was only seven years old, Sardar Charan Singh went to the Great Master with a group of boys and said, "Maharaj Ji, we want to do some seva. Is there something we could do?" The Great Master was pleased by the simple, innocent request and said to Bibi Ralli, "Bring them some sweets." Hazur gave them the sweets as parshad, saying, "There are too many stray dogs here. Drive them out of the Dera. That is your seva."

The other boys left laughing, but Sardar Charan Singh asked Maharaj Ji, "The dogs will not leave unless we beat them. Will we be forgiven for this sin?" Hazur said gently, "Child, there will be no sin when this is done as seva for the sangat." The boy's simplicity and innocence moved the hearts of those of us present, but we thought that the task was beyond such young boys.

In those days, there was hardly any structure worth being called a wall around the Dera. The dogs would come with the sangat and then stay. But young Charan Singh organized the group of boy sevadars so well that within a couple of days there were no stray dogs on the Dera streets.

His childhood friends recall that they could never prevail upon him to do a wrongful act, however much they might pressure him to do so. Though always cheerful and friendly, he possessed from an early age a sense of responsibility and earnestness of purpose that continue to be among his great qualities.

After finishing his primary education at Balsarai, Maharaj Charan Singh attended the high school in the village of Baba Bakala, about a three-mile walk from the Dera. In those days, the way to Baba Bakala was through fields and uneven terrain. Maharaj Charan Singh Ji, even at that young age, used to cover the three-mile distance every morning on foot and walk back in the evening. Thus from early boyhood he became used to long walks and developed a liking for them. At times, when he walked back from the school after playing football and other games, it would be dark by the time he reached Dera.

Kind and tolerant from the very beginning, Maharaj Charan Singh Ji would never complain or bother anyone about his personal needs. Once Bibi Ralli bought him a pair of new shoes for school, but they were a bit small, and therefore uncomfortable for him. He wore these ill-fitting shoes out of the Dera every morning on his way to school, left them in a bush just outside the Dera, and picked them up in the evening on his way home. One day the Great Master was taking an evening walk with Bhai Shadi in the direction of Baba Bakala and saw young Charan returning from school barefoot. When he asked where his shoes were, the boy replied that they were in the bushes because he was unable to walk in them. The Great Master was moved; he asked Bibi Ralli to get new shoes for the boy and cautioned her to be more careful about young Charan Singh's needs and comfort.

From childhood Maharaj Charan Singh developed great love and devotion for his Master. I can still vividly recall how Charan Singh and his brother Shoti[1] used to press the Great Master's feet. At those times, young Charan Singh's face would become radiant with joy, while he pressed the Satguru's feet with great devotion.

---

[1] Maharaj Ji's brother Purshottam Singh was lovingly called Shoti.

The Great Master also had deep affection for him. Shri Durga Das Sehgal relates an incident about young Charan Singh's love for his Master. When he was only ten or eleven years old, he went to the Great Master one day after returning from school and bowed at his feet, almost embracing them. Hazur lovingly patted him on the back and said, "Son, I am very pleased with you. Ask for anything and I'll give it to you." He replied, "I have nothing to ask for." Hazur said once again, "Ask! Whatever you want you shall have." When the boy made the same reply and Hazur repeated the question, Charan Singh replied, "I only want you—nothing but you." Maharaj Ji's face lit up, and with pleasure he said, "Yes, my son, you shall have me."

Even during his school days Sardar Charan Singh always did seva of one kind or another. After his success with driving out the stray dogs, he was given the seva of cleaning the kerosene lanterns. There was no electric power in the Dera in those days, and lanterns were used to light the langar and the streets of the Dera. The lanterns would quickly become blackened with soot and had to be cleaned and filled every day. Although his hands would become black with soot and would smell of kerosene in spite of his washing them with soap and water, Maharaj Ji lovingly did this seva every day.

Taking care of the sangat's shoes during satsang was the next seva he was assigned. I shudder to think now that our Satguru of today used to pick up our shoes with his own hands, look after them, and present them to us at the end of satsang. Many satsangis, feeling embarrassed that a family member of their Satguru was doing the humble seva of picking up their shoes, requested the Great Master not to allow him to do this seva. But the Great Master had his own ways of grooming his future successor, who even today looks upon himself as a sevadar of the sangat.

On 30 January 1933, the Great Master initiated Maharaj Charan Singh, imparting to him the details of the spiritual path of the Saints, on which, in the course of time, he was to lead hundreds of thousands of souls. Although Maharaj Charan Singh Ji never speaks about his meditation, he took to his spiritual practice with such zeal that the Great Master had to tell him once, "It is not yet the time for you to devote so much time to meditation. Give more attention to your studies." Later on, while practicing law, Sardar Charan Singh would quietly retire to the satsang hall next to his house in the town of Sirsa and sit in an upper room in meditation. He would instruct his servant that he was not at home to anyone calling on him at that time.

Sardar Charan Singh passed his high school examinations at Baba Bakala in 1933 and joined Randhir College, Kapurthala, for higher education, studying under the guidance of Prof. Jagmohan Lal Bhatnagar.[1] Since Kapurthala is about twenty miles from the Dera, he could only spend weekends and holidays with the Great Master.

During his summer vacations his seva now included fanning the Great Master during satsang—standing behind the Master, gently waving the large, heavy fan without a stop. This seva was performed, in turns, by his father Sardar Harbans Singh Ji and younger brother Captain Purushottam Singh. But when Sardar Charan Singh was at Dera he would perform it all by himself. In the intense summer heat he would fan Hazur throughout the satsang, which often lasted from one and a half to two hours.

---

[1] A devoted disciple of the Great Master, Prof. Jagmohan Lal attended to the Great Master's foreign correspondence for years. He was very close to Maharaj Charan Singh, having taught him during his college days and later serving him as his personal secretary.

The langar also provided him with seva during his college days. Whether carrying bags of wheat, flour, and pulse, or serving food and water to the sangat, he worked so cheerfully and earnestly that the other sevadars often forgot he was their Master's grandson. At times some of the satsangis serving in the langar would speak roughly to him, but like a well-disciplined soldier he would always obey their orders.

After passing his examinations at Randhir College, Sardar Charan Singh began studying for his B.A. degree at Gordon College in Rawalpindi, and later for his law degree at Punjab University, Lahore. In college, he was fond of sports and played soccer and tennis. He quickly became popular with his fellow students because of his endearing qualities—tolerance, generosity, a good sense of humour, and a sweet and amiable temperament. He has always maintained his college friendships and even today meets his former college friends with the warmth and affection of old.

Always generous and giving, he would not object to some of his classmates taking things from his room for their own use. Once a satsangi going from Dera to Lahore was asked to take Sardar Charan Singh his monthly pocket money. As he was not in his room when the man arrived at the college, the money was left with a fellow student. Shortly afterwards a letter came telling him that his pocket money had been given to that student. When he asked about the money, the boy hesitantly said, "I did get the money, but I spent it all." Maharaj Ji smiled and told him reassuringly, "That's all right. It doesn't matter."

Maharaj Charan Singh Ji never treated the Great Master merely as his grandfather. Rather, he had firm faith that Hazur was the Lord himself and he considered it his first duty to surrender to his Master's will. The Great Master once said to

Sardar Charan Singh, "What would you like to be when you grow up—a son, a bad son, or a good son?" When asked what the difference was between the three, the Great Master explained that a son neither increases nor decreases his inheritance; a bad son squanders his inheritance; and a good son puts his inheritance to proper use, increases it, and so prospers and helps others. Sardar Charan Singh, then in his teens, replied, "Everyone wants to be a good son. But it is all in your hands. Do with me as you will."

Speaking about those early days, Maharaj Charan Singh sometimes says, "Up till the time I was forced to assume the mastership, I never read a single Sant Mat book. For me, Hazur Maharaj Ji himself was Sant Mat." These words are reminiscent of what the Great Master used to say about Baba Ji Maharaj: "I don't need any Vedas, scriptures, or other holy books, or even satsang. For me, Baba Ji's letters are the holiest scriptures."

Sardar Charan Singh Ji received his LL.B. degree from Punjab University, Lahore, in 1942 and began practising law at Sirsa and Hissar. Because of his keen intelligence, industry, and honesty, he soon had a flourishing practice and was recognized as one of the top-ranking lawyers in the area. He always took the entire income from his prosperous practice to the Great Master, who returned what he thought suitable for meeting daily expenses, gave some to the Dera in seva, and kept the rest in savings for him.

Besides having a reputation as a good lawyer, Sardar Charan Singh Ji also became known for his sincerity and uprightness. In 1945, some political leaders asked him to contest a seat in the state assembly. He had never made any important decision without consulting the Great Master and obtaining his approval, so he came to Dera for the Master's permission.

The Great Master knew that family members and well-wishers were keen that Sardar Charan Singh contest the elections and that he himself was quite inclined to do so. The Master, therefore, simply gave a noncommittal reply: "Do what you think best." But when a few older satsangis approached the Great Master on Sardar Charan Singh's behalf for obtaining his permission and blessings for Sardar Charan Singh's success in the elections, Hazur Maharaj Ji said that elections and politics were not meant for him, adding, "Baba Ji has to take some other work from him."

Although he made his views clear to senior satsangis like Sardar Bhagat Singh, the Great Master could not hurt Sardar Charan Singh's feelings by asking him not to stand for the elections. It so happened that a new law was passed by the party in power in Punjab, excluding all new voters from the right to contest the elections. This was done to prevent a particular politician from running for the assembly seat; but it also deprived Sardar Charan Singh of the chance to stand for the elections, for he too happened to be a new voter.

The Great Master, who had great love for his grandson, felt that Sardar Charan Singh would be disappointed at this turn of events. He sent for him and took him on his long satsang tour of those areas which are now in Pakistan.

In 1943 the Great Master arranged for Maharaj Charan Singh's marriage to Rao Bahadur Shivdhyan Singh's daughter, Harjeet Kaur. Hazur Maharaj Ji was pleased with the match, for he knew Bibi Harjeet to be a talented, noble-hearted girl, and her father, Rao Sahib, a devoted satsangi. A prosperous landlord of Pisawah, Uttar Pradesh, Rao Sahib was deeply religious and had spent much time studying the scriptures. When he came to the Great Master's satsang, he accepted the teachings at once and asked for initiation. As a result of his requests, Hazur Maharaj Ji visited Pisawah in May

1943 for satsang,[1] and initiated many of Rao Sahib's family along with other seekers there.

The marriage took place on the morning of 25 November 1944. The Great Master, his family members, and many prominent satsangis accompanied the marriage party to Pisa-wah. The Great Master also gave three satsangs during this visit to Pisawah. Rao Sahib's loving attention to the needs of all members of the marriage party impressed everyone. Even after this close link was formed between his family and the Master's, Rao Sahib continued to exhibit great devotion and humility. When Maharaj Charan Singh became the Master in 1951, Rao Sahib accepted his son-in-law as the Master, without any reservations. From that day onwards he never re-garded Bibi Harjeet as his daughter but treated her with the reverence appropriate to the Satguru's wife.[2]

In September 1943, the Great Master became very sick while in Dalhousie, and the physicians became quite worried, even to the extent of asking Hazur to prepare a will. Some of the family members from Sirsa rushed to Dalhousie, but Maharaj Charan Singh was asked to remain at Sirsa to con-tinue his practice and look after the family farms during the absence of his father. Feeling very sad, he sent a message to the Great Master asking that he be permitted to come for a short while for Maharaj Ji's darshan. Hazur Maharaj Ji, on receiving the message, said, "I am not leaving the world at this time. But when it is my time to go, he will be with me."

The Great Master was seriously ill, and by the end of Sep-tember 1947 had gone to Amritsar for treatment. When Sardar Charan Singh received the news of the Great Master's illness, he at once left his pending cases and drove to Beas. Finding

---

[1] See Chapter Two.
[2] Rao Sahib died on 12 January 1964 at the age of seventy-six.

that Hazur Maharaj Ji was in Amritsar, he drove on to Amritsar. Sardar Charan Singh Ji then remained with the Great Master and served him from October 1947 until 2 April 1948, when the Great Master left this world. During this period of six months, he was away from the Great Master for only two or three days in December, when he was asked by Hazur Maharaj Ji to receive Dr Pierre Schmidt on his arrival in Delhi and escort him to the Dera.

While Maharaj Charan Singh Ji was in Amritsar attending on the Great Master, news came that he had been chosen by the government for a gazetted post in the judiciary. But he did not bother the Master with questions about accepting the appointment. Several of the older satsangis brought up the proposed appointment to Hazur when his health had improved slightly. The Great Master said simply, "No, this position is not for him." Another day, a prominent satsangi (himself a retired sessions judge) again mentioned the appointment to the Great Master. Hazur replied, "What is there in being a judge? What is a judge, after all? Don't put pressure on him to accept the post." Then he said to Sardar Charan Singh, "My son, what is the use of becoming a judge? Wait and see what Baba Ji's will is for you." He paused and then continued, "Give up your law practice now. Your father's health is failing and he needs your help at the farm."

Sardar Charan Singh, bowing to his Master's will, took up the responsibility of running the family farm and sugar factory with the same dedication and efficiency he had shown in college and in his law practice.

Maharaj Ji's Family

Maharaj Charan Singh's father, Sardar Harbans Singh, was the youngest son of the Great Master and was also initiated by him. A man of few words, deeply devoted to the Master, Sardar Harbans Singh was respected and loved by the sangat for his affection, hospitality, and straightforwardness. He treated his father as a Master first, and always implicitly obeyed him. When the Great Master purchased lands in three different villages in the Sirsa area, he took up the work of developing them. Looking on all his worldly work as seva rendered to the Master, he worked very hard to develop the uneven terrain, plough it, and make it fit for production and put in long hours of work. He himself operated the tractor from 2:00 in the morning, putting in long hours. And thus he was largely responsible for the development of these lands. Softhearted and mild-mannered, he was capable of great endurance and physical work.

When the Great Master decided to divide the lands between his two sons and grandson,[1] he called them all to ask their views. Sardar Harbans Singh, indicating his elder brother, Sardar Bachint Singh, submitted, "Hazur, he is my elder brother; please allot him whatever land he chooses." Accepting a completely undeveloped portion of land situated in the village of Sikanderpur, Sardar Harbans Singh once again took up the job of patiently working and developing it into fertile agricultural property.

In reply to some well-wishers' suggestions that he should have taken the land he had worked so hard to develop, Sardar Harbans Singh replied, "I only want Hazur Maharaj Ji's pleasure

---

[1] This grandson was the son of Sardar Basant Singh, the Great Master's second son, who had passed away some years before.

and his blessings." He regularly sent wheat and other agricultural produce from the farm as seva for the Dera langar; and later, when he built a small sugar factory, he sent brown sugar for the use of the sangat.

The Great Master was very much pleased with him and during his visits to Sirsa always stayed in his house. Whenever the Great Master visited Sikanderpur, a large number of satsangis would follow him and stay as Sardar Harbans Singh's guests. Sometimes there would be as many as two hundred people. Sardar Harbans Singh and his wife, Mata Sham Kaur, were both very happy to receive the sangat and looked after them with loving hospitality. Mata Sham Kaur would get up at three in the morning to prepare milk, tea, and breakfast for the sangat. Cooking the meals and personally looking after serving the food, she would eat only after all others had eaten. She would usually work till midnight, but was happy to serve her Master and his sangat in this way.

Once in June—when the summer temperatures reach 120 degrees Fahrenheit—Mata Sham Kaur had finished cooking and serving lunch to the sangat and was planning to eat, when the Great Master called her and said, "Daughter, a group of twenty-five guests has just arrived. Please arrange for their food." It was the hottest part of the day, but immediately she sat down again at the open tandoori oven and began cooking chapattis for the guests. The Great Master's wife, Bibi Kishan Kaur, whom the family called Amma Ji, came down to help her. Mata Sham Kaur rolled the chapattis, putting her hand inside the open oven to stick them to the sides and taking them out with an iron hook when baked; Amma Ji sat nearby, applying ghee to the hot tandoori chapattis and stacking them one on top of another, ready for serving to the guests.[1]

---

[1] *Ghee* is clarified butter commonly used in Indian cooking. *Tandoori chapattis* are chapattis or flat wheat loaves roasted in a clay oven known as a *tandoor*.

When the guests had finished their meal, it was four in the afternoon, and Mata Sham Kaur, in obedience to Amma Ji's directions, ate a little food. As she was coming out of the kitchen area, her clothes drenched in perspiration from hours of working over the oven, she saw the Great Master standing before her, his face beaming with happiness and love. The Great Master patted her and said, "My child, I am greatly pleased with you and your loving seva. Your store will always be full. The grace and blessings of Baba Ji will always be with you."

Even today Mata Sham Kaur loves to serve the sangat and guests coming to Sirsa, and looks to the minutest details of their comfort. She is a living example of devotion and love for the Master, and her affection for the sangat and her large-heartedness have won the esteem of all who have come in contact with her.

The life of Sardar Harbans Singh was a simple, dedicated one—almost that of a Saint. He was never known to have done anything against the wishes of his father and Satguru, Maharaj Sawan Singh Ji. In all matters concerning the farm and the family, he would take the guidance of the Master. And when Sardar Bahadur Maharaj Ji became the Satguru, he accepted him with the same devotion and love that he had for the Great Master. He would ask him to come to Sikanderpur, would seek his guidance in all matters, and looked upon him not only as the Master but also as the head of the family.

When Sardar Bahadur Maharaj Ji appointed Maharaj Charan Singh as the Master, Sardar Harbans Singh's health was declining; he had grown weak and had pain in the joints due to arthritis. He was semi-retired, having already handed over the work of the sugar factory and the farm to Sardar Charan Singh, who was his eldest son. The appointment brought the farm responsibilities back on his ageing shoulders, but ungrudgingly he accepted the situation, bowing to the will of the Master. When Maharaj Charan Singh, concerned over his father's declining health and old age, almost hesitated to accept the responsibility of the mastership, his father reassured him and told him to submit to the Satguru's orders without hesitation. Just as Sardar Harbans Singh had never looked upon the Great Master as his father, always treating him as the Satguru—God in human form—so now he looked upon Maharaj Charan Singh not as a son but as the Master.

In July 1956, when he came to Dera to attend the bhandara, Sardar Harbans Singh became very weak and his health declined rapidly. He was bedridden and could not return to Sikanderpur.

One day Sardar Harbans Singh was in great pain, and when Maharaj Charan Singh was with him, he said, "The pain has become too much, almost unbearable." Maharaj Ji replied, "Chacha Ji,[1] you understand everything. It is better to bear it gracefully and pay off the load than to come back and account for it in another life." From that day onwards, he never complained of his pain.

A few days later, Maharaj Ji's father, having little interest in the physical world, said to Maharaj Ji, "I have no desire to stay here. Why don't you take me?" Maharaj Ji replied, "When Hazur Maharaj Ji left, for days together were you not sad?" His father answered, "Yes, indeed I was." Maharaj Ji said, "Then how can you ask me to take you away?"

Three or four days before his death, Sardar Harbans Singh told his wife, Mata Sham Kaur, "I've given away everything to the children. There are only fifteen rupees that belong to me. Give these ten rupees in seva." And then, after keeping quiet for a moment, he said, "And give these five rupees to Bhagat

---

[1] This is what Maharaj Ji called his father—literally "uncle," "father's younger brother"; children in a joint family in India often address their own parents in the same manner as the other children of the joint family address them.

Singh, the carpenter." Nobody could understand why he had asked that five rupees be given to the carpenter, Bhagat Singh, who lived in the Dera. It was only after Sardar Harbans Singh passed away and the carpenter Bhagat Singh was called to construct the bier that the family realized that the payment to the carpenter had been made in advance by Maharaj Ji's father for the last service rendered.

On or about 8 August 1956, Sardar Harbans Singh said to Maharaj Ji, "I have received the passport from Hazur Maharaj Ji. Now I need the visa from you." Maharaj Ji kept silent for a few minutes and then said, "If Hazur Maharaj Ji has given you permission, how can I detain you?" From that day onwards, Sardar Harbans Singh's attention remained mostly within, and about eight days later, on 16 August 1956, he left the world to merge into the feet of the Satguru.

Before his father's cremation on the following day, Maharaj Ji gave a discourse in the satsang on a shabd from Soami Ji, "O soul, leave thou this home where both grief and joy abound." He spoke for about an hour in his usual sweet and serene voice, which showed no signs of emotion. After satsang, the sangat joined Maharaj Ji's family in the cremation ceremony.

Maharaj Ji's mother, whose account has already been related, is the daughter of the late Sardar Pratap Singh, a respected citizen of Moga (District Ferozepur, Punjab). One of her brothers, Sardar Tara Singh, rose to be a judge in the Patiala High Court; her second brother, Sardar Lal Singh, a tall and handsome man, was a captain in the British Indian Army and, because of his intelligence and imposing personality, rose to become a member of the Viceroy's personal staff. Her third and fourth brothers, Sardar Prem Singh and Sardar Bhag Singh, held responsible posts in the civil administration of Punjab.

Mata Sham Kaur combines in her all the noble qualities of large-heartedness and humility, love and devotion, which are expected in the daughter-in-law of a Sant Satguru and the mother of a great Saint.

Maharaj Ji's younger brother, Sardar Purshottam Singh,[1] after doing his B.A. and LL.B., joined the army and quickly rose to the post of captain. When Maharaj Charan Singh became the Master, Captain Purshottam Singh was due for promotion to the rank of major. Sacrificing his own bright future career, he sought premature retirement to take up the responsibilities of the farm and sugar factory at Sikanderpur. He had to forego his pension, as well as an award for bravery for overpowering a policeman who was shooting at people indiscriminately in Rawalpindi station during the days of Partition. Though himself unarmed, he boldly caught hold of the man, wrestled his gun from him, and arrested him single-handedly. In the process he was wounded and had to be hospitalized. Friendly, serene, and hospitable, he looks after the farm at Sikanderpur with application and devotion of purpose.

Maharaj Ji's youngest brother, Sardar Jagjit Singh, died in August 1948 when he was still in his teens. He was a cheerful and promising young man. He had not received initiation and was very anxious to be initiated. Two days before his death, the Great Master appeared to him within and initiated him.

Maharaj Ji has four sisters, all younger than he. Bibi Satnam Kaur, whose husband died when she was in her early twenties, has one son and a daughter. The three younger sisters are Bibi Gurnam Kaur, married to Col. Tejender Singh Sidhu; Bibi Mahendar Kaur, married to Sardar Gurmukh Singh Dhillon; and Bibi Baljender Kaur, married to Maj. Pritipal Singh Mann.

---

[1] Sardar Purshottam Singh passed away on 20 October 1990.

Maharaj Charan Singh

The Master's wife, Bibi Harjeet Kaur, is the daughter of Rao Bahadur Shivdhyan Singh, who was a devoted satsangi of the Great Master and a landlord in Pisawah, District Aligarh (Uttar Pradesh). She is a noble, intelligent, and able lady, a devoted disciple of the Great Master. When Maharaj Ji was appointed to be the Master, she was only twenty-four, with a small child, and it must have been a great trial for her to accept her husband as the Master and allow him to dedicate his entire life to the service of the sangat. But with courage, calmness, and determination, she bowed her head before the will of the Master and accepted a life of dedication and purity. Seeing the way of life she was faced with at such a young age, all the family members were greatly shaken; but with courage and firm faith in the Satguru, she said to Maharaj Ji, "I do not want to become an obstacle in your accepting the Master's command and taking up the responsibility of guiding the sangat. Please do not hesitate to obey Maharaj Ji's orders, and accept it as his will."

Bibi Harjeet Kaur has great dedication towards service of the sangat. While looking after the three children, she also has studied naturopathy, passed examinations, visited various naturopathic centres in India and abroad; and with the Master's permission she has opened her own nature cure clinic in the Dera. The clinic is developing under her able guidance, and has a trained and dedicated staff of sevadars. More than fifty patients have the benefit of treatment at the clinic every day.

Maharaj Ji's family consists of two sons and a daughter. The elder son, Jasbir Singh, after completing his education, is working in a high post abroad. The younger son, Rana Ranbir Singh, after having completed his education, is helping to run the family farm at Sikanderpur. Maharaj Ji's daughter, Nirmaljit Kaur, is a graduate of Panjab University (Chandigarh) and is married to Dr Parvinder Singh, son of Bhai Mohan Singh of a well-known business family in Delhi. Dr Parvinder Singh, a highly educated young man with a keen intellect and a kind, affectionate nature, is a humble and devoted satsangi of Maharaj Ji.

Successorship

During the few years that Sardar Bahadur Maharaj Ji was the Master, Sardar Charan Singh was helping his father with the farm and involving himself deeply in meditation, often going to the Dera to have darshan and attend Sardar Bahadur Ji's satsangs.

On 22 October 1951, the day before Sardar Bahadur Maharaj Ji passed away, Maharaj Charan Singh returned to Sikanderpur from Ambala, arriving around noon. A little later, when his father, Sardar Harbans Singh, arrived from the Dera, he asked his father about Sardar Bahadur Ji's health. Sardar Harbans Singh said, "Sardar Bahadur Maharaj Ji told me he was much better and asked me to return to the farm." He also conveyed Sardar Bahadur Ji's message to Sardar Charan Singh Ji.[1]

At about four o'clock a telegram arrived, saying, "Send Charan to Dera." Maharaj Ji said, "Why send for me?" He and his father decided that Sardar Bahadur Ji's health must have worsened, so they left immediately in Maharaj Ji's Hillman car.

On the way they were forced to make a detour because of a flooded road, and later were delayed by engine trouble. It took several hours to get the car repaired. Worried about Sar-

---

[1] The message was: "Please tell him not to feel disturbed or upset. What I said about the election was for his own good and on the orders of Hazur Maharaj Ji. Wait and see what Hazur's will for him is. I am very pleased with him."

dar Bahadur Ji's health, they disregarded the late hour and continued their journey. By midnight, more than half the journey still lay ahead. Between 2:30 and 3:00 A.M., Maharaj Charan Singh Ji, who was driving the car, saw dazzling light accompanied by the form of Sardar Bahadur Ji. His attention strayed from his driving, and the car went down a slope on the side of the road and stopped. Resting his head on the steering wheel, he closed his eyes. After a few moments' silence, his father asked, "What is it, son? Are you feeling all right?" Maharaj Charan Singh kept quiet for some time, then said, "Please drive, Chacha Ji. I cannot." His father took the wheel and drove a good distance before Maharaj Ji spoke again. He said, "Sardar Bahadur Ji has gone."

Both were silent for the rest of the night until they reached Moga at daybreak. When they told Maharaj Ji's mother about the telegram, she said, "Only yesterday Sardar Bahadur Ji sent me to Moga, saying that he was much better." His father had a cup of tea in Moga, but Maharaj Ji took nothing. Maharaj Ji's mother joined them on their journey. At Sardar Harbans Singh's insistence, Maharaj Ji took over the driving again, but after a few minutes he stopped the car and said, "I cannot drive. You will have to."

When they arrived, the Dera was still and deserted, for Sardar Bahadur Maharaj Ji's cremation was taking place at the riverside. Maharaj Ji's father said that he knew then that his son's words were true—Sardar Bahadur Ji had gone. Maharaj Ji and his father went to Sardar Bahadur Ji's residence, where they met Bibi Ralli. She began to weep when she saw them. Sardar Harbans Singh said, "Bibi Ji, you could have waited for us. Why do the cremation so soon?" Bibi Ralli answered, "What could we do? Such were his orders."

Maharaj Charan Singh set out for the riverside cremation grounds with his father. He felt immense sorrow at being separated from the Master and at not being able to see him before he passed away. Tears were flowing down his face as he walked towards the cremation ground. As they approached the site, they passed Sardar Bahadur Ji's little granddaughter, Gyan, who was holding on to Miss Louise Hilger's hand. The child, pointing to Maharaj Ji, said to Miss Hilger that he was the new Master. But Maharaj Ji did not hear what she said.

When he arrived at the cremation site, someone said to the sangat, "Here is the new Satguru." At the same time, two of Maharaj Charan Singh Ji's friends, Sardar Gurbux Singh Randhir and Shri Lakshmi Chand Dharmani, came forward and bowed at the Master's feet. He now knew that Sardar Bahadur Maharaj Ji had appointed him as his successor. Tears streaming down his face, he immediately left the riverside for the Dera. Maharaj Ji later said, "At that time it seemed an uphill task even to reach the Dera." Unable to suppress the outburst of his emotions, he went straight to his room and closed the doors.

The passing away of Sardar Bahadur Ji, whom Maharaj Ji loved deeply and whom he looked upon as the manifest form of his own beloved Satguru, Maharaj Sawan Singh Ji, was both a shock and a great personal loss for him. Although Maharaj Charan Singh had great devotion and love for his Satguru and possessed the qualities of kindness and sympathy, tolerance and understanding, serenity and humility—qualities rare among human beings—and although the Great Master, through his own personal association and contact had, it seems, imperceptibly groomed him to bear the burden of mastership, Sardar Charan Singh, on his part, had no desire for this august office. From his own close contact with the Great Master he had seen that the crown of mastership was in reality a crown of nails.

It is hard for us to understand this, for we people of the world, burning with ambition, run after fame and honour; but Saints run from such worldly esteem and reverence. It is only the orders of their Satguru that could force them to accept the responsibility of being the Master. Then they work as dedicated servants of their Master, hiding their unlimited spiritual power behind their humility.

His becoming the Master meant a heavy burden and many sacrifices for Maharaj Ji's family as well. His wife, Bibi Harjeet, only twenty-four years old at the time, had to face the responsibility of raising the three children alone, the youngest just six months old. It hurt the other family members to think of the lonely responsibilities that lay ahead of her, and Maharaj Ji himself was deeply concerned. His father, ageing and in poor health, faced the responsibilities and the strenuous job of looking after the farms at Sirsa, from which he had practically retired; he had been planning to spend more time at the Dera. But Maharaj Ji's father, mother, and wife exhibited great fortitude and patience, and urged him to accept the commands of the Satguru without feeling concerned for them.

Maharaj Charan Singh called to his house all the sevadars who were in close contact with Sardar Bahadur Maharaj Ji during his last days—particularly Pundit Lal Chand, Prof. Jagmohan Lal, Dr Hazara Singh, Gandhi Ram, Bibi Ralli, Rai Sahib Munshi Ram, and Bhai Shadi. He questioned them closely about the will. Their accounts were convincing and there was no reason to doubt that Sardar Bahadur Ji had appointed him his successor.

A day or two later Rai Sahib Munshi Ram went to Maharaj Ji to have a bank cheque signed. He told Maharaj Ji that the bank accounts had been converted by Sardar Bahadur Ji several months before into joint accounts to be signed by

·"either or survivor." Maharaj Ji then remembered the forms he had been asked to sign.

The Dera officials and senior satsangis chose 4 November 1951 as the day for the formal installation of Maharaj Charan Singh Ji as Satguru. Maharaj Ji then went to Sirsa for a few days, returning to the Dera on November 2. The day before the ceremony, Sardar Bachint Singh, Maharaj Ji's uncle, told him that during the ceremony he would present Soami Ji's turban to him and bow at his feet. Maharaj Ji repeatedly asked his uncle not to bow before him; he could not tolerate the idea of his uncle bowing at his feet, for he greatly respected him, not only as the eldest member of the family, but also as a close disciple of Baba Ji Maharaj. Sardar Bachint Singh on his part insisted that though from the point of view of worldly relations Sardar Charan Singh was his nephew, now he was in fact his Satguru and the form of both Baba Ji Maharaj and Maharaj Sawan Singh Ji: "You are no longer my nephew, you are the manifest form of my beloved Satguru. It is my duty and privilege to bow at your holy feet."

On 4 November 1951, a large crowd gathered in the afternoon for the ceremony, and the satsang hall compound was filled to capacity. On this occasion, Baba Pratap Singh of Bhaini Sahib, Baba Deva Singh of Taran-Taran, the spiritual heads from Sri Ramdas Sahib and Sarai Rohilla, and a few other holy men were present. At 2:00 P.M., Babu Gulab Singh gave a satsang on a hymn from Soami Ji's *Sar Bachan*. I then read Sardar Bahadur Ji's will and tried to express to the sangat my impressions of the new Master as a man of seriousness, charity, and great humility—qualities he possessed even as a child. I also related a few incidents from Maharaj Ji's childhood that showed that the Great Master had intended him for this task even then. Babu Gulab Singh spoke again, paying tribute to Sardar Bahadur Maharaj Ji. Then he humbly asked Maharaj Charan Singh to accept the responsibility of the mastership and, in obedience to Sardar Bahadur Ji's command, to guide the satsangis and give them his blessings.

Maharaj Ji came to the dais, bowed in humility, and took his seat. The Master spoke a few emotion-laden words to the sangat. The following is a direct translation from the original:

My love for Hazur Maharaj Ji, the commands of Sardar Bahadur Maharaj Ji, and the affection of the sangat compel me to carry out the wishes of Sardar Bahadur Ji to serve the sangat and the Dera. But when I look at myself and my shortcomings, I feel diffident and find myself unable to decide whether I am really fit for these onerous duties. This struggle has prevented me so far from meeting the sangat, for which I ask your forgiveness.

I wish to tell the sangat quite frankly that I do not make any claims whatsoever to spiritual attainments. I do not find in myself even those excellences that a good satsangi should possess.

I had the good fortune of being at the feet of Hazur Maharaj Ji and of serving him during the last days of his illness, but Sardar Bahadur Ji did not afford me even this privilege. I am so unlucky that I reached here only after his cremation and could not even have his last darshan.

These orders were communicated to me by those fortunate devoted satsangis who were near Sardar Bahadur Ji, and I have no choice but to serve the Dera and the sangat according to his orders. I request the sangat to look upon me as their younger brother and thus help me in serving them and this great institution. If the sangat looks upon me in any other light, it would mean that you do not wish to support and cooperate with me, and that would be doing a great injustice to me.

The passing away of Sardar Bahadur Ji has been a great shock to all of us. We had not yet got over the grief and sorrow caused by Hazur Maharaj Ji's departure when Sardar Bahadur Ji has also left us. Such personalities rarely come into this world. Only a great and highly advanced soul could lead such an immaculate, spotless life, free from all personal motives. We should not become dispirited nor feel helpless in this hour of our calamity, but should try to follow with confidence and firmness the path of Surat Shabd Yoga pointed out to us by Hazur Maharaj Ji and Sardar Bahadur Ji. Hazur Maharaj Ji used to say that he is always with everyone. This assurance stands for all of us and not for me alone. I request all devoted sevadars of the Dera to faithfully carry out whatever duties he had entrusted to them.

The sangat has assembled from far and near to do homage and pay their respects to Sardar Bahadur Maharaj Ji, and for this I thank you with all my heart.

I repeat today before the entire sangat what I said yesterday to a group of devoted satsangis whom I had called for the purpose, namely, that I do not consider myself worthy of putting on the turban of such great Saints. But, compelled by the sangat's love and faith in Hazur Maharaj Ji, I have submitted myself to the sangat, and the sangat can do as they see fit.

Maharaj Ji's sad but serene voice and his words of love and humility deeply moved the sangat. Many eyes were filled with tears.

After the speech, Maharaj Ji's uncle, Sardar Bachint Singh, wrapped around Maharaj Ji the shawl Soami Ji had given to Baba Ji, and presented him with the turban that had been worn by all the Masters of the Dera at the time of their formal installation as the Master. Maharaj Ji reverently touched the turban to his forehead and tied it around his head. Sardar Bachint Singh then bowed to Maharaj Ji, and so did the rest of the sangat, all greeting the new Master with "Radha Soami." Tears were streaming down Maharaj Ji's cheeks, but his face was shining with a spiritual splendour.

My very first meeting with the new Master convinced me that Sardar Bahadur Maharaj Ji had entrusted the work of liberating souls to a person of great spiritual stature. One day, when I tried to express these sentiments to Maharaj Ji, he said, "The joy of living as a slave at the feet of the King of kings, where is that joy in becoming the Master? The chance I had of living at his feet was an incomparable blessing. The bliss of devotion and service to the Satguru cannot be found in the responsibilities of mastership. Had Sardar Bahadur Ji or Hazur Maharaj Ji given me any option, I would have refused to accept this position. My Master was truly great and merciful. If I had had my wish, I would have simply remained one of his obscure devotees all my life."

Hearing these words of devotion and humility, I wanted to ask, "Is 'the true slave of the Lord not like the Lord himself'?[1] Has my Great Master not transformed you into his own divine form? Have the Master and slave not become one?" But overwhelmed with my own emotions, I could not speak and came out of the room.

A few weeks after Maharaj Ji became the Master, some of the politicians who had asked him to run for political office two months earlier came to the Dera to tell him how pleased they were to learn that he was the Satguru of the Radha Soamis. They said, "Now that you are in this position, we want

---

[1]   *Adi Granth*, Maru, M.5, p. 1076.

you to instruct your followers to vote as a block for our party." Maharaj Ji replied that he was unable to give such directions, for "my relationship with the sangat is purely spiritual; it has nothing to do with politics. Every satsangi is free to decide his political views for himself. I am sorry, I cannot interfere in this matter."

Maharaj Charan Singh gave his first satsang at the monthly satsang in February 1952, speaking on a shabd of Tulsi Sahib, "Cleanse thy heart's chamber for the Beloved to come." His soft and sweet voice was inspiring, and his lucid exposition convincing. The sangat felt blessed to hear his beautiful discourse. Bhai Shadi in particular was moved, his face glowing with enthusiasm and delight.

Maharaj Ji had not yet begun to give initiation, though a number of seekers had been making requests for Nam and a few of the older, respected satsangis had asked him to begin initiating. In March 1953, an American lady, Mrs Kinzinger, came to the Dera. Moved by Maharaj Ji's darshan and satsang, she begged for initiation. Maharaj Ji granted her request on 10 April 1953, and then on 5 June 1953 he also initiated three members of the family of Mr K. L. Khanna, who was later to be secretary at the Dera: his mother, Mrs Khanna; his wife, Mrs Satyawati Khanna; and his son, Jitendra Khanna. However, these four initiations were exceptions, for Maharaj Ji had not yet begun general initiations.

The anniversary of Sardar Bahadur Maharaj Ji's death was celebrated at a bhandara on Sunday, 25 October 1953, with an unusually large number of people in attendance. After Maharaj Ji's forceful, one-and-a-half-hour discourse, Babu Gulab Singh, a highly venerated satsangi of Baba Ji Maharaj, rose and asked permission to speak. He said: "Several times I have begged Maharaj Ji to start giving initiation to the many souls thirsting for Nam. The entire sangat is eagerly awaiting that great day. The last time I was in Delhi, some devoted satsangis and seekers pressed me to appeal to you to begin initiations. Once again, Maharaj Ji, on behalf of the sangat and seekers, I humbly and respectfully implore you to open your treasure house and begin to bless seekers with initiation."

Babu Gulab Singh's words touched all of us deeply, especially the seekers, who were overjoyed to hear their feelings expressed so clearly. In the silence that followed, the atmosphere was heavy with anticipation. Finally, Maharaj Ji took the microphone and said:

> *As Babu Ji has said, he and other satsangis have been urging me to start giving Nam. Hazur Sardar Bahadur Ji also left instructions to that effect. I am a slave of the Master and his sangat ...*

Then, his voice choked with emotion, Maharaj Ji paused for a few moments. With tears in his eyes he tried again to speak, but overpowered by his feelings, he got up and left.

The next day, 26 October 1953, Hazur Maharaj Charan Singh Ji opened the floodgates of his grace and mercy and began to give initiation. At 9:00 A.M. he left his house, wearing the shawl that Sardar Bahadur Maharaj Ji had given him, and went into Baba Ji's room in the Great Master's house before proceeding to the satsang hall to initiate the seekers. The sangat stood on each side of the road waiting to have his darshan. When Maharaj Ji emerged from the Great Master's house, his face literally seemed to shine with radiance. He proceeded to the satsang hall and gave initiation to the seekers there. Initiations abroad, which had been suspended after Sardar Bahadur Ji's departure, were also resumed.

Mrs Amy Olivier, an elderly lady living in Durban, South Africa, had become interested in Sant Mat and had requested initiation from Sardar Bahadur Maharaj Ji. She was, however, told by the Master that it was not yet the time for her; her initiation would be arranged at the right time. In 1951, she wrote to the new Master, Maharaj Charan Singh, again asking for initiation. Maharaj Ji replied that he had not yet started initiating, and would inform her as soon as he did. On 26 October 1953, the day Maharaj Ji began to initiate, Mrs Olivier was reading in her room when a bright figure suddenly appeared before her and said, "Initiation has begun. You may come."

Mrs Olivier had not even seen a picture of the new Master, but the vision was so vivid that she was convinced that the magnetic form she saw was Maharaj Ji. She at once began preparing for the long journey, and within one week was on a steamer bound for India. Because of her hurry, she took her smallpox, cholera, and yellow fever inoculations all at once and therefore was ill during most of the voyage. She arrived at the Dera in good spirits in November 1953 and received initiation on 1 January 1954.

Satsang Tours

If we look at the lives of great Saints like Guru Nanak, Kabir, and Ravidas, we find that in spite of the limited means of transportation, they travelled widely, spreading the teachings of Sant Mat and initiating seekers. We have seen how the Great Master made satsang tours until he was eighty-eight years old, often suffering great inconvenience and discomfort. And in spite of his ill health, Sardar Bahadur Maharaj Ji also undertook many tours to give satsang, darshan, and initiation. Maharaj Charan Singh has not only maintained that tradition in India but has even toured abroad, literally around the world, taking the teachings to many countries that have no record of a perfect Saint ever having visited them before.

Although Maharaj Ji did not make a foreign tour until 1961, he began his tours in India a few months after taking up the responsibilities of mastership. Visiting Dalhousie for a break from the heat of the plains in the summer of 1952, he travelled on to mountainous areas nearby to give satsang. Earlier, Maharaj Ji had given one satsang in Amritsar in March 1952, his first satsang outside the Dera. There was a record gathering of satsangis and seekers, and the open compound of the satsang hall was packed to capacity. Maharaj Ji gave two satsangs in Delhi in November 1953, this being his first satsang tour to Delhi. The satsangs were held in the open grounds under *shamiyanas* (canopies), and the gathering was over fifteen thousand.

Bakshi Maluk Chand Ji, an old disciple of the Great Master, narrates an interesting incident of Maharaj Ji's first visit to Delhi in early 1950s:

Maharaj Ji sent for me and said, "An old satsangi of Baba Ji Maharaj, Bhai Narayan Das Ji, lives here in Delhi. Please go and tell him I will visit him tomorrow at 4:00 P.M."

I knew Bhai Narayan Das and used to meet him quite often. I went to his house that very day. When I knocked at his door, he called out, "Come in, Bakshi Ji." I was amazed, and after entering I asked how he knew I was the one knocking at his door. He did not answer my question, but instead asked me to deliver the message I had brought. I knew that he was an advanced soul and spent most of his time now in meditation, so I asked, "Bhai Sahib, tell me, how did you know I was the one at your door and also that I have a message for you?"

*At first Bhai Narayan Das tried to avoid answering
my question. When I pressed him, he finally said that
the day before Baba Ji had appeared inside and said,
"Narayan Das, I will come to you in the physical form
the day after tomorrow at 4:00 P.M."*

*After hearing this I gave him Maharaj Ji's message.
He seemed surprisingly happy and thanked me again
and again for bringing him such a happy message. I protested, "Why thank me when you already had the message?" He replied, "When the inner message of the Satguru is confirmed outside, it is natural to feel joyous."*

*I was present the next day when Maharaj Ji visited
this aged disciple of Baba Ji Maharaj; Maharaj Ji stayed
with him for half an hour. The whole time Bhai Narayan Das gazed fixedly at him, obviously beside himself
with joy, for the Master had come in the physical body
to meet him.*

Maharaj Ji's first long tour of India was in November 1955,
when he held satsangs in Saharanpur, Dehra Dun, Kanpur,
Lucknow, Pisawah, and Delhi. This was followed by Maharaj
Ji's visit to Bombay, Sangli, Indore, Ratlam, Dewas, and Devli.
While in Bombay, from December 2 to 7, Maharaj Ji also gave
satsangs at Kalyan and Chembur. From Bombay he went to
Indore, giving satsangs at Ratlam and Dewas on December
14, and at Devli on December 15; he gave satsangs at Indore
from December 16 to 18. Driving a distance of over three hundred miles, giving satsangs at Ujjain and Shivpuri, and
darshan at the villages of Kanasia and Bilawali on the way,
Maharaj Ji reached Gwalior on the night of December 19.
Here Maharaj Ji gave two satsangs on December 20 and 21,
and arrived back at the Dera on December 23, where the heavy
schedule of Baba Ji's bhandara awaited him.

Two incidents on this long tour remind us that though the outward form of the Masters changes from successor to successor, the Masters are in reality all one. It is interesting that the incident in connection with Maharaj Ji's visit to Dehra Dun involves Dr (Miss) Sinha, who had experienced the oneness of the Masters when she sought initiation from the Great Master but finally received it from Sardar Bahadur Maharaj Ji.[1]

In 1949, Miss Sinha's mother, who was not in very good health, suddenly came from Calcutta to Lucknow, where Miss Sinha was working as a professor in the local college. She told her daughter, "I am going to Beas to have darshan of your Satguru." Since there was to be a college holiday, Miss Sinha said, "Why don't you wait for three days and we'll go together?" The day before they were to leave, however, her mother became so ill that she could not travel to see Sardar Bahadur Maharaj Ji. Deeply distressed, Miss Sinha went on to Beas by herself and told Sardar Bahadur Ji how bad she felt at having detained her mother and thus having deprived her of the Master's darshan: "Maharaj Ji, I will feel consoled if you accept my mother as one of your chosen souls."

With great compassion Sardar Bahadur Maharaj Ji replied, "Very well. Don't worry, from today Maharaj Ji will take care of her soul as one of his own." Still not reassured, Miss Sinha said, "Maharaj Ji, mother is old and probably will not be able to come to Beas. Pray, grant her the blessing that she have your darshan in this birth." Sardar Bahadur Ji answered, "Yes, rest assured, in this very birth she will have the Satguru's darshan. He will himself go to her and give darshan."

As it happened, her mother could not go to Beas, and Sardar Bahadur Maharaj Ji passed away in 1951. In 1955, on his first long tour, Maharaj Charan Singh Ji visited Dehra

---

[1]   See the account of Miss Sinha's initiation in Chapter Three.

Dun, where Miss Sinha's mother was staying with one of her daughters. Miss Sinha, who was working in Delhi at the time, heard of Maharaj Ji's visit and caught the night train to Dehra Dun in order to ask the Master to make a special visit to her mother. She approached Maharaj Ji just before satsang, but before she could speak to him, the Master turned to Mr Bhargava, the secretary of the Dehra Dun satsang and said, "Tell Miss Sinha my programme for today." Mr Bhargava told her, "At 11:00 A.M. Maharaj Ji has scheduled a visit to your sister's house to meet your mother." Maharaj Ji then commented, "You see, sister, it was not necessary for you to come all the way from Delhi." Then Miss Sinha remembered Sardar Bahadur Ji's promise, and with tears in her eyes she bowed to the Master in gratitude.

The other incident from this 1955 tour occurred in Devli, a village where today 90 percent of the inhabitants are satsangis. Devli is located about forty-five miles from Indore but is difficult to reach because the last ten miles must be travelled through the fields by jeep.[1] The Great Master had gone to Devli in 1939, giving satsang from December 13 to 15. When the Great Master was about to leave, the sangat was in tears, and four leading satsangis implored him to visit their village again. The Great Master said, "Don't be dejected. The Satguru is always with you. I am pleased with you and I will visit your village again, not once but twice."

The Great Master was not able to go to Devli, however, and left the world in April 1948. The four satsangis of Devli not only were miserable at the loss of their Satguru, as we all were, but also were perplexed at his not fulfilling his promise. They did not talk about it to others, but felt greatly shaken.

---

[1] Now a regular paved road connects Devli with the main highway, but in the fifties, the Devli satsangis cut a path through their fields for the Master's jeep to pass.

In December 1955, when Maharaj Charan Singh Ji made
his programme for visiting Indore, he said that he would also
go to Devli for satsang. He arrived in Devli and gave satsang
on 15 December 1955. It was on 15 December in 1939 that the
Great Master had promised to visit Devli again. During the
satsang, some older satsangis were thrilled to see the present
Master's form changing into that of the Great Master. When
he scheduled another visit to Devli in December 1956, the village sangat was touched deeply. Their faith in the Satguru was
also strengthened, for they realized the oneness of the Masters. It is truly as Baba Ji said when he made the Great Master
his successor: "A sugar cube dissolves in water, and though
the appearance of the water remains the same, its taste is quite
different." In the same way the Satguru becomes one with his
successor, imparting his power to him so that though the successor looks the same outwardly, inwardly he is one with his
Master.

Maharaj Ji's schedule on that 1955 tour did not allow time
anywhere for giving initiation, but in response to the earnest
prayers of the seekers, he promised to initiate on his next visit.
In December 1956, Maharaj Ji went to Bombay and Indore
for satsang and gave initiation at both places. These were the
first initiations granted by him outside the Dera. During his
1955 and 1956 tours to Indore, Maharaj Ji gave satsang at the
place where the Great Master had stayed during his 1933 visit.

In Indore, during Maharaj Ji's 1956 visit, a satsangi asked
the secretary there for an interview with the Master, but the
secretary informed him that the time for interviews was over.
The man repeatedly asked the secretary and the organizers,
but was told that it was not possible. Then, on the last day,
while giving parshad to the sevadars, Maharaj Ji told the local secretary to bring anyone still wanting an interview. The
satsangi was led into Maharaj Ji's presence and had two or

three minutes with him. When he came out of his interview, the man's eyes were filled with tears and he looked intoxicated with happiness. He told the secretary that he had been initiated twelve years before by the Great Master and, by the Master's grace, had made good progress inside. But then a few years later he committed a sin, and access to the Master within was withdrawn. He said he had spent ten years in great mental restlessness and anguish. He concluded, "Today when I bowed at the Satguru's feet and begged for his forgiveness, his grace returned, my inner eye opened, and the Shabd began to ring within once again."

Maharaj Ji's directions were (and are even today) that there should be no publicity for his satsangs, and the orders were carried out. Yet one fails to comprehend how and from where large numbers gather for his satsangs. In 1955/56 there were hardly three hundred satsangis in Bombay, but in the satsangs the attendance would be no less than five thousand.

From the beginning of those long tours in 1955 until 1961, Maharaj Ji travelled to some sixty cities each year between September and April. He held satsang, granted interviews, and after 1956 gave initiation in almost all the cities he visited. These tours were demanding, exacting, and exhausting —as all who have travelled with the Master know.

In 1962 Maharaj Ji decided to change his approach to touring within India. Sant Mat teachings had spread all over India as a result of his extensive touring for six or seven years. Now, rather than visiting so many small towns and villages each year, he decided to confine his tours to one or two large satsang centres in each state, to which people could come from nearby villages and towns. In this way he could reach satsangis and seekers in various parts of the country, each year giving initiation and satsang for four or five days in each centre. Accordingly, cities, towns, and (in some cases) villages were made satsang centres. These included Delhi, Bombay, Madras, Calcutta, Tatanagar, Nagpur, Indore, Sangli, Jaipur, Ajmer, Sidhpur, Sikanderpur (Sirsa), and a few other towns in India. A *langar* is organized in many of the centres, where food is served to the sangat free of cost. Wherever langar facilities are not provided, food is served in *bhojan bhandars* at the nominal cost of about half a rupee. Land was purchased in these centres, satsang halls built, and all the other necessary facilities constructed—brick sheds for the sangat to stay in, kitchens, bathrooms, water tanks, pipelines, etc.

The consolidated tour programme did turn out to be a more efficient arrangement, but it did not make Maharaj Ji's schedule less demanding, for he still had to travel to thirty or forty different places each year to cover the major centres as well as some smaller centres.

Clearly, a great deal of work goes into organizing the satsang programmes and meeting the needs of the large crowds that come. For example, when Sikanderpur, the location of Maharaj Ji's family farm, became a satsang centre for the state of Haryana, some twenty-five to thirty thousand people had to be accommodated during Maharaj Ji's visits there twice a year. In the beginning, the entire cost of the satsangs was met by Maharaj Ji's family. Under Maharaj Ji's overall guidance, his brother Capt. Purshottam Singh personally supervised the construction of a free kitchen (the langar), a tube well and storage tank, buildings to house the sangat, and the satsang hall, which were built on a nine-acre plot of land from the family farm, donated to the sangat. Maharaj Ji and his family continue to supply most of the wheat, flour, pulse, and vegetables for the langar as well as to accommodate and serve many satsangis who come there for satsang. The Sikanderpur satsang has developed very fast. The size of the gathering now reaches forty thousand, most of the people coming from Haryana and Rajasthan. More land has been donated by Maharaj Ji and his family to meet the growing requirements of the sangat.

Practically every year during the months of August, September, and October, Maharaj Ji visits the hill regions of Punjab, Himachal, and Kangra for satsang. These tours include small towns and villages like Bhota, Sujanpur Tehra, Mandi, Parore, Palampur, Una, and Kalu-ki-Bar. Whenever Maharaj Ji visits Srinagar, Dalhousie, or Mussoorie during the summer months, he gives satsang there every Sunday. After the creation of Pakistan, the hill sangat of Kalabagh, Abbotabad, and other mountain regions came and settled in India in Pinjore, Kalka, and some of the towns of the Simla Hills. In order to give satsang and darshan to them, Maharaj Ji also gives satsangs at Simla and Chandigarh. In Chandigarh the gathering at satsang reaches fifty thousand. In Simla, satsangis and seekers from nearby hill towns like Solan, Singian, Dharampur, Barog, Kandaghat, Uchaghat, Salogan, Subathu, and Chail, and from many tiny hamlets situated in the interior portions of the hills, come down to attend the satsang.

Once, during one of Maharaj Ji's visits to Simla, a few men from Kotgarh, a small hill village about sixty miles away, suggested that Maharaj Ji take a sightseeing trip to their village. Maharaj Ji accepted the invitation and visited Kotgarh for a few hours. During his next visit to Simla in 1966, Maharaj Ji gave one satsang in Kotgarh. The orthodox but simple and pure-minded hill people readily accepted the teachings, and as a result of that one satsang many of them started coming to Simla and the Dera for satsang and initiation.

In October 1968, Maharaj Ji again visited Kotgarh. Situated about nine thousand feet above sea level, Kotgarh had early snow, and the day Maharaj Ji was to arrive it had snowed heavily. Reminiscent of some of the Great Master's tours to remote areas, Maharaj Ji and the party had to walk the last two and a half miles because the road had become impassable due to snow and mud. Maharaj Ji gave three satsangs in Kotgarh and initiated 210 seekers. Just minutes before the initiation began, 3 seekers arrived from a village situated on the Tibetan border. They had walked almost eighty miles through heavy snow because they had heard that a great Mahatma was coming to Kotgarh. Maharaj Ji initiated them along with the others.

Indeed, as we have heard, everything that the Master does has a deep spiritual purpose behind it. Originally he had gone to Kotgarh for a sightseeing trip of a few hours; but actually he was on the mission of collecting his flock for the Father. The hill folk drawn by him began to come for his satsangs in Simla and begged for a satsang in their own village also. Today there are over fifteen hundred satsangis in Kotgarh, and a large number from the Kotgarh area come to Dera every winter for initiation.

The people of Kotgarh and nearby areas had been deeply steeped in rituals and ceremonies. Superstitions, idol worship, and the practice of animal sacrifice prevailed, and caste prejudices had a firm hold on their minds. In such a place, Maharaj Ji boldly explained the teachings of the Saints. His simple discourses appealed to the people and his magnetic personality drew them to the path.

During the last twenty years Maharaj Ji has visited almost all corners of the country. As a result of his strenuous tours, there is perhaps no city in India where at least a few satsangis are not found. After the partition of India some satsangis went and settled in Calcutta. At their request Maharaj Ji began to visit Calcutta also. During the last fifteen years he has made about ten visits to Calcutta and a few Bengali families have come to the path.

In 1964, when Maharaj Ji visited Calcutta—at that time a centre of political upheaval—it was once again embroiled in riots, and there was much gunfire throughout the city. On his way to satsang, Maharaj Ji's car was hit by a bullet. Not surprisingly, the driver panicked, but Maharaj Ji reassured him and told him to drive on to satsang. Gunfire could be heard during the entire satsang; however, Maharaj Ji delivered his one-and-a-half-hour discourse completely unperturbed, and his tranquillity permeated the sangat, quieting their fears.

Like the Great Master and Sardar Bahadur Ji, Maharaj Ji has great regard for the sangat of Ghuman, the village of Baba Ji's birth. He visits Ghuman twice a year, and along with satsangis from Dera and neighbouring places, the entire village gathers to attend the satsang. Although Baba Ji's house is maintained in its original shape, a large, modern satsang hall has been built at Ghuman under Maharaj Ji's direction.

Maharaj Ji has also paid attention to Mehmansinghwala, the Great Master's home village. Baba Ji sometimes used to go to Mehmansinghwala to meet the Great Master's family members and to give satsang there. The Great Master also used to visit his village, but he probably never gave satsangs there.

Mehmansinghwala, fourteen miles from Ludhiana, now has a population of about one thousand. The villagers, traditionally brave and courageous, have always shown preference for military service and have an excellent record of valour and courage during the two World Wars. But they had little interest in Sant Mat. In Baba Ji's time only ten to fifteen persons used to attend the satsangs, out of whom the majority were the Great Master's family members. The villagers regarded the Great Master as a respected elder relation and citizen, but did not concern themselves with his teachings. During the times of Baba Ji and the Great Master, the villagers of Mehman-singhwala, as well as the neighbouring villagers of Raipur and Narangwal, even felt annoyed and repelled by the words "Radha Soami."

Hazur Maharaj Charan Singh Ji decided to hold satsangs at Mehmansinghwala. Surprisingly enough, almost all the villagers attended his first satsang in Mehmansinghwala. They were impressed by the gathering of more than twenty thousand people from the surrounding areas and the thirty or so Western guests from the Dera. It was a matter of pride for them that a man from their village had acquired such distinction. Maharaj Ji gave a powerful discourse on a hymn from the Adi Granth, and the people listened in rapt attention. Still, the villagers understood little of the significance of Sant Mat and were not really interested in the teachings. After the satsang they came to meet Maharaj Ji as a kinsman and fellow villager, and he greeted them appropriately— bowing respectfully to the senior villagers, as one does in India to elders, and displaying affection towards equals. It was like the homecoming of a family member who had been away for a long time.

During this visit Maharaj Ji and his family members donated all their agricultural lands in the village to the satsang. The Great Master's house has been repaired, but it is maintained as it was during his time. Maharaj Ji started giving satsang twice a year in Mehmansinghwala and gradually the people there began to feel attracted to Sant Mat. To the ones who requested initiation, Maharaj Ji said, "If you want initiation, come to Beas." Over the years many of them have since come to the Dera and received initiation.

But even though they regularly attended the satsangs, the people of Mehmansinghwala would not assist in making the necessary arrangements, choosing to remain as guests and spectators. A few years back, just before Hazur was to visit Mehmansinghwala, it rained heavily and the unmetalled roads of the village were rendered undrivable. The trucks carrying the tents had to be stopped a mile outside the village. The difficult approach through the waterlogged streets made it inconvenient to set up the satsang, and it was suggested that the programme be cancelled. Hazur said, "If the people of Mehmansinghwala want the programme to be cancelled, then do so; otherwise do not cancel it."

Meanwhile, the people of a neighbouring village, Narangwal, volunteered to pitch the tents in their village, so the satsang could be held there. Seeing this, the people of Mehmansingwala became enthused, and the whole village came out to repair the approach road. An old dilapidated structure belonging to a villager was pulled down at his request and its debris was used to pave the streets. The road was completed in two days and the satsang was held as scheduled. It was attended by about a hundred thousand people. All arrangements were perfect and the people of the village cooperated to such an extent that they even opened their homes so the sangat could stay comfortably.

Today, as a result of Maharaj Ji's extensive tours, his lucid and forceful discourses, and his loving personality, Sant Mat has spread to almost every part of India. There are thousands of places in India where satsangs are held every week. There are 271 centres that have their own satsang hall or land for satsang. In the face of orthodoxy and ritualism on the one hand and agnosticism on the other, Maharaj Ji has boldly presented the all-embracing teachings of the Saints in the simple, spoken language of the masses. Hundreds of thousands come to attend his discourses at the Dera and other centres, and about half a million have learned the method of inner spiritual practice and meditation from him.

At the base of this dissemination of spirituality is Maharaj Ji's untiring hard labour, his boundless love and grace, and his magnetic personality, which draws true seekers to him like moths to a flame. In fulfilling this great mission of mercy, Maharaj Charan Singh Ji has never spared himself; unmindful of strain and inconvenience, ignoring his own health, he has kept the torch of spirituality burning brightly. And in a world torn with strife and hostility, he has raised a voice of peace and tolerance.

A Significant Reform

Shortly after becoming the Master, Maharaj Ji brought about a basic and significant social reform at the Dera. Though it is no longer even legal in India, the caste system is still firmly entrenched. In this social system, people of the higher castes do not mix with people of the lowest caste, called untouchables. Food and water touched by them are considered polluted and unusable. The Radha Soami Masters have never made distinctions of caste, colour, race, or creed in the people they have initiated or associated with. Even in those early days, Baba Ji's satsangis included people of all castes, and he used to visit the "untouchables" and give satsangs in their houses. The Great Master had many disciples belonging to the lower castes, particularly in the Kangra Hills, and he used to visit their homes and bless them with his discourses. Sardar Bahadur Maharaj Ji also made no distinction of caste or colour, and freely associated with people of all castes.

Yet the deep-rooted social traditions and influences had their hold even on the minds of satsangis. They could not follow the example set by the Masters and continued to practice discrimination against the so-called untouchables. As a result, in the Dera, as at many other places, the sangat used to avoid taking their meals in the company of satsangis belonging to the lower castes. In the langar, "untouchables" would eat separately, away from the rest of the sangat, and in the hills they had a separate langar of their own.

Maharaj Ji decided to rid the sangat of this social evil, and at the July bhandara celebrating the Great Master's birthday, during the satsang he said to the sangat:

> I have been pondering over a serious problem which I want to discuss with you today. All Saints and all scriptures have agreed on one point: that God is the father of us all and that we are all his children, no matter what religion, caste, race, or country we belong to. God has no caste, creed, or country. Our souls are drops of the ocean of the Lord. If the ocean has no caste, how can the drop have any?
>
> God created man; man created the distinctions of castes and creeds and then entangled himself in them. When we leave this world, the Lord will not ask whether we are Hindu or Muslim, Christian or Jew, high caste or untouchable. As Paltu Sahib has said:
>
>> Of his high caste, O Paltu,
>> Let no one be proud;
>> Love alone counts
>> In the court of the Lord.
>
> God is within us all. If a man hates others, he hates God himself. If he looks upon another as low or untouchable, he is calling the Lord himself low and untouchable. The human body is the temple of the living

God; we must remember that the Lord resides in all, irrespective of colour or caste.

Among satsangis there should be no distinctions of caste. We are all brothers—children of the same Lord. I therefore request the sangat from today onwards not to make caste distinctions in the satsang or the langar. Those who persist in such narrow practices will derive little benefit from satsang. In the langar any satsangi who is neat and clean will have as much right to cook in the kitchen or eat in the common eating space as anyone else. Let those who want to do seva there go and serve the sangat. And let the whole sangat sit and eat together in a spirit of love and affection.

A few senior satsangis went to Maharaj Ji after satsang and expressed their misgivings about his decision, saying that the changes in the langar would cause a reaction and some people might stop coming to the Dera. Maharaj Ji was polite and affectionate towards them but firm in the position he had taken.

The following day Maharaj Ji visited the langar himself. He found that although the untouchables were seated in the same langar as everyone else, they were all huddled together a little apart from the rest of the sangat. It was clear that feelings of caste were still there. Seeing this, Maharaj Ji went and sat down among the untouchables. Several prominent Dera administrators, including Maharaj Ji's secretary Rai Sahib Munshi Ram, joined him and ate their lunch with the untouchables.

The next day Maharaj Ji invited all the Dera administrators, sevadars, and elder satsangis to his house for lunch. They included people of all religions and castes; all were seated together and were served the meal in a spirit of great love and respect by the members of the Master's family. Maharaj Ji gave everyone parshad with his own hands.

By his personal, loving example, Maharaj Ji brought about a social revolution at the Dera. Today sixty thousand or more people sit together in the free langar and eat without any awareness of caste. Likewise, satsangis of all castes lovingly prepare the chapattis, dal, and vegetables served in the langar. This influence has reached the sangats outside the Dera as well, and even in the most conservative areas, such as the mountainous Kangra district, a single langar feeds the sangat; no one even bothers to ask anybody's caste.

Tours Abroad

Saints do not come to the world for any particular race, creed, or country, nor are they emotionally attached to any one of them. Social and geopolitical boundaries do not circumscribe their vision. Their love extends to all humanity—all classes, races, and nations are dear to them. Their message is for every human being who is longing to meet the Lord. Their flock includes sheep of many colours and many breeds, who soon learn to respond to the one sound of their voice—the call of love.

The Great Master used to say that Sant Mat has yet to spread in America, Europe, and the rest of the world. American satsangis, anxious to see their Master in his physical form, used to request that the Great Master visit America. But the long sea voyage involved in a trip to the United States, and Hazur's own health and age, would not permit him to undertake a tour abroad.

As narrated earlier, the seed of Sant Mat was sown in the West in 1911, when the American couple, Dr and Mrs Brock, came to the path. Yet until 1953, when Maharaj Charan Singh Ji began initiating, there were only 272 satsangis outside India. As a result of persistent entreaties from the sangat abroad, and in order to meet satsangis in their home towns and bring them in closer contact with the living Master, Maharaj Ji consented to visit various countries in the East and West.

From 1961 to 1971, the Master undertook seven tours abroad. As a result of these long and strenuous tours, there is a sizable sangat in America, Europe, the United Kingdom, South Africa, the Far East, and the Middle East. Even in small countries like Holland and New Zealand there are over one hundred satsangis, and new seekers are regularly coming to the path.

During one of his tours abroad, someone asked the Master how many languages he knew. In his simple and affectionate manner, the Master replied, "Brother, I know only one language, and that is the language of love."

Carrying the message of the Saints in this language of love, Maharaj Ji undertook tours of countries where, in known history, no other perfect Master has set foot. The soft breeze of love and grace that had brought joy to thousands from various parts of this country, now crossed the shores of India to transcend all physical barriers of country, creed, and race, and bring light and solace to seekers of Truth.

In Mexico, a prominent lady said to the Master, "I am very grateful to you that you have come all the way from your country to visit my country." The Master replied affectionately, "Sister, I belong to all countries and all countries are mine."

After his brief visits of a few days, whenever the Master would leave a country, the satsangis and seekers would feel as if a close friend, a dear companion, was taking leave of them. The Saints have never accepted the barriers of any country's borders as a barrier to their message and their love. Today, in almost all countries of the world, there are disciples of the Master.

Nations have been enemies of one another, but not the Master's disciples belonging to them. The white citizens of South Africa, forgetting their feelings of distinction, come to Dera and live with their Indian brother disciples with affection, and serve the sangat with them. A few years back, the relations between the Arab countries and Israel were strained. Several satsangis from both countries were present at the same time in the Dera. They stayed together with great affection, and on their return journey happened to be on the same train to Delhi. They were conversing like close friends and, as Delhi was approaching, they expressed the hope that some day they would again have the good fortune of being together. When their co-passengers learned that they belonged to two countries hostile to each other, they were amazed to see their mutual amity and good will.

Maharaj Ji gave instructions to all representatives and secretaries abroad not to carry out any propaganda or publicity about his visits, either through television and radio or through newspapers, posters, and leaflets. If necessary, a simple announcement giving information about the time and place of satsang could be placed in the local newspapers. These instructions were strictly followed, yet the attendance at the satsangs everywhere was remarkable. In some small centres where there were only fifteen or twenty disciples, the gatherings at satsang were over one thousand. The Saints have their own ways of drawing their marked sheep.

1961: FAR EAST
Maharaj Ji's first tour abroad was to the Far East—Sri Lanka, Burma, Vietnam, Thailand, Singapore, Hong Kong, the Philippines, and Japan. The Master followed the same demanding schedule on this tour as on later tours abroad—busy from morning till night giving satsang, darshan, private interviews,

and initiations. He also gave a few satsangs in Punjabi for the benefit of the Indian satsangis and seekers who were living in these countries. Maharaj Ji left Dera on 8 May 1961 via Delhi and Bombay, with Mr R. N. Mehta accompanying him as his tour secretary, and returned to the Dera on 18 July 1961, in time for the July bhandara.

1962: MIDDLE EAST, EUROPE, UNITED KINGDOM

For almost a decade, the sangats of the United Kingdom and Europe had been asking Maharaj Ji to pay a visit to their countries. But his preoccupation with Dera organization and expansion, and the heavy schedule of tours in India, did not allow him to be away from the Dera for a long tour abroad. At the end of 1961, a group of satsangis from the United Kingdom who had come to the Dera formed themselves into a joint deputation to once again make the request. Maharaj Ji, aware of their keen desire and their need to come in closer contact with the Master, decided to undertake a journey to the United Kingdom and Europe.

Wherever Maharaj Ji went, he left a deep impact on those who came in contact with him. Even non-satsangis, casual passersby, were left looking at his beauty and majesty in awe. Mrs Bea Jauncey, who accompanied the Master on this trip, narrates as an example a small incident during the Master's visit to one of the cities of Italy. Maharaj Ji was walking on a footpath followed by Professor Puri, Mrs Jauncey, and another satsangi lady. A man coming from the opposite direction saw Maharaj Ji from a distance and started gazing at him. When he came near, with eyes still fixed on the Master's face, he kept on walking and bumped into Mrs Jauncey, almost knocking her down. Without turning to look at her but pointing to Maharaj Ji, he said, "Sorry, he is responsible for this."

And the satsangis, many of whom had so far not seen any of the Dera Masters, were thrilled to meet Maharaj Charan Singh Ji. It was a rare blessing to meet the Master in his physical form, and although they had seen his photographs, they soon realized that no camera could ever catch his gracious smile, his kind and loving eyes, and his majestic bearing, nor could words ever describe the feeling of elation and elevation his physical presence inspired.

On 19 April 1962, Maharaj Ji left the Dera for this tour, accompanied by Prof. Janak Puri. In addition to England, the Master travelled to Iran, Lebanon, Turkey, Switzerland, Germany, France, and Sweden, holding satsangs in each country.

After spending a little over two weeks with the satsangis and seekers in the Middle East and Europe, Maharaj Ji arrived in London on Friday, June 8, at 10:45 A.M. About 50 satsangis were present at the airport to receive him. After greeting them with an affectionate "Radha Soami" and a loving smile, Maharaj Ji gave darshan to a sangat of over 250 in a nearby hall. Although Friday was a working day, the hall was packed. It was a thrilling and inspiring scene—all eyes were fixed on the Master's face, not a word was spoken, but hearts were overflowing with love. The twenty minutes of darshan were for them moments of silent communion, filling them with an ineffable bliss. Later, describing her feelings that day, a lady said that she felt "surrounded and enveloped by a love that is altogether beyond human imagination."

After this first darshan in the United Kingdom, Maharaj Ji went with A.V.M. Kundan Sondhi to his flat, which was to serve as the Master's residence during his stay in London. Maharaj Ji's effort was to meet as many satsangis and seekers as possible, individually or in groups. This meant a heavy pressure on his time; and whenever he was at the Sondhis' apartment, a stream of seekers and satsangis continued to come.

From June 9 until the twenty-sixth, Maharaj Ji graced London and the surrounding area with his darshan and gave satsangs in both English and Punjabi. After his English satsangs Maharaj Ji had question-answer sessions which proved both instructive and interesting, and at times Maharaj Ji revealed an unusual sense of recognition and understanding, which brought the sangat closer to him. An instance is given by a satsangi from Swaziland. "Having had severe toothache just before the Master's arrival in England, I asked him whether satsangis should take aspirin or other medicine for the alleviation of pain. Maharaj Ji replied, 'You asked that question before in a letter which I have not yet had time to answer.' This was true, but until that moment I had forgotten having asked this, as the letter had been written more than three months previously. Yet the Master, who receives more than 150 letters daily, about 4,000 between the first and second asking of this question, not only remembered the inquiry but also the person who had asked it, whom he was physically meeting for the first time. This so staggered me that I nearly missed the answer! Maharaj Ji continued that there was nothing against taking aspirin or other medicine. If they relieved the pain, they were meant to do so, but if the pain was written in one's karma and was therefore inescapable, no medicine on earth would be effective."

In any spare time he had, the Master visited as many private homes as possible. The tour organizers were soon exhausted, but Maharaj Ji somehow remained always fresh and buoyant. In order to meet more informally with a smaller group of satsangis, Maharaj Ji accepted a request to attend a tea at a satsangi's house outside London. When Maharaj Ji arrived, the organizer of the party said, "Maharaj Ji, four seekers who could not reach London in time for the initiation are here today and are very anxious to be initiated."

Maharaj Ji smiled and said, "Brother, I can do only one thing or the other—we can have the tea party or the initiation, but there is no time for both."

The satsangi replied, "Just seeing you here is enough for us. If it is proper, perhaps you could give initiation to these seekers." Thus instead of a tea party, the satsangis who were present, after a quick cup of tea with the Master, enjoyed the quiet and serenity of the initiation. (Among those initiated was Mrs Dorothy Hoare, the mother of Sir Frederick Hoare, the Lord Mayor of London.)

The effect of this tour on satsangis in the countries the Master visited was tremendous. Three letters received at the Dera capture some of this impact:

My Beloved Satguru—Radha Soami. I am writing this short letter just to thank you for your kindness and benevolence. I have lately witnessed a strange incident. Whether it would appear strange to you or not I cannot say. You would remember my having told you here one morning after the satsang that during the satsang I had noticed you had assumed a different form. At that time I could not identify the form as that of any Saint, but seeing a photograph today I realized that it resembled that of Soami Ji Maharaj. This morning after meditation, I read in a book that Soami Ji Maharaj had departed from this world at 2:00 P.M. on 15 June 1878. Thereupon I was reminded that you had visited us at 2:00 P.M. on 15 June 1962. There may be no relationship between these two events. I am merely mentioning them as an instance of a strange coincidence.

When you were last with us, we were overwhelmed by a sense of extreme happiness and peace of mind. One

evening, on the eve of your departure, when I said good-
bye to you after the satsang and you conferred upon me
the signal honour of allowing me to touch your hands, I
felt as if a bright light emanating from your person had
touched me and purged me of all my impurities. A sense
of extreme bliss and happiness came over me. I was con-
scious of this feeling long afterwards; in fact, I am still
under its influence and it has affected the course of my
life and thoughts: I cannot find the words to express and
thank you adequately for what you have done for me.

As you know, Hazur Maharaj Ji's visit to this country,
by which we feel honoured, has acquired historical im-
portance. Who knows but that it may be the first time
that a perfect Master has ever set foot on our soil, and
Hazur may be the first such Master. In any case, his visit
is an unforgettable event not only for this island but for
all those who were eagerly looking forward to it. Merely
to have the darshan of Hazur Maharaj Ji was a truly
wondrous experience. Even a man of my mean intelli-
gence could feel as if love personified stood before him.
He was radiating peace and benevolence all around and
we felt as if we were in the presence of God Almighty. It
is not easy to give expression to the glory of such rare
moments in one's life. When my eyes fell on his radiant
face for the first time, they filled with tears, and my heart
with pure love and joy.

After this memorable and, for the British sangat, historic
visit, the Master left London on June 26 for Spain, his last
port of call before returning to India. At the last satsang in
London, Colonel Sanders made a short speech thanking
Maharaj Ji for coming and for all his kindness. The Master's

reply was gracious and benevolent; he concluded it with the words: "The way is clear. Keep straight, for if you keep straight, the path also will be straight and easy."

Maharaj Ji left London on June 26 for Spain and, after a few more stops, arrived in Delhi on July 7. He gave darshan to the Delhi sangat before travelling to Sikanderpur. It was not until July 11, in the evening, that Hazur returned to the Dera. Anyone who has experienced the Master's absence from the Dera knows how dramatically the colony changes both when he leaves and when he returns.

The Master's visit to the United Kingdom and Europe was a deeply felt experience for the satsangis and seekers, an experience summed up by them thus: "We received the love of God, given to us in the full and overflowing measure by one of His devoted sons—our Satguru." And when he returned to the Dera after being away from us for twelve weeks, it was also a stirring experience for us. Our bodies had withered in the severe summer heat, and so too our hearts in separation from him. With the ambrosia of his satsangs he revived our spirits, and with his one look of love and compassion, with his one radiant smile, he brought new life and cheer to our wilting hearts.

1964: Far East, America, United Kingdom, Europe
The Saints disregard their own rest and comfort while fulfilling their divine mission. When we recollect how the Great Master and Sardar Bahadur Ji never spared themselves in the performance of their duties, and when we see how Maharaj Charan Singh Ji undertakes long and incredibly strenuous tours, we realize the meaning of the Great Master's words, "Toil and discomfort is the legacy of the Saints."

The year 1964 was a significant one for the American sangat. Maharaj Ji had already made tours abroad in 1961 and 1962, but he had not yet visited the Western country to which

Sant Mat had first spread in 1911—the United States. In 1962, when Maharaj Ji was in London, in the stream of visitors who daily came to see him were a number of Americans who had come over from the States, some from the faraway Pacific Coast, to renew in person their pressing invitation for him to visit America. Maharaj Ji agreed to come "in the summer of 1964, if possible." When this was announced, satsangis in the Far East and England begged him to stop in their countries on his journey to America. Maharaj Ji accepted their requests and decided to travel through the Far East to California, then across America to the East Coast, stopping in London on his return to India.

Maharaj Ji's 1964 tour began on April 25 with a 5:15 A.M. flight to Bangkok, Thailand, in the company of A.V.M. Kundan Sondhi, his tour secretary, and Dr Randolph Stone and his niece Miss Louise Hilger—both of whom had been living at the Dera for about six months a year for many years, serving in their own capacities as a labour of love. Maharaj Ji had just completed the April bhandara and the initiations, followed by satsangs and initiations in Delhi. He had been extremely busy while at Delhi and had had little time to do any packing for the long tour. It was past midnight when he finished his packing, and after a little over an hour's rest he had to get up in order to be ready to leave for the airport, the reporting time being 4:00 A.M. After a tiring day and a night without sleep, when Maharaj Ji alighted from the plane at Bangkok, his first stop of the tour, he was looking fresh and cheerful. Satsangis, their friends and relatives, and a few heads of local religious bodies, waiting at the airport to greet him, were captivated by the Master, whose face was radiant with kindness and affection.

Although there were only ten satsangis in Bangkok, the attendance at satsangs was almost two thousand. The Master gave three satsangs in Bangkok, met all the disciples individually, gave interviews to seekers, and, before leaving for Singapore, granted initiation.

The small sangat of Singapore was completely dwarfed by newcomers to the satsang and by seekers asking for interviews with Maharaj Ji. On his last day in Singapore, so great was the pressure of people wanting to meet him that the Master had to give interviews, individually and in small groups, till midnight. He also granted initiation before leaving.

Reaching Saigon at 11:00 A.M. on May 1, Maharaj Ji had the same busy programme as at the previous two centres. But here he was scheduled to stay for only twenty-six hours; as his further programme was already fixed, his stay could not be extended. During this time he could have only very little rest: the whole day of May 1, part of the night, and the following morning—until his flight for Hong Kong at 12:00 noon on May 2—were fully taken up by satsang, by meeting satsangis and seekers and answering their questions with great patience and affection, and by giving time to the local organizers to solve their problems regarding satsang. Some of the seekers' questions involved long explanations of Sant Mat, taking much time.

In spite of the pressure of lack of time, Maharaj Ji could not disappoint some of the keen seekers, and so he gave initiation, explaining the method of spiritual practice to them in detail.

After two days' busy programme in Hong Kong, Maharaj Ji flew to Tokyo on the evening of May 5. Leaving Tokyo at 9:30 P.M. on May 7, he arrived in Honolulu on May 8 at 9:15 A.M. local time. His twenty-five-hour stay at Honolulu again combined the busy schedule of interviews, question-answer sessions, explaining Sant Mat to seekers, and even an initiation. On the morning of May 9, Maharaj Ji began the most

significant part of the trip—his first visit to the mainland
of the United States of America. The end of the flight from
Honolulu "would be the beginning of a mission of love, the
fulfilment of a promise," wrote A.V.M. Sondhi. "He would
meet in the flesh hundreds of disciples and seekers after Truth,
most of whom knew of him only as others had described him
or from photographic representations, the best of which fail
to convey the true image and grandeur of the real Master in
human form."

For years, even decades, the disciples had been looking
forward to the Master's visit to America. His visit was a great
event in the life of the American satsangis, particularly for
the large number of disciples who had not yet seen the
Master in his physical form. A satsangi described the first arrival of the Master thus:

*"What will he be like? Will he be as wonderful as they
say?" We have accepted, in a typical Western, very ra-
tional fashion, a philosophy, because it answers all our
questions. But the living person behind this philosophy—how will our analytical faculties respond to him?
And when the jet airplane bringing their divine guest
was coming in for landing, the satsangis felt a "great
surge of joy well up" within them. When the Master
entered the waiting hall, not one of us could take our
eyes off the one man who was standing at the door ...
And this is Maharaj Ji ... How can we describe him? He
looks like his photographs, of course, but there is something more, something infinitely more. All our hopes are
fulfilled—even hopes we never before realized we had,
are fulfilled.*

*One thing is certain, the well-memorized list of cri-
teria of a perfect Master has been forgotten. Not because*

it is overlooked, but because we have passed into some new kind of experience where analysis and comparison are meaningless.

"What is he like?" they ask us later. How can there be an answer to that? We can only say to those who ask: You must see for yourselves. We will talk about his visit for days, months, and years; we will use millions of words; but only when you see that happiness that we have, only when you feel the feeling of love that we feel, only when you know the blessings we have received, will you begin to understand.

The Master's arrival in Los Angeles was an unforgettable experience for all those who were fortunate enough to witness it. Instead of a "quiet arrival," as Maharaj Ji had requested, the airport was thronged by many—not only local satsangis but also by others who had travelled from as far away as San Francisco, Arizona, and Texas. The Master, it seems, was deluged by the love and devotion of the disciples, and so were the disciples by the boundless compassion and overflowing love of the Master, whose happiness at meeting his disciples found expression through his radiant smile. The whole atmosphere was flooded with invisible rays of spiritual serenity and bliss.

Such was the radiance and majesty of the Master's personality that all eyes were fixed on him; and as he walked past, people respectfully gave way and stood in an almost awestruck silence, looking at him all the while. This was the historic arrival of the Master on the West Coast of America, where, fifty-three years before, the first two American seekers were accepted by the Great Master for initiation into the practice of Shabd.

Here, as in other states of America, Maharaj Ji's sweet smile, keen sense of humour, affectionate behaviour, and above all, his love for his disciples, generated such an atmosphere of warmth that the barriers of formality were removed. The satsangis felt they had known Maharaj Ji for years, and meeting him was only the renewal of an earlier friendship. So quickly did the Master dispel qualms about how to act or speak in his presence that the satsangis forgot their self-consciousness and became captivated by the radiant happiness that surrounds him.

After Maharaj Ji arrived in Los Angeles, he was formally introduced at the Biltmore Hotel by his representative, Mr Harvey Myers, who welcomed the Master and thanked him for visiting America. Thanking everyone for the gracious welcome and hospitality he had received, the Master said:

> For me, personally, this event is one of considerable significance, not only for the honour being shown to me on a great continent to which I have been able to come for the first time, but more especially because I find myself today on that part of American soil which can claim to have the oldest association with the Dera. It was to the West Coast that Sant Mat first came in the first quarter of this century when someone, on behalf of Hazur Maharaj Ji, our Great Master, initiated the first American. It is here that the Radha Soami philosophy in America slowly took root and where I think we have the highest concentration of American satsangis.

Continuing, the Master said, "I bring you the hearty Radha Soami greetings and good wishes of all the many hundreds of thousands of satsangis in India." Speaking about the programme of the six-week visit, Maharaj Ji said it would be his endeavour to meet the maximum number of satsangis possible, individually and in groups, either at the residence of his hosts or in the satsangis' own homes. He also requested that those satsangis whose homes he could not visit should try to understand and appreciate the practical difficulties. And Maharaj Ji assured the sangat—a gathering of about eight hundred satsangis and seekers—that as predicted by the Great Master, "Sant Mat has a great and promising future in this wonderful country of yours." Concluding the speech Maharaj Ji said, "We should try to be a living example of the principles of Sant Mat."

The pattern of the busy and strenuous schedule of Maharaj Ji's visit to the United States was set at Los Angeles, where besides a satsang and a session of questions and answers, the Master gave interviews from 8:30 A.M. to 1:00 P.M. and again from 6:00 to 7:30 P.M. He also permitted satsangis to join him at his meals. He visited satsangis in their homes, such trips taking a good portion of his time. In the words of A.V.M. Sondhi, "No one who applied for a personal interview with the Master was denied it and no limit was set on the time for interviews, which often went on till after midnight."

A.V.M. Sondhi added, "The fact that he had to be ready quite early the following morning to start on another equally heavy schedule at the same centre, or to travel by air several hundred miles away to the next one, seemed to him to be of no consequence. There is no doubt that such a tempo involved an enormous physical strain which would have worn out an ordinary mortal. But the Master has a capacity for hours of sustained effort, which is as amazing as his ability to look perfectly fresh, relaxed, cheerful, and keen at the end of it. He simply took in his stride, without question or hesitation, any unscheduled commitment that arose, even at the expense of necessary respite."

A few times, during the days of particularly strenuous, incessant activity, if it was suggested that the schedule be altered to provide him with some rest, the Master would dismiss the suggestion with a smile, saying, "Don't worry, I am all right."

The question-and-answer sessions at Los Angeles, as at other centres in the States, were an elevating and joyful event for the satsangis and seekers. His answers—simple, to the point, and given with a deep sense of understanding and compassion—always deeply moved the disciples. His lively sense of humour, captivating smile, and affection brought the sangat close to him. His answers always conveyed much more than mere words said in reply to a query; they were a subtle and profound communication direct to the hearts of the audience.

And, "although all the carefully thought-out questions are meaningless, large groups of people sit asking Maharaj Ji questions. We become aware that we want to ask question after question, not so much for the answers as to keep him with us and to listen to him and see him, because being here in the Master's presence is the answer."

In one of the meetings, a satsangi asked him, "Why can't I seem to think of anything to say to you?" Maharaj Ji softly replied, "There are no words needed here." And indeed, all communications between the Master and his disciple is above and beyond the medium of words.

An initiate one evening expressed a keen desire to learn Punjabi, the language in which Maharaj Ji gives satsangs in India. The Master simply shook his head and said, "It is not necessary." Looking gently at his disciple, he added, "The language of love needs no words."

Completing his tour of the West Coast—San Diego, Whitewater, San Francisco, Seattle, and Vancouver (British Columbia) Maharaj Ji flew to Minneapolis, Minnesota, in the central United States on May 26.

As a result of someone's notifying the press about Maharaj Ji's arrival, a member of the ABC television network contacted the Master at the house of Colonel Berg, the Master's representative in the Midwest, and asked the Master to appear on a television interview. Maharaj Ji refused to do so as his schedule was already full; but the persistent interviewer, Louise Leopard, appeared personally on May 27 at the next place he visited in Minneapolis and prevailed upon him, A.V.M. Sondhi, and Colonel Berg to get into her waiting car and go directly to the television studio. In the interview that followed, Louise Leopard asked Maharaj Ji about some aspects of the Sant Mat teachings and about who he was.

A.V.M. Sondhi, in his report of the tour, says, "Before the Master faced the television cameras for his brief explanation of the Sant Mat philosophy, he was told by the interviewer how the tense and agitated atmosphere that normally prevailed in the studios had been almost dramatically transformed by his presence into one of peace and tranquillity, and was asked the reason for this extraordinary change. With his characteristic smile, he replied simply, 'If one's mind is at peace, it also radiates peace.'"

At one point in the interview, Miss Leopard paused and again made the same remark, saying, "I am much impressed, Sir, with the aura of peace that seems to surround you, and complete—what would I say—almost satisfaction, contentment, or something that is a mysterious quality about you. Is this true of most people who practise your philosophy?"

Maharaj Ji answered, "Thank you. You see, unless we have peace within ourselves, we can never have peace outside.

Everybody wants peace, but our search for peace is generally in worldly achievements or in worldly possessions. The more we run after these things, the more frustrated and unhappy we are becoming every day. If we try to search for that peace within ourselves, we get that peace. Then we will also find peace even around us."

On May 28, a satsang was held at the Unitarian Society Auditorium, Minneapolis, which was attended by a large number of seekers and satsangis. Colonel Berg gave a speech to introduce and welcome the Master; he also gave a brief account of the Dera activities and, concluding the speech, said, "Indian mystics and all true Saints have proclaimed throughout the ages that only a perfect *living* Master can take one along the path to liberation. The Master and God are one. God has sent down millions of souls to this universe, and himself comes down to the earth in the form of a Master to take back to Him the souls who are ready to come back home. And we are fortunate and indeed blessed to have such a Master in our very midst today—Maharaj Charan Singh Ji in person!"

Reporting about the Master's reply to Colonel Berg's speech, A.V.M. Sondhi says, "With grace of speech, gentleness, and extreme humility, which are but a few of the noblest human virtues that the Master embodies, he told his 'sisters and brothers' that he had come to the United States not as a preacher nor as a head of any particular religious group; he was there to convey the significance of what 'we call in India the Sant Mat philosophy or the teachings of the Saints, the aim of which is none other than God-realization through self-realization.' He reminded them that this was not a new philosophy, nor was it confined to any country or people. It was, in fact, the true heritage of all mankind, the essence of all religions."

At Chicago the satsang leaders had arranged for him to stay at a motel some forty miles from the city. Satsangis from many places across the United States had also booked rooms in that motel in order to be in the same place as their Master. The motel turned out to be located on a major highway, travelled day and night by cars, buses, and trucks. Because it was very noisy, the satsang organizers offered to arrange for another motel for the Master, where he could get some much-needed rest. But Maharaj Ji refused to change motels, because he did not want to disappoint all the satsangis who were staying at the same motel as he was.

After stops at Detroit and Pittsburgh, the Master arrived in Washington, D.C., on June 11, where he stayed in the apartment of Mr and Mrs Henry Weekley. During his five days in Washington, Maharaj Ji left the Weekleys' apartment only three times for brief periods—such was the intensity of his schedule of satsang, interviews, and initiation.

Whenever the Master stayed in a satsangi's home, the host was asked to invite satsangis and seekers in groups of thirty or forty to meet the Master during his free time. These meetings would usually take the form of question-answer sessions and would sometimes run well into the night.

At one such meeting in Washington, a newcomer tried to draw Maharaj Ji into an argument. Though the man appeared to be educated and well-bred, his haughty tone and rude language belied his appearance. He was not an initiate of Maharaj Ji's; nor was he a seeker, for he had knowledge of Sant Mat and knew well the importance of a perfect Master. He was, however, disrespectful, almost hostile in his talk and was not willing to look on Maharaj Ji as a Master.

The man tried to provoke the Master into anger by rude questions and comments, and his tone had a calculated edge. The satsangis and seekers present felt greatly embarrassed and upset by him, but Maharaj Ji replied to his questions with perfect composure and humility, in a voice full of softness and love. After this extraordinary dialogue, the man cooled down, thanked Maharaj Ji, and before leaving said in an emotion-laden voice, "Master, I feel that all the time I have been talking to the Lord himself."

The Master has his own way of drawing his chosen ones to the path. When the news of his arrival reached the Sikh temple in Washington, the local Sikhs decided to ask the Master to visit the temple and address the congregation. A young Sikh, Joginder Singh Sarai, was asked to contact Maharaj Ji for this purpose.

Joginder Singh arrived at the Weekleys' apartment to ask Maharaj Ji, on behalf of the Washington Sikh sangat, to give a discourse at the gurdwara. Mr Weekley was in the middle of introducing the young man to Maharaj Ji when Joginder Singh fell to his knees, touched his head to Maharaj Ji's feet, and tearfully requested initiation. After Maharaj Ji asked him to get up, the young man, with tears streaming down his cheeks, again asked Maharaj Ji for initiation.

Maharaj Ji smiled at him and said, "When did you last eat meat?" The young man replied, "This morning." Maharaj Ji said, "You won't eat it any more?" "No, Maharaj Ji," he said, "I'll never eat it again." Maharaj Ji then said, "Good. Attend satsang for two days and then come to me here on Monday at 8:00 A.M."

On hearing this assurance, Joginder Singh completely forgot his purpose in visiting Maharaj Ji and got up to leave. Mr Weekley said, "Maharaj Ji, this young man originally came to ask you to give a satsang at the gurdwara here in Washington." Maharaj Ji readily agreed to speak there.

On Monday, June 15, the Master initiated Joginder Singh in Punjabi, with about twenty-five Americans present. After his initiation, Joginder Singh revealed to Mr Weekley the background of what had happened to him. Having obtained a job at the Indian Embassy, he had come to Washington a few years before from the village of Balsarai, right next to the Dera, yet he had never seen Maharaj Ji and had never gone to satsang; a few words of the Master's discourses would sometimes fall on his ears because of the Dera loudspeakers, but he had never paid attention to what was being said. On seeing the Master for the first time, he was completely overwhelmed with awe and devotion, and could not prevent himself from asking for initiation.

With the Sikh gurdwara filled to capacity, Maharaj Ji delivered an impressive discourse in Punjabi for about forty minutes. He explained that Nam or Shabd, as mentioned by the Saints, is not a written or spoken word. It is not anywhere outside; it is within our own body and can be seen and heard only on going within. The Lord, the Supreme Being, is also within our body. He is not to be found in mountains or forests, nor in any man-made temples, churches, or mosques. The Master went on to explain the importance of a living Master, who alone can put the seeker on the path, connect him to the Shabd within, and lead him back to the Father. The audience listened to Maharaj Ji's words with rapt attention, their eyes fixed on him.

When Maharaj Ji prepared to leave Washington on June 15, Mr Weekley voiced the feelings of all the satsangis who had gathered to say good-bye: "Maharaj Ji, we can never repay you for all the gifts you have bestowed on us by your coming." "I am not leaving this place empty-handed," the Master said quite seriously. "The beautiful smiles, the laughter, the love they have given me—I will need extra luggage to carry this back to India with me."

From Washington, the Master went by car to Atlantic City, New Jersey, before driving on to New York City on June 16.

Greatly concerned that the Master needed a few days rest, the organizers of his tour in America strongly suggested that he travel to England by sea, a journey of five or six days. Maharaj Ji accepted the proposal. The satsangis in New York, out of this same concern, had lightened Maharaj Ji's programme to include just one satsang a day plus a little time for interviews with seekers. As soon as he studied the programme, Maharaj Ji reinstated the two daily satsangs and added three sessions for interviews—morning, midday, and evening. Any time left over was to be spent in visiting satsangis' homes.

At the request of a few satsangis, Maharaj Ji visited the United Nations building on June 19. When he was being shown one of the great auditoriums where the delegates can tune their earphones to hear a speech translated into any of the major languages, he said softly, almost to himself, "If we learn just one language, the language of love, all our conflicts would cease." It was also here, in the huge assembly hall, when he was shown groups of seats allotted to the representatives of the various nations, that he commented, "Only if we were one nation, not many, could we live in peace. And such unity could only be achieved on a spiritual platform."

On Sunday, June 21, America was celebrating Father's Day, and some of the satsangis were feeling very happy and fortunate that their Satguru, the true Father, was with them on this day. For like a father he had herded them all into one fold of love, had given them a feeling of belonging—of belonging to the Master and his flock. With these feelings in his heart, one satsangi said to the Master, "Maharaj Ji, happy Father's Day!" Maharaj Ji looked at him and said with a soft, loving smile, "Are all days not the Father's days?" In the words of a satsangi, they only later realized the true import of what at first appeared to them as a light-hearted, casual reply: All days belong to the Lord, our Father; He has given them to us; we should spend them with our thoughts always on Him, live them in His company, in His service, in His love.

New York was the Master's last stop in his strenuous six-week tour of the United States. It was a fruitful visit for the satsangis and seekers—inspiring and exalting. At the end of a full programme of satsangs, interviews, and initiation, Maharaj Ji met the satsangis for the final satsang, concluding it with these words:

I leave the States happy in the thought that my visit has served the purpose for which I came, and this was to bring me closer to the hearts and minds of the American satsangis. I know that a great deal of love and devotion has been generated in the fulfillment of this purpose, and I have no doubt that the same love and grace of my beloved Great Master will bring me back into your midst again.

On 24 June 1964, Maharaj Ji boarded the ocean liner *Queen Mary,* bound for England. A large number of satsangis and seekers had come to see him off. The Master shook hands with each one of them, blessed them with a word of thanks, a look of love, and assured them that he would again come to the States. With tears of farewell clouding their eyes and Master's love overflowing from their hearts, the sangat, with raised hands and a soft "Radha Soami," bade farewell to Maharaj Ji as he boarded the ship. As the large ocean liner pulled out from the dock, the crowd on the deck of the ship parted in two, and "like the sun shining from between clouds," the Master walked through the crowd and appeared at the railing of the deck. He raised his right hand, waving good-bye to his loving devotees. The sangat was thrilled by this unexpected darshan. The ship moved away, but still the Master was standing on the deck with his hand raised. Gradually the ship receded, becoming a small point before it vanished from their sight.

The sangat's hearts ached at parting from the Master, and eyes were filled with tears. "But we also felt grateful for the precious gift the Master gave us during his visit—the gift of his love."

The five-day voyage on the *Queen Mary* provided Maharaj Ji with much-needed rest. None of his co-passengers on the ship had any idea of his identity. But what could veil the magnetic personality and a certain elevating and soothing aura about him? Those passengers who had the good fortune of coming in contact with him wanted to know who this extraordinary person, Mr C. S. Grewal, really was. Who was this person who looked always at peace with himself and radiated peace around him?

The liner docked at Southampton on June 30. Some of the passengers came to know the identity of Maharaj Ji when Colonel Sanders and a few Indian and Western satsangis came aboard the ship to receive him. A few of the passengers later contacted the Master's representative in England and obtained books on Sant Mat; some of them in course of time also applied for initiation.

Maharaj Ji's 1964 trip was mainly to visit the United States; therefore only seven days could be spared for his visit to the United Kingdom. The shortness of this visit, however, proved to be very taxing for Maharaj Ji, as he tried to give almost all available time to the sangat. The interviews lasted until midnight, and his day began at 4:00 A.M.

As Maharaj Ji had to reach Dera by the middle of July in order to be in time for the July bhandara, he could not visit the various satsang centres on the Continent. Satsangis from Europe and a few from South Africa had come to London for satsang and darshan, and Maharaj Ji met all of them during his short stay.

After a busy schedule of satsang, question-answer sessions, interviews, and initiation, Maharaj Ji was to leave England on July 6 for Geneva. At his last satsang in England, the Master gave his farewell message in a few words; and though addressed to a small congregation, it is of universal application—true and significant at all times. In his sweet, well-modulated voice, vibrant with love and compassion, the Master said:

> I can only say a few words; I have nothing more to give in advice—the books are full of the teachings—but I can only suggest that satsangis and everybody should try to love one another. The more you are nearer to one another, the more you will be nearer and dearer to me. The more we are nearer and dearer to one another, the more we are nearer and dearer to the Lord. So this we should always try to keep in our minds. We should, in our group meetings, always be in harmony; there should always be love, affection, and understanding. Try to help one another. Try to strengthen one another's faith; try to strengthen one another on the path. That is the real service we can do for one another. And so I always advise that our group meetings should be open to everybody; our arms should be open to everybody. We should give a warm welcome to whomsoever wants to come and join us. But for that we must develop love and affection within ourselves. That is the only thing which can welcome others. If there is no love within ourselves, if there is no love within our group meetings, I think we are not coming up to the mark that Sant Mat expects from us. So I can only ask you again, as Christ also taught you, "Love one another."

The trip back to Delhi was via Geneva, Rome, and Bombay, with Maharaj Ji finally arriving back at the Dera on July 16. He had left firm orders that no Dera administrator, sevadar, or satsangi, or even any of his own relatives, was to travel to Bombay or Delhi to receive him, nor was there to be an official welcome at the Dera.

Longing for the Satguru for almost twelve weeks, braving the hot summer winds and the burning desire to see him, the sangat at Dera was thrilled to receive the news that the Master had arrived in India on July 13. His scheduled arrival at the Dera was a great day for us—the day of his triumphant and safe return from abroad. We were anxious to celebrate it, but Maharaj Ji, who never approves of such outward expressions of emotion, directed us not to do so. We submitted to his will quietly, the memory of twelve weeks' agony of separation erased from our minds by the first moment of his darshan.

1966: SOUTH AFRICA

In May 1966, Maharaj Ji undertook another major foreign tour—this time principally to visit South Africa, with stops in Kenya, Tanzania, Europe, and Israel. Sant Mat began in South Africa at the end of the Second World War when Sir Colin Garbett, Major Little, and Dr Lander retired after their service in India and settled in South Africa. Till 1951, there were only four satsangis in South Africa. When Maharaj Charan Singh Ji granted Nam to a few seekers from South Africa in 1954, the sangat began to grow, and by the end of 1965 there were 350 satsangis. For several years, a few satsangis from South Africa had been visiting the Dera each year for Maharaj Ji's darshan, but most of the initiates in South Africa had not yet seen Maharaj Ji. After his tour of America in 1964, the South African satsangis hoped he might also visit their

333

country, and many began writing to the Master requesting such a visit. They had to wait two years more before their request was graciously fulfilled.

After the April bhandara and initiations at the Dera, Maharaj Ji gave satsang in Delhi, followed by initiation. The Master then visited Indore in the last week of April, and after a week's programme of satsang and initiations at Indore, he had planned to return to Dera for four days' work before leaving for Africa. Maharaj Ji was scheduled to fly from Indore to Delhi and then leave by train the same evening in order to reach Dera by the morning of April 30. After the four days of work at Dera, he was to leave for Delhi again and then on to Bombay, where he was to catch his flight for Nairobi.

However, due to some technical problems, all flights from Indore airport were suspended for a few months, and therefore, instead of flying to Delhi direct from Indore, Maharaj Ji had to drive to Bhopal from Indore at 5:00 A.M. on April 29. On reaching Bhopal airport, we were told the plane would be late by two hours. After two hours, at 10:00 A.M., we were told that the flight would be further delayed and was now due at 5:00 P.M. As waiting at the airport for seven hours was not a happy prospect, it was suggested to Maharaj Ji that we drive down to Sanchi, a place of historical interest dating from the B.C. era. A Western satsangi, who had joined us at Indore and was flying with Maharaj Ji to Delhi and on to Beas, was quite happy at the prospect of seeing Sanchi. Although it was a hot day and Maharaj Ji was tired after continuous satsang programmes since the bhandara at Dera, he agreed.

I had accompanied Maharaj Ji on this tour as his secretary and was scheduled to leave Bhopal by train at 12:00 noon, along with the *pathi* and Maharaj Ji's personal servant. When I reached the Dera on the evening of the thirtieth, I was surprised—rather, shocked—to find that the Master, who should have arrived at 6:00 A.M., had not yet arrived, and that the secretary was making frantic calls to find out where and how Maharaj Ji had been delayed.

We later learned that after three hours in the car and about three hours in Sanchi, the Master had reached Bhopal airport at 4:00 P.M. But the plane was reported to be further delayed and was due to land at 6:00 P.M. The delays continued, and finally it was announced at 10:00 P.M. that the flight had been cancelled. By this time, the last train of the day from Bhopal to Delhi had already left. The Master was keen to reach Dera as early as possible, for he had to discuss many important matters with the Dera staff before leaving for South Africa. He decided to drive to Delhi immediately, so as to catch the morning flight for Amritsar, the closest airport to Dera.

After driving nonstop all through the night and half a day, and covering a distance of five hundred miles, Maharaj Ji reached Delhi at 3:00 in the afternoon on April 30, missing both the flight and the day train to Amritsar.

After a bath and lunch in Delhi—the previous meal he had had was twenty-six hours earlier at Sanchi, with only a few cups of sugarless tea to sustain him during this entire period—the Master was ready to discuss certain important matters relating to his tour and bookings with the organizers at Delhi.

Leaving Delhi by train that night, Maharaj Ji reached Dera the next morning, May 1. After three days of hectic activity—discussions with staff members, clearing mail that had been pending for so many days, giving directions to the engineers regarding the construction work, meeting satsangis—the Master left for Delhi on the night of May 3, and on the morning of the fourth he left for Bombay. He flew to Nairobi on May 5, to begin his eagerly awaited tour of South Africa, East Africa, and Europe.

In Nairobi, satsangis and seekers had gathered from Uganda, Zambia, Kumasi in Ghana, Swaziland, and Rhodesia to meet the Master and have his darshan. He spent two days giving satsang and interviews to all of them. Late in the evening of May 7, a group of satsangis and seekers from Tanzania arrived for darshan. On reaching Nairobi, they were greatly disappointed to learn that the satsang programme was over and that the Master would be leaving for Johannesburg early the next morning. Anxious to obtain just a glimpse of the Master, they went straight to his hotel. When they arrived at the hotel, Maharaj Ji had already retired to his room for the night. Characteristic of his disregard for his own comfort, when Maharaj Ji heard of their arrival he left his bed, dressed, and came out to the sitting room. The few minutes of darshan soon turned into a question-answer session when one of the group, a seeker, asked a question about the main tenets of Sant Mat. When Maharaj Ji finally took leave of them, after a full one and a half hour of questions and answers, it was past midnight. Because of their distress at having missed satsang, the Master promised that he would try to visit them in Tanzania on his return journey.

Maharaj Ji arrived in Johannesburg, South Africa, on 8 May 1966. Sam Busa, Master's representative in South Africa, and a few others received him at the airport. After the immigration formalities, the Master drove straight to the B.P. Centre, where satsangis and seekers were waiting for his darshan, many to see him for the first time in their life. In the words of a South African satsangi, "The hall was packed to capacity, and as Maharaj Ji walked in, everyone stood with folded hands. How can one describe love? During darshan it became something tangible, something that could be seen, felt, experienced. Professor Puri's description was all-embracing. He

336

said that the satsangis were in perfect rapport with their Master, and their love was expressed in silent eloquence."

During the eighteen days of the Master's visit to South Africa, he gave private interviews to over six hundred people, gave satsangs, held question-answer sessions, visited satsangi homes, and attended to his mail. Maharaj Ji had asked the organizers not to refuse anyone wanting an interview, and in order to meet as many satsangis and seekers as possible in small groups, one-and-a-half-hour garden parties were arranged daily with forty to fifty people invited to each. Even lunch was used as a time for meeting ten to fifteen satsangis.

Many, in fact most of the satsangis and seekers were seeing the Master for the first time, and sometimes they felt hesitation and nervousness while approaching him for their interviews. They were unsure how to behave in his presence. But the Master's warmth and his affectionate and relaxed approach dispelled their nervousness; his kind and loving words gave them the feeling that they had known the Master for many years and that they were meeting an old friend.

One evening a satsangi asked the Master, "Could I please know how I am to address Maharaj Ji in private conversation?" The Master leaned towards the questioner with an expression of gentleness and love. "Brother," he said, "we are all travellers on the same path. There is no special form of address. It must be heart to heart."

On May 12, the Master left Johannesburg early in the morning and, driving 270 miles, reached Swaziland a little after noon. He gave darshan to the sangat on arrival, had lunch in their company, and gave individual interviews to each one of them, as well as satsang in the evening. This was followed on the next day by another long trip by car—early morning till 1:00 P.M.—to White River. Here the Master stayed only for a short time, as he had to be back in Johannesburg the same night. He spent the whole time in the company of the sangat, even during lunch attending to their queries regarding the path. After lunch he gave satsang and interviews. After two very busy, non-stop days, he arrived back in Johannesburg at 10:00 P.M.

In spite of this tiring programme, the Master was cheerful, fresh, and radiant as ever. The staggering schedule of satsangs, interviews, visiting satsangis in their homes, and giving them time even during lunch, of starting the day early and often ending it after midnight, left the organizers exhausted—but not the Master. Sam Busa, who along with Professor Puri accompanied Maharaj Ji during his entire tour of South Africa, says:

Although Maharaj Ji had only been in South Africa for five days at this stage, I was able to experience at first-hand the tremendous pace at which he lives. No normal human being could live his life, day after day, month after month, year after year, this way. Whether he is in India, South Africa, Europe, or anywhere else, it does not matter; his life is always the same. I had the privilege of being the first to see Maharaj Ji in the morning, usually around 4:30 A.M., when I took him his morning tea, and last at night when I accompanied him up to the door of his bedroom. It was more often than not around midnight before he retired. By this one can gauge how little sleep he really has. All I can say is that even after so short a time as five days, Professor Puri and I were starting to show signs of wear and tear. During the evening satsangs many people laughed at us and said we were quite a study while we struggled to look intelligent and bright, as our sleepy eyelids insisted on closing every now and then during the Master's talks.

Maharaj Ji left Johannesburg for Cape Town on May 18. After an equally busy schedule in Cape Town and Durban, he returned to Johannesburg on the morning of May 26. He was to leave for the United Kingdom the same evening, but that did not prevent him from spending the entire day in darshan, satsang, and initiation. At the last meeting in Johannesburg, the Master bade farewell with these words—words meaningful and inspiring to a sangat sad at the prospect of parting, assuring them that their love and devotion would enable him to visit them again:

My stay in your beautiful country comes to an end today. During my short stay, I am glad I have been able to visit almost all our satsang centres and have been able to see you individually and collectively at meetings, at garden parties, at luncheons, or at such odd places as the airport, and even at the roadside.

I am glad to find spiritual hunger in your hearts. I am grateful to you, all of you, for your warm reception, your affectionate greetings, your love and your devotion. I assure you that, although my stay has been very short in this country, your love and devotion will enable me to visit you more often in the near future....

I would like to remind you of what Jesus Christ told us two thousand years ago. He said, "My first commandment is, love thy Lord with all thy heart, with all thy might, with all thy soul." Then he said, "My second commandment is, love thy neighbour as thyself." But do not forget that this whole universe is our neighbour and the Lord is within every one of us, so we have to love one and all—everyone—whomsoever the Lord has created. The teachings of all the prophets, of all the sages, of all the saints in the world, are broadly based on these

*two commandments. If we adhere to these command-
ments, we grasp the gist of the teachings of all the saints
and of all the prophets.*

*You know your destination, you know the path lead-
ing to your destination. I can only advise you to perse-
vere on the path with all your love and devotion.*

Maharaj Ji's South African tour gave new life to the sangat.
From 350 satsangis, the sangat has grown to over 2,000 today
in the twenty or so satsang centres, with many seekers studying the teachings and trying to adopt a vegetarian diet. Above
all, the Master's visit, as his physical presence always does,
awakened in the satsangis a new enthusiasm for living the
teachings; it increased their love for the Master and their
affection for one another.

Although the Master's eighteen-day visit to South Africa
was short, its impact on satsangis and seekers was profound.
A few incidents reported by satsangis from South Africa illustrate the impression made by the Master.

The wife of one satsangi had no interest in Sant Mat, and
though she did not try to prevent her husband from following the principles of the path, she was a regular meat eater
and fond of non-vegetarian dishes. When the Master arrived,
out of curiosity she decided to see what her husband's Guru
was like. In her words, "When the Master entered the room
and walked down the aisle to the dais, I felt truly blessed in
seeing such an extraordinary 'man'. As long as he sat before
me, I sat still, silent and spellbound, tears of happiness running down my cheeks. I knew then that my husband's Master
was also my Master; I knew that here was my father, mother,
friend, and guide, who would show me the path."

An officer of the South African Department of Police and
Internal Security had been assigned to watch Master's activities

in South Africa. His assignment was to attend Maharaj Ji's discourses and report any adverse criticism of the national, political, and ethnic policies of South Africa. After faithfully carrying out his duty, he ended up making a tearful request for initiation. Today he is a most loving and enthusiastic satsangi.

In South Africa, a country subscribing to the apartheid policy, over 90 percent of Maharaj Ji's disciples are white. Forgetting all feelings of distinction, they sit at the Master's feet, associate with their Indian and African satsangi brothers with regard and affection, and come to India and serve the sangat with satsangis of all castes, colour, and creeds.

During this trip to South Africa, wherever the Master went, everyone—even government officials—forgot all race distinctions in his presence. When Maharaj Ji was crossing the border into South Africa from Swaziland, he happened to present his passport to the South African policeman standing under the "Europeans only" notice. Seeing him, the police officer stood up, checked the passport, and respectfully returned it to him. He did not ask Maharaj Ji to move over to the counter for non-whites. A satsangi who was there commented, "He addressed the Master on every occasion as 'Sir', but not the rest of us."

On another occasion, on one of the automobile journeys between satsang centres, Maharaj Ji's car became separated from the second car, which was carrying snacks and coffee for breakfast. Seeing that they were getting late for the Master's coffee, Sam Busa stopped at a beautiful restaurant in a small town that came on the way. As the restaurant was meant only for whites—others were not even permitted to enter it—Mr Busa intended to bring breakfast out for everyone. When the car stopped, Maharaj Ji got out and started walking towards the restaurant. Sam Busa and his companions were dumbstruck, not knowing what to do, for they were afraid the restaurant owner might be rude and disrespectful toward Maharaj Ji. A few minutes later, they entered the restaurant to find the Master sitting at the central table with the waiter respectfully taking his order. The proprietor was also there, and he and his staff members served the Master with unusual courtesy and respect, all the time gazing at him. A feeling of joy and peace filled the restaurant.

On May 26, Maharaj Ji left Johannesburg on the British and European part of his tour. A satsangi gives this account of the departure: "We arrived at the airport at about 6:15 P.M. There were between three and four hundred people waiting to see the Master off. Somehow or other he was able to shake everyone by the hand before he left. Even people who had not come to see him off, joined the queue. One lady said she simply had to shake the hand of 'that wonderful person', although she did not know who he was."

During his eighteen-day stay, the Master gave personal interviews to seven hundred persons, listening to and solving their problems. Apart from this, every day he met forty to fifty people at a time, over lunch and tea. Though, as instructed by Maharaj Ji, no publicity was made, yet seven to eight hundred persons attended every satsang. Hazur gave initiation to ninety-seven persons, in all, at three places. Among these, only three were Indians.

The sangat was sad; the wonderful days that had brought the Master among them had passed away like an unbelievably exhilarating dream. The Master was now preparing to go through customs for boarding the plane. His face was glowing, more radiant then ever, and his smile was full of ineffable love and mercy. A new initiate, with tears in his eyes, suddenly spoke out the thoughts of all those present: "Master, I am very sad that you are leaving us." The Master turned to him and gently replied, "Am I leaving you?"

And when the majestic jet soared towards the sky, carrying the most extraordinary passenger on earth, tears were running down the cheeks of the satsangis. Yet they were feeling a unique inner rapport with their Master—although in his physical body he was moving away from them, in his Radiant Form he is always with every one of his disciples.

As he had promised, Maharaj Ji stopped in Dar-es-Salaam, Tanzania, on May 27 to meet those satsangis who had missed the satsang he had given in Nairobi, Kenya, on his way to South Africa. In spite of being unwell from the gruelling routine he had followed, he graciously held satsang there for two days and continued with the usual engagements of his programme. The Master then went on to Cairo, Egypt, for a few days before travelling to London on June 5.

Maharaj Ji's plane was due to arrive at London airport on the afternoon of Sunday, 5 June 1966, at 4:35 P.M., but the plane arrived in London nine and a half hours late—at 2:00 A.M. on June 6. About three hundred people had come to the airport in the afternoon and stayed into the night, patiently waiting to meet him. Seeing such a large crowd waiting for so many hours, the airport authorities sent a police sergeant and a few constables to watch the crowd. The sergeant asked several people who they were waiting for, and was told, "Our Satguru." This reply did not relieve his apprehensions, so he stayed on. When Maharaj Ji finally arrived at 2:00 A.M., the crowd of three hundred stood silently before him, gazing with perfect stillness at his face.

One satsangi described the Master's arrival in London thus:

"And then he came, walking towards us, dressed in ivory white and not, seemingly, at all tired. So majestic and still he stood, full of love and understanding. His eyes looked individually at ours. Not only were we entranced, but the policemen, too, seemed awed by his presence and, instead of watching over the crowd, were intent on gazing at him!"

Later, the sergeant told one of the satsangis that in his twelve years' service at the airport he had never witnessed such discipline and such a moving sight of devotion and love.

It was a little past 3:00 A.M. when the Master arrived at the flat where he was to stay while in London. A few satsangis were waiting for his darshan at the flat. The Master, always thoughtful of others' feelings, knew that they had been waiting for several hours and sat with them in the drawing room instead of retiring to rest after his strenuous tour and exacting flight. It was past 4:00 A.M. when he retired to his bedroom. It must have been a night without any sleep for him, because we at the Dera know that the Master cannot sleep after 3:00 in the morning.

During this entire tour, Maharaj Ji had little time for sleep or rest. When a satsangi pointed this out to the Master and expressed his concern, Maharaj Ji replied, "I am happy to be able to do my duty."

Maharaj Ji was in London for three weeks, following his usual programme, after which he flew on to Frankfurt on June 25. One evening the German sangat asked the Master if he could travel to his next stop, Geneva, by car instead of by plane, so that they could all travel with him. Even though this meant exchanging a one-hour plane trip for an eight-to-ten-hour car journey, Maharaj Ji, not wanting to disappoint them, accepted their proposal. Leaving Frankfurt in the morning, Maharaj Ji and the party arrived in Geneva at 7:00 in the evening.

The Master stayed in Geneva for five days before going on to Vienna, where an Indian lady from Ghana, who had missed seeing the Master in both Nairobi and London, finally caught up with him and received initiation. On his way back to India, Maharaj Ji stopped in Israel for a three-day stay with the five satsangis and a few seekers there. As a result of his visit, more seekers are inquiring about the path, and a few Sant Mat books have been translated into Hebrew.

The Master arrived in Bombay on July 14 and at the Dera on the sixteenth. His hard-worked human frame must have needed rest after the long tour, but the pending mail, Dera work, and the oncoming July bhandara did not allow it.

1968: FAR EAST, AUSTRALIA, NEW ZEALAND

On 6 May 1968, the Master once again travelled abroad to meet satsangis and seekers—this time in the Far East, Australia, and New Zealand. He was accompanied by Mr Madan Mehta as his travelling secretary, and Mrs Bea Jauncey, a devoted English satsangi, who at that time was in the process of moving from England to New Zealand. The Master's first stop was Bangkok, Thailand, where he spent five days giving darshan, satsang, and interviews, and initiating seekers on the last day before going on to Hong Kong on May 11.

In Hong Kong, Maharaj Ji was invited to give a satsang in the Sikh gurdwara, which was filled with a capacity crowd, including only thirty or so satsangis. A prominent Sikh gentleman, who undertook to introduce the Master to the audience, ended his speech by warning Maharaj Ji, in a harsh tone, against saying anything that might offend their beliefs. The Master always avoids controversy, but he also does not hesitate to explain the real meaning of the teachings of the Saints. For one and a half hours, Maharaj Ji, in his even, mellow voice, and in a language direct, simple, and full of love, outlined the real meaning of the teachings of Guru Nanak. He explained that Nam and Shabd, mentioned in so many verses of Guru Nanak's writings, refer to the power that is the Lord himself and can be found only within the body, not in the scriptures.

He also made clear the necessity of a living Master if one wishes to obtain Nam. The people were absolutely quiet, deeply impressed with Maharaj Ji and his discourse. At the conclusion of Maharaj Ji's discourse, the same Sikh gentleman, visibly moved, thanked him warmly for his excellent talk and for coming to give darshan to the sangat.

The Master continued his tour on May 16, flying on to Japan, where he visited Tokyo, Kobe, and Osaka. Then he returned to Hong Kong for more satsangs and initiation before going to Singapore on May 31. After his Singapore itinerary, the Master flew to Jakarta, Indonesia, for four hectic days and then on to Sydney, Australia, for his first visit to that continent. At that time there were only eleven satsangis scattered all over Australia. Maharaj Ji initiated a few more on this tour and appointed Max Valentine as his representative. Today Australia has over one hundred satsangis.

From Sydney the Master flew to Christ Church, New Zealand. Sant Mat was introduced to New Zealand in 1964 when an English couple "accidentally" stopped at the Dera on their way from England to settle in New Zealand. Travelling overland in a camper, they had driven through Europe, the Middle East, Afghanistan, and Pakistan to India. They arrived in Amritsar, where they had planned to rest for three or four days, but crowds of spectators kept gathering around their vehicle—hardly a restful experience. When they inquired about a more secluded spot where they could rest, someone suggested they go to the Dera, where Westerners are no novelty. They arrived at the colony and were given permission to park their camper in the Guest House compound. They were much impressed by the general efficiency and the administration of the Dera. When they learned that the Dera is a spiritual centre with a Master who gives discourses on the path, they felt it would be lack of courtesy on their part not to attend the satsangs. The Master greatly impressed and attracted them, and instead of a few days' rest at Dera, the couple stayed here a whole month, eventually receiving initiation. When they continued their journey, they took Sant Mat with them to New Zealand.

Maharaj Ji stayed in New Zealand from June 21 to June 30. He gave three satsangs in Auckland, the capital, where almost everyone attending requested and was given a private interview. The Master's visit has led to further growth of Sant Mat in New Zealand; today there are many satsangis in this beautiful country, and many seekers are applying for initiation.

From New Zealand the Master proceeded to the Fiji Islands on June 30, meeting satsangis and seekers, and then back again to Singapore on July 8. In spite of what was by then quite a long tour, he continued his usual busy satsang programme. Though no provision had been made for it, he also gave initiation to a group of seekers, which included eight Chinese. The initiation took three hours, after which Maharaj Ji had to go straight to the airport to catch his flight back to Bombay. He landed in Bombay after midnight on July 10, and returned to Dera on July 11.

1970: EUROPE, UNITED KINGDOM, AMERICA, ASIA

The main purpose of Maharaj Ji's 1970 foreign tour was to visit the North American centres, but he also included on this trip many centres in Europe and Asia. Right from its beginning, this tour made extraordinarily heavy demands on the Master. He left the Dera immediately after the April bhandara initiations to give two satsangs in Delhi on April 19 and 20. Without taking a break, the Master flew out of Delhi on April 21, bound for Greece. He was accompanied by his tour secretary, Prof. Janak Puri. After almost twenty-four hours without sleep, Maharaj Ji arrived in Athens to find that the sangat had arranged a sightseeing tour of the historical sights of Athens, beginning a few hours after his arrival. The entire sangat in Greece, about thirty people, had made plans to accompany the Master in the tour bus. Professor Puri tried to persuade the Master to cancel the trip and take a little rest, but Maharaj Ji did not wish to disappoint the sangat and agreed to go with them to whatever places they wanted.

On reaching the hotel, Maharaj Ji took a bath and breakfast and was ready to join the sangat for the tour of Athens and its environs. The tour was followed by interviews. Thirty people were expected at the satsang that evening, but the organizers were surprised to find a gathering of over one hundred. After the satsang the Master permitted the audience to ask questions, which he answered with his usual lucidity, humility, and sense of humour. The meeting ended at 10:30 P.M., and the Master retired after a day which for anyone else would have been long and tiring.

The strenuous beginning in Athens set the tempo for the entire 1970 tour. Originally the Master had not planned to give initiation at any of the centres on this tour, in order to devote more time to meeting satsangis and seekers. But he did not have the heart to disappoint the seekers, so from Athens onwards he held initiation in almost every city on his itinerary.

From Athens, Maharaj Ji proceeded to Geneva, where satsangis and seekers from Germany, Italy, France, Holland, Norway, Sweden, South Africa, and even from America had come to have his darshan. The Master gave interviews to all of them during his three days' stay, gave three satsangs, and initiated a few seekers through his German representative, Mr Rudolf Walberg.

The Master's next stop was Amsterdam, where the daily schedule called for a brief period of darshan in the morning and satsang in the evening. But on the very first morning during darshan, a seeker asked a question of the Master, which he replied to at length, and the twenty minutes of darshan turned into a question-and-answer session of over an hour. This routine continued throughout his stay of four days. The Master gave interviews to over 125 people during this time. The sangat in Holland was less than 100, but the attendance at satsangs was over 250. Before leaving for London on 1 May 1970, Maharaj Ji initiated seekers and met the satsang organizers.

In view of the many countries the Master was scheduled to visit during this tour, only five or six days were allotted to the programme in England. The result was an extremely crowded daily programme for the Master, which included, besides numerous interviews, two satsangs—10:00 A.M. till 12:00 noon in English for the Western sangat, and 3:00 till 5:00 P.M. in Punjabi for the Indian sangat settled in the United Kingdom. The English satsangs were attended by over one thousand people, while the Punjabi ones had an audience of about three thousand.

The Royal Theatre Hall, where Maharaj Ji gave his discourses in Punjabi, could accommodate 2,300 people, but the gathering was much larger. After allowing about 3,000 people to enter, many of whom had to stand, the organizers were forced to close the doors. Those who could not get admission stood outside on the street in order to have the Master's darshan when he came out after the satsang. Such a large crowd on the street naturally attracted the attention of the city police, who sent policemen to control the crowd in case of trouble. They were, however, amazed to see the order and discipline of the sangat, who quietly waited for their Master to come out of the hall and then dispersed after he had left.

After his short visit to the United Kingdom, described by the Master's representative, Colonel Sanders, as "a whirlwind visit," the Master left London on May 6, making a short tour of the West Indies and Mexico on his way to the United States. In just ten days he visited Bermuda, Barbados, Trinidad, and Jamaica. This portion of his travels typified the difficulties he suffered throughout the tour, for because of the time change on the flight from London to Bermuda, Maharaj Ji was without sleep for a full twenty-four hours and had no time to rest in Bermuda or Barbados, as he had only one day in each place. Regardless of the strain and discomfort, the lack of sleep and irregular meal times, the Master meticulously kept to the busy schedule laid out for him by the local satsang organizers.

Maharaj Ji arrived in Mexico on May 16 for a four-day visit, flying on to Washington, D.C., on May 20. In a trip reminiscent of the Master's early train tours in India, sangats turned out at the airport to have Maharaj Ji's darshan at the two places where the plane stopped on its way to Washington —San Antonio and Dallas. In Dallas two hundred satsangis even sang a song of welcome to the Master, hardly usual for American airports. Maharaj Ji stayed with the Weekleys for his two days in Washington, following his usual schedule and even finding time to meet a group of Indians from the diplomatic corps. In a letter from Washington to the Dera secretary, Mr K. L. Khanna, the Master described some aspects of his tour thus far:

> Thanks for your affectionate letter. I am glad all is well at Dera and everything is peaceful and running smoothly. It couldn't be otherwise. I have left everything—all the Dera affairs—in the hands of the most loving and loyal devotees of Hazur Maharaj Ji. Over and above everybody, he is always there to look after his own interest. We are just puppets and doing our duty according to the best of our ability.

By Maharaj Ji's grace, my tour is just wonderful from a satsang point of view. I am collecting a lot of audiences everywhere I go, as you know from Janak's letters. People are hungry for spirituality and they realize now that material achievements have not led them to any happiness or peace of mind. They have started thinking openly and are trying to come out from the traditional beliefs.

My health is fairly good, though these long flights are terrible. Then, also, the delays and change of timings give one many sleepless nights. But I am very happy in the discharge of my duty and in finding people full of love and devotion and so receptive to Maharaj Ji's teachings. No doubt, sometimes it is very tiring to go through the same routine every day, but then it gives one a strange consolation and happiness when one feels that Maharaj Ji's mission is being fulfilled by His grace.

I feel quite relaxed and happy to attend to my satsang activities. Besides, people's love and devotion just make one forget oneself.

One interesting difference from his 1964 tour of America is that Maharaj Ji added a new feature to his schedule—coffee breaks. One of the satsang organizers described them thus:

The difficulty in all cities came in the fact that only a small percentage of those desiring personal interviews got them. However, an informal coffee break was held in all cities and those desiring but not getting an interview were included. Actually, after the first day, coffee was excluded from the "coffee breaks" as nobody would touch the coffee or anything as long as Master was present. So, we had a running joke about our "coffeeless coffee breaks." In fact, those attending the "breaks" got much more than coffee, for in this way they had forty minutes or so in relative closeness to the Master, and many told me their questions were fully answered.

Another unusual feature of the 1970 tour is that satsangis often travelled with Maharaj Ji from centre to centre. In a letter to the Dera, the Master made this comment: "Satsangis are following me from one centre to another centre, and three-fourths of the plane in which I travel is usually filled with satsangis, and the hotels where I stay are crowded with them. I think I am giving good business to the airlines and the hotels as well as to the photographers' supply houses, without getting any commission from them!"

On May 22, when the Master flew on to New York, he was accompanied not only by Professor Puri and Mr Weekley, but also by forty or fifty satsangis who had booked themselves on the same flight Maharaj Ji was taking. On the plane, the air hostesses were amazed when such a large section of the passengers refused meals with meat and eggs and would not drink any alcohol; they could not believe it was happening.

Arriving in New York in the late afternoon, the Master gave a satsang at 7:00 P.M., attended by eight hundred people. After finishing interviews and finalizing his schedule, it was almost 11:00 at night. Apart from a cup of tea in the afternoon, Maharaj Ji had not taken anything and had missed his dinner because of satsang activities. Realizing this, Mr Weekley suggested they go to a restaurant and have some milk or coffee. Maharaj Ji agreed and, accompanied by Professor Puri and Mr Weekley, went to a small cafe. At that late hour the small restaurant appeared deserted and Mr Weekley said with a laugh, "Maharaj Ji, we have succeeded at last in getting away from the satsangis. You can have a few moments of rest." The

Master smiled and said, "No, Mr Weekley, you are wrong. Some satsangis are sitting at that table behind us." And Maharaj Ji was right. At a table in the corner of the restaurant, behind Maharaj Ji, sat a group of six satsangis who had just come to New York. They had never seen Maharaj Ji before, nor had Maharaj Ji seen them, for they had been initiated through his representative. But the Satguru always recognizes his chosen souls.

One day, during a question-answer session in New York, a young man of about twenty asked the Master with great devotion and humility, "Master, we all know our pain, but what is your pain?" While the young man was speaking, Maharaj Ji was looking at him with great love. Then he answered sweetly, "Brother, your pain is my pain ..." There was a hushed, tearful silence throughout the auditorium as the Master continued, "When my disciples are miserable and unhappy, then I am miserable and unhappy. When they are happy, I am happy. So, be happy."

The next day, when the Master asked Mr Weekley how he was, he replied that after what the Master had said the day before, he had no option. And the Master replied, "That is right, you have no option."

In New York, Maharaj Ji granted interviews to satsangis and seekers every morning. One morning, while sixty or seventy people were waiting for their interviews in the Statler-Hilton lobby, two members of the hotel staff, a plumber and a maid, appeared before Mr Weekley with a bag of tools and a work order to repair a leaking faucet in the bathroom of Maharaj Ji's hotel suite. Mr Weekley told them to wait and, going through the room where Maharaj Ji was giving interviews, checked the bathroom, to find nothing wrong with the taps. "There must be a mistake, the taps are fine," he told them. After a moment's silence the plumber said, "Yes, you are right. We made this up ourselves because we want to see the man with the beautiful eyes." Mr Weekley was so touched by his guileless confession that, ignoring the line of satsangis waiting outside, he took the plumber and maid into Maharaj Ji's room and said, "Please pardon me, Maharaj Ji, but I could not help bringing these people to see you." The Master got up from his chair before Mr Weekley had finished speaking and stood looking at the couple, a soft, compassionate smile on his face. They gazed at "the man with the beautiful eyes," neither speaking nor moving. Then the Master shook hands with them and patted them on the shoulder as he said good-bye. They were both from Haiti, the "plumber" being a general repairman, and the woman a cleaning maid on one of the floors of the hotel. They emerged from the Master's room after their silent interview, joy and happiness on their faces and tears in their eyes—and they did not even know who he was!

On the morning Maharaj Ji left for Detroit, there was a wonderful scene in his hotel corridor: a large number of the hotel workers—maids, waiters, and repairmen, none of them satsangis—had gathered outside the Master's room to say good-bye and have a final glimpse of "the man with the beautiful eyes." When the Master came out, he quietly walked down the long corridor, responding to the greetings of each one of them with a smile or a nod; his entire personality seemed to pour out divine rays of compassion and love.

Maharaj Ji arrived in Detroit on May 26, continuing with his usual busy routine of satsang, darshan, interviews, and initiation. One afternoon, an incident occurred that adds meaning to the oft-repeated statement that we must become like little children. The Master was with a group of children—babies of a few months up to children of ten years. The children beamed on seeing Maharaj Ji, and a few could not contain themselves and ran up to him. One four-year-old boy caught hold of the Master's two index fingers and stared up at him. The boy held on as the Master moved his hands about, playing with him. Finally Maharaj Ji laughingly asked, "Do you have any friends?" "No," he whispered, "Just one." "And who is that?" Maharaj Ji asked. And the little boy, angelically looking into the Master's face from a distance of about one foot and still hanging on to his fingers, withdrew his right hand and, pointing his finger right at the Master's nose, said, "You."

This brief dialogue deeply moved all the satsangis present, for in this world of changing relationships guided by selfishness, who else but the Master is our true friend?

Following his visits to Chicago and Minneapolis, the Master flew to the city of Calgary, Canada, on June 8 and was met by his representative from Vancouver, Dr Jitendra Khanna. He travelled through the Canadian Rockies with Dr Khanna and his wife, and arrived in Vancouver on June 11.

After travelling to Victoria on June 13, Maharaj Ji left Canada on the fourteenth for California. This was the busiest part of his tour because California has the largest concentration of satsangis in America. He spoke to gatherings of 1,000 in Palo Alto, and more than 1,500 in Pasadena (Los Angeles), giving more private interviews than in any other part of the tour, sometimes 150 in a day. It was also in California that the Master initiated the largest group of seekers; 178 were initiated in one session in Pasadena.

On this tour Maharaj Ji's endeavour was to meet the maximum number of satsangis individually or in small groups, and give time to all seekers. This involved an extremely heavy schedule which provided him almost no rest, keeping him busy till midnight every night. One of the organizers commented that the speed of this tour of Maharaj Ji was such that no human being could keep pace with him. Maharaj Ji himself admitted, in one of his letters to the Dera secretary: "I don't think I have ever worked so hard on any other satsang tour, but by Maharaj Ji's grace I am keeping fairly good health."

After his journey by ship to Honolulu, the Master went on to Tokyo and Hong Kong, spending several days in each place meeting satsangis and seekers before flying to Bombay on July 14. On July 15 he gave darshan and a short discourse in Bombay, and darshan to the Delhi sangat on the same day, returning to Dera on July 16, bringing showers of grace and love to our hearts parched by the long separation. Little rest awaited the Master after this round-the-world tour. The Satguru's work never ends, and hardly ever lessens. The work piled up during his absence—the big heap of pending correspondence, the numerous decisions waiting for his guiding word—and the preparations for the approaching July bhandara reminded us of the physical burden the Saints have to bear in the world, not to speak of the endless burden of their disciples' karmas.

1971: FAR EAST

When the Master made his tour of the United States in 1970, his stops in the Far East were very short and only whetted the satsangis' appetite for darshan. They begged Maharaj Ji to visit them for a longer time, and the love and longing behind their requests resulted in his 1971 tour of the Far East. With Mr Krishin Babani, the secretary of the Bombay satsang, as his travelling secretary, the Master went to Hong Kong, the Philippines, Thailand, Japan, Taiwan, Singapore, Indonesia, and Sri Lanka between May 15 and July 9.

After giving three satsangs in Hong Kong and assuring some applicants that he would initiate them on his return journey, Maharaj Ji reached his second stop, Manila (Philippines), on May 20. An unexpectedly large crowd of five hundred turned out for satsang on the first night, overflowing the auditorium, and a larger hall had to be engaged for the following night. Maharaj Ji granted interviews to many seekers and found that a surprising number had adopted the vegetarian diet even before his arrival in Manila. Thirty-four requested and received initiation. In Bangkok the numbers attending satsang swelled from seven hundred on the first night to fifteen hundred on the next.

On these tours, the Master often has to answer unusual questions. Following a discourse in Bangkok, one gentleman asked: "Maharaj Ji, for centuries we have been trying to find the Lord in the same old way. Yet science has made rapid progress and has opened new horizons to man. We have even reached the moon. Then why is it that we are following the same outdated ways to realize God? Can the path not be changed? Can some concessions not be made so that one can realize God without having to give up eating meat and drinking alcohol?"

Maharaj Ji smiled gently and replied, "You are right, brother, much has changed; human intellect and science have made enormous progress. But please do not forget that in spite of all the changes, birth and death are changeless realities. In this ever-changing world, the law of karma is irrevocable. As we sow, so have we to reap. God is the same, was the same, and will always be the same. He is beyond all changes, and so is the path leading to Him. It cannot be changed. There is no favouritism at His door, no bribe is accepted, and no concessions given. There can be no relaxation in the mode of living for those who tread the path, nor are special favours available, as the path is the same for all." Then the Master laughed softly and said, "But if you change the old God into a new one, you will surely be able to change the way to meet Him."[1]

Two long car journeys also marked the 1971 tour. These trips gave those disciples who lived between major cities a chance to have Maharaj Ji's darshan en route. The first car journey—seventeen hundred miles from Bangkok to Singapore—took five days to complete.

In Singapore, Maharaj Ji had a very busy schedule. He gave four satsangs, many interviews, visited satsangis in their homes, and on June 20 initiated Indian seekers in Punjabi and, in the evening, other seekers in English. The evening session of initiation included some Chinese seekers settled in Singapore. The satsang on the last day of this visit was attended by over one thousand people. Sant Mat in Singapore was originally limited to the Indians settled there, but now with the Master's visits to this small country, local people and the Chinese who have settled there are also taking an interest in the path.

Shortly after arriving in Surabaya, Indonesia, at 5:30 on the evening of June 25, Maharaj Ji gave a satsang which was attended by three hundred people, including a large number of seekers. The next day in Surabaya was a very busy one for the Master: in a sixteen-hour, non-stop day, there were crowded initiations, interviews, and a two-hour satsang. He could just manage a few minutes for a hurried dinner at 10:00 P.M., which was followed by a meeting with the local satsang organizers and workers. The next morning Mr Babani was scheduled to give a satsang. Originally Maharaj Ji was not scheduled to attend this satsang but was to relax and complete his packing for the next leg of the journey—a 550-mile car trip to Jakarta. But at the last moment the Master decided

---

[1] This conversation was translated from the original Punjabi.

to be present at the satsang, and the sangat was thrilled at this unexpected darshan.

As in Surabaya, the satsang at Jakarta was attended by a large number of seekers. The unprecedented gathering of over six hundred was kept spellbound by Maharaj Ji's lucid and powerful discourse. During this short visit, Maharaj Ji gave interviews to about one hundred seekers and initiated fifty-six. His last activity scheduled for Jakarta was giving parshad to the sevadars. After the parshad was blessed by the Master and distributed to the sevadars, Maharaj Ji gave a few words of encouragement and advice to them. He urged them to maintain harmony and love in the sangat, to serve the sangat with love and a spirit of dedication, to be regular in meditation, and to lead the life of an ideal satsangi.

On July 4, Maharaj Ji flew to Colombo, the capital of Sri Lanka, with a stopover in Singapore on the way. After several days of satsang in Sri Lanka, the Master finished his Far East tour on July 10 and returned to India—only to plunge once again into preparations for the July bhandara after a two-day stay in Sikanderpur.

The full significance of Maharaj Ji's long and strenuous tours to different countries around the world will only be known in the course of time, but the immediate impact of his visits is apparent. For satsangis, the Master's visits instilled in them more love and understanding and greater enthusiasm for the path. Many satsangis had the opportunity of seeing their Satguru in his physical form. They realized the beauty, dynamic majesty, and grace of the physical Master. They realized that the physical form of the Master—the Word made flesh—has the unique ability to spiritually elevate and enthral devotees; it has the ineffable power of generating love and devotion in their hearts. In many countries the Master visited, a hunger for spirituality, an interest in vegetarianism, and the keenness to lead a pure life have definitely spread among seekers. Another visible outcome of Maharaj Ji's foreign tours has been the number of young people coming to the path in almost every country he visited.

Many young people who had turned to intoxicating drugs in their search for peace and happiness have given up these harmful pursuits and received initiation. One such young couple found their way to the Dera. They attended Maharaj Ji's satsangs and were deeply impressed both by the Master and the spiritual path he expounds. Feeling remorse for their past way of life, they gave up the drugs without which they had not been able to live even for a day. After about two weeks they begged the Master for initiation, and when it was granted, they worked hard at their meditation. When their three-month visit at the Dera came to an end, they went to the Master and confessed that they had jumped bail in America just before they were to come to trial for narcotics. They also explained that they had lived together outside of marriage before coming to the Dera, though they had lived separately during their visit here. Maharaj Ji listened patiently and then advised them first to get married, because a settled householder's life is an aid in following the path; and further he advised them to go to Delhi and surrender themselves to the American ambassador. If they were punished, he told them to accept the sentence cheerfully as part of God's will and as a settlement of their karmic account.

The couple accepted his advice completely; their previous fears of serving a jail sentence were relieved and they were happy to follow the Master's directions. After saying goodbye to Maharaj Ji, they immediately went to Delhi and handed themselves over to the American ambassador. The ambassador and his staff were greatly impressed with the attitude of these young people. They were married in the embassy and then sent back to the United States where they confessed their guilt and accepted their jail term in a spirit of self-surrender. After serving their term, they were released from jail and began to earn their own living, leading the life of good satsangis and giving daily time to their meditation.

The Master had drawn people from various walks of life—young apostates strongly reacting against traditional religious practices, as well as priests and monks confined to the precincts of formalism. A trappist monk in America had led an austere life in a monastery for fourteen years, practising penances such as fasting, vows of silence, and long hours of prayer, without any apparent results. Finally he asked permission from his superior to leave the monastery to search for spiritual truth. Receiving permission, he began attending meetings of different spiritual groups, but found no solace until the day an acquaintance gave him the book *Path of the Masters*. After only a little study of the book, he realized he had found the path he had been seeking. He began to attend satsang meetings and soon received initiation. With the Master's grace, he attained that divine love for which he had undertaken severe austerities for fourteen long years. In his own words, he experienced that "sublime and elevating feeling of love" that he had never imagined to be possible.

Perhaps for the first time in known history, a perfect Saint has travelled to the far corners of the world carrying the message of the Saints to people of different nations, races, religions, and languages; and while fulfilling his mission, the Master has had to face numerous inconveniences and work extremely hard, overlooking his own comfort and even his health.

The seed of Sant Mat sown in the West by Maharaj Sawan Singh Ji in 1911 has sprouted and is growing. Maharaj Charan

Singh Ji has tended it with care and attention, nurtured it with the divine water of love and grace; it is now growing day after day, its branches providing shelter to seekers all over the world.

From North America, Mexico, South America, and the West Indies, to the United Kingdom, Europe, the Middle East, South and East Africa; from Japan, Hong Kong, Thailand, Malaysia, and Indonesia, to the Fiji Islands, Australia, and New Zealand, seekers and satsangis from all over the world are today praying to Maharaj Ji to visit them again.

Though the Master has provided more accommodations for the visiting seekers and disciples from abroad, and though over five hundred come every year, there are many thousands whose circumstances do not permit them to make the journey to the Dera and who long for the Master as much or even more than we at the Dera do whenever he goes on a tour.

In spite of the daily increasing burden of work at the Dera, the Master—all kindness and mercy—will surely grant their heartfelt prayers and visit them many times more.[1]

Dera Timetable

At the Dera, a daily routine of meditation, satsang, and seva is followed throughout the year. Whether it is the icy cold nights of the winter months or the hot sultry nights of the Punjab summer, the Dera siren resounds at 3:00 A.M. The devotees, after a period of quiet sleep, get up from their beds in the serene early morning atmosphere of the Dera and sit in meditation with a relaxed mind. Thus each day given by the Lord is begun in devotion to Him.

[1] After the author wrote this, the Master undertook tours of the United Kingdom and Europe, the Far East, North Africa, East Africa, and South Africa.

After two and a half to three hours of meditation, the sangat gets up at about 6:00 A.M. From 7:00 till 8:30, according to the season of the year, is the time for morning seva; those who want to, gladly take part in it. Satsang is held every morning at about 8:30 in the summer and 9:30 in the winter. When Maharaj Ji is at the Dera, he either delivers the discourse, speaking with his melodious voice in simple, clear language, or he gives darshan while one of the senior satsangis authorized to give satsang delivers the discourse. When the Master is out of the Dera, daily satsang is held as usual, as are all of the other Dera activities.

The rest of the morning is spent in seva—in the langar, in the fields, or in various other departments of the Dera. Then comes lunch and an afternoon rest. At 3:00 P.M. the siren sounds, calling the sangat to seva—usually either earth seva or brick seva. When Maharaj Ji is at the Dera, he is almost always present for this seva. After two hours or so of seva, the sangat returns home around dusk. From 6:00 to 8:00 P.M., the satsangis have their dinner and rest, and by the time it is 9:00, they retire to bed after a short period of meditation. Thus, according to the Dera routine, the satsangi's day of sixteen to seventeen hours is divided between meditation, satsang, and seva. The seva is always voluntary and there is no compulsion on anyone to do seva or to do it for any particular length of time. Similarly the Dera routine is there for satsangis and seekers to take advantage of, but there is no compulsion on anyone to rigidly follow the routine. However, out of love and devotion, the sangat follows the entire routine with enthusiasm and enjoys doing so.

Maharaj Ji's concern for the comfort of each person is expressed through the untiring work of the sevadars, who see that transportation, housing, and food are provided for everyone. This is certainly no small task, especially at the bhandaras, as people begin to arrive in huge numbers eight to ten days before the actual bhandara day. They come by car, bus, truck, tractor, trolley, van, scooter, bicycle—and are happy to travel by whatever form of conveyance they can obtain. As the sangat arrives, so also do the sevadars. To facilitate travel to the Dera, special buses are run from major towns and cities to the Dera. A permanent bus stand has been built for these buses, as well as for those shuttling visitors to and from the Beas railway station.

Hundreds of sevadars are on hand to welcome bhandara visitors, carry their luggage, and direct them to accommodations that have been set up just for this occasion. Scenes of the langar during the bhandaras are truly amazing to behold. Hundreds of ladies help cook chapattis on the huge ovens, even in the blazing heat of May and July, while the sevadars serving the food almost have to run to get around the vast field where thirty to forty thousand people are eating at each shift. And what is most beautiful and inspiring about all the selfless service is the love of the Master that motivates it.

During bhandara times the daily routine changes only slightly, but the Dera is transformed from a quiet retreat into a bustling city of several hundred thousand people who come for satsang, darshan, and seva.

The Master has an equally long but much more strenuous day. Metaphorically speaking, the running of the entire Dera rests on the Master's shoulders because he is the inspiring and guiding force. Physically also he bears the load, because he looks after the daily working of the various departments in their minutest details and devotes considerable time and energy to it. His day, like that of all other Dera residents, begins at 3:00 in the morning. After meditation, bath, and breakfast, he comes downstairs to his office at 7:30. His personal secretary comes with important letters and documents, and is followed by the department heads and engineers, who come to discuss and receive instructions about the day's work. The Master then goes on a short round of the various sites where work is in progress, such as road making, erecting walls or shifting them, digging sewerage canals, working in the fields, and other construction work. He meets the sangat at each place seva is being done and personally gives directions about further work.

The Master then arrives at satsang—at 8:30 A.M. in summer or 9:30 in winter—and sits through the satsang, giving the discourse at least twice a week. During bhandara days he gives the discourse every day and, in view of the large gathering, explains the principles of Sant Mat and its various aspects in a discourse that is usually one and a half hours long.

After the satsang the Master meets with the various department heads of the Dera until lunch time. During bhandara days he visits the langar each morning at about 11:30, moving through every corner of the free kitchen where the food is cooked. Because of the large number of people fed during the bhandaras—about two hundred thousand at each meal—the ladies cooking the chapattis do not come for satsang. The Master himself walks down the aisles between the large ovens and huge iron plates where chapattis are cooked, blessing the sevadars with his darshan.

Afterwards, the Master returns to the satsang grounds, and from about 12:00 noon till 1:30 P.M. he gives darshan to the sangat who file past, offering their voluntary contributions to the Dera Trust. The Master also gives interviews at this time to those satsangis who need some guidance regarding their inner progress. In between the satsang and the visit to the langar, the Master also meets the group of Western satsangis staying in the Guest House and gives them darshan and individual interviews.

It is almost 2:00 P.M. by the time the Master sits down for lunch, and after about forty minutes' rest he dictates replies to the numerous letters he receives every day. At 4:00 the Master goes to the place where the sangat is doing seva. He sits in a chair on a platform so that the sangat can see him— for he is the source of inspiration for the sangat, who accomplish in a few hours the work that would normally take days. During seva, the Master is kept busy giving interviews, discussing plans with the engineers, and answering letters in the various Indian languages.

No sooner does he reach his residence at about 5:30 P.M. than the Dera secretary comes to discuss urgent matters and seek his guidance. A little after 6:00, the Master again visits the langar to give darshan to the sevadars and bless the food. From 7:00 till 8:00 the Master is at the evening meeting in the Guest House, answering the questions of the large number of Westerners who visit the Dera between the last week of September and the middle of April. He answers questions that range from the principles of Sant Mat and the method of meditation to the satsangis' problems—marriage, divorce, jobs, bringing up children, and the vegetarian diet. For the last few years during the meetings, the Master has sometimes given discourses on the Bible, bringing out the hidden gems of spirituality from the symbols and parables of Jesus Christ.

After the English meeting, the Master returns to his residence, takes his dinner, and gives time to his family members and a few long-time satsangis. The Master's day is always full—incredibly busy and strenuous. He rises with the sangat at 3:00 A.M. and rarely retires before 9:30 P.M. Before retiring to his room, the Master spends some time in the office completing any pending work of that day, or going through a new manuscript. Then Maharaj Ji retires to his bedroom. After about ten minutes of reading, he puts out the light.

After a strenuous nineteen-hour day, whether our beloved Master gives attention to the centre of sleep in the physical body or transcends all physical barriers to travel into the inner regions of pure joy and bliss, he alone knows. A highly advanced friend of mine once told me that in the Court of the Supreme Being—in whose will and command the perfect Masters act—there is no such thing as a holiday or a recess for the Satguru, not even in his sleep. But the Great Master used to say that when the devotee merges himself in the Shabd or the Word within, the Word gives him such energy and freshness that he has hardly any need for sleep.

And the Saints themselves are the Word personified.

Dera During the Wars

Whenever their followers have to go through a major catastrophe, the Saints, moved by compassion, protect and comfort them. At such times they often take the heavy load of the satsangis' karmas on themselves and alleviate their suffering. During the partition of India in 1947, a period of great violence and bloodshed, Maharaj Sawan Singh Ji protected his disciples and even their kith and kin, helping them to reach places of safety. In order to reduce the sangat's burden of misery, the Great Master himself had to undergo pain and serious illness and even sacrifice his own life. Numerous refugees, both Hindu and Muslim, who experienced the Satguru's help and grace at that time, are still living to tell the tale of their Master's immense love for them.

Later, when the war between India and Pakistan broke out on 6 September 1965, Maharaj Charan Singh Ji was in Dalhousie. As soon as he heard the news on the radio, he left Dalhousie for the Dera in order to be with the sangat. He had to pass through areas close to the battle zone, but he took no notice of the danger, even though the sound of bombs and cannon fire could be heard almost throughout the 125-mile drive. The Master's arrival gave the sangat much reassurance and confidence, and though the Dera was close to the border, they were relaxed and happy, while the rest of the country was in a state of tension and anxiety.

The numbers at the Dera swelled to bhandara-size crowds as satsangis poured into Beas from towns on the western front of the war. The satsangis and even many others from the two border villages of Chhamb and Jorian—which were devastated during the first two or three days of the war—came and took shelter at the Dera. Incidentally, Maharaj Ji had visited Chhamb in the late Fifties and gave one satsang there. Many people from Jullundur, Kapurthala, and other cities south and southeast of Dera left their homes and went further south, away from the danger zone. But satsangis from these areas preferred to be near the Master and came to the Dera, though it was closer to the Indo-Pakistan border than their own towns were.

Though we could hear bombs exploding throughout the day and night, sometimes even close enough to make our windows and doors rattle, the usual routine of the Dera continued, with the Master at the centre. Satsang was held daily, and Maharaj Ji was always present throughout the afternoon seva. During the enforced blackouts at night, the Master used to go around the Dera himself to make sure no breaches in this regulation occurred.

The army authorities advised the Dera organizers to suspend satsang and seva activities at the Dera and to move the satsang to some other province in India. They strongly recommended this step because the colony is only forty miles by air from the border and comes in the danger zone. But with Maharaj Ji's grace, the satsangs, which had to be held in the open grounds under shamiyanas because of the large attendance, continued daily without any interruption.

Before the second Indo-Pakistan war, during the last week of November 1971, Maharaj Ji was not well. On his return from the satsang tours of Ajmer and Jaipur, the Master had a severe heart attack in Delhi, and the satsang tours of Chandigarh and Bombay had to be cancelled. On December 3, when the war broke out, the Master was in a Delhi hospital and had been advised complete bed rest by the physicians. At the suggestion of the doctors, the news of the outbreak of the war was not given to him and the radio was quietly removed from his room in the hospital; even newspapers were not brought to him. But on the morning of December 4, Maharaj Ji called for a radio and listened to the news. As soon as he heard about the war, he decided to return to the Dera. The doctors said it would be harmful to his health even to leave his bed, much less travel. Maharaj Ji's family members and the satsangis with him begged him to give up the idea, but his decision was final. He said it was his duty to be with the sangat at such a time, and he returned to the Dera on 6 December 1971.

On reaching the Dera, Maharaj Ji could not be dissuaded from coming to the satsang and meeting the sangat. Once again he stayed in the Dera throughout the period of hostilities. There were numerous satsangis in border areas like Chhamb, Naushehra, Jammu, Pathankot, and many other small border towns and villages. The satsangis coming from these areas gave us many accounts of the Master's grace and protection in the face of grave danger and devastation. The Satguru, in his love and mercy, came to the aid of the sangat; but he had to pay the price by enduring sickness and physical suffering.

As in the previous war, though once again in what was called the danger zone, Dera and its usual atmosphere of peace and quiet remained undisturbed. When the war broke out, there were about sixty Western satsangis at the Dera. They were offered the option of moving to Delhi as a place of greater safety, but declined and said they did not want to leave the colony.

During both this war and the 1965 war, I had the good fortune of being with Maharaj Ji. He was relaxed and unperturbed; the daily changing aspects of the war could not disturb his calm. I never saw signs of anxiety or agitation on his face; his compassion was unaffected by any feelings of hostility. He seemed to transcend all considerations of creed and nationality. One day when a satsangi expressed his feelings of hostility towards some of the countries involved in the war, the Master advised him to adopt a broad outlook, one of tolerance and understanding, for whatever was happening was the outcome of our own karmas. A satsangi should fulfil his obligations towards his country and society, but should never bear malice or ill will towards any religion or country. Man has learned to hate man in the name of God; it is time he learned to love in His name.

Dera Development

Two small thatched huts built by Baba Jaimal Singh Ji in 1891 marked the beginning of what today has grown into the Radha Soami colony, a centre of remarkable physical and spiritual dimensions. The details of its growth during the time of the Great Master have been given earlier. During the period of Sardar Bahadur Maharaj Ji, the main well—built during Baba Ji's time—was cleaned, made deeper, and a pump installed; and the Dera lands were consolidated.

When Maharaj Charan Singh Ji became the Master, day by day the sangat began to increase and soon there was an acute shortage of space—for the sangat's accommodation, for cooking and serving food in the langar, and for seating the sangat in satsang. The bhandara gatherings, which during Baba Ji's time were about one hundred people and during Great Master's time about thirty thousand, soon exceeded one hundred thousand.

The sangat grew so rapidly that all the facilities were becoming inadequate. The number of people to be fed in the langar at bhandaras increased to over fifty thousand in a very short time. Since only three or four thousand people could be fed at a time, the langar was operating almost twenty-four hours a day in order to feed everyone, and the sound of cooking and serving in the langar could be heard till late at night.

One night during the April bhandara in 1954, Maharaj Ji was kept awake until 2:30 in the morning by the noise of activity in the langar. He sent someone to find out what was happening there and learned that the sangat was still eating, while several thousand more were waiting to be served their supper. It distressed him greatly that people had to wait for their evening meal until 2:00 or 3:00 in the morning. The next day he went with Rai Sahib Munshi Ram and Mr Ahluwalia, the Dera secretary, to inspect the langar. Maharaj Ji said that enough space was needed to seat at least twenty thousand people at a time, so that everyone could be served in two or three shifts. The cooking area could be expanded a little, but not the courtyard where the food was served. On three sides of the langar were the Dera buildings, and on the fourth side, ravines thirty to forty feet deep.

Maharaj Ji pointed out that the langar could be extended only on the east side where the ravines were, and added that the only way seemed to be to fill the ravines and level the ground. "But Hazur," protested Mr Ahluwalia, "the ravines are so wide and deep that it would be impossible to fill them. Even if we tried to fill them, it would take at least ten or twelve years, perhaps more." Rai Sahib Munshi Ram, one of the seniormost satsangis of the Great Master's time, agreed, saying, "Let the langar go on as it is—somehow we are pulling on." But Maharaj Ji replied, "Even if it does take ten years, it doesn't matter. At least then the sangat will be able to eat in comfort."

The next day at the end of satsang, Maharaj Ji announced that the filling of the ravines would begin as a form of seva. For the first few days, this new seva of carrying earth in baskets on one's head proceeded so slowly that ten years seemed an optimistic estimate. But then the Master began the practice of being present for the entire period of seva, both morning and evening, and the huge craters began to fill up. At bhandara times, eight thousand or more people at a time were engaged in this earth-moving seva, and over a million cubic feet of earth were carried by the sangat to fill the ravines and level the land. The job which according to many of us was going to be long and laborious was accomplished by the sangat's love and the Master's grace in the unbelievably short period of two years. Now twenty thousand people could indeed be fed at one sitting in the langar.[1]

This was just the beginning of *mitti-ki-seva*, as this earth-moving seva is called. The growth of the sangat has made this seva in some ways more important than the other types

---

[1]   This is the place where the major part of the cooking is done today and where the shed with the corrugated cement roof stands.

of physical seva. Four to five million cubic feet of earth are moved in a year, levelling ravines and gullies to provide space for satsang, langar grounds, and more buildings. The expanded langar of the Fifties became inadequate after a few years, so two more terraces were built on land levelled by mitti-ki-seva. Today a new langar, which can feed sixty thousand people at a time, has been constructed on these levelled plains, and an expanded cooking area has been added.

Mitti-ki-seva is an unforgettable sight. At bhandaras literally tens of thousands of people from all walks of life—rich and poor, educated and illiterate, old and young—work together carrying baskets of earth on their heads in a spirit of loving service. Once, a group of men from a foreign television company happened to visit the Dera during mitti-ki-seva. They asked what the labourers were paid and could not believe it when they were told it was a labour of love. How could they understand that the wages of this loving seva, done with humility and dedication, are the one compassionate glance of the Master, the one brief glimpse of his radiant face, for which the disciple would sacrifice everything!

On another occasion a distinguished authority on Sikh history visited the Dera and witnessed two days of mitti-ki-seva, satsang, and langar. He made this comment: "In studying Sikh history I have read a great deal about the Gurus, their activities, and the love and devotion of the sangat. I have read about these things but could never imagine what they must have been like in reality. On coming here I feel that I am actually seeing the glory of the Gurus and the love of the disciples for them."

Concerning the spirit of mitti-ki-seva, Sir Colin Garbett, one of the earliest South African satsangis, related that once when he was sitting next to Maharaj Ji at mitti-ki-seva, he asked, "Some people carry tremendous loads while others have hardly a handful in their basket. What is the use of their seva when they are carrying so little?" The Master replied, "Sir Colin, it is not how much is carried that is important, but the love and devotion with which the seva is done."

Today over two hundred thousand people are fed in the langar at each meal. Despite the fact that food is served to such a large gathering, the langar is kept clean; and after the sangat has eaten, no one could guess that such a large number of people has eaten there. The entire seva in the langar is done by sevadars who volunteer and come from various parts of the country to do the variety of jobs connected with the langar—cutting vegetables, making dough, baking chapattis, cooking dal and vegetables, cleaning the huge cooking vats, and serving food and water to the sangat.

The sight of the sangat's seva in the langar leaves a lasting impression on the visitor, and when the Master visits the langar on bhandara days, it is an unforgettable event. Even during the hot days of the May bhandara, when the temperature rises to 120 degrees Fahrenheit, and in the sultry, suffocating monsoon days of July when the breeze ceases to blow, ladies sit for hours at the furnaces and huge hot plates baking chapattis, their bodies bathed in perspiration. They cook chapattis with great devotion, and when the Master visits them their eyes are filled with tears, their faces shine with love and joy. The Master's radiance, his unbounded love, is the moving force that enables them to cook the food under such hard conditions. Once, a few visitors—intellectuals—seeing this sight, remarked that nowhere in the world had they even seen such a sight of devotion and joy. Nor had they imagined that such devotion and selfless love was possible in this world.

The satsang hall compound could not accommodate the increased number of satsangis and seekers attending the monthly satsangs and bhandaras, and in 1954 a number of thatched hutments inside the satsang hall compound had to be demolished. Even then, the grounds were too small, for the sangat had swelled to over fifty thousand.

In 1955 the large attendance at the April and July bhandaras necessitated the shifting of satsang outside of the satsang hall compound. The sangat, through persistent mitti-ki-seva, levelled the uneven ground to the south of the satsang hall so that two hundred thousand could be seated at satsang. Within four or five years this also became insufficient, so four adjacent acres were levelled and added to the new grounds; this became a permanent satsang ground for bhandaras and even monthly satsangs.

With the increase in the sangat, there was additional pressure on accommodation arrangements, bathrooms, tea stalls, and the cafeteria. A process of continued building work was started under Maharaj Ji's direction and, one by one, buildings, sheds, and bathrooms have come up in the Dera. A shed of twenty thousand square feet (two hundred feet by one hundred feet) was built in the langar to provide shelter for the sangat during the rainy season; twenty-five sheds have been built in the reclaimed area to the south of the langar, which are used to accommodate the sangat. Even this does not suffice, and hundreds of shamiyanas and tents are erected during each bhandara. The Master has built a large number of one-, two-, and three-bedroom houses with all amenities: fans, electricity, running water, flush toilets, a courtyard, and a lawn. These houses are allotted to old satsangis and permanent sevadars at the Dera. All houses are connected by broad roads, and are interspersed with open grassy areas. The entire colony today has a well-organized water supply system, with three large water storage tanks of fifty thousand gallons each, sixty feet above ground, fed by deep tube wells. A number of small wells in the colony have been filled in so that the water is supplied only through the large tanks under controlled, hygienic conditions. With the availability of water, large lawns and gardens have come up in the Dera, and flowering trees and shrubs have been planted along all the roads.

In the reclaimed ground on the west side of the Dera, thousands of trees have been planted and the sangat rests in their shade on summer days.

For greater security for the sangat, a high wall has been built around the entire Dera. On each side there are large gates with living quarters for the sevadars who are on duty at the gates. In December 1970 Maharaj Ji decided to remove the hedge on the river side of the Dera and replace it with a six-foot-high wall. Thirty-five hundred feet long, with three gates and eleven rooms, the wall was erected by the sangat in the remarkably short time of two weeks. Maharaj Ji used to sit in seva every day—before satsang, after satsang, and at least two hours in the afternoon—during the construction of this wall.

In spite of the large number of people coming and staying here, the Dera is a clean and hygienic place, and the sevadars do their best to keep it so. The tarmac roads are washed every morning; other roads are swept daily by sevadars; periodically the Dera is sprayed to protect the sangat from mosquitoes, etc.; and over four thousand water taps and fifteen hundred flush toilets have been provided for the sangat, with separate bathrooms for men and women.

Maharaj Ji has provided many other facilities to the devotees coming from outside the Dera. Although the langar is open to all and serves free food, there are some who want to pay for their food. For them a bhojan bhandar has been built, where meals are served at the nominal cost of less than five U.S. cents. The food is excellent and there is no limit to the quantity one is allowed to eat. The bhojan bhandar and a cafeteria serving tea and snacks are both subsidized by the Dera Trust.

The sole purpose of the Saints' coming into this world is to save us from the cycle of birth and rebirth, not to make the world a better place to live in. But they also tell us that we must help one another. They show us by their example the way to help others in a spirit of love and detachment, without expecting rewards for our good actions. During his tours of the villages in the rural and mountainous areas, Maharaj Ji noticed a large number of people suffering from cataracts and other eye diseases. In view of their inability to afford or even find the needed medical attention, the first Dera eye camp was held in February 1965. Eye specialists from the Sitapur Eye Hospital near Aligarh (Uttar Pradesh)—Dr J. M. Pahwa and his team—came at the Dera's invitation and treated some two thousand patients, free of charge. All the 950 major operations and the 300 minor ones they performed were successful.

The eye camp has become a yearly feature of Dera life, providing a wonderful opportunity for seva. Satsangi doctors come to the Dera from all over India and abroad to serve in the eye camp. A number of educated satsangis from other professions—lawyers, government officials, businessmen—also come to Dera in a spirit of loving devotion to perform many tasks not requiring medical expertise. The eye camp is open to all, and no distinction is made between satsangi and non-satsangi patients.

From the preparation of the grounds to the organization of the hospital, the eye camp is carefully planned. Each camp begins with the sevadars thoroughly cleaning and disinfecting the whole area. The patients are housed in twenty-five dormitories, each a separate ward under the supervision of two doctors and a group of sevadars acting as nurses, working in shifts throughout the day and night. The patients are provided with food, beds, clean linen, medicines, all the needed medical tests, and eyeglasses—free of charge—and their relatives are also given the use of all Dera facilities. The large operation theatre is divided into separate areas for the different stages of the operation. After the operation, the patients recuperate in their wards until they can return to their villages. In addition to cataract operations, patients are treated for other eye ailments as well.

In eye operations, success depends largely on the postoperative care of the patient. Dr Pahwa, who is renowned for his skill, spirit of service, and dedication, has remarked that the efficient arrangements, cleanliness, and untiring service of the sevadars play a vital role in the success of the Dera eye camps. By the Master's grace, not a single operation to date has been unsuccessful.

Maharaj Ji himself visits the eye camp two or three times every day. He walks through each ward, meets the doctors, and inquires about the progress of the operations and the convalescing patients. His grace and mercy and, above all, his loving concern for the patients—the majority of whom are not satsangis—inspire the sangat to serve the patients in a spirit of selfless dedication. For the entire period of the eye camp, the sevadars do not come to the satsangs and mostly stay at the camp.

Once, at the request of the Punjab Government Health Department, Maharaj Ji allowed the Blood Bank Society to visit Dera for blood donations. At a word from the Master, satsangis flocked to donate blood; their number was so great that the team did not have sufficient arrangements either for collecting the blood or for its storage and preservation. The Blood Bank Society now visits the Dera once or twice a year according to their needs. The number of donors here is so large that many satsangis who want to give blood are unable to do so, because the Blood Bank does not have the means to collect and preserve the blood of the thousands of devotees who line up to give their blood.

Year-round medical services, free of cost, are also available at the Dera. The Maharaj Sawan Singh Hospital, run by qualified doctors and nurses, treats people from the Dera and also patients from the surrounding villages, where no medical help exists. It has sixteen beds, a small laboratory, and a small operating room. The hospital staff is often supplemented by doctors and nurses visiting the Dera, such as the Naidu family from South Africa, who devote much of their time attending to the patients.

Bibi Harjeet Kaur, Maharaj Ji's wife, runs a Nature Cure Clinic in the Dera where patients are treated through a special programme of diet, exercise, and naturopathic therapies using mud, water, steam, sunrays, and so on. She opened the clinic in Pisawah House, the house belonging to her father, Rao Bahadur Shivdhyan Singh. The clinic is comparatively smaller than many others in India, but because of her devotion, hard work, and selfless service, it is recognized today as one of the well-managed naturopathic centres in the country. Bibi Harjeet Kaur, interested in naturopathic cures from early youth, studied this system at various centres in North India and passed examinations before opening the centre at the Dera. The patients are treated free of cost, and in the beginning all expenses were met by Bibi Harjeet Kaur herself; now the Dera has taken over the financial responsibility. Under her able guidance, a group of devoted sevadars are looking after a large number of patients each year.

Dr Randolph Stone, a highly devoted American disciple of the Great Master, has been coming to the Dera for about six months a year for the last fifteen years. A scholar and author, he is a specialist in his own method of treatment, known as polarity therapy, which deals with the various energy currents in the body. He has been practising in America since 1914 and has successfully treated a number of patients suffering from incurable ailments, both here and abroad. With the Master's permission, he treats patients in the Dera free of charge. Though he is now eighty, he is physically very fit and devotes many hours every day to treating patients.[1]

Till 1951 there was only one guest house for seekers and satsangis coming from abroad. It consisted of only four bedrooms, and during the entire year there were only four or five visitors. Maharaj Ji brought new life to Sant Mat abroad by appointing more representatives in the United States, Europe, and South Africa, where the sangat had started to grow. In 1955, a small annex, consisting of three rooms and two bathrooms, was built onto the guest house in order to accommodate the growing number of visitors from abroad. The Rani-ki-Kothi, a two-storey house in the Guest House compound, built in 1954 by Indumati Rajwade for herself and her family, was offered by her to the Master as a guest house, and thus a few more visitors could be accommodated.

After Maharaj Ji's foreign tours in the 1960s, the number of satsangis abroad began to grow rapidly. Naturally, more and more satsangis wanted to visit the Dera, and in 1965 a two-storey guest house of thirty-seven rooms was built to accommodate more foreign guests. It is a beautiful building with a reception lounge on the ground floor and a meeting hall on the upper floor, which has a seating capacity of around 150. It is in this meeting hall that Maharaj Ji holds daily meetings with the guests from abroad, either giving a discourse or

---

[1] Besides writing many books about his own system of therapy, Dr Stone wrote an excellent analysis of the mystic elements in the Old and New Testaments, *Mystic Bible,* which has been popular among both satsangis and seekers. In 1973, at the age of eighty-three, Dr Stone settled permanently at the Dera; he passed on in December 1981.

answering questions in English. At the back of this guest house is a kitchen and dining hall to provide meals for the Western guests.

As with all the building projects at the Dera, Maharaj Ji supervised the plans for this building and all the details of its construction. The laying of the roof terrace on the new guest house in July 1965 is an example of the way in which Maharaj Ji inspires the sangat to do seva—and then rewards bountifully for the work he has inspired. The engineers wanted the entire roof to be laid in a single day in a continuous process, so that the expanse of concrete would mature into one jointless block. At 7:00 A.M. the day the work was to be done, Maharaj Ji gave a fifteen-minute discourse and then called for the sangat's help in laying the roof.

The seva began at 7:30 in the morning and continued until 3:00 in the afternoon without a break for lunch. Maharaj Ji was present the whole time, and though the sangat had five or six breaks for a cold sweet drink, he only had one cup of coffee during the eight hours in the intense monsoon heat. After the roof was successfully laid, Maharaj Ji had food brought from the langar, asked the sangat to be seated, and served chapattis to them with his own hands. It was a beautiful sight, for Maharaj Ji's face seemed full of affection for the sevadars, who had obviously forgotten their exhaustion in the bliss of their Master's darshan and his pleasure with them. Only after the sangat had finished eating did Maharaj Ji go to his house for lunch, around 4:00 in the afternoon.

But this new guest house soon proved to be insufficient because the number of people from abroad increased every year. Visitors started coming not only from Canada, the United States, South Africa, and Europe, but also from South America, East Africa, Israel, the West Indies, and the Far East—Japan, Hong Kong, Thailand, Singapore, Australia, and

New Zealand—lending a truly international colour to the Guest House. The number of annual visitors from abroad has risen to about five hundred, with the guests staying for two to ten weeks. In view of this, Maharaj Ji has started two new buildings in the Guest House complex, providing forty-five additional rooms.

Because of the increasing numbers attracted to the path, the Dera has grown into a small township—probably the most carefully planned and cared for township in the world, as it is planned and cared for by the Lord in human form.

Today the physical Dera consists of a sizable expanse of land within the boundary walls and a big tract outside its walls. In addition to the section of older houses built during the Great Master's time, Maharaj Ji has had a new section of modern houses constructed: one-, two-, and three-room cottages, fully equipped with modern amenities, to accommodate permanent residents and regular Indian visitors to the Dera. More houses are under construction, all of which are made available to satsangis at less than cost price. Waterworks, drainage, and hygienic arrangements have received special attention to ensure cleanliness even when the huge bhandara crowds are there. Besides the free kitchen, or langar, a variety of arrangements have been made to feed the sangat: a bhojan bhandar, a vegetable and fruit stall, and a provision store, where essential articles are sold at subsidized rates.

From the very beginning of his mastership, Maharaj Ji has taken a keen interest in every detail of the Dera's growth. All building and construction plans are first submitted to him, and even skilled engineers find his suggestions invaluable. It is Maharaj Ji's close personal attention to all seva projects that has inspired the sangat to work so enthusiastically at developing the Dera.

One of the first projects to which he gave his attention was making books on Sant Mat available in many languages. Until 1951, the Dera had published only five or six books in English and a couple of books in Punjabi. Under his guidance, books on Sant Mat are now being published in almost every Indian language, including Hindi, Punjabi, Urdu, Sindhi, Marathi, Gujarati, Bengali, Tamil, Telugu, and Kannada. Books available in English number more than forty, including eleven books by Maharaj Ji himself. Many of these have been translated outside India into French, Spanish, Dutch, German, Greek, Italian, Polish, Arabic, Indonesian, Chinese, and other languages. Indian-language books published by the Dera are generously subsidized to make them available at less than cost price to satsangis and seekers.

One book that Maharaj Ji has particularly close association with is *Spiritual Letters,* a collection of inspiring letters written by Baba Ji Maharaj to Maharaj Sawan Singh. These were the letters which the Great Master said he cherished as his only scripture. Maharaj Ji sometimes relates how the letters came into book form. A day or two before the Great Master made his will, he handed over a beautiful jewel chest lined with velvet to Maharaj Charan Singh Ji. Before parting with the box, he raised it to his forehead and kissed it with reverence.

The Great Master's eyes were moist and he said to Maharaj Ji, "My son, this is my rarest and most precious treasure. Today I am handing it over to you—treasure it with love and care." This casket contained the letters written by Baba Ji Maharaj to the Great Master during the days he was a disciple and are of great spiritual and historical value.

Maharaj Ji says: "I little realized at that time how precious the gift was and what a fund of esoteric knowledge of Sant Mat it contained. But as I went through the letters in later years, I was deeply impressed with their profundity and practical character and felt that this great gift must be shared with as many satsangi brothers and sisters as possible, not only in our country but also abroad."

During the Great Master's time, on the persuasion of Dr Johnson and a few satsangis at the Dera, the Great Master released eleven of Baba Ji's letters and they were printed in Punjabi and Hindi. They were also translated into English and circulated among Western satsangis. In 1952/53, Miss Louise Hilger,[1] during her long stay at the Dera, heard about the letters and took Maharaj Ji's permission to have them read out and translated to her. With the Master's permission, Prof. Jagmohan Lal Bhatnagar translated the letters to Miss Hilger and she noted them down in shorthand. Later, in response to her keen desire to share the letters with the growing number of English-speaking satsangis, the Master permitted them to be printed. He also allowed them to be printed in Punjabi, Hindi, Urdu, and other Indian languages.

This was the beginning of an extensive publication programme, inspired and guided by the Master, who has made Sant Mat literature available to the masses in India and to satsangis abroad.

All Saints are waves emanating from the Supreme Being. They rise from that ocean, come to the shore of this physical world, and merge back into the ocean. After they leave, the world forgets their true message of going within and meeting the Lord. People adopt various external practices, divide

---

[1] Miss Louise Hilger, who had been coming to the Dera since 1951 and spending about six months here every year, permanently settled here in 1973. She has been responsible for the editing, typing, and proofreading of almost all English books printed by the Radha Soami Satsang Beas in the last thirty years. Besides this, her personal notes, typed transcriptions of satsang translations, and letters to satsangis abroad are an inspiring treasure.

themselves into formal allegiances, and lose sight of the truth that the Saints once taught them. Again the Saints come to reveal the hidden truth of the teachings and to show mankind the real path to God.

In his monumental two-volume work, *Gurmat Sidhant* (abridged and translated as *Philosophy of the Masters,* five volumes), the Great Master discusses the teachings of the ancient sages and medieval Saints of India and the Middle East, pointing out that the message of all Saints is the same. Maharaj Charan Singh Ji likewise reveals the gems of spiritual knowledge hidden in the parables of the New Testament. Only a Saint can unfold the true meaning of a past Saint's writings, for he holds the key to the secret of the Word.

In his discourses on the New Testament, Maharaj Ji has brought out the esoteric meaning of the teachings of Jesus Christ, clearly pointing out that Jesus, like all other Saints, teaches that God is within and can be realized by the practice of the Word, or Shabd. Maharaj Ji explains that there are clear references to the importance of the Word and the physical Master, and to the law of karma and transmigration of souls. Maharaj Ji's unique contribution has been a revelation to many Western seekers and satsangis, who have taped most of his discourses on the Bible and transcribed them into manuscript form. At their request, Maharaj Ji permitted their publication in book form. His discourses on the Gospel of Saint John were brought out in 1967, and those on the Gospel of Saint Matthew are being printed.[1]

---

[1] These books, *Light on Saint John* and *Light on Saint Matthew,* are currently in print.

Creation of the Trust

In 1957, Maharaj Charan Singh Ji made a most significant and radical change in the organization of the Dera. He created the Radha Soami Satsang Beas, a trust society, and transferred ownership of all the satsang property to this society. When he first proposed this idea, some of the senior satsangis, such as Rai Sahib Munshi Ram, Rai Bahadur Shankar Dass Sondhi, and a few others, opposed it. They argued that in accordance with Sant Mat tradition, the Master is the sole owner of all satsang property and it should remain in his name. But Maharaj Ji said that, in fact, the Masters had always been trustees rather than owners because they hold this property in trust for the sangat, never using it for personal needs but always for the benefit and development of the sangat. Maharaj Ji said this principle of trusteeship should now be given a legal and well-defined shape for the benefit of the sangat and for more efficient management of all these properties. The Master added that this arrangement would also relieve him of much responsibility and give him more time to serve the sangat in other ways.

On 11 October 1957, Maharaj Ji created and registered the Society, Radha Soami Satsang Beas, nominating some trusted devotees of the Great Master and of Sardar Bahadur Maharaj Ji to serve on the board of the Society. In a deed registered on 25 October 1957, Maharaj Ji declared himself the trustee, not the owner, of all the satsang properties. On that same day he transferred all this trust property to the Society, which continues to run the Dera to this day.

The entire Dera administration is managed by devoted sevadars who come from all parts of India and from various walks of life. They include retired government officers, business executives, bankers, professors, lawyers, physicians, engineers, men from the armed forces, and many technicians proficient in the various types of work required at the Dera. They all serve free of charge and support themselves on their personal income or pension.

Besides these sevadars, a large number of satsangis and visitors from outside the Dera, from India as well as abroad, come and do seva at various places—such as the langar, the bhojan bhandar, the hospital, the nature cure clinic, the library, the engineering department, and the publications department. The way the sangat and sevadars do this seva is an inspiring sight. Their love and devotion has to be seen to be believed; but behind the love is the driving force of the Master. He is the real doer, the true architect of the entire development, the inspiration behind every activity here. The ripples in the lake glow in the light of the sun, but the credit goes to the brilliant rays of the sun itself. The love of the sangat is only a reflection of the deep love of the Satguru for his fold.

Following the Master's example, the entire emphasis of life at the Dera is on meditation and service. Indeed, it must be one of the most unusual cities in the world. The administrators receive no salary, living on their pensions and doing their jobs out of their love for the Lord and the Master. In Dera anyone can eat free of charge, so there are no beggars. Of course, the most striking feature of the Dera is that it has had a perfect Master overseeing its development since Baba Ji first built his mud hut here. The atmosphere, the fragrance in the Dera, is of the love, devotion, and spiritual serenity of the Master.

From the day Baba Ji laid the foundation of the Dera in 1891, it has grown into a vast colony with manifold activities. It has become a spiritual centre drawing true seekers from all parts of India and the world. With the expansion of the Dera's dimensions, both physical and spiritual, its activities have increased. But the atmosphere of peace and serenity has continued unchanged. As Maharaj Ji often says, "We can only find peace in the physical world when we are at peace with ourselves. When we experience true peace within, we radiate peace all round." Life in Dera runs throughout the year in this atmosphere of spiritual calm, and the emphasis has been, and today still is, on spiritual practice, on meditation, and on going within.

The Dera is a unique township in the world; the law here is sympathy, understanding, and love. In a world overcast by hatred, Dera radiates love; in a world blinded by prejudice, it encourages understanding; in a world of selfish pursuits, it is an example of selfless dedication; in a world battered by strife and enmity, by distrust and jealousy, Dera is an abode of peace. The Master, himself a living example of inner peace and love, teaches seekers to develop, act, and live in love. He is the storehouse of the energy that illuminates the entire colony. Under his guidance and care, Dera is today a heaven on earth, providing spiritual solace irrespective of caste, creed, colour, or nationality, to men and women who long to become one with God.

Addresses for Information and Books

INDIAN SUB-CONTINENT

INDIA
The Secretary
Radha Soami Satsang Beas
P.O. Dera Baba Jaimal Singh 143204
District Amritsar, Punjab

Mr. Krishin Babani
Buona Casa Bldg., 2nd Floor
Sir P.M. Road, Fort
Bombay 400 001

NEPAL
Mr. Prakash Gauchan
RSS(B)—Nepal
P.O. Box 1646
Sundarighat, Kirtipur, Kathmandu

SRI LANKA
Mr. D. H. Jiwat
c/o Geekay Ltd.
33 Bankshall Street, Colombo 11

SOUTHEAST ASIA

INDONESIA
Mr. Gope L. Nanwani
Jl. Kelinci Raya No. 32A
Jakarta Pusat 10710

MALAYSIA
Dr. Narjit Singh Dhaliwal
Kumpulan Perubatan SMP
18 Lorong Sempadan, Jalan 16/7
or (P.O. Box 7081)
Shah Alam 40702

SINGAPORE
Mr. Sajan Shankardas Nanwani
Beas Enterprises
111 North Bridge Road
#04-40 Peninsula Plaza
Singapore 0617

THAILAND
Mr. Harmahinder Singh Sethi
ASA International Ltd., Part.
43/17/-18, SOI Sawasdee,
Sukhumvit SOI 31, Bangkok 10110

ASIA PACIFIC

AUSTRALIA
Mrs. Janet Bland
P.O. Box 3, Oaklands Park
Adelaide, S. Australia 5046

HONG KONG
Mrs. Cami Moss
T.S.T., P.O. Box 97739, Kowloon

JAPAN
Mr. Jani Mohinani
1-1-10 Akamatsu-cho, Nada-ku
Kobe 657

NEW ZEALAND
Mr. Tony Waddicor
10 Maxine Place, Tauranga

PHILIPPINES
Mr. Kay Sham
P.O. Box 2346
MCC Makati, Metro Manila

TAIWAN R.O.C.
Mr. Larry T. Nanwani
No. 57 Tun Hwa South Road Sec. 1
Room 808, Choo Woo House
or (P.O. Box 68-1414), Taipei

NORTH AMERICA

CANADA
Mr. John W. Abel
701-1012 Beach Ave.
Vancouver, B.C. V6E 1T7

Dr. Peter Grayson
177 Division Street South
Kingsville, Ontario N9Y 1R1

UNITED STATES
Dr. Eugene Ivash
4701 Shadow Lane
Austin, TX 78731

Dr. Vincent P. Savarese
3507 Saint Elizabeth Road
Glendale, CA 91206

Dr. John Templer
114 Verdier Road
Beaufort, SC 29902

Dr. Frank Vogel
7 Pelham Terrace
Arlington, MA 02174

Science of the Soul Study Center
Route 24, Box 79
Fayetteville, NC 28306

CARIBBEAN ISLANDS

CARIBBEAN ISLANDS
Mr. Sean Finnigan
Villa Rosa, Canape Vert.
or (P.O. Box 2314)
Port-au-Prince, Haiti

BARBADOS
Mr. Bhagwandas Kessaram Gopwani
c/o Kiddies Corner, 43 Swan Street
or (P.O. Box 603)
Bridgetown

TRINIDAD (WEST INDIES)
Mr. Thakurdas Chatlani
8A Saddle Road, Maraval

CENTRAL AMERICA

MEXICO
Mr. Jorge Angel Santana
Cometa 2821, Jardines del Bosque
Guadalajara, JAL 44520

For the following countries, contact:
Mr. Jorge Angel Santana, MEXICO

BELIZE
COSTA RICA
GUATEMALA
HONDURAS
NICARAGUA
PANAMA
SAN SALVADOR

SOUTH AMERICA

BRAZIL
Mr. Alberto Cancio Ferreira
See PORTUGAL.

COLOMBIA
Mr. Alberto Garcia Botero
Calle 147 #23-19, Bogota

ECUADOR
Mr. Gonzalo Vargas Noriega
Calle Montalvo No. 200, Oficina 201
Edificio Ponce Larrea
or (P.O. Box 17-21-1477)
Quito

GUYANA
Mrs. Rajni B. Manglani
c/o Bhagwan's Store
18 Water Street, Georgetown

PERU
Mr. Gonzalo Vargas Noriega
See ECUADOR.

VENEZUELA
Mr. Jose Antonio Penaherrera
Calle Mohedano Con Sucre
Edif. Don Jose, Local 2
Apartado Postal 63-436
Chacaito, Caracas 1.016

EUROPE

AUSTRIA
Mr. Hansjorg Hammerer
Sezenweingasse 10
Salzburg A-5020

BELGIUM
Mr. Jacob Hofstra
See NETHERLANDS.

BULGARIA
Mr. Emil Saev
P.O. Box 342, Sofia 1000

CYPRUS
Mr. Heraclis Achilleos
18 Kyriacou Matsi, Flat 101
or (P.O. Box 9077)
Pallouriotissa, Nicosia 116

CZECH REPUBLIC
Mr. Vladimir Skalsky
Maratkova 916, Prague 4, 142 00

DENMARK
Mr. Rudolf Walberg
See GERMANY.

FRANCE
Mr. Pierre de Proyart
7 Quai Voltaire
Paris 75007

GERMANY
Mr. Rudolf Walberg
P.O. Box 1544
D-65800 Bad Soden/Taunus

GIBRALTAR
Mr. Sunder T. Mahtani
Radha Soami Satsang Beas
401 Ocean Heights

GREECE
Mr. Dimitrios Sotiriou
Moschoula 4, Penteli
Athens 152-36

ITALY
Mrs. Wilma Salvatori Torri
Via Bacchiglione 3-00199
Rome

NETHERLANDS, THE (HOLLAND)
Mr. Jacob Hofstra
Geulwijk 6, Leusden 3831 LM

NORWAY
Mr. Rudolf Walberg
See GERMANY.

PORTUGAL
Mr. Alberto Cancio Ferreira
Urb. do Buzano
Av. Comandante Gilberto
Duarte e Duarte, Lote 2, 3° Esq.
S. Domingos de Rana 2775

SLOVENIA
Mr. Marko Bedina
Brezje PRI, Trzicu 68, 4290 Trzic

SPAIN
Mr. Hiro W. Balani
Radha Soami Satsang Beas
Loma Del Valle, Cruce del Pinar
Alhaurin de la Torre
or (P.O. Box 486)
Malaga 29012

SWEDEN
Mr. Lennart Zachen
Norra Sonnarpsvagen 29
S-286 72 Asljunga

SWITZERLAND
Mr. Olivier de Coulon
Rue du Centre
Tolochenaz (VD) CH-1131

UNITED KINGDOM
Mrs. Flora E. Wood
Haynes Park
Haynes, Bedford MK45 3BL

AFRICA

BENIN
Mrs. Priya J. Vaswani
c/o Mr. Jaikumar Vaswani
B.P. 951, Cotonou

GHANA
Mr. James Osei Kojo Sekyi
P.O. Box 4615, Accra

KENYA
Mr. Surinder Singh Ghir
P.O. Box 39993, Nairobi

MAURITIUS
Mrs. Doolaree Nuckcheddy
17 Leconte de Lisle Ave.
Quatre Bornes

MOROCCO
Mr. Hiro W. Balani
See SPAIN.

NIGERIA
Mr. Nanik N. Balani
120 Awolowo Road
or (G.P.O. Box 10407)
Ikoyi, Lagos

SOUTH AFRICA
Mr. Sam Busa
P.O. Box 41355, Craighall 2024

TANZANIA
Mr. Diljeet Nath Pandit
83 Lugalo Rd., East Upanga
or (P.O. Box 1963), Dar-es-Salaam

UGANDA
Mr. Sylvester Kakooza
Alanda Ltd., Plot 64, William Street
or (P.O. Box 31381), Kampala

ZIMBABWE
Mrs. Dorothy Roodt
102 Suffolk Rd., Strathaven
or (P.O. Box 7095), Harare

MIDDLE EAST

BAHRAIN, U.A.E.
Mrs. Shiela Chand
P.O. Box 3079

DUBAI, U.A.E
Mr. Chander Bhatia
Shabnam Trading Co.
P.O. Box 2296

ISRAEL
Mrs. H. Mandelbaum
P.O. Box 22121, Tel Aviv 61221

BOOKS ON THIS SCIENCE

SOAMI JI MAHARAJ
  Sar Bachan

BABA JAIMAL SINGH
  Spiritual Letters (to Hazur Maharaj Sawan Singh: 1896-1903)

MAHARAJ SAWAN SINGH
  The Dawn of Light (letters to Western disciples: 1911-1934)
  Discourses on Sant Mat
  My Submission (introduction to Philosophy of the Masters)
  Philosophy of the Masters (Gurmat Sidhant), 5 vols.
    (an encyclopedia on the teachings of the Saints)
  Philosophy of the Masters (abridged)
  Spiritual Gems (letters to Western disciples: 1919-1948)
  Tales of the Mystic East (as narrated in satsangs)

MAHARAJ JAGAT SINGH
  The Science of the Soul (discourses and letters: 1948-1951)

MAHARAJ CHARAN SINGH
  Die to Live (answers to questions on meditation)
  Divine Light (discourses and letters: 1959-1964)
  Light on Saint John
  Light on Saint Matthew
  Light on Sant Mat (discourses and letters: 1952-1958)
  The Master Answers (to audiences in America: 1964)
  The Path (first part of Divine Light)
  Quest for Light (letters: 1965-1971)
  Spiritual Discourses
  Spiritual Heritage (from tape-recorded talks)
  Teachings of the Saints (first chapter of Die to Live)
  Thus Saith the Master (to audiences in America: 1970)
  Truth Eternal (a discourse)

BOOKS ABOUT THE MASTERS
    Call of the Great Master—Diwan Daryai Lal Kapur
    Heaven on Earth—Diwan Daryai Lal Kapur
    Treasure Beyond Measure—Shanti Sethi
    With a Great Master in India—Julian P. Johnson
    With the Three Masters, 3 volumes—from the diary of Rai Sahib
      Munshi Ram

BOOKS ON SANT MAT IN GENERAL
    The Holy Name—Miriam Bokser Caravella
    In Search of the Way—Flora E. Wood
    The Inner Voice—Colonel C. W. Sanders
    Liberation of the Soul—J. Stanley White
    Message Divine—Shanti Sethi
    Mystic Bible—Randolph Stone
    The Mystic Philosophy of Sant Mat—Peter Fripp
    Mysticism, The Spiritual Path, 2 volumes—Lekh Raj Puri
    The Path of the Masters—Julian P. Johnson
    Radha Soami Teachings— Lekh Raj Puri
    A Soul's Safari—Netta Pfeifer
    Teachings of the Gurus— Lekh Raj Puri
    Yoga and the Bible—Joseph Leeming

MYSTICS OF THE EAST SERIES
    Bulleh Shah—J. R. Puri and T.R. Shangari
    Dadu, The Compassionate Mystic—K. N. Upadhyaya
    Dariya Sahib, Saint of Bihar—K. N. Upadhyaya
    Guru Nanak, His Mystic Teachings—J. R. Puri
    Guru Ravidas, Life and Teachings—K. N. Upadhyaya
    Kabir, The Great Mystic—Isaac A. Ezekiel
    Kabir, The Weaver of God's Name—V. K. Sethi
    Mira, The Divine Lover—V. K. Sethi
    Saint Namdev, His Life and Teachings—J. R. Puri and V. K. Sethi
    Saint Paltu—Isaac A. Ezekiel
    Sant Charan Das—T. R. Shangari
    Sarmad, Jewish Saint of India—Isaac A. Ezekiel
    Sultan Bahu—J. R. Puri
    Tukaram, Saint of Maharashtra—C. Rajwade
    Tulsi Sahib, Saint of Hathras—J. R. Puri and V. K. Sethi